CONTINUED ON BACK ENDPAPER ⟩

Barker

ENGLISH
GRAMMAR AND
COMPOSITION

10

JOHN E. WARRINER

Head of the English Department
Garden City High School
Garden City, New York

CHAPTERS ON SPEAKING AND LISTENING
AND PARLIAMENTARY PROCEDURE BY

FRANCIS GRIFFITH

Principal, Richmond Hill High School
Richmond Hill, New York

HARCOURT, BRACE & WORLD, INC.

New York • Chicago • Atlanta • Dallas • Burlingame

THE AUTHORS: **JOHN E. WARRINER** has taught English for 32 years, in junior and senior high schools and in college. He is the author of *Warriner's Handbook of English: I* and *II* and a coauthor of the *English Workshop* series. **FRANCIS GRIFFITH,** who has done graduate work at Columbia University and includes in his experience advanced courses at the National University of Ireland, was for many years Chairman of English and Speech in a Brooklyn, New York, high school.

> The photograph on the cover of this book shows part of a type case containing the printing type Perpetua, a face designed in 1932 by the English artist Eric Gill. The chapter headings throughout the book are set in this type. Cover photograph by Lew Merrim from Monkmeyer.

Preface

English Grammar and Composition: Grade 10 is the fourth book in a new six-book series, which has grown out of requests from many teachers for a textbook for each grade that presents needed material in a concise and thorough manner. Like the other members of the series, this textbook states clearly the facts about language and the conventions of usage; it gives full explanations of important skills in writing, speaking, and listening; and it includes enough drills and exercises to meet any teaching demand. The *English Grammar and Composition* series has been planned to appeal to all teachers who prefer to handle motivation themselves, but who need a textbook which presents the subject matter of English arranged for efficient teaching as well as for reference, and functions as a storehouse of carefully prepared exercise materials.

The specific function of the tenth-grade volume is to establish the fundamentals of good English. The book provides both a summary of the materials taught in the seventh-, eighth-, and ninth-grade books and a thorough preparation for the more advanced language study covered in the eleventh-grade book and in the twelfth-grade, the final volume of the series. The work in sentence structure, for example, while it goes beyond the ninth-grade treatment, does not attempt more advanced items such as subordination, parallelism, clear reference, and the research paper, topics which are appropriately treated in the upper years of the senior high school. The goal is the thorough clinching of basic skills rather than the teaching of refinements of style.

Part One reviews the traditional terminology of grammar, a logical and usually necessary study in preparation for the year's work, especially in the tenth grade, which in many school systems is the first year of the senior high school. In Part Two, grammar is immediately applied to the writing of correct and effective sentences, the emphasis shifting from the facts about language to their application in the right use of language. Chapter 10, "Special Problems in Good Usage," is a glossary of usages which a tenth-grader should know but which, for the most part, are matters of word meaning and custom rather than matters of grammar.

The five chapters of Part Three, *Composition*, teach the basic skills of theme writing. The expository paragraph and the longer composition receive especially thorough treatment and are accompanied by a great many helpful suggestions as to what to write about. A chapter on the use of the library and reference tools aids in acquisition of material for writing. The chapter on narrative writing gives specific help in creative writing as distinguished from exposition. The letter-writing chapter contains the important conventions to be observed in informal and business correspondence. In all these chapters, as in all books of the series, the usual textbook motivation has been omitted, leaving space for basic skills and forms.

In Part Four, Mr. Griffith's handling of social conversation, an increasingly important subject for students in their early teens, is realistic. He proceeds from the proper way to make social introductions through the courtesies of conversation to specific problems, such as extending thanks and apology and asking for a date. Listening is an especially important topic in today's English classes. Mr. Griffith's treatment of this subject avoids the pitfall of nebulousness by giving concrete advice on how to listen intelligently. The student is shown how to be a purposeful, accurate, and critical listener. In democratically run classes, clubs, and student government, high school students need to know the fundamentals of parliamentary procedure. Chapter 18 covers these fundamentals concretely by explaining how to write a constitution and how to conduct and participate in a meeting.

Part Five, *Mechanics*, is the most extensive treatment of capitalization, punctuation, and spelling to be found in any of the six books of the series. Teachers will recognize the importance of this thorough treatment in the tenth year, when students are expected to demonstrate a grasp of the mechanical skills so that in the succeeding years they may be free to consider less pedestrian aspects of written English.

The final chapter on vocabulary development, written by Dr. Paul Schweitzer of the Bronx High School of Science, New York, describes various ways of enlarging one's vocabulary, an important matter in itself and especially important in this day when tests of verbal aptitude are so commonly used for diagnosis and evaluation of high school students.

The teaching in the *English Grammar and Composition* series is direct and concise. These characteristics appeal to both students and teachers. Typographically the handbook-type arrangement, with rules in color, makes learning easier. The colored reference tabs, the charts in the end papers, and the complete index expedite efficient use of the book for reference.

With the exception of the grammar review chapters, which necessarily precede their application in the chapters on correct and effective sentences, the arrangement of the book is not sequential. Each chapter is an independent unit and may be taught at any time in the course. The chapters themselves are so organized that teachers may easily skim the parts their students already know and concentrate on the parts which need emphasis. A separate test booklet containing summary tests for each "testable" chapter is available from the publishers at a small cost. For the end of the work on each chapter the teacher thus has for each student a printed test which the student has not seen in advance.

Diagraming is included in the grammar chapters and used for illustrative purposes elsewhere because many teachers find it a useful visual aid for making word relationships clear. The diagrams, however, are an accessory, not an integral part of the teaching method. They can be ignored if the teacher wishes.

Author and publisher wish to acknowledge the valuable help of many experienced teachers who have assisted in

criticized the entire manuscript: Brother Charles A.
Conefrey, Power Memorial Academy, New York; Miss Olga
Achtenhagen, Plainfield High School, Plainfield, New
Jersey; and Mr. A. T. Krider, John Adams High School,
South Bend, Indiana. Special thanks are due Miss Mary
Evelyn Whitten of North Texas State College, who assisted
in the revision of the manuscript and contributed the
chapter "Narrative Writing," and to Miss Hildegard
Schmalenbeck, Texas College of Arts and Industries, for
her critical reading of this chapter. Other readers of the
series, who have given valuable criticism, are: Mrs. Elizabeth
White, Board of Public Instruction, Miami, Florida;
Miss Martha Davis, Winn Seale Junior High School,
Corpus Christi, Texas; Miss Anna Fort, Deal Junior High
School, Washington, D.C.; Miss Margaret B. Dietrich,
Westfield Senior High School, Westfield, New Jersey;
Mrs. Gladys Kronsagen, Glenbard Township High School,
Glen Ellyn, Illinois; Sister Mary David, O.P., Junipero
Memorial High School, Monterey, California.

Finally, the author is deeply indebted to his wife for her
effective collaboration at every stage in the making of
this book.

J. W.

Contents

PART TWO

Correct and Effective Sentences

PART SIX

Vocabulary

PART ONE

GRAMMAR

CHAPTER 1

The Word

SPOTTING THE PARTS OF SPEECH

How much time you should spend working on Chapter 1 will depend on how well you remember the grammar you have learned so far in school. Do you know the names of words? Words are the materials you work with in your study of language. It is just as necessary to know their names as it is to know the name of anything else you wish to talk about.

Words are named according to the work they do in the sentence. There are eight kinds of work to be done in the sentence. The words that perform them are called the *parts of speech*. The names are:

noun	adverb
pronoun	preposition
adjective	conjunction
verb	interjection

As a result of your study of this chapter, you should be able to name the part of speech of almost any word in any sentence, to "spot the parts of speech."

The Noun

1a. A *noun* is a word used to name a person, place, thing, or an idea.

Your own name is a noun. The name of your home town is a noun. *Book* is a noun. The names of things

2

which you cannot touch or see are nouns; for instance, *strength, happiness, emotion, thought, meaning, width.* Although these words do not name objects, they do name qualities or ideas. The name of a quality or an idea is just as truly a noun as the name of anything which has size and shape.

● EXERCISE 1.   There are 25 nouns in the following paragraph. Make a list of them. Do not be misled by words which may be used as nouns in one place but as some other part of speech in another place.

1. A hurricane would not have left the room in so big a jumble.   2. From the door to the long window opposite and from the fireplace in the left wall to the piano on the other side, lay a collection of junk impossible to imagine. 3. The scene spoke of haste, of sudden departure, of great carelessness.   4. Black pieces of broken records, deflated footballs, battered hockey sticks, banners and pennants, books, rugs, and chairs were strewn about the floor.

● EXERCISE 2.   How many nouns can you spot in the following paragraph? List them on your paper. Place before each noun the number of the sentence in which it appears.

1. A lamp, once tall and proud, lay twisted and shattered across a corner of the floor.   2. Pictures of athletes sitting in staring rows had been thrown into the pile, their frames splintered and their glasses in pieces.   3. The door to the closet hung open, revealing stark emptiness. 4. Articles had been hurled into the room, leaving the shelves bare.   5. The bright hues of a hundred neckties added color to the scene as the warm rays of the sun played upon them.   6. Jagged pieces of a jigsaw puzzle challenged me to try to fit them together, but the clean-up job which faced me was puzzling enough and at the time required a greater effort than I knew I could manage. 7. Quietly I reached for the doorknob.   8. I would shut

the ugly sight from view.   9. The knob came off in my hand!

THE PROPER NOUN AND THE COMMON NOUN

Nouns may be divided into two classes: proper nouns and common nouns. A proper noun names a particular person, place, or thing. A common noun does not name a particular person, place, or thing. *Millville* is a proper noun; *village* is a common noun. *Jean* is a proper noun; *girl* is a common noun. Proper nouns are capitalized. Examine the following proper nouns: [1]

PARTICULAR PLACES	Europe, Paris, Main Street
PARTICULAR PERSONS	Thomas Edison, Captain Kelley
PARTICULAR THINGS	Chrysler Building, Field Museum, Statue of Liberty, the *Flying Cloud* (ship), the *Zephyr* (train), Atlantic Ocean

● EXERCISE 3.   List a proper noun to make each common noun listed below more specific. For instance, for the common noun *school*, you could list *Garden City High School, Notre Dame*, or any other particular school.

1. comedian
2. river
3. street
4. movie
5. champion
6. magazine
7. automobile
8. hotel
9. mountain
10. war

The Pronoun

1b. A *pronoun* is a word used in place of one or more nouns.

You ask your teacher, "Is there any *ink* there?" Your teacher replies, "No *it* is all gone." In place of the noun *ink*, the teacher has used the pronoun *it*.

[1] Further study of proper nouns will be found under Capitalization, pages 412–423.

A friend says to you, "I am looking for *Harry and the boys*. Have you seen *them?*" Here your friend has used the pronoun *them* in place of the nouns *Harry* and *boys*.

● EXERCISE 4. By filling in the blanks in the following sentences orally, show what pronouns you would use in referring to the italicized nouns. Do not write in this book.

1. The *books* are on the library table. Please bring —— to me.
2. *Mary* and *Harold* are going to bring *Betty* and *Jean*. —— will arrive before lunch.
3. I asked *Jim*, "Will —— please help me?"
4. Wondering whether the pen belonged to *Jack*, I asked ——, "Is this *pen* ——?"
5. "No," he replied, "—— is not ——."

The words with which you filled in the blanks are all pronouns because, as you see, they are used in place of the nouns to which they refer.

Learn to recognize the following words as pronouns.[2]

> I, me, my, mine, myself
> you, your, yours, yourself, yourselves
> he, him, his, himself
> she, her, hers, herself
> it, its, itself
> we, us, our, ours, ourselves
> they, them, their, theirs, themselves
> who, whom, whose
> none, someone, anyone, everyone
> somebody, anybody, everybody

[2] More complete discussion of pronouns will be found on pages 117–142. The purpose of the discussion above is merely to help students to *identify* pronouns.

1b

Below is a list of words that are often used as pronouns. (Sometimes these words are *adjectives*, the part of speech which you will study next.)

> this, that, these, those
> which, what
> one, other, another
> each, either, neither, all, any, both, some, many

● EXERCISE 5.   List on your paper the pronouns in the following sentences. You should find 25. Before each pronoun write the number of the sentence in which it appears.

1. While we quarreled with the umpire, the fans roared for justice.   2. Someone cried out, "That is no strike, and you know it!"   3. Another screamed, "Let me at him! We need a hit!"   4. Some began to clap their hands. 5. Others were silent.   6. But all were deeply concerned. 7. Then the umpire, shaking his fist and scowling at both of us, stated emphatically, "I make my decisions and hold to them."   8. Our final score, which was 5 to 4, showed everybody in our league the effect of what he had said.

The Adjective

1c. An *adjective* is a word used to modify a noun or pronoun.

Modify means to change. In grammar, to modify a word means to change the meaning of the word by making the meaning more definite. Adjectives, then, are words used to *make the meaning* of nouns or pronouns *more definite.* An adjective may modify a noun or pronoun by telling *what kind* it is. For example: *green* dress; *tall* building; *great* beauty; *strong* man; he is *fat.* An adjective may point out *which one;* for example: *this* box, *these* pencils, the *approaching* train, the *last* car. An adjective may tell *how many;* for example:

many players, *few* lessons, *three* dollars. The commonest adjectives are the little words *a*, *an*, and *the*. They are frequently called *articles*.

An adjective is not always placed next to the word it modifies. It may be separated from the word it modifies by other words.

The **boys** were very **tired**.   [*tired* boys]
The **box** seems much too **heavy**.   [*heavy* box]

An adjective modifying a pronoun is almost always separated from the pronoun.

She looks **happy.**

They are **late.**

● EXERCISE 6.   In the following paragraph the adjectives (except *a*, *an*, and *the*) are printed in italics. Make a list of the adjectives and after each one write the word it modifies.

1. Dad drove us up and down the *busy* street for *twenty* minutes.   2. The day was *hot;* Dad was *impatient.*   3. From the *back* seat we looked ahead, trying to spot a *parking* space.   4. We learned the location of *every* hydrant and *bus* stop.   5. Finally, we saw *two* men climb into a *parked* jeep just ahead of us.   6. Our *sudden* yell nearly scared Dad into a *head-on* collision with an *approaching* truck.   7. With *rising* hope we waited until, to our *great* relief, the jeep pulled out.   8. Dad summoned his *last* bit of strength to back the *long* car into the *short* space left by the jeep.   9. His task was *difficult* and took *several* minutes.   10. After the *tiresome* hunt in the *crowded* car, we crawled out onto the *hot* sidewalk to start our shopping.   11. Then we saw the *awful* sign which no one had noticed before: "Post Office. *Five-Minute* Parking."

● EXERCISE 7.   Copy the following sentences, supplying adjectives in the blank spaces. Try to supply

1c

meaningful, interesting adjectives. Read the paragraph through before you copy it.

Late in the afternoon we had our first view of Osborne's camp. It lay in a —— valley between two lines of —— hills. The river was a —— band of light cutting through the center of the camp. From our —— position we could see only the —— tops of the —— cabins and the —— line of the flagpole rising through the —— foliage. A —— column of —— smoke rose straight up in the —— air. The —— sound of the —— bell urged us on down the —— road ahead. The view was a —— prospect after a —— day of hiking.

● EXERCISE 8. Write a paragraph, about 100 words in length, describing some scene familiar to you. Underline the adjectives once and the words they modify twice. Try to have at least ten adjectives in your paragraph. Be sure that your adjectives are not all of the same kind. Use some that tell *what kind*, some that tell *how many*, and some that tell *which one*.

PRONOUN OR ADJECTIVE

Now that you understand what an adjective is, you should be able to tell whether such words as *this*, *which*, etc. (see the words in the second list on page 6), are used as adjectives or pronouns. In the first sentence in each pair below, the words are used as pronouns to *take the place of* nouns. In the second sentence they are used as adjectives to *modify* nouns. Tell what nouns are modified.

PRONOUN   The blue pen is better than **this.**
ADJECTIVE   The blue pen is better than **this** pen.

PRONOUN   I want **that.**
ADJECTIVE   I want **that** box.

PRONOUN   We found **many.**
ADJECTIVE   We found **many** shells.

● EXERCISE 9. Study the italicized words in these sentences. Make two columns on your paper, labeling one column *pronouns*, the other *adjectives*. List the italicized words in the proper column. How the word is used tells you what kind of word it is. Before each word, write the number of the sentence in which it appears.

1. Your brother insists that *this* gun is loaded.
2. *That* is the gun *which* he says is not loaded.
3. *Which* gun will you use in the rifle match?
4. *Both* are old, and *neither* is in good condition.
5. *All* guns are dangerous, but *some* are more dangerous than *others*.
6. There are *several* guns in my collection, but *all* are useless now.
7. *Those* weapons in *this* collection belong to Mr. Fay.
8. *Many* were used for hunting, but *this* was used in the Civil War, *which* occurred a hundred years ago.
9. *Each* of these pistols is older than the *other* guns.
10. *Few* collectors own *more* guns than Mr. Fay.

● EXERCISE 10. The following words may be used as either pronouns or adjectives. Write a pair of sentences for each word. In the first sentence of each pair use the word as a pronoun; in the second, as an adjective.

1. this	5. either	8. **all**
2. each	6. one	9. other
3. any	7. both	10. **what**
4. some		

The Verb

1d. A verb is a word which expresses action or helps to make a statement.

THE ACTION VERB

You will have little difficulty recognizing verbs which express action, provided you realize that verbs

1d

like *think* and *believe* are action verbs even though the action cannot be seen. Typical examples of action verbs are: I *run*, he *plays*, they *fight*, you *make*, they *reply*, I *think*, we *know*.

THE LINKING VERB

Some verbs do not express action, but they do help to make a statement by acting as a link between two words. They are called *linking* verbs. The verb in each of the following sentences does not express action. It acts as a link between the other words on either side of it.

1. He **is** a lawyer.
2. You **look** tired.
3. Arnold **seemed** angry.
4. Jane **appeared** excited.
5. Henry **feels** sick.
6. He **became** overconfident.

The following are the most commonly used linking verbs: [3] *be, become, seem, grow, appear, look, feel, smell, taste, remain, sound, stay.*

THE VERB TO BE

The commonest verb in any language is the verb *to be*. It is a linking verb. Below is a list of the many forms of this verb.

am	have been	could be (can be,
are	has been	may be, might
is	had been	be, must be,
was	shall be	should be)
were	will be	could have been
be	shall have been	(can have been,
being	will have been	etc.)

Like the other linking verbs, the verb *to be* is usually followed by a noun or an adjective which fills out or completes its meaning.

1. I **am** his *brother.*
2. John **is** the *winner.*
3. You **may be** *sorry.*
4. The children **are** *happy.*
5. Carolyn **will be** my *partner.*
6. Someone **had been** *thoughtless.*

[3] **Linking** verbs are also called *state-of-being* verbs.

VERBS OF MORE THAN ONE WORD — THE VERB PHRASE

A verb frequently has one or more *helping verbs*. The verb and its helping verbs work together as a unit which is called a *verb phrase*.[4]

Commonly used helping verbs are: *to be* (in all its forms), *will, shall, has, have, had, can, could, may, might, must, ought, should, would, do, does, did*.

1. The boys **had been playing** football.
2. A large ship **was lying** in the harbor.
3. Very few people **would enjoy** such a long journey.
4. John **might have been shot** that night.
5. I **did clean** the carburetor.
6. **Will** you **wash** the car tomorrow?

● EXERCISE 11. Study each italicized verb in this paragraph. Tell whether it is an action verb or a linking verb.

1. "Early to bed and early to rise" *is* good advice for a high school student. 2. If you *do* your homework when you *feel* sleepy, you *will make* mistakes in it. 3. Problems which *seem* hard late at night *look* easy in the morning when you *are* wide awake. 4. *Set* the alarm clock so that it *will awaken* you early. 5. You *will discover* how much more work you *can finish* in one hour before breakfast than you *could have done* at bedtime; furthermore, if you *stay* awake too late at night, you *will become* sleepy in school the next day. 6. Your homework *will have been done* poorly, and you *will sleep* through your classes. 7. You *will miss* important explanations about the next assignment, and the work *will seem* harder than ever.

● EXERCISE 12. In the following paragraph there are 25 verbs. Write them in a column on your paper. Be sure to include all the helping verbs, especially when the parts of the verb are separated by other

---

[4] You will find further treatment of verb phrases on page 28.

words. The word *not* in a phrase such as *could not see* is not a verb. The verb is *could see*.

1. Ruth waited hopefully for Bob in the center of the hall.   2. She clutched her books in one hand, scratched a mosquito bite with the other, and hoped Bob would stop.   3. Bob, who was the new senior in Room 31, strolled down the corridor, looked at Ruth, hesitated, and walked on.   4. Tears of desperation came to Ruth's eyes.   5. Nice dates had been scarce lately.   6. Though Bob, she felt sure, would be a wonderful date, he had not asked her yet.   7. Maybe, thought Ruth, I could ask him.   8. After all, he is the new one around here, and I am a senior too.   9. Ruth summoned her courage, raced down the hall, breathlessly accosted Bob and said, "Hi, Bob. How about the dance Friday? Will you come with me? The whole gang will be there."

● EXERCISE 13.   Write in a column on your paper all the verbs in the following paragraph. Include all the parts of every verb.

1. At first we could not discover the cause of the fight which had attracted our attention.   2. It seemed as though all the dogs on our block were in it.   3. They snarled, growled, barked, and leaped around in a circle until we could hardly tell big dogs from little dogs.   4. Flashes of black, tan, and white were mixed with rust and a nondescript gray.   5. Suddenly a fawn-colored nose appeared, and then a dirty tan-and-white pup emerged triumphant from the noisy pack and tore across the street with a huge bone in his teeth.   6. He was followed at once by a string of dogs.   7. Although the sounds of the fight could have been heard throughout the neighborhood, the chase was breathlessly quiet.   8. You might have thought they were playing a game if their quiet seriousness had not shown that this was an animal struggle for food.

● EXERCISE 14.   Write a paragraph of 150 words or more relating an incident which happened in one of your classes recently. Underline all the verbs and verb phrases. You can make your paragraph interesting by choosing vivid, lively verbs.

The Adverb

1e. An *adverb* is a word used to modify a verb, an adjective, or another adverb.

ADVERBS MODIFYING VERBS

Just as there are words which modify nouns and pronouns (adjectives), there are words which modify verbs. For example, the verb *walk* may be modified by such words as *slowly, rapidly, awkwardly, gracefully,* etc. The verb *jump* may be modified by *fast, high, far, suddenly,* etc. *A word which modifies a verb is an adverb.*

● EXERCISE 15. There are 12 adverbs in the following sentences. Make a list of them. After each write the verb which it modifies.

1. The swarthy man came swiftly around the corner. 2. A monkey, which was dressed in a striped playsuit, followed timidly. 3. Tony turned smilingly to his pet and gestured hopefully to him. 4. The monkey danced quickly and gracefully; he jumped nimbly into the air and landed neatly on the organ grinder's shoulder. 5. Tony set him on the ground where the monkey performed happily in front of an ever-growing crowd of children who laughed delightedly as the little animal minced toward them and begged slyly, confidently, for pennies.

Adverbs, in modifying verbs, usually tell one of four things about the action of the verb. They may tell *when* the action was done; they may tell *where* it was done; they may tell *how* it was done; they may tell *to what extent* (how long or how much) it was done.

1. Jim swam **then.** [The adverb *then* tells *when* Jim swam.]

1e

2. Jim swam **there**.   [The adverb *there* tells *where* Jim swam.]
3. Jim swam **rapidly**.   [The adverb *rapidly* tells *how* Jim swam.]
4. Jim swam **far**.   [The adverb *far* tells *to what extent* Jim swam.]

● EXERCISE 16.   Give two adverb modifiers for each of the following verbs.

1. fled
2. moved
3. pushed
4. left

5. rowed
6. drove
7. spoke

8. saw
9. said
10. wrote

ADVERBS MODIFYING ADJECTIVES

You should be able to name the part of speech of every word in this sentence except *very:*

We followed a very narrow road.

If you will ask yourself just what *very* does in the sentence, you will probably find that it modifies *narrow*. It tells how narrow the road was. You know that *narrow* is an adjective because it modifies the noun *road*. *Very* modifies an adjective. *A word which modifies an adjective is an adverb.*

● EXERCISE 17.   In each of the following sentences there is an adverb modifying an adjective. List these adverbs on your paper and after each one write the adjective which it modifies.

1. The very sad camel named Gloomy gazed out from his cage.
2. He saw a surprisingly small boy struggling to climb up to the railing.
3. An extremely dirty little girl helped the boy to see.
4. He got a fairly good hold on the railing.
5. He stared with startlingly blue eyes at the camel.

6. Gloomy stared back with an <u>amazingly</u> snobbish expression.
7. Then a <u>rather</u> surprised look came over the camel's face.
8. He peered at the <u>spotlessly clean</u> sweater the boy wore.
9. It was <u>extremely</u> fluffy camel's hair!
10. Gloomy, who was <u>somewhat</u> sad, almost smiled.

ADVERBS MODIFYING OTHER ADVERBS

You have learned that an adverb may modify a verb or it may modify an adjective. *Some adverbs modify other adverbs.* There is an example of this in the following sentence:

Father drove the car rather skillfully.

From your study of the parts of speech, you can spot *skillfully* as an adverb modifying the verb *drove*, telling *how* Father drove. You can also see that *rather* modifies the adverb *skillfully*, telling *how* skillfully. Here, then, is an adverb modifying another adverb. *An adverb is a word used to modify a verb, an adjective, or another adverb.*

▶ CAUTION: As you may have discovered, many adverbs end in *–ly*. But do not make the mistake of thinking that all words ending in *–ly* are adverbs. For instance, the following words are adjectives: *costly, lovely, friendly, deadly.*

● EXERCISE 18. There are 20 adverbs in the following paragraph. Make a list of them. After each write the word which the adverb modifies and tell whether this word is a verb, an adjective, or another adverb.

1. I had plenty of very good reasons for doubting Alec's stories about the dog he formerly owned. 2. Alec told the stories so well that all of us greatly enjoyed listening to

them. 3. He told them rather convincingly and, I suppose, fooled many people. 4. According to Alec, his dog Skipper possessed an unusually keen sense of smell. 5. When something was lost around the house, Skipper, who would usually be put on the scent, would manage somehow to find the lost article. 6. Then Alec decided to put this trait to some more practical use. 7. He played a lot of golf during the summer and frequently suffered the annoyance of having to hunt for a lost ball. 8. One day it suddenly occurred to him to use Skipper to hunt the missing balls. 9. He rubbed each ball in an extremely smelly bone-dust fertilizer which his father had recently spread over the front yard. 10. Anything which had come into contact with the fertilizer was very attractive to Skipper. 11. Alec took Skipper with him on his daily round of golf, and never did the dog fail to recover a lost ball. 12. "Sometime," Alec would add seriously, "I will tell you about the way he used to caddie for me."

● EXERCISE 19.   Use each of the following adverbs in a sentence. Draw an arrow from the adverb to the word it modifies.

1. quickly	3. happily	5. tomorrow	7. now	9. out
2. often	4. rather	6. very	8. too	10. again

● EXERCISE 20.   The following words may be used as either adjectives or adverbs. Write a pair of sentences for each word. In the first sentence use the word as an *adjective;* in the second, as an *adverb.*

EXAMPLES Spelling drill is a **daily** occurrence.
Our English class meets **daily.**

1. weekly	3. more	5. late
2. high	4. fast	

● EXERCISE 21.   Write a paragraph vividly describing a scene at a football game or some other athletic event. Get action as well as excitement into your word picture. When you have finished, *underline all adjectives and adverbs.* Note how important these parts of speech are in making a good description.

● REVIEW EXERCISE A. List the 35 italicized words in the following paragraph. After each word tell what part of speech it is. In a third column write down the word modified by each italicized adjective and adverb. In this and other exercises in this book, the words *my, your, his, her, our, their, whose* are called possessive pronouns, although some people prefer to think of them as adjectives.

1. One of *our favorite games* when *we* were boys was a vicious little *pastime* known as "duck on a rock." 2. I do not remember the *rules* of the game *now,* nor do I recall *very clearly* what the object of *it was.* 3. What is still very vivid is *my mental picture* of the game. 4. On *summer* evenings as the arc lights came on and people *sauntered* out to *their* front porches and yards, the boys gathered at the corner for a game of "duck." 5. The wide, unpaved street, illuminated by the hanging street lamp, *provided* an excellent playground. 6. Only an occasional horse-drawn carriage disturbed us. 7. I *remember* how we respected the older boys. 8. *They managed* the game, using us youngsters as extras, laughing at *us* and praising us. 9. *Each* boy equipped himself with a rock big enough to carry an impact, yet small enough to be rolled *easily.* 10. There was a great deal of throwing of rocks and hopping out of their way, and many a lad *dropped* out of the game with a sore toe or a *bruised* shin. 11. The game was, theoretically at least, played on the ground, but rocks do bounce. 12. On a *large* boulder at either side of the street sat a smaller rock — the duck. 13. The enemy, from the *opposite* curb, tried to dislodge it by throwing rocks. 14. By the same means we tried to defend our duck and to dislodge *theirs.* 15. What happened when *ours* fell defeated in the dust or what rewards we won upon dislodging their duck, I have no *idea.* 16. The game usually lasted until

the younger boys were called *home* to bed, and the older
boys wandered *off* to find *more adult* amusements.

The Preposition

**1f. A word used to show the relation of a noun or
pronoun to some other word in the sentence
is a *preposition*.**

In the following sentences the prepositions are in
heavy type. They show the relation to each other of
the words in italics. In Sentence 1, for instance, the
preposition *on* shows the relation of *rugs* to *floor*.

1. The *rugs* **on** the living room *floor* are beautiful.
2. The *boys* **in** the *boat* are good sailors.
3. The *seat* **behind** *me* is vacant.
4. We *left* **before** *dawn*.
5. Jerry *is working* **with** his *father*.

**1g. A group of words which begins with a prepo-
sition and ends with a noun or pronoun is a
prepositional phrase.**

These four groups are prepositional phrases:

of the *story*	**in** the *house*
on the *train*	**from** *him*

The following are commonly used as prepositions:

aboard	at	by
about	before	concerning
above	behind	down
across	below	during
after	beneath	except
against	beside	for
along	besides	from
amid	between	in
among	beyond	into
around	but (*meaning* except)	like

of	through	until
off	throughout	up
on	to	upon
over	toward, towards	with
past	under	within
since	underneath	without

Some prepositions consist of more than one word: *in spite of* my warning; *on account of* the storm; *according to* Bill.

▶ CAUTION: Do not confuse prepositions with adverbs. Remember that a preposition begins a phrase and must have with it a noun or a pronoun.

PREPOSITIONAL PHRASE   I fell *down the hill*.
ADVERB   I fell *down*.

In both sentences, the italicized words tell where I fell, but the adverb *down* is not followed by a noun or pronoun.

● EXERCISE 22.   Use the following words as prepositions in sentences. Underline the phrase which each preposition introduces. Be able to tell between which words the preposition shows relationship.

1. in   3. like   5. with   7. at   9. across
2. on   4. over   6. during 8. by   10. for

Use the following words as adverbs in sentences.

11. over   13. in   15. under
12. across   14. around   16. down

The Conjunction

Study the use of the words in heavy type in the following sentences:

Mary **and** her sister wanted to go home, **but** they had no way to get there.

Homework must be done at home **or** in study hall.

1f-g

You should observe that each of these words joins parts of the sentence together. In the first sentence, *and* joins *Mary* and *her sister; but* joins the first idea, *Mary and her sister wanted to go home*, to the second idea, *they had no way to get there*. In the second sentence, *or* joins the two ideas as to where homework must be done.

1h. A word which joins together words and groups of words is a *conjunction*.

There are three kinds of conjunctions: *co-ordinating* conjunctions, *correlative* conjunctions, and *subordinating* conjunctions.

Co-ordinating conjunctions. The co-ordinating conjunctions are *and, but, or, nor,* and *for.*

Correlative conjunctions. Some conjunctions are used in pairs. Examples of these are: *either . . . or; neither . . . nor; both . . . and; not only . . . but also.* Study the *pairs* of conjunctions in the following sentences. Conjunctions of this kind, which are used in pairs, are called *correlative conjunctions.*

1. **Either** the president of the Student Council **or** the principal will take charge of our meeting.
2. **Neither** the treasurer **nor** the secretary could remember who had paid dues.
3. **Both** the freshmen **and** the sophomores wanted to give a dance.
4. **Not only** hot dogs and hamburgers were sold at the snack bar, **but also** candy and ice cream.

Subordinating conjunctions will be studied later in connection with subordinate clauses. See page 73.

● EXERCISE 23.   List the co-ordinating and correlative conjunctions in the following paragraphs.

1. Baseball and track are probably the most popular spring sports in our schools and colleges.   2. One is largely

a team sport, but in the other, runners, jumpers, and weight men perform as individuals.   3. Team play among the members of a track team is not possible except in the relays, but co-operation among the players on a baseball team is of supreme importance.   4. In both baseball and track, however, the success of the team depends on every player's doing his part.

5. Lacrosse is a spring team sport popular in some sections of our country, but quite unknown in others.   6. This is somewhat strange, for it is the only completely American sport we have.   7. It was played originally by the Indians and was adopted from them by the early French explorers in Canada.   8. Once a very brutal game used by the Indians in training for war, lacrosse today has been "civilized" and is played by both schools and colleges.

9. The lacrosse ball must be not only caught but also carried and thrown only with the crosse, or stick. 10. There is always danger of injury from a wild swing of the crosse, and helmets with metal face guards provide head and face protection.   11. The crosse itself is a raw-hide net supported by a wooden handle.   12. In both lacrosse and hockey the object of the game is the same — to put the ball into the goal at the end of the field. 13. The playing field is about the size of a football field; there is considerable running, and the game is physically strenuous.   14. In neither the East nor the West is lacrosse regarded very generally as a major sport, but it may some day rival baseball and track in popularity.

The Interjection

There are a few words which are used as exclamations to show strong feeling, such as anger, surprise, excitement, etc. Examples of these are *Oh! Brother! Wow! Jeepers! Heck! Gee whiz!* These words are usually followed by an exclamation mark.

EXAMPLES   **Wow! What a game!**
           "Gosh!" he said, "you must be crazy."

1h

1i. **Words expressing emotion and having no grammatical relation to other words in the sentence are *interjections*.**

● EXERCISE 24.   Make a list of 10 interjections other than those given above.

Determining Parts of Speech

1j. **What part of speech a word is depends on how the word is used.**

In the following sentences you will see that one word is used as three different parts of speech.

What part of speech is *play* in each sentence?

On Fridays the girls **play** games during gym period.
The seniors gave a **play** in assembly.
The children's **play** hour came in the middle of the morning.

● EXERCISE 25.   Number in a column on your paper from 1 to 15. Study the use of each of the italicized words in the following sentences. On your paper after the proper number write the part of speech of the word. Be prepared to explain to the class why the word is that part of speech. For example, in the first sentence *light* is a noun. It is the name of something.

1. We were blinded by the *light*.
2. Please *light* the fire.
3. The box looked heavy, but it was really very *light*.
4. This year we are studying *plane* geometry.
5. One of the boys in the shop will *plane* these boards for you.
6. A small *plane* circled overhead.
7. He has an *air* of self-confidence.
8. The chairman will *air* the grievances of the strikers.
9. An *air* gun can be very dangerous.
10. He never has *any* money.
11. I don't care for *any*, thank you.

12. She has just gone *out*.
13. She went *out* the back door.
14. I shall *room* at the Whites' home.
15. The *room* is a large one.

● REVIEW EXERCISE B. Write 3 sentences for each of the following words, using the word as a different part of speech in each sentence. At the end of the sentence write the part of speech.

    1. stone   2. mail   3. water   4. store   5. star

● REVIEW EXERCISE C. Now that you have learned eight parts of speech, you should be able to classify every word in the following paragraph. Arrange the 30 italicized words in columns, leaving a space between the columns. After each word write what part of speech it is. You should be able to tell why, and you should make a score of 100 per cent. The underlined expression is regarded as one word.

    1. I *had looked forward* a long time *to my first visit* to Washington.   2. *Everyone* had told me the *sights* I should see, *and* I had a *rather long list in* my hand as I *walked from* the Union Station.   3. *There* and *then* my list was forgotten because *almost immediately I* saw the dome of the Capitol in the *distance* and *headed toward* it.   4. *This* building was not the *top* item on my list, *but* it was as *good* a place as *any* for the start of a tour *like mine.*

● REVIEW EXERCISE D. Arrange the 30 italicized words in columns on your paper, leaving a space between columns. After each word write what part of speech it is.

    1. The *Indians* who lived *on* the islands in the Caribbean Sea before the *arrival* of the white man were *well* acquainted with the great cyclonic storms *that* arose frequently in *that* area.   2. *They* called these storms "hurucans," an *Indian* word meaning "evil spirits."   3. The *early* Spanish ex-

plorers *adopted* the Indian term, which has *now* become our word "hurricane."

4. As *everyone* on the Atlantic Coast knows, a hurricane is a dangerous storm *with* rain-bearing winds whirling *about* a center *at* speeds in excess of 75 mph. 5. The storm *itself* moves *rather* slowly, usually in a *northwesterly* direction. 6. It *menaces* shipping *and* coastal regions and *sometimes* continues *inland* with great force.

7. More than a thousand hurricanes have been recorded and *studied* by meteorologists. 8. In recent years, with the *help* of *both* scientific instruments and airplanes, *weather* men have been *able* to spot a hurricane almost as soon as it forms. 9. Early warnings have done *much* to diminish loss of life and property. 10. No one knows exactly why a hurricane forms *or* what determines its course, and no one has ever found a way to stop or divert *one*.

● REVIEW EXERCISE E. From memory, list and define the eight parts of speech. Illustrate each definition by correctly using the part of speech in a sentence. Underline the illustrative word.

● REVIEW EXERCISE F. Since a monotonous style often occurs when too many consecutive sentences begin with a noun or pronoun, your knowledge of the parts of speech can enable you to construct more interesting and varied sentences. Work for variety by writing four sentences, each beginning in a different way as follows: Begin sentence 1 with a prepositional phrase; sentence 2 with an adverb; sentence 3 with an adjective; sentence 4 with a correlative conjunction.

CHAPTER 2

The Sentence

SUBJECT AND PREDICATE, SINGLE-WORD MODIFIERS

Most of your thinking, a very large part of your writing, and a smaller part of your speaking are done in sentence form. The sentence is the basic unit of expression. No matter whether you write a book of a thousand pages or a simple explanation of why you were absent from school recently, you will do it by means of sentences. Your purpose now is to understand the structure of a sentence so that you can write good sentences with ease.

2a. A *sentence* is a group of words containing a verb and its subject and expressing a completed thought.

The sentence is used chiefly in written expression. In our ordinary speech — our conversations with friends, our practical exchange of ideas on the athletic field, etc. — we do not use sentences very regularly. For example, you meet someone in the corridor after class:

"Hello, Joe. Going home?"
"Yes. Coming?"
"No. Cafeteria. See you tonight."

In this conversation, which is perfectly good *colloquial* English, there is, strictly speaking, not even one

2a

sentence. Your *thoughts* are complete, but your *expression* of them is incomplete because you and Joe are in a hurry. How unnatural the hurried conversation would sound if it were carried on in sentences!

"Hello, Joe. Are you going home?"
"Yes, I am going home. Are you coming?"
"No. I'm going to the cafeteria. I'll see you tonight."

These are your thoughts, but so far as you and Joe are concerned, you have expressed them in the first example quite adequately. However, when you are writing a careful explanation or an important letter, when you are trying to be convincing on paper or to state clearly what you know in an examination, you want to be as clear in your writing as you are in your thoughts. At such times you are careful to express your thoughts completely. To do this you make sure to write in sentences. At such times each group of words you use is a completely expressed thought. It begins with a capital letter and ends with a period (or, of course, a question mark or an exclamation point).

Subject and Predicate

2b. A sentence consists of two parts: the *subject* and the *predicate*. The *subject* of the sentence is that part about which something is being said. The *predicate* is that part which says something about the subject.

Subject   Predicate
The largest planes | are not the most efficient.

Predicate   Subject
Strong and weatherbeaten and happy were | the returning campers.

Subject   Predicate
The old trapper | was telling one story after another.

● EXERCISE 1. In the following sentences tell what the subject is and what the predicate is. If your teacher directs you to copy the sentences onto your paper, draw one line under the complete subject and two lines under the complete predicate. Bear in mind that, as in the second example on page 26, the subject may come *after* the predicate. Do not write in this book.

1. Frances sang three songs at our concert.
2. A tall, gray-haired man attracted our attention.
3. All around us rose the snow-capped peaks.
4. The light drizzle became a downpour in the afternoon.
5. Many of your best friends will be waiting for you.
6. The new automobiles are faster and safer.
7. Freddie threw off his coat and began to work.
8. In the water was a large diving raft.
9. Jerry received a pen and pencil set as a birthday gift.
10. The king of France treated his subjects with indifference.

THE COMPLETE PREDICATE AND THE VERB

You have learned that the predicate of a sentence is that part which says something about the subject. This part is really the *complete predicate*. Within the complete predicate there is always a word (or group of words) which is the "heart" of the predicate, the key word or words in the predicate.

2c. The principal word or group of words in the complete predicate is called the *simple predicate* or, more commonly, the *verb*.

EXAMPLES   A squadron of Army planes **flew** low over the school. [Complete predicate: *flew low over the school;* verb: *flew*]

Several curious students **were standing** outside the door. [Complete predicate: *were standing outside the door;* verb: *were standing*]

2b-c

THE VERB PHRASE

When a verb form is accompanied by helping verbs, it is a verb phrase. The following are examples of verb phrases: *am going, will be, has seen, has been seen, did send, would have been.* In the following sentences, the verb is printed in heavy type; the rest of the complete predicate is italicized. Study the sentences carefully so that you will be able to pick out the verb in the sentences in the next exercise.

1. The principal **spoke** *to us this morning about our conduct.*
2. He **had entered** *the auditorium slowly and solemnly.*
3. Nearly everyone in the room **expected** *a scolding.*
4. The quiet tension **was felt** *by everyone.*
5. The president of our student council **arose** *stiffly from his seat.*

● EXERCISE 2. Number in a column on your paper from 1 to 10. Find the verb in each of the following sentences and write it after the proper number on your paper. If you find a verb phrase, be sure to include all the helping verbs.

1. Six o'clock is the busiest time of day for the gateman at the Main Street crossing.
2. Four express trains go through the village within a space of ten minutes.
3. The traffic on Main Street becomes very heavy at this time.
4. Pete puts the gates down at six o'clock.
5. Three minutes later he raises them.
6. They are lowered a second time at 6:06.
7. Two flyers thunder by in a cloud of smoke and cinders.
8. Once again up go the gates.
9. At 6:10 Pete cranks them down again for the *Cannonball.*
10. By this time dozens of cars are waiting.

THE COMPLETE SUBJECT AND THE SIMPLE SUBJECT

As you know, the subject of a sentence is that part about which something is being said. This part is really the *complete subject*. The principal word in the complete subject is called the *simple subject*.

2d. The *simple subject* is a word naming the person, place, thing, or idea about which something is being said.

EXAMPLE   *A heavy red* **truck** swung around the corner. [Complete subject: *A heavy red truck;* simple subject: *truck*]

In naming the simple subject, consider proper nouns as one word.

EXAMPLE   *The* **Empire State Building** *in* New York is the tallest skyscraper in the world. [Complete subject: *The Empire State Building in New York;* simple subject: *Empire State Building*]

▶ CAUTION: Remember that *noun* and *subject* do not mean the same thing. A *noun* is the name of a person, place, thing, or an idea. *Subject* is the name of a part of a sentence; it is usually a noun or pronoun.

Throughout the rest of this book the word **subject** *will be used to mean the* **simple subject**.

HOW TO FIND THE SUBJECT OF A SENTENCE

Because the subject may appear at almost any point in the sentence, you will find it easier to locate the subject if you will pick out the verb first. For instance:

The hero of the expedition led his men to safety.

The verb is *led*. Now ask yourself, "Who or what led?" Your answer is *hero;* hence *hero* is the subject. In the sentence:

In the middle of the morning came the mail.

2d

the verb is *came*. Ask yourself, "Who or what came?" Your answer is *mail;* hence *mail* is the subject.

The best way to find the subject of a sentence is to find the verb first and then ask yourself, "Who or what.....?"

● EXERCISE 3.   Number on your paper from 1 to 10. Write the verb and the subject of each of the following sentences after the proper number on your paper. Select the verb first.

1. A creaking sound startled me.
2. From out of the darkened hallway came a blinding flash.
3. The brilliant beam moved quickly.
4. It picked out the stairway at once.
5. To my ears came a muffled cry.
6. This unexpected sound indicated more than one visitor.
7. A few cautious footsteps on the stairs were followed by a dull thud.
8. The suspense became too much for me.
9. With a shout I leaped from my hiding place.
10. The hall lights revealed nothing.

● EXERCISE 4.   Number in a column from 1 to 10. In each sentence select the verb and the subject and copy them on your paper after the proper number.

1. A tall boy almost always has an advantage.
2. A few extra inches may make a lot of difference in a basketball game.
3. Height is of especial advantage under the basket.
4. Shots from beneath the basket are hard for a short player.
5. Long arms are a great help in retrieving the ball from the backboard.
6. The player with long arms and legs has an advantage in tennis, too.
7. Some tall, long-legged boys are clumsy in their movements.

8. A short and fast athlete runs rings around them.
9. Certain positions on a baseball team are played better by a short, heavy-set boy.
10. Most famous catchers have been stocky in build.

THE SUBJECT IN AN UNUSUAL POSITION

There are two kinds of sentences whose word order you must usually change when you wish to find the verb and its subject. These are (1) sentences which begin with the words *there* or *here*, and (2) sentences which ask a question.

1. *Sentences which begin with* **there** *or* **here**

When the words *there* and *here* come at the beginning of a sentence, they may appear to be subjects, but usually they are not subjects. Following the formula for finding the subject of a sentence will prevent your mistaking *there* and *here* for the subject.

EXAMPLE   **There were many reasons for leaving.**   [Verb:
were   What were? *reasons (were)*]

2. *Sentences which ask a question*

EXAMPLE   **What were you doing?**

A question should be changed into a statement: *You were doing what.* Now you can see that *were doing* is the verb, and *you* is the subject.

The words in a verb phrase may be separated from one another by other words. In the sentence *Did he help you?* the verb is *did help.* The subject *he* separates the parts of the verb phrase.

Other examples of verb phrases separated in this way are:

	Verb Phrase
Where have you been?	have been
Does he expect you?	does expect
Have you been playing football?	have been playing
Will your father be coming soon?	will be coming

● EXERCISE 5.   Number in a column from 1 to 10. Select the verb and the subject in each of the following sentences and write them after the proper number on your paper. Rearrange the sentences if necessary. Select the verb first. Be sure to write down all parts of a verb phrase.

1. There are ten boys in the class.
2. Where is the teacher of this class?
3. Where were you going?
4. There will be a pep rally this evening.
5. There is no reason for your taking such an attitude.
6. Did John take your book?
7. There are two strange books in my locker.
8. Where did he spend his summer vacation?
9. Are there any voters in favor of this plan?
10. Here are a few arguments against your idea.

SENTENCES IN WHICH THE SUBJECT IS UNDERSTOOD

Whenever you make a request of someone or command someone, you usually leave out of your sentence the subject, which is the word *you*.

EXAMPLES   **Please bring me that pen.**
                  Go home at once!

In the first sentence the verb is *bring*. Who is to do the bringing? What the sentence means is "*You* please bring me that pen." In the second sentence, the verb is *go*. Who is to go? "*You* go home at once!" Hence the subject in both sentences is *you*, even though the word does not appear in the sentence. A subject of this kind is an *understood subject*.

COMPOUND SUBJECTS AND VERBS

2e. When the subject consists of two or more connected words, it is called a *compound*

subject. **The commonest connecting words are** *and* **and** *or.*

EXAMPLE   **James** and his **sister** *have gone* to a new school. [Verb: *have gone;* compound subject: *James* (and) *sister*]

2f. When the verb consists of two or more verbs joined by a connecting word, it is called a *compound* **verb.**

EXAMPLE   On our fishing trip we **paddled** more than a hundred miles and **caught** dozens of fish. [Compound verb: *paddled* (and) *caught;* subject: *we*]

● EXERCISE 6.   Write 3 sentences containing a compound subject, 3 containing a compound verb, and 3 containing both a compound subject and a compound verb.

2g. The subject is never in a prepositional phrase.

A prepositional phrase is a group of words which begins with a preposition and ends with a noun or pronoun: *in the morning, of them.* Finding the subject when it is followed by a phrase may be difficult.

EXAMPLE   One *of these boys* will be elected.

You see, at once, that the verb is *will be elected.* When you ask, "Who will be elected?" you are likely to make the mistake of answering *boys.* However, that is not what the sentence says. The sentence says, "*One of these boys will be elected.*" The subject is *one.* You notice that *boys* is part of the phrase *of these boys.* In many sentences you can easily isolate the verb and subject simply by crossing out all prepositional phrases.

EXAMPLE   The building ~~with large wings on either side~~ looks ~~like ours in the state capital at home.~~

Verb: **looks**   Subject: **building**

2e-g

● EXERCISE 7. Write 2 sentences containing an understood subject, 2 containing a compound subject, 2 containing a compound verb, 2 in which the subject follows the verb, and 2 in which the subject is followed by a prepositional phrase.

● EXERCISE 8. Number on your paper from 1 to 10. Write down the verb and before it the subject of each sentence. If the subject of the sentence is understood, write down *you* as the subject.

EXAMPLES
1. **Unfortunately there is no acceptable excuse for your actions.**
   1. excuse   is

2. **The boys and girls work hard at their studies and play hard at their games.**
   2. boys   girls   work   play

1. There will be plenty of time later.
2. Is one of your brothers going to college?
3. Bring your violin.
4. How beautiful are the mountains and the hills!
5. Where have you and Betty been sitting?
6. Both of these shoes are mine.
7. There are many vacant desks in Room 5.
8. How many people have you told this to?
9. Leave at once and go back to your class!
10. Will neither of those covers fit this box?

2h. A sentence expresses a completed thought.

You have just learned that a sentence contains a verb and its subject. This does not mean that all groups of words containing a verb and its subject are sentences. To be a sentence such groups of words must also express a *completed thought.*

In *when he was in high school* there are a verb and its subject — the verb is *was;* the subject is *he.* Yet the group of words is not a sentence because it does not express a completed thought. It is a fragment, a part of a sentence. Contrast: *He played varsity football when he was in high school.* Now you have a *sentence.* The thought has been completed.

● EXERCISE 9.   Some of the following groups of words are sentences and some are sentence fragments.[1] Number on a sheet of paper from 1 to 20. Read each group of words thoughtfully. (Reading aloud will be better than reading silently.) If it is a sentence, put an *S* beside the corresponding number on your paper. If it is not a sentence, write an *F* for fragment. Ask yourself whether the group of words has a verb and its subject and *whether it expresses a completed thought.*

S   1. She is coming on the afternoon train.
F   2. Leaving the rest of us stranded.
S   3. I don't remember him very well.
F   4. My favorite television programs.
S   5. The teachers held a meeting.
S   6. No one could understand the speaker.
F   7. Which my father made for me.
S   8. In the front of the room sat our headmaster.
F   9. If you want to go with us.
S 10. You ought to think before you speak.
F 11. Riding in the back part of the truck with boxes, crates, and baskets.
S 12. You will receive your reports tomorrow.
F 13. While the President was speaking on the radio.
F 14. After I had finished my homework last night.
F 15. As Walker stepped into the room and everyone turned to greet him.
S 16. If you will be patient, you will get what you want.
F 17. With four children of her own and two nephews to care for.
S 18. A committee was appointed to study the problem.

2h

---

[1] Further treatment of sentence fragments will be found in Chapter 4, "Writing Complete Sentences."

ᴵᶠ
19. Day after day and night after night.
⌒⌐ 20. Please give me another day for this assignment.

● EXERCISE 10.   There were 10 sentence fragments in the preceding exercise. Write these on your paper and, by adding to them, make each one a complete sentence. The words you add may be placed before or after the fragment.

2i. Sentences may be classified according to their purpose.[2]

There are four kinds of sentences: (1) declarative, (2) imperative, (3) interrogative, (4) exclamatory.

(1) A sentence which merely makes a statement is a *declarative* sentence.   Its purpose is to *declare* something. Most of the sentences you use are declarative.

EXAMPLES   At the end of the day everyone was exhausted.
            I told my brother to do his own homework.

(2) A sentence which gives a command or makes a request is an *imperative* sentence.

EXAMPLES   Raise your right hand.
            Please bring your literature books to class.

(3) A sentence which asks a question is an *interrogative* sentence.   To *interrogate* means to *ask*. An interrogative sentence is followed by a question mark.

EXAMPLE   Where have you been?
           Isn't he tall?

(4) A sentence which expresses strong feeling is an *exclamatory* sentence.   It exclaims. A declarative, imperative, or interrogative sentence may be spoken in

---

[2] Classification of sentences according to *structure* is taught in connection with the study of modifying clauses on pages 78–80.

such a way that it will be exclamatory. Then it should be followed by an exclamation mark.

EXAMPLES   **That is enough!** [Declarative becomes exclamatory.]
Bend over!   [Imperative becomes exclamatory.]
Isn't he tall! [Interrogative becomes exclamatory.]

● EXERCISE 11.   Classify the sentences in Exercise 8 according to the four kinds you have just learned.

● EXERCISE 12.   Write 3 sentences which could be read as declarative, interrogative, or exclamatory, according to the speaker's purpose. For instance, look at the following sentence:

> **Johnny's coming.** [declarative]
> **Johnny's coming!** [exclamatory]
> **Johnny's coming?** [interrogative]

Diagraming Sentences

Many students find that they can understand sentence parts better when they use a diagram. A diagram is a means of arranging a sentence in a kind of picture form. The picture shows clearly how the various parts of the sentence fit together and how they are related. You may find diagraming useful to you, and for that reason this book contains an explanation of how to diagram each of the parts of a sentence.

The first thing to do in making a diagram is to draw a straight horizontal line on your paper. Somewhere to the left of the center of the line draw a short vertical line crossing the horizontal one. This vertical line is the dividing point between the complete subject and the complete predicate of your sentence. The

2i

subject and all words that relate to it (in other words, the complete subject) go to the left of this vertical line; the verb and all words that relate to it (in other words, the complete predicate) go to the right.

1. *Diagraming the subject and the verb*
On the horizontal line to the right you place the verb. To the left you place the subject.

| Subject | verb |

2. *Diagraming the understood subject*
For an understood subject use the word *you* in parentheses as the subject in your diagram.

Go at once. | (you) | go |

3. *Diagraming modifying words*
Modifiers of the subject and the verb (adjectives and adverbs) are written on slanting lines connected to the subject or verb.

An ancient jalopy rattled noisily by.

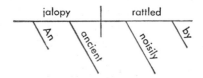

4. *Diagraming compound subjects and verbs*
When you have a sentence with a compound subject or a compound verb, diagram it as shown on the next page.
Notice in the diagram how the word *together*, modifying both parts of the compound verb, is diagramed so that it clearly is related to both parts. The

same method is used when a word modifies both parts of a compound subject.

Children and adults worked and played together.

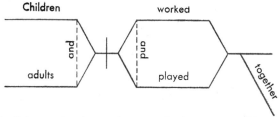

5. *Diagraming* **here, there,** *and* **where** *as modifiers*

When the words *here, there,* and *where* are modifiers of the verb, diagram them as in the following illustrations.

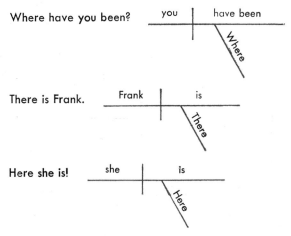

6. *Diagraming* **there** *when it does not modify any-thing* [3]

---

[3] In this use *there* does not tell where. It merely helps to start the sentence. When used in this way, *there* is called an *expletive* (Latin, *filling up*). The word *it* may also be used as an expletive; for instance, *It* is fun to play ball.

When *there* begins a sentence but does not modify either the verb or the subject, it is diagramed on a line by itself as in the following illustration.

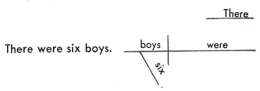

There were six boys.

7. *Diagraming a modifier of a modifier*

A word which modifies another modifier is diagramed like *very* in the following illustration.

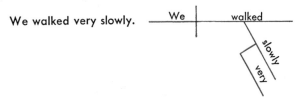

We walked very slowly.

● EXERCISE 13.   Diagram the following. Diagrams of the first five sentences are provided for you to copy and fill in.

1. We started early.

2. Our train traveled rapidly.

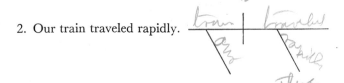

3. There was a loud explosion.

4. Our neighbors arose early today and went away.

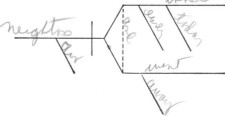

5. Stand still immediately.

6. The workmen left early.
7. A small package came today.
8. Both girls studied late.
9. Some Mexican girls came here today.
10. The gorgeous red sun was setting slowly.

● EXERCISE 14.   Diagram the following sentences.

1. We will play tomorrow.
2. The other girls disagreed bitterly.
3. Beyond lies Manchuria.
4. There are no large cities here.
5. Where are your English books?
6. Come here immediately.
7. Has my father arrived?
8. She dances very gracefully and skates beautifully.
9. Study harder.
10. An old skipper and his grandson live and work here.

● REVIEW EXERCISE A.   Before continuing your study of the parts of a sentence, you should review what you have learned thus far. Be sure that you understand thoroughly everything you have covered because you will be building constantly upon what you have just learned. Can you give in your own words a definition of each of the following and make up an example to illustrate it?

1. A sentence
2. A complete subject
3. A complete predicate
4. A subject (simple)
5. A compound subject
6. A verb (simple pred.)
7. A verb phrase
8. A compound verb
9. An understood subject
10. A prepositional phrase
11. A declarative sentence
12. An imperative sentence
13. An interrogative sentence
14. An exclamatory sentence

● REVIEW EXERCISE B.   Number in a column on your paper from 1 to 15. Select from each of the following sentences the verb and the subject and write them after the proper number on your paper. Be especially careful to include all parts of a *verb phrase*. This is a mastery test to show that you can identify the verb and its subject.

1. Give me your opinion of him.
2. Where has your brother been?
3. What did Mother say?
4. Tell him your story and note his reaction.
5. What were Jean and she doing?
6. Will one of you boys bring your dictionary to class?
7. There could have been several other reasons for his attitude.
8. Do you and Ralph see each other often?
9. All of these vegetables have spoiled.
10. Our journey will probably take us to Europe.
11. A handsome young fellow in an officer's uniform was approaching from the opposite corner.
12. There will be a lot of presents for everyone.
13. None of my relatives live in the East.
14. Where did Phil leave my books?
15. Where will you and the other boys eat and sleep?

Complements

Every sentence has a base. This base may be compared to the foundation of a building or to the backbone of an animal. It is that part of the sentence upon which are built or from which are suspended all the other parts of the sentence. Sometimes the base itself is composed of only two parts. These are the subject and the verb.

EXAMPLES   The **kettle** of boiling water **exploded.** [Base: *kettle exploded*]
The **mystery** of the haunted house **was explained.** [Base: *mystery was explained*]

Most sentences, however, have a base which is composed of three parts: the subject, the verb, and the *complement*.

2j. The *complement* is a word or group of words which completes the meaning begun by the verb and subject.

The following example will show you how the complement does this.

The firemen extinguished the blaze.

	Subject	Verb	Complement
BASE	firemen	extinguished	blaze

You can see that the complement *blaze* is a necessary part of this sentence base. The subject *firemen* and the verb *extinguished* by themselves would not be enough to make a complete thought. Study the following sentences and their bases. The bases are printed in heavy type. Name the part of speech of each complement. For instance, in the first sentence, the complement *captain* is a noun. In the second sentence, the complement *tall* is an adjective.

1. **Harold is** our **captain.**
2. Their **captain is** very **tall.**
3. **Jimmy defeated** his **brother.**
4. **Everyone** in the car **was** probably **afraid.**

2j

5. Both **Matt** and **Paul knocked** the **ball** over the fence.
6. His little **house looked** quite **attractive.**
7. Our club **secretary read** the **minutes.**
8. The new **planes make** a terrifying **roar.**
9. This small donkey **engine can pull** a long **string** of cars.
10. **Jane** always **seems** quite **happy.**

● EXERCISE 15. Using your imagination, construct sentences from the following sentence bases. Do not be satisfied with adding only one or two words. Make *interesting* sentences.

SUBJECT	VERB	COMPLEMENT
1. team	defeated	opponents
2. sky	was	blue
3. officer	caught	boys
4. visitors	departed	
5. teacher	is	friend
6. father	is	foreman
7. storm	was	violent
8. building	seemed	tall
9. dog	is	mine
10. bells	rang	

● EXERCISE 16. Number in a column on your paper from 1 to 17. Select from each of the following sentences the sentence base. Write the base after the proper number on your paper.

1. His victory surprised all of us.
2. Everyone in school was proud of him.
3. For his achievement he received a gold medal.
4. The spectators cheered him.
5. The townspeople held a banquet in his honor.
6. The school bought twenty-five new typewriters.
7. The commercial students were very glad.
8. The old typewriters had been good machines in their day.
9. The new typewriters were noiseless.

10. I shall take typing next year.
11. That is the course for me.
12. Have you been ill?
13. A timely warning may save many lives.
14. She will be an excellent addition to the faculty.
15. You should not believe his tall tales.
16. Not one of the members of the club knows the new applicant for membership.
17. The team from Australia won every match.

THE SUBJECT COMPLEMENT

You may have noticed as you were selecting the bases of the sentences above that the complements are of several kinds. Some of them refer to the subject: for example, in Sentence 9, in the base *typewriters were noiseless*, *noiseless* refers to the subject *typewriters*. Also, in Sentence 8, in the sentence base *typewriters had been machines*, *machines* refers to the subject, explaining what the *typewriters had been*.

2k. Complements which describe or explain the simple subject are called *subject complements*.

There are two kinds of subject complements. If the subject complement is a noun or a pronoun, it is a *predicate nominative*. If the subject complement is an adjective, it is a *predicate adjective*.

Predicate nominatives (nouns and pronouns) and adjectives are linked to the subject by linking verbs only. (See page 10.) The common linking verbs are *be*,[4] *become, feel, smell, taste, look, grow, seem, appear, remain, sound, stay*.

● EXERCISE 17.   Number on your paper from 1 to 10. Select the subject complement from each of the following sentences and write it after the corresponding number on your paper. *Your work will be*

_____

[4] For the other forms of *be*, see page 10.

2k

easier if you first find the verb and its subject. After each complement write what kind it is: predicate nominative or predicate adjective.

1. The large, awkward-looking machines in the fields were reapers.
2. Your trip may be dangerous.
3. When rescued, the explorers were ill.
4. The uniformed attendants were foreign soldiers.
5. The plane from South America was a beauty.
6. That is he.
7. Our days in prison seemed endless.
8. His account of the accident was a good story.
9. Beside him I felt very small.
10. The new teacher certainly looks young.

DISTINGUISHING BETWEEN SUBJECT AND COMPLEMENT

When the subject is not in its normal position before the verb, as in questions and "turned around" sentences, the complement may seem to be the subject. However, if you always determine the subject in the usual way, you will have no difficulty distinguishing between subject and complement.

EXAMPLES   **A strong man was Mr. Bush.** [Verb: *was*   Who was? *Mr. Bush*   Complement: *man*]

           Are these boys your friends? [Verb: *are*   Who are? *boys*   Complement: *friends*]

DIAGRAMING THE PREDICATE NOMINATIVE AND THE PREDICATE ADJECTIVE

A subject complement (predicate nominative or predicate adjective) should be placed on the same horizontal line with the simple subject and the predicate verb. It comes after the verb, and a line *slanting toward the subject* and drawn upward from the horizontal line separates it from the verb. The line slants toward the subject to show that the subject complement is closely related to the subject. The following example shows how to diagram a subject complement.

PREDICATE NOMINATIVE **Our storekeeper is a fat man.**

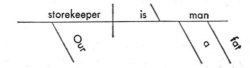

PREDICATE ADJECTIVE **Our storekeeper is fat.**

● EXERCISE 18. Diagram the following sentences.

1. The new president is a capable man.
2. Does that apple taste good?
3. That might have been they.
4. The thief probably was he.
5. The last few miles were very tiring.
6. Yesterday's homework seemed too difficult.
7. Are you the manager?
8. Jack will undoubtedly be our next pitcher.
9. The new mayor is a banker.
10. Mr. Jones was once my neighbor.

THE OBJECT COMPLEMENT

There is a kind of complement, however, which does not refer to the subject. Instead, *it receives the action of the verb or names the result of the action.* Notice the word *opponents* in the following sentence.

EXAMPLE **The first *team defeated* their *opponents* easily.**
[Base: *team defeated opponents*]

Here, you see, the complement *opponents* receives from the subject an action stated by the verb *defeated*. In other words, the verb tells what the subject did to the complement. In sentences of this kind, in which the complement receives the action of the verb, the complement is called an *object complement*. Object complements are usually called simply *objects*. There are two kinds of objects, the *direct* and the *indirect*.

21. The *direct object* is a word or group of words that directly receives the action expressed by the verb or names the result of the action.

EXAMPLES   Father took **us** with him.
James built a **boat**.

In the first sentence, *us* is the *direct object*. It directly receives the action expressed by the verb *took*. In the second sentence *boat* is the direct object, telling the result of the action *built*. Objects are used after *action* verbs only. Verbs like *think, believe, imagine*, which express mental action, are action verbs just as truly as verbs like *hit, fight, play, write*, which express physical action.

● EXERCISE 19.   List the direct objects. Be able to tell the verb whose action the object receives.

1. George's father caught some fine trout.
2. He used a new kind of fly.
3. He makes his own flies.
4. Mr. Stark enjoys fishing.
5. Sometimes he takes George and me with him.
6. We have no expensive equipment like his.
7. I need a pair of rubber boots.
8. George received a new rod and reel for his birthday.
9. Last week I caught my first trout.
10. I threw the little fish back into the stream.

▶ CAUTION: Like the subject, the object of a verb is never part of a prepositional phrase.

2m. An *indirect object* is a noun or pronoun in the predicate that normally precedes (comes be-

fore) the direct object. It usually tells *to whom* or *for whom* the action of the verb is done.

Study the following sentences:

The postman left a letter for me.
The postman left me a letter.

You recognized *letter* as a direct object in both sentences. It receives directly the action of the verb. In the second sentence you have another word which seems to receive, indirectly at least, the action of the verb. That word is *me. Me*, which comes before the direct object, tells *for whom* the letter was left. It is an *indirect object.*

What is the *indirect object* in this sentence?

I sent Harold a letter.

Letter is the direct object; *Harold* is the indirect object. It is Harold *to whom* the letter was sent.

If the words *to* and *for* are used, the word following them is part of a prepositional phrase and not an indirect object. Compare the following pairs.

1. I read a story **to her.**   [No indirect object]
   I read **her** a story.   [*Her* is the indirect object.]
2. Mother made a new dress **for me.**   [No indirect object]
   Mother made **me** a new dress.   [*Me* is the indirect object.]

▶ CAUTION: When identifying complements, do not be confused by adverbs in the predicate.

   We went **home.**   [adverb telling where]
   We have a new **home.**   [direct object complement]

● EXERCISE 20.   Make two columns on your paper. Label one column *direct objects.* Label the other column *indirect objects.* List in the proper column all the direct and indirect objects in the following sentences. You will not find an indirect object in every sentence.

1. We planned a long hike through the pine forest.
2. Our head counselor gave us permission.
3. He lent me his canteen.
4. The forest held no fears for such seasoned campers.
5. Usually they give campers a guide for this trip.
6. I gave George the compass.
7. He gladly gave me the maps.
8. I showed the boys a short cut through the swamp.
9. We told the younger boys stories about being lost.
10. We followed the fire lanes through the woods.

COMPOUND COMPLEMENTS

Complements may be compound.

COMPOUND PREDICATE NOMINATIVE (NOUN)   The winners of the contest were **Helen** and **Dot**.

COMPOUND PREDICATE ADJECTIVE   He is **intelligent** and **industrious**.

COMPOUND DIRECT OBJECT   Father sent my **brother** and **me** to camp.

COMPOUND INDIRECT OBJECT   The coach gave **Jim** and **me** varsity letters.

● EXERCISE 21.   Write 2 sentences containing a compound subject, 2 containing a compound verb, 2 containing a compound predicate nominative, 2 containing a compound predicate adjective, 2 containing a compound direct object.

DIAGRAMING THE DIRECT AND THE INDIRECT OBJECT

The *direct object* is diagramed in almost the same way as the predicate nominative. The only difference is that the line separating the object from the verb is *vertical* (not slanting), as in the following examples.

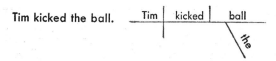

Tim kicked the ball.

We heard jokes and stories.   [compound direct object]

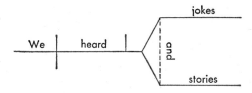

The *indirect object* is diagramed on a horizontal line beneath the verb of which the word is the indirect object.

Esther's friends gave her a party.

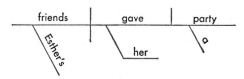

● EXERCISE 22.   Diagram the following sentences.

1. August is usually a hot month.
2. Everyone seems hot and tired.
3. The muggy weather bothers animals.
4. Our dog follows my sister and me everywhere.
5. We gave him a cool bath yesterday.

● REVIEW EXERCISE C.   Copy the numbered italicized words in a column on your paper. After each write the correct one of the following identifications, using these abbreviations: subject, *s*; verb, *v*; predicate adjective, *p.a.*; predicate nominative, *p.n.*; direct object, *d.o.*; indirect object, *i.o.*; object of preposition, *o.p.*

Are there any (1) *coins* in your pocket? If so, you are (2) *lucky*. At one (3) *time* in the world's history, (4) *cattle* were the only (5) *money*. Using cattle as money today would be rather (6) *awkward*. You could hardly give a (7) *storekeeper* a (8) *calf* in payment for a new dress. "Pecunia" is the Latin (9) *word* for money. It comes from "pecus," which means cattle. Fortunately, your remote (10) *ancestors* eventually (11) *found* a kind of (12) *money* more portable than cattle. Various materials besides metal have been used for money. Men have given their (13) *creditors* (14) *payment* in such interesting things as stones, elephant tails, shells, and salt. Our word "salary" comes from the Latin word "sal," meaning salt. Caesar gave his (15) *soldiers*, as part of their pay, money to buy salt. Our slang phrase "shell out" is a (16) *reminder* of the old custom of using shells as payment.

In seventeenth-century America, pioneers used (17) *furs* for money. A good gun was (18) *valuable*. (19) *It* was worth a pile of beaver (20) *pelts* as high as the gun was long. At one time, Tennessee (21) *paid* its (22) *governor* an official (23) *salary* of 100 deerskins a year. In Virginia for many (24) *years*, tobacco was the only legal (25) *tender*.

The first coin of the United States Government was authorized in 1787. It was a (26) *cent* and (27) *bore* the inscription "Mind Your Business." Today American coins bear the phrase "In God We Trust." Most people, of course, would rather carry paper (28) *money* than coins. Our government (29) *prints* bills at the rate of more than two billion a year, including all denominations. Still the handy (30) *checkbook* is our real (31) *means* of exchange. The fourteen million (32) *checks* written every day in the United States (33) *cover* 90 per cent of all the exchange of money, both personal and business.

CHAPTER 3

The Sentence

PHRASES AND CLAUSES

For complete understanding of correct sentence structure you need to know phrases and clauses — how the various kinds are formed and what they do in a sentence. Since phrases and clauses are advanced items in grammar, you will probably want to study this chapter carefully.

The Phrase

You know that a group of words used as a verb is a *verb phrase. Have been sleeping, is sleeping, will be sleeping* are verb phrases. Groups of words may also be used as adjectives, adverbs, and nouns.

3a. A group of words used as a single part of speech and not containing a verb and its subject is called a *phrase.*

PREPOSITIONAL PHRASES

3b. A group of words which begins with a preposition and ends with a noun or pronoun is a *prepositional phrase.*[1]

EXAMPLES   by + the old mill **stream**
to + **him**

[1] Do not confuse the infinitive form of a verb (*to see, to run*) with a prepositional phrase beginning with the preposition *to — to me, to the store.*

3a-b

3c. The noun or pronoun which concludes the prepositional phrase is the *object of the preposition* which begins the phrase.

EXAMPLES   **In** the *summer* Bob went **to** a *camp* **for** *boys.*
[*Summer* is the object of the preposition *in; camp* is the object of the preposition *to; boys* is the object of the preposition *for.*]
During the entire *afternoon* I waited **for** *him.*
[*Afternoon* is the object of the preposition *during; him* is the object of the preposition *for.*]

THE PREPOSITIONAL PHRASE USED AS AN ADJECTIVE [2]

If you will study the phrases in heavy type in this sentence, you will see that each modifies a noun:

EXAMPLE   A lady **in the front row** was wearing a hat **with a big red feather**.

The phrase *in the front row* tells *which* lady, and since it thus modifies the noun *lady*, it is used as an adjective, for only adjectives modify nouns. The phrase *with a big red feather* describes the noun *hat*. It modifies a noun; it is an *adjective phrase*.

3d. A phrase that modifies a noun or a pronoun is an *adjective phrase*.

If you thoughtfully examine the pairs of sentences below, you will see just how a phrase is used as an adjective.

1. The **morning** delivery was late.
   The delivery **in the morning** was late.
2. The **wood** pile grew taller as the men worked.
   The pile **of wood** grew taller as the men worked.
3. The **Boston** papers opposed his election.
   The papers **in Boston** opposed his election.

[2] For work on the correct use of adjective phrases see "Misplaced Phrase Modifiers" on page 176.

● EXERCISE 1.   Each of the following sentences contains two adjective phrases. List them in order on your paper. After each phrase write the noun it modifies.

EXAMPLE   The man at the gate gave me a bundle of tickets.

Phrase	Word Modified
at the gate	man
of tickets	bundle

1. My friend in England sent me a book of short stories.
2. The men at work envied those on vacation.
3. This book by Charles Dickens gives a picture of nineteenth-century England.
4. We had a piece of cake with chocolate frosting.
5. People from the South have an accent of their own.

THE PREPOSITIONAL PHRASE USED AS AN ADVERB [3]

3e. A phrase that modifies a verb, an adjective, or an adverb is an *adverb phrase*.

Compare the sentences in each of the groups below.

1. Our homeroom team won the game **easily.**
   Our homeroom team won the game **with ease.**
2. The spectators celebrated the victory **enthusiastically.**
   The spectators celebrated the victory **with enthusiasm.**
3. **Earlier** we had eaten a big breakfast.
   At an earlier hour we had eaten a big breakfast.

Name the modified verb in each sentence.

As you know, adverbs may also modify adjectives and other adverbs. Hence adverb phrases may likewise be used as modifiers of adjectives and adverbs.

EXAMPLES   The new coat was too large **across the shoulders.** [adverb phrase modifying adjective *large*]
Later **in the day** the rain stopped. [adverb phrase modifying adverb *later*]

[3] For work on the proper use of adverb phrases, see "Misplaced Phrase Modifiers" on page 176.

3c-e

Adverb phrases modify other words in the same ways that adverbs modify other words. An adverb phrase may tell *how, when, where, why,* or *to what extent.*

● EXERCISE 2.   Each of the following sentences contains two adverb phrases. List these phrases in order on your paper. After each phrase write the word the phrase modifies.

EXAMPLE   **He arrived at ten o'clock and left after lunch.**

Phrase	Word Modified
at ten o'clock	arrived
after lunch	left

1. We went by ourselves but returned with the boys.
2. Gerald and I stood on the corner and talked for an hour.
3. Mr. Sikes walked into the room and put the assignment on the blackboard.
4. John arrived at dawn and left before nightfall.
5. In Detroit I stayed with my uncle.

DIAGRAMING ADJECTIVE AND ADVERB PHRASES

Prepositional phrases used as adjectives and adverbs are diagramed in much the same way as adjectives and adverbs. The preposition which begins the phrase is placed on a slanting line leading down from the word the phrase modifies. The noun or pronoun which ends the phrase is placed on a horizontal line drawn from the slanting line.

EXAMPLE   **The owner of the car waited for several hours.**
[*Of the car* is an adjective phrase modifying the noun *owner. For several hours* is an adverb phrase modifying the verb *waited.*]

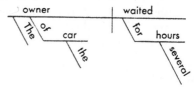

● EXERCISE 3. Diagram the following sentences.

1. Closely I watched the changes in the clouds.
2. A few of the wispy clouds vanished before my eyes.
3. About dusk a heavy group gathered along the horizon.
4. After dark I saw sharp flashes of lightning.
5. Soon strong gusts of wind warned me of imminent danger.

● EXERCISE 4. Write 5 sentences containing an adjective phrase and 5 sentences containing an adverb phrase. Underline each phrase and draw an arrow from the phrase to the word the phrase modifies.

The Verbals: Participial, Gerund, and Infinitive Phrases [4]

In Chapter 1 you learned that there are eight parts of speech. There are some words, however, which cannot be classified in any one of these eight classes because these words are really two parts of speech in one. These words are called *verbals* because they are formed from verbs and act very much like verbs. They are, however, used as other parts of speech. There are three kinds of verbals: the *participle*, the *gerund*, and the *infinitive*.

THE PARTICIPLE

A *participle* is a word formed from a verb and used as an adjective to modify a noun or a pronoun. From the verb *swim* you can form the participle *swimming*, as in the sentence:

The **swimming** beaver dived out of sight.

In this sentence the word *swimming* is partly a verb because it carries the action of the verb *swim*. Further-

---

[4] For work on the proper use of verbals, see "Dangling Modifiers" on page 172.

more, it is partly an adjective because it modifies the noun *beaver*. It is a participle. Study the use of the word *standing* in the following sentence:

Standing in the back of the auditorium, we could not hear the speaker.

In this sentence *standing* is a participle because it gives the action of the verb *stand;* yet, like an adjective, it modifies the pronoun *we.*

3f. A word which acts as both a verb and an adjective is called a *participle*. Participles which end in –*ing* are called *present participles*.

▶ CAUTION: Not all words ending in –*ing* are participles. When used as a verb, a word ending in –*ing* is part of a verb phrase. Study the difference in use between the words ending in –*ing* in the following sentences.

Walking home from school, Jack **was whistling.** [*Walking* is a participle; *whistling* is a part of the verb phrase *was whistling.*]

Jean, **looking** out the window, **was watching** the children **playing** in the street. [*Looking* is a participle; *was watching* is a verb phrase; *playing* is a participle.]

● EXERCISE 5.   From the following sentences select the present participles and list them in a column. After each participle write the noun or pronoun which it modifies.

1. Hurrying from one shop to another, the foreman was soon exhausted.
2. Helen, working rapidly, finished the dishes in a few minutes.
3. Pete is the boy carrying the flag.
4. Believing he was right, the speaker would not listen to any arguments.
5. Jim, seeing the danger, called us back.

6. The books lying on the table are mine.
7. Expecting visitors, we turned on the porch light.
8. We saw a number of fish lying under the bank.
9. Carrying furniture upstairs, Father strained his back.
10. I saw Jim driving the car.

● EXERCISE 6.   Improve the following choppy sentences by using present participles. By your revisions, eliminate wordiness and the childish style.

EXAMPLES   1. **The baby was crying. It was thirsty.**
            1. **The crying baby was thirsty.**

1. The jewels sparkled. They attracted my attention.
2. He leaped into action. He pounded violently on the cell door.
3. The train creaked and groaned. It managed to get through the tunnel.
4. We traveled west. We soon reached the crossroads.
5. The horses galloped. They climbed mountains and crossed ravines.

Participles which end in *–d, –ed, –t, –en,* or *–n* show action in the past and are called *past participles.* Study the words in heavy type in the following sentences.

She was an excited little girl.

Since *excited* in this sentence carries the action of the verb *excite* and at the same time modifies the noun *girl,* it is both verb and adjective — therefore a *participle.*

The dog, left alone in the house, kept all intruders away.

You can see that *left* carries the action of the verb *leave,* but it is an adjective too because it modifies the noun *dog.* Hence *left,* being both verb and adjective, is a *participle.*

● EXERCISE 7.   Select from the following sentences all the participles, both present and past. List them

3f

on your paper, and after each one write the word which the participle modifies.

1. Our teacher, annoyed by our conduct, kept us after school.
2. The boxes shipped from abroad came by air.
3. Awakened by the noise, Harold sprang to his feet, trembling with fear.
4. Seeing the problem clearly, I was able to solve it.
5. The days spent at the seashore improved my health.
6. Looking for the treasure buried by the old Spanish explorers, we uncovered many ancient relics.
7. Surprised by the sudden appearance of George wearing a new white suit, we rushed to meet him.
8. She came bringing gifts for us and left loaded with presents from us.
9. Sensing a disturbance in the back of the room, the professor called for order.
10. Angered by his attitude, the clerk refused to listen.

THE PARTICIPIAL PHRASE

3g. When a participle introduces a group of related words, all of which act together as an adjective, this word group is called a *participial phrase*.

The participial phrase in each of the following sentences is printed in heavy type. An arrow points to the noun or pronoun which the phrase modifies. Note that Sentences 1–5 contain present participles (ending in *–ing*) and Sentences 6–10 contain past participles (ending in *–ed, –d, –t, –en, –n*).

1. **Getting up from her desk,** Jane approached the teacher.
2. I found the child **crying for his mother.**
3. **Jumping with perfect form,** he cleared the bar at six feet.

4. **Working in his office all day,** Father gets very little exercise.

5. It was a shock to see you **coming around the corner.**

6. We were sorry for the dog, **chained to a stake all the time.**

7. **Admired by everyone,** he became conceited.

8. **Swept off his feet by the charge,** our quarterback was thrown for a loss.

9. **Taken completely by surprise,** the enemy was forced to surrender.

10. The sloop, **torn from its moorings,** ran aground.

● EXERCISE 8.   You have learned to identify adjective, adverb, and participial phrases. Select the adverb, adjective, and participial phrases from the following sentences and copy them on your paper. After each phrase write the word it modifies and tell what kind of phrase it is. Do not copy separately prepositional phrases that are part of a participial phrase.

When identifying participial phrases, do not be misled by verb phrases containing a word ending in *–ing* or *–ed: were talking, have been working, has jumped,* etc. (See CAUTION under **3f,** page 58.)

1. My cousins from Chicago are spending the summer with us.
2. Disturbed by the commotion, we could not sleep.
3. In the afternoon we played tennis with Jimmy and him.
4. The girls living in the next house helped us with our work.
5. Attracted by the promise of easy money, he accepted the job.
6. Bored with the party, I looked around the room for the pretty girl in the red dress.
7. Determined to get a hit, the man at the plate swung hard at the ball coming toward him.

3g

8. Acting on a hunch, the police stopped a small truck carrying coal and found the goods hidden in it.

THE GERUND

3h. The *gerund* is a word formed from a verb and used as a noun.

Study the darker words in the following sentences. They are *gerunds*. Prove that each word is part verb and part noun. For instance, *eating* in the first sentence is formed from the verb *eat;* yet it names an action. It is the name of something; therefore it is used as a noun. Further proof that *eating* is used as a noun is its use as subject of the sentence.

1. **Eating** is a great pleasure.
2. **Skiing** is my favorite winter sport.
3. We enjoyed **cooking** our dinner over a campfire.
4. The clever **playing** of the catcher saved the game.
5. **Controlling** the breath is important in **singing**.

You can see that each of the darker words is used as a noun. In some sentences it is used as the subject; in others it is used as the object of the verb. How is *singing* used in the fifth sentence? Unlike participles, gerunds always end in *–ing.*

● EXERCISE 9.   From the following verbs make gerunds and use each one in a sentence which will show clearly that your gerund is used as a noun. It may be one of the following in the sentence: subject of verb, object of verb, predicate nominative, object of a preposition.

1. be	3. swim	5. walk	7. talk	9. serve
2. run	4. hear	6. look	8. wait	10. sleep

THE GERUND PHRASE

3i. A *gerund* *phrase* is a phrase containing a gerund.

1. **Getting up early** is very painful.
2. **Eating breakfast hurriedly** will give you indigestion.
3. Fran's trouble is **being late for school.**
4. I dislike **studying late at night.**
5. By **dieting for a month,** she lost ten pounds.

Go back over the preceding examples and tell how each gerund phrase is used in the sentence. Is it the subject, the predicate nominative, the direct object, or the object of a preposition?

● EXERCISE 10. Write 5 sentences, each containing one or more gerund phrases. Underline each phrase and write above it how it is used — *s.,* subject; *o.,* object; *p.n.,* predicate noun; *o.p.,* object of a preposition. Include an example of each use.

THE INFINITIVE

3j. An *infinitive* is a verbal consisting of *to* followed by the verb. An infinitive is generally used as a noun, but may also be used as an adjective or an adverb.

To go, to see, to work are examples of infinitives. Study the infinitives in the following sentences and note how each is used.

1. **To skate** on thin ice is dangerous. [noun, subject of *is*]
2. We like **to study** in the library. [noun, object of *like*]
3. They had plenty of water **to drink.** [adjective, modifies *water*]
4. He played **to win.** [adverb, modifies *played*]
5. **To see** is **to believe.** [nouns, subject of *is* and predicate nominative after *is*]

3h-j

● EXERCISE 11. List on your paper the infinitives in the following sentences. After each infinitive, tell how it is used — as subject, object, predicate nominative.

1. To work rapidly in hot weather is impossible.
2. She promised to do her best.
3. I don't want to wait.
4. His ambition was to swim the channel.
5. To eat is a necessity as well as a pleasure.
6. She expects to see you.
7. To work by yourself is efficient.
8. To leave in the midst of such a storm would be to ask for trouble.
9. I love to listen to records.
10. She attempted to prevent my going.
11. We intend to win.
12. Their plan was to steal the blueprints.

THE INFINITIVE PHRASE

3k. A phrase which contains an infinitive is an infinitive phrase.

Study the make-up of the infinitive phrases in the sentences below.

1. My plan was **to leave early.**
2. The principal duty of the fire squad is **to prevent fires.**
3. Do you expect **to beat the champion?**
4. **To be a professional ballplayer** was Andy's ambition.
5. Jack has gone **to see his brother.**

● EXERCISE 12. Write 5 sentences, each containing one or more infinitive phrases.

Since a verbal is part verb, it may, like a verb, have modifiers and complements.

EXAMPLES   I spoke to the girl **standing** *behind me.* [The participle *standing* is modified by the adverb

phrase *behind me*, which is part of the participial
phrase *standing behind me*.]
After collecting *his wages,* Allan quit. [*Wages*
is the object of the gerund *collecting*.]
We asked Phil **to take** *our picture.* [*Picture* is
the object of the infinitive *to take*.]

● REVIEW EXERCISE A.   Each of the following sentences contains verbal phrases. List the phrases on
your paper; there are 20 of them. After each, tell
what kind it is: participial, gerund, infinitive. Modifiers and complements of a verbal are considered part
of the phrase.

1. Expecting praise, we were surprised to find ourselves
   being scolded.
2. Eating between meals is his favorite pastime, but sleeping in class gives him the greatest pleasure.
3. I watched the stream rising inch by inch and tried to
   warn the people living nearby.
4. Listening to music is a good way to relax.
5. I found the dullest part of the work was writing the book
   reports assigned every month.
6. The boys do not like practicing every day, but they all
   want to make the team.
7. Hindered by a painful thumb, Bert was unable to swing
   a bat hard enough to get a hit.
8. Thinking it was due today, I tried to write my essay
   riding to school on the bus.

● REVIEW EXERCISE B.   There are 20 phrases of
all kinds in the following paragraph. Copy them in
order on your paper. After each, tell what kind it is:
prepositional (adjective, adverb), participial, gerund,
infinitive. Some of the verbal phrases contain a prepositional phrase. In such cases, do not list the prepositional phrase separately.

Driving a car is a skill learned only by much experience.
Some beginners think they have learned to drive when they

3k

can start a car, steer it around the block, and stop it. Anyone above the age of five can start a car by turning a key and by pressing the accelerator. Steering a car through deserted streets is child's play. Handling an automobile, however, requires quick judgment and automatic responses based on experience. Taking the car out, you face a series of emergency situations demanding quick action. You may run into a traffic jam; you will almost certainly have to make a left turn when you are facing traffic. A driver must always anticipate the actions of other drivers. Perhaps most difficult of all is estimating distance and speed when you are passing a car going in the same direction.

The Clause [5]

31. A group of words that contains a verb and its subject and is used as a part of a sentence is called a *clause*.

DISTINGUISHING BETWEEN PHRASES AND CLAUSES

Study the following examples of phrases and clauses.

PHRASE a man *with a black hat*
CLAUSE a man **who wore** *a black hat* [The verb in this clause is *wore;* the subject of the clause is *who.*]

PHRASE *Climbing the ladder,* he lost his balance.
CLAUSE *While* **he was climbing** *the ladder,* he lost his balance. [The verb is *was climbing;* the subject is *he.*]

The difference between a clause and a phrase is that a clause has a verb and a subject; whereas a phrase does not.

DISTINGUISHING BETWEEN MAIN AND SUBORDINATE CLAUSES

3m. A *main* (or *independent*) *clause* is a clause that expresses a completed thought and can stand by itself as a sentence.

[5] For work on the proper use of clauses see "Misplaced Clause Modifiers" on page 178.

Standing by itself, a main (independent) clause would be called a sentence, but when written as a part of a sentence it is called a clause. For example, the two sentences below become main clauses when they are combined into one long sentence.

SENTENCES (completed thoughts) The train is pulled as far as Harrisburg by an electric locomotive.

From Harrisburg on, it is pulled by a diesel locomotive.

MAIN CLAUSES (parts of a sentence) The train is pulled as far as Harrisburg by an electric locomotive, *but* from Harrisburg on, it is pulled by a diesel locomotive.

The two main clauses in this sentence are joined into one sentence by the conjunction *but*.

3n. A *subordinate* (or *dependent*) *clause* is a clause which does not express a completed thought and cannot stand alone.

EXAMPLES When the shop door opened ....;

..... who was the shopkeeper

..... that someone was in the shop

These clauses depend upon a main clause to make their meaning complete. Note how they become meaningful when linked to a main clause (completed thought).

When the shop door opened, **a bell rang.**
Mr. Simon, who was the shopkeeper, **heard the bell.**
He knew that someone was in the shop.

● EXERCISE 13. The following list contains sentences, subordinate clauses, and some word groups

3l-n

which are not clauses — do not have a verb and subject. Number on your paper from 1 to 15. Identify each group of words and tell what it is (*sentence, subordinate clause, neither*) after the corresponding number on your paper. Be able to support your opinion.

1. To whom he was talking.
2. The conversation lasted ten minutes.
3. Since he had very little to say.
4. Although she bought us tickets for the game.
5. On the day of the big game.
6. The stadium stands on a small hill.
7. Which is an ideal location.
8. Standing outside the stadium.
9. During the intermission between halves.
10. While the referee and umpires discussed the penalty.
11. The crowd roared its biased opinion.
12. As soon as a decision had been reached.
13. One of the best games of the season.
14. If they hadn't been so overconfident.
15. The result might have been different.

RELATIVE PRONOUNS IN SUBORDINATE CLAUSES

Read the following sentences, noting especially the words in heavy type. These words are the subjects of the clauses in which they appear. Do you know what part of speech these words are?

1. I can't remember the name of the girl **who** spoke to me.
2. This is the book **that** contains the best recipes.
3. It is this coat **which** fits you best.
4. Wait for Jim, **who** is coming later.

The subjects of these clauses are, as you have discovered, all pronouns. They *relate* to another word somewhere in the sentence.

In Sentence 1 *who* relates to *girl*.
In Sentence 2 *that* relates to *book*.

In Sentence 3 *which* relates to *coat*.
What word does *who* relate to in Sentence 4?

3o. A pronoun which introduces a subordinate clause and *relates* to another word or idea is called a *relative pronoun*.

The relative pronouns are *who, whom, whose, which,* and *that*. Relative pronouns are frequently used as subjects of subordinate clauses. They may also be used as objects and as predicate nominatives. The pronoun *which* relates to things only; *that* relates to things or people; *who, whom, whose* relate to people only.

COMPLEMENTS AND MODIFIERS IN SUBORDINATE CLAUSES

The verb in a subordinate clause may have an indirect or a direct object, a predicate nominative or a predicate adjective. Naturally, it may also be modified by an adverb.

1. There is the man **whom I saw.**   [*Whom* is the direct object of *saw*.]
2. I couldn't tell **who it was.**   [*Who* is a predicate nominative: it was *who*.]
3. Although she bought **us tickets** for the game . . . . .   [*Us* is the indirect object of *bought; tickets* is the direct object of *bought*.]
4. If they hadn't been so **overconfident** . . . . .   [*Overconfident* is a predicate adjective.]
5. While he was working **for me** . . . . .   [*For me* is an adverb phrase modifying *was working*.]

● EXERCISE 14.   Copy on your paper the italicized subordinate clauses in the following sentences. In each clause name the kinds of words listed below by writing the proper abbreviation over that kind of word if you find it in the clause.

3o

ABBREVIATIONS

s.	subject	*i.o.*	indirect object
v.	verb	*p.n.*	predicate nominative
d.o.	direct object	*p.a.*	predicate adjective

If the verb is composed of more than one word, label each word.

EXAMPLE   When she has finally given us her permission, I will thank her.

1. I'd like to know *who did this.*
2. I know *who the captain was,* but I don't know *which team won the game.*
3. He is the player *whom you were watching.*
4. Is this the suit *that you wore to church?*
5. We saw a man *who was very tall.*
6. *When you see Joe,* please give him my message.
7. He left *before I could give him the message.*
8. *Although he had waited for me,* I missed him.
9. Do you know *when he sent us the order?*
10. *If you can possibly spare a dollar,* give it to him.

● EXERCISE 15.   Write 10 sentences containing subordinate clauses. Underline the clauses and, using the abbreviations in Exercise 14, name each part of the clause.

THE ADJECTIVE CLAUSE

3p. An *adjective clause* is a subordinate clause used as an adjective to modify a noun or pronoun.

EXAMPLE   Bill has a horse **that jumps beautifully.**

That jumps beautifully is a subordinate clause. *That* is its subject, and *jumps* is its verb. The clause modifies the noun *horse.* Therefore it is an *adjective clause.*

EXAMPLE   It is she **whom I mean.**

Whom I mean is a subordinate clause. Its subject is *I;* its verb is *mean;* its direct object is *whom.* The clause modifies the pronoun *she.* It is an *adjective clause.*

DIAGRAMING THE ADJECTIVE CLAUSE

Since a subordinate clause has a verb and a subject and includes complements and modifiers, it is diagramed very much like a sentence. An adjective clause beginning with a relative pronoun is joined to the noun it modifies by a slanting dotted line. The line runs from the modified word to the relative pronoun.

The knife that Father carries on his watch chain has a pearl handle.

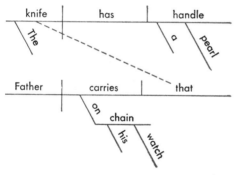

● EXERCISE 16. Copy on your paper the italicized clauses in the following sentences. Label the subject, the verb, and the complements, if any. After each clause write the word it modifies.

1. Jane invited several girls *whom she had met recently.*
2. This is the one *about whom I was telling you.*
3. The gift *which you selected* pleased me most.
4. It was she *who told me the story.*
5. That was the time *when he made a grave mistake.*

From your study of the preceding sentences you may have noticed that adjective clauses usually begin

3p

with the relative pronouns *who, whom, whose, that,* and *which*. However, Sentence 5 shows that an adjective clause may begin with some other word.

● EXERCISE 17.   Each of the following sentences contains an adjective clause. Write the adjective clauses on your paper. Label the verb and the subject. After each clause write the word which the clause modifies.

1. The line which formed at the ticket window was very long.
2. The line was filled with people who wanted to go to the circus.
3. I was standing behind Mary, who had arrived early.
4. She was the girl whom I had met at school.
5. She proved to be a friend that I could trust.
6. She took the money which I had brought.
7. The tickets that she bought were good ones.
8. They were for seats that were in the front row.
9. I thanked Mary, who had helped me.
10. There were others in line who got their tickets through friends.

THE ADVERB CLAUSE

3q. An *adverb clause* is a subordinate clause used as an adverb to tell *how, when, where, why, how much,* or *under what conditions*.

Study the following sentences and note how the adverb clause tells:

HOW   **He played as though he had been inspired.** [*As though he had been inspired* tells *how* he played.]

WHEN   **She found the door locked when she reached home.** [*When she reached home* tells *when* she found the door locked.]

WHERE — I will go **wherever you send me.** [*Wherever you send me* tells *where* I will go.]

WHY — **Because there is so much to do,** we must hurry. [*Because there is so much to do* tells *why* we must hurry.]

HOW MUCH — Sam ate more **than I did.** [*Than I did* tells *how much* more Sam ate.]

UNDER WHAT CONDITIONS — **If you help us,** we will finish sooner. [*If you help us* tells *under what conditions* we will finish sooner.]

THE SUBORDINATING CONJUNCTION

Adverb clauses are introduced by conjunctions. Conjunctions of this kind are *subordinating conjunctions*. *To subordinate* means to reduce something to a position of less importance, to a *sub order*. A subordinate clause is less important than the main clause in a sentence. The conjunction which introduces it is, therefore, known as a *subordinating conjunction*.

It may help you to learn a list of subordinating conjunctions. The following are the commonest ones. Usually, but not always, these words are used to introduce adverb clauses.

COMMON SUBORDINATING CONJUNCTIONS [6]

after	because	so that	when
although	before	than	whenever
as	if	though	wherever
as if	in order that	unless	while
as long as	since	until	

DIAGRAMING THE ADVERB CLAUSE

An *adverb clause* is written on a horizontal line below the main clause and joined to the main clause by the subordinating conjunction, which is written on a

[6] *After, as, before, since,* and *until* may, as you know, also be used as prepositions.

3q

dotted line running from the word the clause refers
to down to the verb in the clause.

Someone called to me as I was leaving.

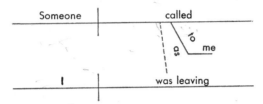

● EXERCISE 18.   From each of the following sentences copy onto your paper the adverb clause. Label
the subject and the verb of the clause. After each
clause state whether the clause tells *how, when, where,*
or *why.*

1. Frank works as though he enjoys working.
2. I will use the wheelbarrow while you shovel sand.
3. We will build the walk wherever you want it.
4. We must get some water so that we can mix cement.
5. After he has unloaded the cement, Andy will help us.
6. Put the cement where you can reach it easily.
7. Because the cement was poor, the old walk crumbled.
8. As soon as the walk is finished, I will go swimming.
9. When you see Dad, tell him the truth.
10. He talks as though he is an authority.

● EXERCISE 19.   List on your paper the subordinate
clauses in the following sentences. After each clause
state whether it is an adjective clause or an adverb
clause.

1. The party which the sophomore class gave was the best
   of the year.
2. When the decorations were planned, everyone wanted
   simple decorations.
3. There were green and gold streamers that hung from
   the ceiling.

4. Although the orchestra was small, it was very good.
5. John, who was the treasurer, reported a profit.
6. Since most of our dances had lost money, the sophomores were praised for their achievement.
7. The dance that lost the most money was the Senior
   Prom.
8. It lost money because the seniors would not admit
   underclassmen.
9. Since they had a crowd, the sophomores made money.
10. After the party was over, some of us went to Joe's.

● EXERCISE 20. Diagram the sentences in Exercise 19.

● EXERCISE 21. Write 10 sentences, using in each a different one of the subordinating conjunctions in the list on page 73. After each sentence state whether the clause tells *how, when, where, why, how much,* or *under what conditions.*

THE NOUN CLAUSE

3r. A *noun clause* is a subordinate clause used as a noun.

Compare the two sentences in each pair below. Notice that in the second sentence in each pair *a subordinate clause takes the place of a noun in the first sentence.*

Tell whether the clause in each of the following pairs of sentences is used as the subject, object, or predicate nominative.

1. Nobody knew the **answer.**
   Nobody knew **what the answer was.**

2. The **defeat** made very little difference to the spectators.
   That the team was defeated made very little difference to the spectators.

3. The award goes to the **winner.**
   The award goes to **whoever wins.**

3r

4. The winner will be the best **player.**
   The winner will be **whoever plays best.**

5. I could not understand her **question.**
   I could not understand **what she asked.**

THE SUBORDINATE CLAUSE NOT INTRODUCED BY A JOINING WORD

Sometimes, especially in everyday speaking, we use a subordinate clause without a word to join it to the rest of the sentence. Compare the subordinate clauses in the paired sentences below.

1. I know **that** *he will be on time.*
   I know *he will be on time.*   [The joining word *that* has been omitted.]

2. He is the man **whom** *I saw.*
   He is the man *I saw.*   [The joining word *whom* has been omitted.]

● EXERCISE 22.   There are 10 noun clauses in the following sentences. Copy them on your paper. Label the subject and the verb. After each clause tell whether it is the subject of the sentence, the object, the predicate nominative, or the object of a preposition.

1. I do not remember who told me this.
2. The storekeeper knows what you want.
3. Whoever wants a high mark must work hard.
4. I know she is coming.
5. I will work with whoever is appointed.
6. He asked me what I was doing.
7. The captain will be whoever wins the election.
8. He surprised us all by what he did.
9. They wanted what they could not have.
10. Whoever wants library privileges must sign this card.

DIAGRAMING A NOUN CLAUSE

A clause used as subject, object, predicate nominative, or object of a preposition is supported by an upright line resting on the line of the subject, object, predicate nominative, or object of a preposition.

NOUN CLAUSE AS SUBJECT   **What he said** surprised us.

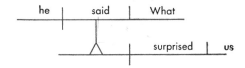

NOUN CLAUSE AS OBJECT   We knew **that he was guilty.**
[*That* introduces the clause but plays no part in it.]

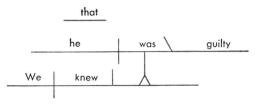

● EXERCISE 23.   Diagram the sentences in Exercise 22.

● REVIEW EXERCISE C.   Copy each clause on your paper. Label the verb and the subject, and name the kind of clause.

1. Father objected when he heard our plans.
2. He asked who was going with us.
3. That he took this attitude surprised me.
4. He told me that it would be late.
5. What we disliked was taking a chaperone.
6. It was Margaret who finally solved the problem.
7. She invited her older sister, whom everyone likes.
8. As soon as everyone was ready, we told Margaret where we were going.
9. Everyone said that it was the best outing of the entire summer.

Sentences Classified According to Form or Structure

3s. Classified according to structure, there are four kinds of sentences — simple, compound, complex, compound-complex.

(1) A *simple sentence* is a sentence with one main clause and no subordinate clauses.

Simple sentences are not necessarily short.

EXAMPLE
Subject
Philip, a young friend from Marblehead, Massa-
Verb
chusetts, and a born sailor, can handle a sailing yacht with all the skill of an experienced mariner.

(2) A *compound sentence* is composed of two or more main clauses but no subordinate clauses.

EXAMPLES
s.   v.
Franklin is an excellent yachtsman; *nevertheless,*
s.   v.
he was no match for Philip.   [two main clauses]
s.   v.   s.
His yacht was neither new nor handsome, *but* it
v.   s.   v.
was trim, *and* it won every race.   [three main clauses]

Conjunctions most commonly used to join the clauses of a compound sentence are *and, but, nor, or, for.* When so used, these conjunctions are usually preceded by a comma.[7]

Other words used to join the clauses of a compound sentence are *consequently, therefore, nevertheless, however, moreover, otherwise,* etc. When so used, they are preceded by a semicolon.[8]

Each main clause in a compound sentence is diagramed like a separate sentence. A dotted line joins

[7] For punctuation of compound sentences see pages 448–451.
[8] These joining words are called *conjunctive adverbs.*

them together. This line is drawn between the verbs of the clauses.

EXAMPLE   Franklin is an excellent yachtsman, but he is no match for Philip.

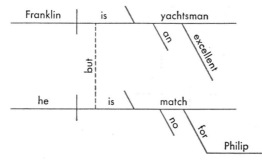

▶ CAUTION: Do not confuse the compound predicate of a simple sentence with the two subjects and two predicates of a compound sentence.

s.   v.   v.
She left the room hurriedly *and* returned at once.
[simple sentence with a compound predicate]
s.   v.   s.   v.
She left the room hurriedly, *and* she returned at once.
[compound sentence with two main clauses]

(3) A *complex sentence* is a sentence containing one main clause and one or more subordinate clauses.

EXAMPLE   **When the whistle blew,** everyone ran.

Since you have already learned how to diagram subordinate clauses (adjective, adverb, and noun clauses), you have learned to diagram a complex sentence. If you wish to refresh your memory, turn back to pages 71, 74, and 77.

(4) A *compound-complex sentence* contains two or more main clauses and one or more subordinate clauses.

EXAMPLE   **The book that I read was written by Kenneth Roberts, and I enjoyed it.**   [two main clauses and one subordinate clause]

3s

In diagraming a compound-complex sentence, first diagram the main clauses [see 3s (2)]. Then attach the subordinate clauses to the words they modify.

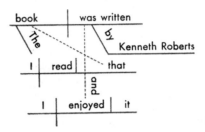

● EXERCISE 24.   Write and label 2 simple sentences, 2 compound sentences, and 2 complex sentences.

● EXERCISE 25.   What kind of sentence is each of the following? Be prepared to prove your answer.

1. After the plans have been completed, we will produce this complicated apparatus.
2. We appreciate the inconvenience which the delay caused, and we regret it very much.
3. Telephones must be placed where the need is greatest.
4. If you will limit your call to five minutes, we shall appreciate it.
5. Leave when you are ready.
6. I could hear his voice very clearly.
7. He was in San Francisco, and I was in New York.
8. She eagerly picked up the receiver and listened.
9. We take the telephone for granted, but we should appreciate it more fully.
10. The service which it gives us is remarkable.

● EXERCISE 26.   Diagram the sentences in Exercise 25.

● REVIEW EXERCISE D.   Copy on your paper **the** numbered italicized word groups in the following passage. After each, write the correct one of the following identifications: *adj. ph.* (adjective phrase); *adv. ph.* (adverb phrase); *part. ph.* (participial phrase); *ger. ph.* (gerund phrase); *inf. ph.* (infinitive phrase); *adj. cl.* (adjective clause); *adv. cl.* (adverb clause); *n. cl.* (noun clause).

(1) *Although most great athletes are popular*, the public sometimes singles out (2) *for special acclaim* an athlete (3) *who has an unusual history.* Such an athlete is Glenn Cunningham, (4) *who was in the 1930's the greatest miler in the world.* (5) *Being a world champion* is a great achievement, but (6) *overcoming Glenn Cunningham's physical handicap* was an even greater one. Other milers have since broken his record, but none has had (7) *to rise above the discouragements* (8) *which faced Glenn.* (9) *When he was eight years old,* Glenn, (10) *trying to rescue his brother from a flaming building,* was severely burned. (11) *Reduced almost to charred bones,* his legs were useless. He lost the toes (12) *of his left foot,* and his arch was all but destroyed. (13) *Because they thought he would never walk again,* the doctors (14) *attending him* recommended amputation. (15) *Giving in to Glenn's pleas,* his parents refused (16) *to permit amputation.* After (17) *spending months in bed,* Glenn, (18) *determined to prove the doctors wrong,* made his first attempt to stand and walk. Slowly his bravery and persistence brought results. He learned not only (19) *to walk again* but also to run. He ran (20) *wherever he went.* (21) *As his legs grew strong,* so did the rest of his body, and he became an outstanding high school athlete. (22) *Succeeding as a high school runner* does not mean, of course, (23) *succeeding in college competition.* But (24) *at Kansas University,* Glenn captured the national intercollegiate title and went on (25) *to the Olympics and world renown.* At the time he retired (26) *from competition,* he had defeated all the greatest runners (27) *of his day.* With deformed legs and a toeless foot, he had become, (28) *through sheer courage and persistence,* the fastest miler in the world. Sports fans admired (29) *what he had achieved as a boy* just as much as they admired (30) *what he had done as a man.*

PART TWO

CORRECT AND

EFFECTIVE

SENTENCES

CHAPTER 4

Writing
Complete Sentences

This chapter is for those of you whose compositions frequently contain incomplete sentences. When parts of sentences are written as though they were complete sentences, they are called *sentence fragments*. Many times sentence fragments get into your writing because you are careless in your punctuation, but they may also appear because you do not know very clearly what a sentence is or what the common sentence fragments are. This chapter will help you to avoid writing fragments as sentences.

In your study of the grammar of the sentence in Chapter 2 you learned that in order to be a sentence, a group of words must express a completed thought. You learned, furthermore, that a sentence contains a verb and its subject. If these terms are not now completely clear to you, return to page 25 and refresh your knowledge of them.

In analyzing your own sentences, you should ask yourself two questions: (1) Does this group of words express a *completed* thought? (2) Does it contain a verb and its subject? As you know, a subordinate clause [1] contains a verb and its subject; yet it is not a sentence because its thought is not completed. It

[1] See page 67.

depends upon the rest of the sentence for its meaning. By itself it is only a *fragment* of a sentence.

● EXERCISE 1. On your paper write *S* for each complete sentence, *F* for each sentence fragment (not a completed thought).

1. When the soldiers came back.
2. The missing dog having been found.
3. Waiting several hours for the bus.
4. While the ladies prepared the food.
5. The fire of the camp could be seen miles away.
6. Eagerly leaning out the window and looking down the street.
7. Please stop teasing the girls.
8. The penalty for cheating is very severe.
9. On the afternoon of the second day of school.
10. Low over the frightened crowd swung the blimp.

Common Types of Sentence Fragments

4a. The subordinate clause must not be written as a sentence.

Although a subordinate clause does have a verb and a subject, it depends upon the main clause of the sentence for its complete meaning.

WRONG The principal advised us to take typing. Which will be useful in all our courses.

RIGHT The principal advised us to take typing, which will be useful in all our courses.

WRONG We left the party early. After we had reached home. We discovered we had lost the door key.

RIGHT We left the party early. After we had reached home, we discovered we had lost the door key.

NOTE: In combining an adverb clause with a main clause, the adverb clause can either precede or follow the main clause.

4a

ADVERB CLAUSE FIRST. **If you want to go swimming,** I will take you to the beach.

MAIN CLAUSE FIRST. I will take you to the beach **if you want to go swimming.**

● EXERCISE 2. Add a main clause either at the beginning or at the end of each of the following subordinate clauses to make 10 complete sentences. An adverb clause at the beginning of a sentence is followed by a comma.

1. As we were rounding a bend in the river
2. While I was sitting in the barber shop
3. If you see my sister
4. Which I have never read
5. Until he had finished reading the book
6. That the victory had been announced
7. Who helped us with our work
8. Before you decide what to do
9. When the storm began
10. What left us completely exhausted

● EXERCISE 3. In the paragraph below there are several sentence fragments. They are all subordinate clauses which should be attached to a main clause. Copy the paragraph, changing the punctuation so that there will be no subordinate clauses standing by themselves. In your copying, omit the numbers.

1. Helen and I are baseball fans. 2. Of course, we can't equal Jimmy Sullivan. 3. Who knows the batting average of nearly every player in the league. 4. We keep up on the standing of the teams, and we do know a lot about the Dodgers. 5. Which is usually our favorite team. 6. Whenever we can get our dads to take us. 7. We go into the city to a game. 8. This isn't very often. 9. Because our dads are busy men without many free afternoons. 10. We have suggested that they take us to a night game. 11. And that they take our mothers along. 12. We especially enjoy night games. 13. Because we can stay

out late.   14. Although we can't see many games.   15. We can watch them on television.   16. Helen and I are arm-chair fans.   17. Who watch baseball mostly in our living room.   18. Which is more comfortable than a ball park.

4b. Participial phrases and gerund phrases must not be written as sentences.

You will recall from your study of pages 60–63 that the present participle and the gerund are verbals ending in –*ing*. *Words ending in* –**ing** *cannot be used as verbs unless they have with them a helping verb. By themselves they can never be used as the verb in a sentence.* With a helping verb like *am, are, has been, will be,* etc., they become complete verbs.

WRONG   **The girls making fudge**   [A phrase; no verb]

RIGHT   **The girls were making fudge.**   [A sentence; a helping verb *were* has been added.]

WRONG   **A thunderstorm threatening in the east.**   [A phrase; no verb]

RIGHT   **A thunderstorm was threatening in the east.**   [A sentence; a helping verb *was* has been added.]

A participial phrase containing a past participle must not be written as a sentence.

WRONG   **We finally found him. Bound and gagged and in great pain.**

RIGHT   **We finally found him, bound and gagged and in great pain.**

A participial phrase or a gerund phrase appears as an error in writing usually because of incorrect punctuation which leaves the phrase standing alone, un-attached to a sentence.

WRONG   **John was nearly drowned. Swimming in the forbidden pit on Farmer Bowle's property.**

RIGHT   **John was nearly drowned, swimming in the forbidden pit on Farmer Bowle's property.**

4b

WRONG   In going to the opposite shore. The commander lost his way.

RIGHT   In going to the opposite shore, the commander lost his way.

WRONG   Ben walked slowly along the street. Having only a few pennies in his pockets. He could not buy anything to eat.

RIGHT   Ben walked slowly along the street. Having only a few pennies in his pockets, he could not buy anything to eat.

WRONG   Left alone in the deserted house. Marilyn was terrified.

RIGHT   Left alone in the deserted house, Marilyn was terrified.

WRONG   The final speaker was Mr. Lambert. He argued a long time. Determined to change the minds of his audience.

RIGHT   The final speaker was Mr. Lambert. He argued a long time, determined to change the minds of his audience.

In the sentences above marked *Right*, the phrase is not left standing by itself but is attached to a main clause. The phrase has become part of a sentence; this is the only way it should be written.

● EXERCISE 4.   Using the phrases listed below, write 10 complete sentences.

1. Springing upon the platform and waving his arms wildly
2. Upon reaching home after the celebration
3. Abandoned by his comrades
4. Hiding behind a tree just to the right of the front porch
5. Playing center on the varsity
6. Pleased by the excellent performance of the school actors
7. Creeping forward between two projecting boulders
8. Riding all day across the prairie

9. After waiting patiently for several hours
10. Praised by everyone

● EXERCISE 5. Some of the following groups of words are sentences. Others are fragments, or contain fragments. On your paper place an *S* after the number corresponding to each complete sentence; correct the others by making them parts of complete sentences and write your sentences after the proper numbers.

1. Believing that he had lost the match, Jimmy stopped trying.
2. We were thrilled at our first view of the harbor. Which is one of the finest in the world.
3. If he had not given up so soon.
4. The coach scolded Jimmy for his lack of fight. Telling him he'd never make a champion that way.
5. Delighted by the news that he had won a fortune.
6. I couldn't identify any of the ships. Which were lying at anchor there.
7. Because his opponent was more tired than he.
8. Suffering from the heat and tired from our long walk. We decided to go directly to bed.
9. He handled his money carelessly. Giving it away in large amounts to people. Who didn't know how to handle it.
10. We enjoyed watching the antics of some sailors. Who apparently had just come ashore. After a long voyage.

4c. An appositive must not be written as a sentence. An *appositive* is a word or group of words which means the same thing as the noun it follows. Usually it identifies or explains the noun.

EXAMPLES   Mike, **the custodian,** is the best-natured man in our building. [*The custodian* is an appositive. It is in apposition with *Mike.*]

4c

> My good friend, **the pastor of St. Luke's Church,**
> has consented to speak to us. [*The pastor of*
> *St. Luke's Church* is in apposition with *friend*.]

Sometimes a hasty writer will treat an appositive as a complete sentence and leave it standing alone, although it has neither verb nor subject and does not express a complete thought.

WRONG   We were talking about Mr. Altman. The newly appointed member of the board of directors.

RIGHT   We were talking about Mr. Altman, **the newly appointed member of the board of directors.** [apposition with *Mr. Altman*]

Since an appositive is usually set off from the sentence by commas, the way to correct the error in the sentence above is to use a comma instead of a period after *Altman*.

WRONG   Today the President had a long conference with an old friend of his. Our new ambassador to England.

RIGHT   Today the President had a long conference with an old friend of his, our new ambassador to England.

WRONG   I received my most valuable information from Mr. Scott. An experienced explorer who knows the arctic regions thoroughly.

RIGHT   I received my most valuable information from Mr. Scott, an experienced explorer who knows the arctic regions thoroughly.

4d.   Avoid other sentence fragments.

You have been studying how to improve your writing by not letting subordinate clauses, participial phrases, and appositives stand by themselves, unattached to a main clause. There are other kinds of fragments which you should know so that you will not let them stand alone either. These other fragments do have names, but it will not be necessary for you to learn them. Study the following examples of rather common fragments. Notice that each *wrong* item is corrected by attaching the fragment to a main clause. Then do the summary exercises which follow.

WRONG   Sally was delighted with everything she saw on the farm. Especially the baby chickens and the new colt.

RIGHT   Sally was delighted with everything she saw on the farm, especially the baby chickens and the new colt.

WRONG   I begged Ray to let me go with him. To see a major league ball game.

RIGHT   I begged Ray to let me go with him to see a major league ball game.

WRONG   A freshman has many things to learn. Such as the plan of the high school, the student customs, and the best way to study.

RIGHT   A freshman has many things to learn, such as the plan of the high school, the student customs, and the best way to study.

WRONG   He made a great many friends. Became the most popular boy in his class and was elected class president.

RIGHT   He made a great many friends, became the most popular boy in his class, and was elected class president.

● EXERCISE 6.   Each of the following contains a sentence fragment. Rewrite each item so that there will not be a sentence fragment in it.

1. We can profit from the mistakes of others. Taking care not to make the same mistakes ourselves.
2. I enjoy literature more than grammar. Because I like to read better than to write.
3. Walter worried about his math. Having failed it the first term. He found the second term even harder.
4. We felt sorry for Joyce. Kept after school for not doing her homework. She had to miss the game.

4d

5. I promised that I would do my best. To get George the kind of portable radio set he wanted.

6. Our class wrote letters of congratulation to Senator Warren. The first graduate of our school to become a national figure.

7. We listened to everything Captain Cooper had to say. About life in the Air Corps. Which we thought the most exciting branch of the service.

8. My parents reserve the living room radio for themselves. Insisting that Jane and I listen to our programs on our own sets.

9. Sam picked up his books and raincoat with a flourish. As he left the room. He stumbled on the threshold. Lost his balance and went down in a heap.

10. The foreman sent us out on the highway. To shovel crushed stone onto the new road.

The Run-on Sentence

It is not enough just to be able to avoid writing *parts* of sentences (subordinate clauses, participial phrases, appositives, and other fragments) as though they were whole sentences. It is equally important always to recognize where one sentence ends and the next one begins.

4e. **A sentence should be followed by an end mark (period, question mark, exclamation point).**

Sentences should not be separated by commas. To use a comma between sentences is an error in thought as well as in punctuation. In the following exercises are examples of poor writing in which sentences are not separated from each other properly. *Such constructions, because they consist of several complete sentences all run on together as though they were one sentence, are called* **run-on sentences.** *Avoid them.*

● EXERCISE 7. Read the following aloud. Your ear will tell you where the complete thoughts begin and end. Write the last word in each complete sentence on your paper. Place the proper mark of punctuation after it. Then write the first word of the next sentence, beginning it with a capital letter.

EXAMPLE 1. **We sailed out of the harbor just before dusk, a stiff breeze was blowing, lowering clouds forecast a storm coming from the north.**
1. dusk. A
blowing. Lowering

1. I found it hard to believe his stories they were all too full of miraculous happenings, they didn't sound like true accounts of what had actually happened I doubt whether he believed them himself.

2. Having been excused early, we hurried to the locker room and changed to our baseball suits, when the coach called us, we were ready to go the big bus drew up in the drive, and just as we had done a dozen other times, we piled in and took our usual seats this trip was different, however, every boy knew how different it was we would return either as champions of the state or as just another second-rate ball team.

3. It was the hottest day we could remember, coming down the street, we were sure we could see heat waves rising from the sidewalk, we felt as though we'd never get home we ambled up the street in a daze, hoping we'd last just one more block, we knew if we could make it there would be wonderful bottles of ice-cold cokes awaiting us.

4. Working on a lake steamer all summer was monotonous, it was also better than any other job I could have obtained, I loved the water and the ships and the rough and ready men with whom I worked, the food was good the work was not too strenuous, if it hadn't been for the sameness of the routine day after day, I should probably never have left.

4e

● EXERCISE 8. Copy the following paragraphs on your paper. Add punctuation and capital letters necessary to divide them into complete sentences.

1. When our evening chores were done, we'd gather in the lot behind the barn, lie down on our backs, and watch the nighthawks they would be circling, sailing, and diving above us it was a matter of pride to see which of us could spot a diver first, the low whirr of the birds coming out of their dives was a music we loved to hear.

2. Spring was descending on Mr. Bush, the neighbor to our left to anyone else it might mean birds in the trees, green things, blossoming catkins all over the place to Mr. Bush it meant only one thing, the grim business of planting his garden day after day we would see him digging like mad, turning over soil, raking, fertilizing then came the all-important planting, the moment toward which all his efforts had been bent, he dropped each seed in, carefully muttering to himself meanwhile as though he were ordering each bit to grow and grow well for him it was wonderful to see him he concentrated so hard on what he was doing that he didn't hear even the ringing of the telephone, and he paid no attention whatever to his wife's strident call to dinner he was happy making mere seeds come to life.

3. Maybelle was a cute girl she used to have the nicest clothes when she walked, she always swished a little, making taffeta-like sounds all the boys, the ones on our block anyway, whistled when she came by Maybelle pretended she didn't hear them, never pausing in her jaunts down the street she knew that she made them all want to date her her blue eyes were very blue her long yellow hair blew carelessly in the breeze, and her pretty legs seemed to twinkle as she sauntered by Maybelle was a cute girl, the boys said she thought so too I never liked Maybelle.

● EXERCISE 9. Copy the following selection on your paper, inserting punctuation so that there will be no sentence fragments and no run-on sentences.

Every sentence must have a verb and its subject and must express a complete thought.

The airport was an exciting place we stood on a high platform near the observation tower, which was a glass-inclosed room in the distance the wide runways formed a huge white cross their pavements glistened in the sun, which was directly overhead great planes with the sun flashing from their sides turned and taxied on the large concrete apron above the roar of motors I shouted to George, and he shouted to me he was pointing to the blue water beyond the field, a part of Flushing Bay then he began to pound me on my back where I was sunburned I finally saw what he was pointing at a huge seaplane was coming in sweeping down to the bright blue water in a graceful glide, she was like a great white gull effortlessly she slid across the waves leaving a broad wake of white, blue, and green water behind her we turned to leave the airport thinking that it could offer nothing to surpass this final picture.

CHAPTER 5

Making Words Agree

AGREEMENT OF SUBJECT AND VERB

5a. A verb agrees with its subject in number.

In order to speak and write correctly you must be able to make the words you use *agree* with one another grammatically. If you will study the following pairs of sentences you will see at once how words *agree*.

1. Three **girls** from our class **were** going to the theater the following day.
   One **girl** from our class **was** going to buy the tickets.

2. **Many** of the tickets **were** lost.
   One of the tickets **was** found.

3. The **pupils** in our class **have** been looking for the other tickets.
   Our **teacher has** been hunting too.

In these sentences you can see how, in order to be correct, the verbs agree with their subjects. When the subject refers to *several* things, as in the first sentence in each pair, the verb takes a certain form to agree with that subject. When the subject refers to *one* thing, as in the second sentence in each pair, the verb changes to agree with the changed subject.

SINGULAR AND PLURAL NUMBER

5b. **When a word refers to one thing, it is singular in number. When a word refers to more than one thing, it is plural in number.**

In the sentences on page 96, which words are singular? Which are plural? [1] As you see, verbs change their number to agree with the number of their subjects.

● EXERCISE 1. List the following words on your paper. After each plural word write *plural;* after each singular word write *singular*.

1. children	6. either
2. many	7. anyone
3. one	8. few
4. each	9. several
5. both	10. somebody

Have your list checked to be sure it is correct before going on to the next exercise.

● EXERCISE 2. Decide which one of the words in parentheses should be used to agree with the subject given.

1. children (ask, asks)	9. no one (appear, appears)
2. many (has, have)	10. few (go, goes)
3. one (seem, seems)	11. women (is, are)
4. each (believe, believes)	12. neither (look, looks)
5. both (play, plays)	13. several (use, uses)
6. either (was, were)	14. somebody (work, works)
7. anyone (leave, leaves)	15. anybody (lose, loses)
8. books (appeal, appeals)	

▶ CAUTION: *Is, was,* and *has* are singular. *Are, were,* and *have* are usually plural, except when used with singular

5a-b

[1] See pages 502–504 for rules governing formation of plural of nouns.

I and *you* (I *have*, you *are*) and in sentences like the following, beginning with *if*.

SINGULAR   **If I were** boss, I'd change the working hours.
             If she were here, I'd tell her what I think.

Most verbs ending in a single *s* (*looks, meets, dresses*) are singular. Most verbs not ending in *s* are plural except when used with singular *I* and *you*.

SINGULAR	PLURAL
He appeals	They appeal
He believes	They believe
He learns	They learn
He leaves	They leave
He looks	They look
He makes	They make
He suits	They suit
He seems	They seem
He works	They work
He wants	They want
He goes	They go
He tries	They try

5c. The number of the subject is not changed by a prepositional phrase following the subject.[2]

One construction which may prove difficult for you is that in which a prepositional phrase comes between the subject and its verb.

1. **One is** late.
   One of the teachers **is** late.
2. **Both are** courteous.
   Both of the men in the office **are** courteous.

The subject is never in a prepositional phrase. The prepositional phrase cannot change the number of the subject, and so it cannot affect the number of the

---

[2] The pronouns *some, any, none, all,* when used as subjects, are exceptions to this rule. See **5e.**

verb which agrees with the subject. A diagram will make this point clear.

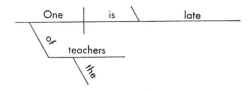

In the following exercises, do not be misled by phrases coming between subject and verb.

● EXERCISE 3. In each of the following sentences you have a choice of verbs. Write the subject of each verb on your paper. Remembering that verb and subject must agree in number, select the one of the two verbs in parentheses which agrees in number with the subject. You are now applying a grammar principle to usage.

1. The girls in the office (work, works) long hours.
2. A tree with wide-spreading branches (were, was) brushing the house.
3. The sound of the branches (was, were) weird.
4. The players on the first team (were, was) the best.
5. The buildings along the waterfront (seem, seems) to be unoccupied.
6. This book for boys (make, makes) good reading.
7. The train with the beach crowds (leave, leaves) at noon.
8. Some guards from the sheriff's office (were, was) trying to calm the mob.
9. Games of skill (was, were) taught to the campers.
10. Both of the players on our team (look, looks) good.
11. A box of these books (weigh, weighs) ninety pounds.
12. Sails for a boat like this (cost, costs) $500.
13. The work of riveters (is, are) sometimes dangerous.
14. The opinions of a critic often (determines, determine) the success of a play.

5c

15. Our loss of these games (has, have) hurt our chances.
16. The sound of airplane motors (was, were) deafening.
17. The girls in my class (seem, seems) older than I.
18. For the citizen, a knowledge of school and community problems (are, is) important.
19. Larry, like his older brothers, (plays, play) a good game of golf.
20. The luck of some players (are, is) astounding.

5d. The following common words are singular: each, either, neither, one, everyone, everybody, no one, nobody, anyone, anybody, someone, somebody.

These words and the words listed in **5e** are called *indefinite pronouns* because they refer only generally, *indefinitely*, to some thing or person. Many people, however, are confused by the plural noun in the phrase following the subject. Thinking this word to be the subject, they make the verb plural to agree with it, thus throwing the verb out of agreement with its true subject, the indefinite pronoun.

WRONG   **One of the apples are ripe.** [Verb is incorrectly made to agree with *apples*, which is not its subject.]

RIGHT   **One of the apples is ripe.** [Verb agrees with its subject, which is *one*.]

Study the use of the indefinite pronouns in the following pairs of sentences.

1. **Each is** present.
   Each of the members **is** present.
2. **Either (Neither) seems** good.
   Either (Neither) of the plans **seems good.**
3. **One has** been answered.
   One of our questions **has** been answered.
4. **Everyone looks** happy.
   Every one of the youngsters **looks** happy.

5. **Everybody takes** the same course.
Everybody in those classes **takes** the same course.

5e. The following common words are plural: *several, few, both, many. Some, any, none, all,* and *most* may be either plural or singular.

When the words *some, any, none, all,* and *most* are
followed by a phrase, the phrase often helps you to
decide whether the words are plural or singular. The
phrase makes clear whether or not the writer is
thinking of *several* things or *one* thing.

PLURAL **Some** of the pencils **are** sharp.
SINGULAR **Some** of the food **has** spoiled.

PLURAL **Have any** of the girls been here?
SINGULAR **Has any** of the order been shipped?

PLURAL **None** of his reasons **were** sound.
SINGULAR **None** of his money **was** taken.

PLURAL **All** of the tires **were** new.
SINGULAR **All** of the gasoline **was** spilled.

● EXERCISE 4. *Oral Drill.* Repeat each of the following sentences *aloud* 5 times, stressing the italicized
words.

1. *One* of these *is* mine.
2. *Every one* of them *looks* good.
3. *Neither* of the books *has* a clean cover.
4. *Some* of them *are* willing.
5. Not *one* of these stories *appeals* to me.
6. *One* of us *is* sure to win.
7. *Neither* of the teams *was* defeated.
8. *Either* of your proposals *is* acceptable.
9. *Several* of us girls *were* looking for you.
10. *Every boy* on the team *respects* the coach.

● EXERCISE 5. Number from 1 to 10 on your paper.
Select from the pair of verbs in each sentence the

5d-e

correct one to agree with the subject. Write this verb after the proper number on your paper.

1. (Is, Are) every one of these pens yours?
2. Neither of the ladies (were, was) afraid to work.
3. Every one of our trees (was, were) uprooted by the storm.
4. Each of the bushes (need, needs) trimming.
5. Both of your brothers (is, are) leaving school.
6. Several of the players (seem, seems) nervous.
7. Not one of these boys (has, have) finished the homework.
8. Everybody in the European countries (knows, know) what war is like.
9. One of your arguments (is, are) easily refuted.
10. A few of the boys in my class (were, was) on the honor roll.

● EXERCISE 6. Number in a column on your paper from 1 to 20. Read each of the following sentences *aloud*. If the sentence is correct, that is, if the verb and the subject are in agreement, write a plus (+) after the proper number on your paper. If the sentence is incorrect, write a zero (0) after the proper number.

1. Every one of us have tried out for the tennis team.
2. One of the boats looks like a sloop.
3. Either of the older boys are able to do the job.
4. Some of the pages in this book are torn.
5. Every one of you have to report to the principal.
6. Each of those girls work conscientiously.
7. Neither of your arguments is convincing.
8. Both of the escaped prisoners was captured.
9. One of us has to be on time.
10. Several of our Presidents have come from Ohio.
11. All of the children look healthy.
12. Neither of my friends know how to dance.
13. Are one of the boxes large enough?

14. Either of your offers seems fair.
15. Each of the contests is sure to be close.
16. Every one of these dogs are thoroughly trained.
17. Some of the students was rather noisy.
18. Many of my answers were wrong.
19. Not one of us were going to tell on you.
20. If any one of you boys and girls knows the answer, raise your hand.

5f. *Don't* and *doesn't* must agree with their subjects. With the subjects *I* and *you*, use *don't* (do not). With other subjects use *doesn't* (does not) when the subject is singular, and *don't* (do not) when the subject is plural.

EXAMPLES   **I don't** know how.
You don't know my brother.
It (He) doesn't work.
They don't want to go.

The commonest errors in the use of *don't* and *doesn't* are made when *don't* is incorrectly used after *it, he,* or *she.* You can remove these common errors from your speech and writing if you will remember always to use *doesn't* after *it, he,* or *she.*

WRONG   **It don't** seem possible.
RIGHT   **It doesn't** seem possible.

WRONG   **He don't** know the answer.
RIGHT   **He doesn't** know the answer.

● EXERCISE 7.   Write in a column on your paper the correct form (*don't* or *doesn't*) for the following sentences.

1. This —— worry me.
2. It —— look right.

5f

3. He —— appear until the second act.
4. They —— want any money.
5. We —— have enough time.
6. That —— sound right.
7. She —— know any better.
8. He —— feel well.
9. It —— matter.
10. You —— look very tall.
11. Fred —— study very hard.
12. My sister —— like college.
13. Some of the boys —— like the captain.
14. It —— appeal to me.
15. This work —— please the boss.
16. —— she believe in miracles?
17. This —— seem possible.
18. —— he ever get tired?
19. —— it make sense?
20. It ——.

● EXERCISE 8.   Choose the correct one of the two verbs given in parentheses in the sentences below and list them in a column on your paper.

1. Mr. Bright, one of my teachers, (believe, believes) in more homework.
2. The ship which is crowded with sightseers (sail, sails) at ten o'clock.
3. The other ship, which carries freight and passengers, (leaves, leave) earlier.
4. It (don't, doesn't) matter how you go so long as you get there.
5. Harold says he (doesn't, don't) want to go.
6. Christmas, of all the holidays in the year, (appeals, appeal) most to us.
7. Some of us in the class (learn, learns) faster than others.
8. (Wasn't, Weren't) you surprised?
9. He (don't, doesn't) like to be kept waiting.
10. They (wasn't, weren't) at all helpful.

THE COMPOUND SUBJECT

5g. Most compound subjects joined by *and* are plural and take a plural verb.

EXAMPLES   Lewis *and* he **were** arguing.

               The automobile *and* the train **are** not yet outmoded.

               The beginning *and* the end of your story **are** good.

Some compound subjects joined by *and* are singular and take a singular verb.

EXAMPLES   *Bread and butter* **is** a poor diet.

               Running and diving into the pool **is** prohibited.

               The *stress and strain* of flood waters on the bridge **was** carefully prepared for.

In compound subjects in which the *idea* is singular, the verb must be singular. In the sentences above, *bread and butter*, *running and diving*, *stress and strain* are thought of as units — as one food, one action, one force. When so thought of, they are naturally singular.

5h. Singular subjects joined by *or* or *nor* are singular and take a singular verb.

EXAMPLES   *Either* Fred *or* Jerry **is** coming.

               Neither my brother *nor* my sister **was** at home.

               Has *either* George *or* his mother called yet?

               Neither Helen *nor* Jane **works** as fast as you.

               Neither the president *nor* his secretary **speaks** very highly of the candidates.

(1) The word *either* may be omitted, but the number of the subject is not changed so long as its parts are joined by *or*.

EXAMPLE   Mary *or* her sister **was** trying to make a telephone call.

5g-h

(2) Do not confuse this *either . . . or, neither . . . nor* construction with the other correlative conjunctions *both . . . and*, which take a plural verb.

EXAMPLES   *Both* the cat *and* the dog **are** very friendly.
Neither the cat *nor* the dog **is** very friendly.

5i. When two subjects, one of which is singular and the other is plural, are joined by *or, nor*, the verb agrees with the nearer word.

ACCEPTABLE   Either the President or his Cabinet *members* are to be held responsible.

It is best to avoid such constructions entirely.

BETTER   The responsibility will be placed upon either the President or his Cabinet members.

● EXERCISE 9.   From the parentheses in the following sentences choose the correct verb. Write the verbs in a column on your paper.

1. Neither James nor his brother (care, cares) for sports.
2. Both Jack and she (are, is) graduating this year.
3. Neither the teacher nor his pupils (were, was) right.
4. Either the principal or the class adviser (are, is) going with us.
5. Neither their team nor ours (have, has) a chance in the tournament.
6. Either the captains or the umpire (call, calls) time out.
7. Doris and he (was, were) dancing together.
8. The school or the village (pay, pays) the expenses.
9. Neither Marion nor Janet (seem, seems) to approve.
10. Both George and Joan (look, looks) like you.

● EXERCISE 10.   *Oral Drill*. Repeat each of the following sentences *aloud* 5 times, stressing the italicized words.

1. *Each* of us *has* finished.
2. *Neither* Beth *nor* Ned *is* at home.
3. A *few* of his ideas *are* excellent.

4. *Either* Julia *or* she *has* your pen.
5. *One* of my fingers *was* broken.
6. *Every one* of these seats *is* too small.
7. *Both* Don and Dave *are* absent.
8. *Each* of these magazines *looks* interesting.
9. *Not one* of your friends *has* been here.
10. *Several* of them *were* here yesterday.

OTHER PROBLEMS IN AGREEMENT

5j. When the subject and the predicate nominative are of different numbers, the verb agrees with the subject, *not* with the predicate nominative.

	Subject		Predicate Nominative
RIGHT	The ship's cargo	was	bananas.
RIGHT	Bananas	were	the ship's cargo.
BETTER	The ship carried a cargo of bananas.		

5k. When the subject comes after the verb, as in sentences beginning with *here is*, *there is*, and *where is*, be especially careful to determine the subject and make sure that it and the verb agree.

WRONG	There is too many in this car.
RIGHT	There **are** too many in this car.

In our daily conversation we increase the likelihood of error by hurrying over *there is*, *there are* and making contractions of them.

WRONG	Here's the pencils you ordered.
RIGHT	Here **are** the pencils you ordered.

WRONG	Where's Harry and Joe?
RIGHT	Where **are** Harry and Joe?

5l. *Together with*, *in addition to*, *including*, *as well as*, and similar constructions following the

5i-l

subject do not affect the number of the subject.

The tendency of a careless writer might be to consider the subject with such a construction plural, but strictly the subject is singular and requires a singular verb.

EXAMPLES   Mr. Leary, together with his two sons, **has** left for California.

The trapeze performer, as well as the spectators, **was** frightened.

This error, in addition to those made by the other players, **was** responsible for our losing the game.

Perhaps the logic of this rule will be clearer to you if you rearrange the sentence about Mr. Leary.

Mr. Leary **has** left for California with his two sons.

● EXERCISE 11. *Oral Drill.* Repeat each of the following sentences *aloud* 5 times, stressing the italicized words.

1. Where *are* those *papers?*
2. *Francis*, with several others, *has gone* to the movies.
3. *Both* Keith *and* Larry *are* with him.
4. There *are* your *notebooks.*
5. *Ruth* as well as Dot *is* taking chemistry.
6. *Either* Grace *or* Grant *has* a slide rule.
7. *One* of the officers *has* resigned.
8. The *superintendent*, together with the principals, *is* attending a convention.
9. *Neither* of them *feels* like playing.
10. Here *are* the *skates.*

● EXERCISE 12. Number in a column on your paper from 1 to 20. Read each sentence aloud. If the verb agrees with the subject, put a plus (+) on your paper after the proper number. If the verb does not agree with the subject, write a zero (0).

1. Here's your skates.
2. One of these stories is about the Revolutionary War.
3. Neither this book nor the other interest me.
4. Where's the gloves I left here?
5. Both you and he are taller than I.
6. Either Fred or Joe has been injured.
7. Macaroni and cheese are a popular dish in our family.
8. There are several answers to your question.
9. Every one of his themes are interesting.
10. There's several cars in the driveway.
11. Mr. Wheaton, with his two sisters, are going to Denver.
12. Have either of the dogs returned?
13. Your uncle and aunt, together with your cousins, are spending the summer on a ranch.
14. Both Frank and she have been abroad.
15. Do every one of your friends go to your school?
16. Neither of the policemen uses strong-arm methods.
17. Edward, as well as Ernest and Eugenie, were at home.
18. Here's your test papers.
19. Don't he like to swim?
20. Each of us wants a vacation.

5m. Collective nouns may be either singular or plural.

You may be puzzled at times by words which name a *group* of persons or objects. Such words are known as *collective nouns*. They are puzzling because *they may be used with a plural verb when the speaker is thinking of the individual parts of the group; they may be used with a singular verb when the speaker is thinking of the group as a unit.* Study the following pairs of sentences.

1. The jury **was** locked behind closed doors. [*Jury* is thought of as a unit.]
   The jury **were** arguing among themselves. [*Jury* is thought of as individuals.]

5m

2. The class **was** a very large one.
   The class **were** not all present.
3. The family **has** arrived.
   The family **have** given their consent.

Following is a list of common collective nouns:

jury	crowd	flock	committee
herd	class	group	audience
club	troop	swarm	squadron
army	fleet	team	faculty

● EXERCISE 13.   Select 5 collective nouns and write 5 pairs of sentences like those given above, showing clearly how the words you choose may be either singular or plural.

5n. Words stating amount (time, money, measurement, weight, volume, fractions) are usually singular.

EXAMPLES   *Two weeks* **is** the usual vacation.
Five dollars **was** more than I had expected.
Four tons **is** what I ordered.
Three quarters of our time **has** passed.

5o. The title of a book, even when plural in form, takes a singular verb.

EXAMPLE   *Short Stories for Boys* **is** worth reading.

● REVIEW EXERCISE A.   In some of the following sentences the verbs agree with their subjects; in others, the verbs do not agree. Number in a column on your paper from 1 to 33. If the verb and subject agree in a sentence, write *A*, for agreement, after the proper number. If the verb does not agree with its subject, write the correct form of the verb after the proper number.

1. The committee was unable to agree among themselves.
2. Neither of the men leaves until five o'clock.
3. Several of the boys in the office are absent today.
4. Bacon and eggs is a tasty dish.
5. Either Joan or Betty are using my sled.
6. She don't mind very well.
7. Each one of them has a bike.
8. There are one set of books left on the shelf.
9. Do every one of you agree to take the test later?
10. Several of the boys seem to have colds.
11. She, together with her friends, seems to have come late.
12. Neither of us care to go.
13. He, as well as his brothers, seem to have gone out.
14. There is too many automobiles in this parking space.
15. Not one of them was invited.
16. *Popular Sports Stories* have been read by every member of the class.
17. Where's the books I gave you?
18. Some of the horses were running away.
19. Both of the students have good reports.
20. Few of Mother's friends like to play bridge.
21. One of our teachers seem like a good sport.
22. There is in this room two books which must be found now.
23. Basketry and riding is two things we do at camp.
24. Each of us has a long way to go.
25. Everyone in these rooms are excused for the day.
26. Here comes Mary and Jim.
27. At the grocery store on the corner are several bushels of wheat.
28. Was there a book, compass, and ruler in that drawer?
29. Lying on the bed was both of the kittens.
30. Down goes the red handkerchiefs!
31. When do little white lies become black?
32. There in the rusty trunk was her old love letters.
33. Doesn't all this noise distract you?

5n-0

Agreement of Pronoun and Antecedent

5p. A pronoun agrees with its antecedent in number and gender.

So far in your study of *agreement* you have learned how to make subject and verb agree. The next type of agreement is the agreement of a pronoun with its antecedent. A careful study of the following sentences will show you what is meant by the term *antecedent* and how the pronoun which refers to the antecedent agrees with it in number and gender.[3]

1. **One** of the players broke **his** racket.
2. **Each** of the girls did **her** best.
3. **Everyone** brought **his** own lunch.
4. **Neither** of the ladies recognized **her** child.

In each of these sentences the first pronoun (*one, each, everyone, neither*) is the *antecedent* of the second pronoun, which refers to it. *Antecedent* means *going before* (Latin *ante*, before + *cedens*, going). Notice that the first pronoun is singular in every case and that the second pronoun, which refers to it, is also singular. If the antecedent is plural, the pronoun which agrees with it is also plural.

Several *members* of the team failed to play *their* best.

If you will keep in mind all that you have learned about agreement of subject and verb, you will have no difficulty in making pronouns and antecedents agree. Keep in mind, for instance, that the indefinite pronouns — *each, either, neither, one, everyone, everybody, no one, nobody, anyone, anybody, someone, somebody* —

[3] *Gender* indicates *sex:* feminine, masculine, neuter. When the antecedent may be either masculine or feminine, use the masculine form of the pronoun. Example: Each of the boys and girls was eager to do *his* part.

are singular. They are referred to by singular pronouns: *he, she, him, her, his, hers, it,* and *its*. Keep in mind that a prepositional phrase following a subject does not alter the number of the subject.

One (of the artists) destroyed **his** own masterpiece.

(1) Two antecedents joined by *and* should be referred to by a plural pronoun.

EXAMPLE   Sid **and** Bill did **their** best.

(2) Two or more singular antecedents joined by *or* or *nor* should be referred to by a singular pronoun.

EXAMPLE   **Neither** Sid **nor** Bill did **his** best.

● EXERCISE 14.   Number in a column on your paper from 1 to 12. For each blank in the following sentences select a pronoun which will agree with its antecedent and write it after the proper number on your paper.

1. Not one of the captives would give —— own name.
2. Either Steve or George can bring —— father's car.
3. One of my friends forgot —— hat.
4. No one in the group seemed sure of —— own destination.
5. Each girl in the troop had to make —— own bed.
6. Several members of the club were told to make —— protests to the president.
7. One of the children asked directions of us, but we told —— we were lost too.
8. Philip and his brother helped —— uncle harvest his wheat.
9. Every soldier is responsible for —— own equipment.
10. Both of the applicants brought —— credentials with them.
11. Neither did —— best.
12. Neither Molly nor she could do —— homework.

5p

(3) When the idea of the sentence (the meaning of the antecedent) is clearly plural, the plural pronoun is acceptable, even though grammatically the singular may be preferable.

For example, in the following sentences, the idea of the speaker is so definitely plural that to use a singular pronoun would be unnatural. Usage here differs somewhat from grammar.

Did everybody have a good time at Jack's party? Yes, they seemed to.

If everyone comes, it will be impossible to seat them.

● REVIEW EXERCISE B.   In some of the following sentences subject and verb, and pronoun and antecedent, agree; in others they do not. Number on your paper from 1 to 20. If a sentence is correct, place a + after the corresponding number; if it is incorrect, place a 0.

1. Neither of the roads were paved.
2. One of the girls brought her little sister to class.
3. Tim, with several other boys, have gone swimming.
4. Neither Ted nor Tom had finished their work.
5. Both Eileen and she make their own dresses.
6. Where's your brother and sister?
7. A few of the boys offered their services.
8. Either Thelma or Judy will bring her records.
9. Each of the campers cooked their own supper.
10. Neither of the boys wanted to do their homework.
11. Every one of the schools is closed.
12. Either of them could get an A, if he would work.
13. Here's the books I promised you.
14. Would anyone treat their dog so cruelly?
15. Some of the musicians own their instruments.
16. Each boy had their own locker.
17. If anyone has not done their homework, they should see me.
18. No one could believe his eyes.

19. Where's the money your father gave you?
20. Both Byron and Lloyd string their own rackets.

● **EXERCISE 15.** *Oral Drill.* Repeat each of the following sentences *aloud* 5 times, stressing the italicized words.

1. *Both* of the bats *were* cracked.
2. *Neither* of them *was* usable.
3. *One* of the workmen lent me *his* knife.
4. *Each* sailor did *his* own laundry.
5. Where *are* your *books?*
6. If *one* of the boys calls, ask *him* to wait.
7. *Neither Dad* nor *Mother* would give *his* consent.
8. *Each* of the students asked what *his* grade was.
9. *One* of them did not sign *his* name.
10. If *anyone* asks you, tell *him* your name.

Agreement of Adjective and Noun

5q. The adjectives *this, these, that, those* agree in number with the word they modify.

When the pronouns *this* (plural, *these*) and *that* (plural, *those*) are used as adjectives they agree in number with the noun they modify. For example, in the sentence *Those papers are valuable* the adjective *those* must also be plural to agree with *papers.*

There are very few cases in which any English-speaking person would make an error in using the plural form of these adjectives. In fact, the only common error of this kind is illustrated in the following constructions.

WRONG   I like these kind of books. [Incorrect because *these* is plural and *kind* is singular]
RIGHT   I like **these kinds.**
RIGHT   I like **this kind.**

Other words frequently used as *kind* is used in these sentences are *sort, sorts* and *type, types.*

5q

● EXERCISE 16. For the blanks in the following sentences choose the correct form of a suitable word: *this, these, those, kind, sort, type.* When your sentences have been corrected, repeat each *aloud* 5 times.

1. Mother prefers these —— of ice cream.
2. I don't care for those —— of people.
3. Which —— do you want, these or those?
4. I always buy —— kind.
5. If you use —— type of paper, you will get better results
6. We sell these —— only.
7. —— sort of argument is foolish.
8. These —— can be found in any store.

● REVIEW EXERCISE C. Number on your paper from 1 to 20. In each sentence select the correct one of two forms given in parentheses and write it after the corresponding number on your paper.

1. If you help one of the girls, (she, they) will help you.
2. Neither of these knives (look, looks) sharp.
3. I never read these (kind, kinds) of magazines.
4. Each of the candidates (seems, seem) well qualified.
5. Mr. Nye, as well as his children, (enjoys, enjoy) skiing.
6. Either Pete or his brothers (is, are) responsible.
7. Both trains and buses (were, was) delayed.
8. Do you like (this, these) type of uniform?
9. A few of our men (were, was) wounded.
10. (Here's, Here are) the groceries you ordered.
11. If anyone wishes to see the doctor, (he, they) must wait.
12. Neither of them could help (himself, themselves).
13. I don't like (these, this) kind of apples.
14. Several of the students (was, were) tardy.
15. Neither of the boats could find (its, their) way.
16. Where (are, is) the girls?
17. If someone will help me, I'll pay (him, them) well.
18. I asked the clerk for a pound of (those, that) kind.
19. Everyone in our family (has, have) (his, their) duties.
20. Either could do better, if (he, they) would work.

CHAPTER 6

Using the Correct Case of Pronouns

In the English language nouns and pronouns may be in one of three cases: *nominative, objective,* and *possessive.* Nouns and indefinite pronouns have the same form in the nominative and objective cases; they change form only in the possessive case, when they require either an apostrophe and *s* or just an apostrophe.

Nominative [subject]	Objective [object of verb]	Possessive

The **captain** saw another **captain** reading the **captain's** orders.

Nom.	Obj.	Poss.

Anybody there may ask **anybody** else. Has **anybody's** reply been received?

On the other hand, personal pronouns change their forms to denote the various cases. Since this changing results in so many different pronoun forms and each form has a definite use, there are many personal-pronoun problems in usage. For example, in our speaking and writing we are continually having to decide whether to use *I* or *me, he* or *him, she* or *her, we* or *us, they* or *them, who* or *whom.* Modern usage may ignore these distinctions in a few special constructions, but in general the educated person must know how to solve pronoun case problems. You must master these case forms and know when to use them.

THE CASE FORMS OF PRONOUNS [1]

Examine the following table presenting the various case forms of pronouns in the singular and plural numbers.

PERSONAL PRONOUNS

Singular

	NOMINATIVE CASE	OBJECTIVE CASE
FIRST PERSON	I	me
SECOND PERSON	you	you
THIRD PERSON	he, she, it	him, her, it

Plural

	NOMINATIVE CASE	OBJECTIVE CASE
FIRST PERSON	we	us
SECOND PERSON	you	you
THIRD PERSON	they	them

RELATIVE AND INTERROGATIVE PRONOUNS

NOMINATIVE CASE	OBJECTIVE CASE
who	whom
whoever	whomever

● EXERCISE 1.   Referring to the table above, list on your paper in a column the pronouns which change their forms according to their case. Which pronouns keep the same form in both cases?

By doing the exercise just above, you have learned

[1] Personal pronouns are those pronouns which change form in the different persons. There are three persons, first, second, and third. The meaning of *person* is as follows:

1st person is the person speaking: (*I*, *We*) come.

2nd person is the person spoken to: *You* are coming.

3rd person is the person spoken about: *He* (*She*, *It*, *They*) will come.

Who and *whom* (*whoever* and *whomever*) are not personal pronouns. They may be relative pronouns (see page 69); when used to ask a question they are interrogative pronouns.

that the pronouns *you* and *it* do not undergo any changes. Therefore, these pronouns do not present any usage problem. Omitting them from consideration, you will have the following list of pronouns whose nominative case form is different from their objective case form. Memorize these lists.

NOMINATIVE CASE	OBJECTIVE CASE
I	me
he	him
she	her
we	us
they	them
who	whom
whoever	whomever

● EXERCISE 2. Your teacher will read to you a mixed-up list of pronouns. You are to write the case of each pronoun. With practice you should be able to do this quickly, automatically.

● EXERCISE 3. Write the following personal pronouns:

1. Third person plural objective case
2. First person plural nominative case
3. Third person plural nominative case
4. First person singular objective case
5. Third person singular objective case, feminine gender
6. First person singular nominative case
7. Third person singular nominative case, feminine gender
8. Third person singular objective case, masculine gender
9. First person plural objective case
10. Third person singular nominative case, masculine gender

When you have thoroughly memorized the nominative and objective pronouns, and not until then, you will be ready to study the correct use of pronouns as explained in the following pages.

120   *Using the Correct Case of Pronouns*

The Nominative Case

6a. The subject of a verb is in the nominative case.

Notice that the pronouns in the sentences below are in the nominative case because they are used as subjects.

He and **I** went to the wrestling match. [*He* and *I* are subjects of the verb *went.*]

Who played in the backfield? [*Who* is the subject of *played.*]

We girls believe that **they** told the secret. [*We* is the subject of *believe,* and *they* is the subject of *told.*]

● EXERCISE 4. Number your paper from 1 to 12. Choose correct pronouns for the blanks in the following sentences. Vary your pronouns. Omit *you* entirely.

1. Jimmy and —— make a good team.
2. Jack and —— played against them yesterday.
3. She and —— argued about the score.
4. My partner and —— practiced for several days.
5. The Browns suggested to us that —— and —— go on a picnic.
6. Tom and —— preferred to play golf.
7. Sara and —— are twins.
8. Neither Betty nor —— are on the committee.
9. —— and —— asked our dads to play with us.
10. —— boys accused them of being afraid of us.
11. Yesterday —— and —— played by ourselves.
12. Dad said that Mr. Brown and —— could have made better scores than ours.

● EXERCISE 5. *Oral Drill.* Recite *aloud* 5 times each of the following sentences, stressing the italicized words. By *hearing* and *speaking* the correct form you will make your tongue and ear sensitive to it, and help yourself to speak correctly.

1. *He* and *I* are friends.
2. *You* and *I* will work together.

3. *Betty* and *I* expect to win.
4. *We* and *they* are cousins.
5. *We* boys (or girls) were late.

● EXERCISE 6.   Number in a column on your paper from 1 to 20. Read each of the following sentences *aloud*. Decide whether the italicized pronouns are in the correct case. If all of them in a sentence are correct, put a + after the proper number on your paper; if any one of them is not, put a 0 and write the correct form of the pronouns.

1. Bill and *I* believed that you and *she* would help.
2. You and *I* will have to solve the problem.
3. Your friends and *him* are troublemakers.
4. *We* players respect the coach.
5. *Him* and *me* were going skating.
6. Helen and *her* preferred to ski.
7. The principal and *he* knew the whole story.
8. You and *I* ought to get together.
9. I wish you and *she* were more friendly.
10. You and *them* came from the same town.
11. Where do your aunt and *he* live?
12. *He* and *she* live on Tenth Street.
13. *Him* and *me* will graduate at the same time.
14. *Us* boys must stick together.
15. I think you and *she* are bound to win.
16. *Her* and *I* arrived an hour early.
17. My uncle and *they* were not able to come.
18. Sally and *I* will bring the sandwiches.
19. Bill and *me* decided to go to college together.
20. Hank and *he* enlisted in the Navy.

6b. A predicate nominative is in the nominative case.

A review of pages 45–47, where you previously encountered this predicate construction, will remind you of the following facts:

6a-b

(1) A predicate nominative is a word which completes the meaning of the verb and means the same thing as the subject.

EXAMPLE   **That must be they.**

(2) The forms of the verb *to be* are the only verbs followed by a predicate nominative. The forms of *to be* are *am, is, are, was, were,* and verbs ending in *be* or *been*.

EXAMPLES   **That is she.   I'd hate to be she.**
            It might have been they.

● EXERCISE 7. Remembering that a predicate nominative is in the nominative case, supply the predicate pronouns specified for the following.

1. I thought it was ———. (third person singular masculine)
2. These are ———. (third person plural)
3. I thought it might be ———. (third person singular feminine)
4. It couldn't be ———. (third person plural)

▶ NOTE: Observance of this rule among educated people varies greatly. In at least one instance, custom has changed the case of a predicate nominative. This instance is the expression "It's *me*." The objective pronoun *me* is correct. Of course *It's I* is still correct, too.

In listening to conversations, you will often hear the objective case used after a form of *to be*. Expressions like *That's him, That was us, Had it been us* may be fairly classed as acceptable, everyday, *oral* English but should probably be avoided in *written* English. Your drills in this book contain only a few of these generally accepted constructions. They are included for the sake of drilling you on the rule which you should understand and be able to apply in case of need: *A predicate nominative is in the nominative case.*

● REVIEW EXERCISE A. Number in a column on your paper from 1 to 20. Write after the proper number the pronouns which will correctly fill the spaces in the following sentences. You should be able to make a perfect score. Try to use *as many different pronouns* as you can. Omit *you* entirely. Be ready to explain the reason for your choice.

1. Sally and —— made the highest scores.
2. It might have been ——.
3. I didn't know that you and —— were sisters.
4. —— girls refused to agree to the plan.
5. When I asked them, both Jean and —— gave me the money.
6. I was sure that the family and —— wouldn't let you down.
7. Did you think it was ——?
8. The party leaders and —— were unable to get together.
9. Jill and —— tried to persuade them.
10. Are you sure that it was ——?
11. Jimmy and —— stayed at my house all afternoon.
12. Was that Mr. Bartlett or ——?
13. —— boys asked our parents.
14. Jed and —— are old friends.
15. The two captains are Albert and ——.
16. My uncle and —— came to call on us.
17. I thought it probably was ——.
18. I think that —— boys have a good chance to win.
19. —— and —— entered school the same year.
20. —— and —— are traveling in the same car.

The Objective Case

6c. The object of a verb is in the objective case.

So far in your study of the correct use of pronouns, you have learned that *the nominative forms are used as subjects and as predicate nominatives.* Having learned the uses of the nominative pronouns, you are now

6c

ready to learn the uses of the objective pronouns. The objective pronouns, as you know, are:

me	us
you	you
him	them
her	whom
it	whomever

These pronouns are used as objects. There are two kinds of objects: objects of verbs, and objects of prepositions. You learned to identify the object of a verb in your study of complements on page 47. To refresh your knowledge of verbs and their objects, study these examples. The object is in heavy type.

(1) The object of a verb receives the action of the verb.

EXAMPLES   Fire *had* nearly *destroyed* the **barracks**.
Which **book** *did* you *choose?*

(2) An object may be compound.

EXAMPLE   The teacher *put* **Hank** and **me** in the front row.

● EXERCISE 8. In the following sentences, select the objects of the verbs.

1. We are expecting you at four o'clock.
2. They invited us.
3. Captain Brill booted the ball.
4. Did you defeat May or her?
5. Did you help Fred and him?
6. The family left me behind.
7. We shall expect you and your brother at one.
8. I believed him completely.
9. I tested Jerry and him.
10. Why have you been avoiding Roy and me?

Failure to use the objective pronouns as objects of the verb leads to rather serious errors in usage.

Such errors can be avoided with a little thought, a little care, and a large amount of drill.

WRONG   I have met Andy and he.
RIGHT   I *have met* Andy and **him.**

WRONG   They frightened Joe and I.
RIGHT   They *frightened* Joe and **me.**

Most errors in the use of pronouns are made when the subject or object is compound — that is, has two parts. In the following sentence the subject is compound: *Jean and (I, me) did the dishes.* You can often arrive at the correct form by simply dropping the first word of the two in the compound subject: *I did the dishes.* Your ear tells you that *I*, not *me*, is correct. You would not say *Me did the dishes.* Similarly you can determine the correct form when an object is compound: *Mr. Johnson hired Jack and (I, me).* If you drop *Jack*, you will find that the correct form is *me:* Mr. Johnson hired *me.*

● EXERCISE 9.   Remembering that the pronoun objects are always in the objective case, supply the correct pronouns for the blanks in the following sentences. Avoid using the same pronoun throughout. Omit *you* entirely.

1. She met Mother and —— at the store.
2. I left Mother and —— together.
3. Have you seen either your father or ——?
4. Did you take Mary or ——?
5. She couldn't convince either Roy or ——.
6. Don't tell Jeff and —— what I told you.[2]
7. Did you ask Dr. Jones and —— for their opinion?
8. Mother refused to leave the baby and —— alone.

[2] The indirect object, like the direct object, takes the objective case.

DIRECT OBJECT   I took Mother and **him.**
INDIRECT OBJECT   I took Mother and **him** a book.

9. Please give —— and —— a better book.
10. They sent —— boys several letters.

● REVIEW EXERCISE B. Remembering what you learned about the case of subjects and predicate nominatives as well as what you have just learned about the case of objects of the verb, fill the blanks in the following sentences. Use a variety of pronouns. Omit *you* entirely.

1. Please give Helen and —— extra time for our compositions.
2. You and —— had better ask for more time.
3. Did you and —— get an allowance of extra time?
4. Miss English refused Joyce and —— any special consideration.
5. It was Helen and ——.
6. Mrs. Lord and —— assigned Bill and —— some extra work.
7. Mr. Fletcher took Allen and —— to the game.
8. Jack and —— were the only soldiers the general could trust.
9. Were you chasing Alice or ——?
10. He sent my friend and —— on a dangerous mission.
11. Did he want you or ——?
12. The winner will be either Carl or ——.
13. —— and —— are going steady.
14. Have you seen Janet or ——?
15. Why do you think it was ——?

● REVIEW EXERCISE C.

Write 3 sentences containing pronouns used as subjects of verbs.

Write 3 sentences containing pronouns used as predicate nominatives.

Write 4 sentences containing pronouns used as objects of verbs.

After each sentence tell how the pronoun is used: subject, predicate nominative, or object of verb.

● REVIEW EXERCISE D. Number in a column on your paper from 1 to 20. Select the correct one of the two pronouns in the parentheses and write it after the corresponding number on your paper. Be ready to explain your answers.

1. Our guide called Sandy and (I, me).
2. Sandy and (he, him) knew the woods and streams well.
3. (He, Him) and (I, me) were at the head of the line of canoes.
4. Fred and (they, them) were at the end of the line.
5. The guide gave (he, him) and (I, me) some good advice.
6. The guide and (we, us) boys told the hikers the trip was dangerous.
7. They refused to believe Sandy and (I, me), but they did believe him.
8. (They, Them) and (he, him) were on the best of terms.
9. It was (he, him) who collected the fees.
10. He knew it was (they, them) who paid the money.
11. The guide agreed to pay Sandy and (I, me) a small amount of money.
12. It must have been (they, them).
13. Her husband and (she, her) had never been in the north woods.
14. When their canoe capsized, (him, he) and (her, she) were thrown into the water.
15. Sandy and (I, me) swung our canoe toward them.
16. The guide and (us, we) realized our responsibility.
17. Mrs. Stanley, however, was not helpless. It was (she, her) who saved her husband.
18. When the guide and (we, us) reached them they were sitting calmly on a large boulder in midstream.
19. Neither her husband nor (she, her) was injured in the accident.
20. The rest of the party congratulated Mr. Stanley and (her, she) on their escape.

● REVIEW EXERCISE E. *Oral Drill.* Recite *aloud* 5 times each of the following sentences, stressing the italicized words.

1. *He* and *I* are neighbors.
2. Do you mean Bill or *me?*
3. You resemble your mother and *her.*
4. Frank and *I* called you and *him.*
5. Sally and *we* are in the same class.
6. Ask Jean and *her.*
7. Is that *he?*
8. I saw both Bob and *him.*
9. I know Frank and *her.*
10. He caught Pat and *me.*
11. It might be *they.*
12. Jeff and *he* are on the team.

● REVIEW EXERCISE F. Using the pronouns below, write 10 correct sentences of your own. Include sentences with pronouns used as subjects, predicate nominatives, and objects of verbs. After each sentence tell how the pronouns are used.

1. they	6. we boys
2. he and I	7. us boys
3. him and me	8. you and me
4. my mother and she	9. Ed and him
5. my mother and her	10. Tom and them

● REVIEW EXERCISE G. Prepare a drill exercise of 10 sentences for use with your classmates. Pattern your exercise after Review Exercise D on page 127. Be sure that every sentence presents a real problem in the correct use of pronouns. Because errors in the use of pronouns are usually made when the subject or object is compound, you should use compound subjects and objects in your sentences. Do not put the answers on your paper. You may test someone with your exercise in class.

6d. The object of a preposition is in the objective case.

You will remember from your study of the parts of speech that a preposition is a word which shows the relationship between a noun or a pronoun and some other word in the sentence. There is a list of common prepositions on pages 18–19. A preposition begins a prepositional phrase:

on the **train**   *for* my **father**
in the **house**   *of* the **story**
          above the **trees**

The final or principal word in a prepositional phrase is the *object of the preposition* which begins the phrase. The words in heavy type in the phrases above are the objects. They are in the objective case. *When the object of a preposition is a pronoun, you must be careful to use the objective form.* The following pronouns are used as objects of prepositions: *me, you, him, her, it, us, you, them, whom, whomever.*

Examine the following sentences carefully to see how pronouns are used as objects of prepositions. The objects given are compound because it is the compound form that usually leads to errors in usage.

1. I am expecting letters *from* **Jane** and **her.**
2. The argument was *between* **John** and **me.**
3. These orders are intended *for* **you** and **them.**
4. He wrote *to* our **friends** and **us.**

● EXERCISE 10.   In the following sentences pick out the prepositions which take pronoun objects and list them on your paper. After each write the correct one of the two pronouns given in parentheses.

1. Send a letter to his father and (she, her).
2. He stood between Helen and (me, I).

6d

3. I played against Stuart and (him, he).
4. Behind Carl and (me, I) was an angry rattlesnake.
5. The book was written by his brother and (him, he).
6. I ran into Alice and (them, they).
7. My aunt is coming after you and (we, us).
8. The picture of Paul and (me, I) is on her desk.
9. I'll go with you and (her, she).
10. Are you looking at Pam or (me, I)?

● EXERCISE 11.   Select the correct one of the two pronouns in parentheses and write it on your paper.

1. This decision must be made by you and (I, me).
2. Between the Republican candidate and (he, him) there is a mutual feeling of respect.
3. Let's go to the movies with Dad and (she, her).
4. She told the secret to Martha and (I, me).
5. Packages were left for you and (them, they).
6. I was surprised to run into Fran and (her, she) in New York.
7. Everyone except (she, her) was looking at Bob.
8. The police were standing directly behind (them, they) and (we, us).
9. Why did you come without the family and (them, they)?
10. Did anyone ask about the Whites and (us, we)?

● EXERCISE 12.   Write sentences of your own, using each of the following prepositions with a compound object, one of whose parts is a pronoun.

EXAMPLE   **She was looking for** *Barbara* **and** *me*.

1. between	6. with
2. at	7. near
3. to	8. toward
4. of	9. by
5. like	10. except

● EXERCISE 13.   *Oral Drill.* Read *aloud* 5 times each of the following sentences, stressing the italicized words.

1. The letters are *from* my brother and *her.*
2. They write *to* Alice and *me* regularly.
3. The mail is delivered *by* either Mr. Owen or *him.*
4. Mr. Owen had letters *for them* and *us.*
5. She refused to come *with* either Anne or *me.*
6. Who was sitting *between you* and *them?*
7. They played a trick *on* the boys and *us.*
8. *Without you* and *her*, I won't go.
9. Were you talking *about him* and *me?*
10. He looks *like* both *you* and *her.*

Who and Whom as Interrogative Pronouns

Like the use of the correct form of the pronoun as a predicate nominative (page 122), the use of *who* and *whom* in questions can no longer be reduced to a strict law. In modern *conversational* English usage the distinction between *who* and *whom* is gradually disappearing, and *whom* is going out of use. Among educated people, one sometimes hears *Who do you mean? Who do you know?* According to the rule you have learned about the case of the object of the verb, the speaker should say *whom* in these sentences. *In everyday conversation* you may use *who* for *whom* as an interrogative pronoun. *In written English* you should observe carefully the distinction between *who* and *whom.*

WHO AND WHOM AS RELATIVE PRONOUNS

When the pronouns *who* and *whom* introduce a subordinate clause, they are relative (not interrogative) pronouns. (See page 69.)

6e. The case of a relative pronoun is determined by its use in the clause which it introduces.

EXAMPLE   **It was James who spoke to me.**   [*Who* is in the nominative case because it is the subject of the verb *spoke* in the subordinate clause.]

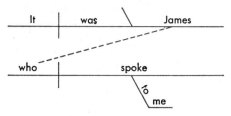

EXAMPLE   **It was James whom I saw.**   [*Whom* is in the objective case because it is the object of the verb *saw*, the verb in the subordinate clause.]

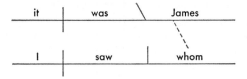

EXAMPLE   **I can remember who was absent.**   [*Who* is in the nominative case because it is the subject of the verb *was* in the subordinate clause. The object of the verb *can remember* is not *who* but the entire subordinate clause, which is a noun clause.]

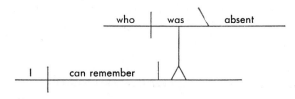

EXAMPLES   He is the friend **of whom I spoke.**
            He is the friend **whom I spoke of.**   [*Whom* is in

the objective case because it is the object of the preposition *of* in the subordinate clause.]

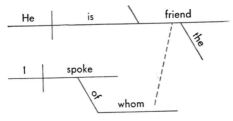

EXAMPLE   **Do you know who it was?**   [*Who* is in the nominative case because it is a predicate nominative after the verb *was*. This is clear when you change the clause around so that the sentence rather nonsensically reads: Do you know *it was who?*]

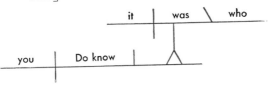

▶ CAUTION: Interrupting expressions like *I think* and *I believe* do not affect the case of the relative pronoun.

EXAMPLES   **He is the one who, I believe, will win.**   [*Who* is the subject of the clause *who will win.*]
I asked Maggie, who, I thought, would know.   [*Who* is the subject of the clause *who would know.*]

There is a modern tendency to use only *who* as a relative pronoun in conversation, but in writing, the distinction between *who* and *whom* is still carefully observed.

What can we conclude about the proper use of *who* and *whom?* In your daily conversations you need not be too much concerned about the distinction, especially in questions.

6e

In your writing, you should observe the distinction. The practice exercises which follow will contain *who* and *whom* problems, therefore, to help you in your written English. Since correct use of these pronouns is very difficult, you may wish to look back at the examples on this and the preceding page for help.

When you are deciding whether a clause calls for *who* or *whom*, first remove the clause from the sentence. Then ask yourself how the pronoun is used *in its own clause:* subject of verb; predicate nominative; object of verb (direct or indirect); object of preposition. When you know how the pronoun is used, you can select the correct form.

EXAMPLE   **She is the teacher (*who, whom*) I admire most.**
[Clause: (*who, whom*) I admire most. Use of pronoun: object of verb (I admire *whom*). Correct: *whom* I admire most.]

You may find it helpful to think of *who* as equivalent to *he*, and *whom* as equivalent to *him*.

EXAMPLES   **He is a man (*who, whom*) everyone likes**
[Everyone likes *him;* hence *whom*.]
He is a man (*who, whom*) in time will succeed.
[*He* in time will succeed; hence *who*.]

● EXERCISE 14.   Copy on your paper the clause in each sentence, writing (*who, whom*) at the beginning of the clause. On the line below the clause, write the use of the pronoun in the clause: subject of verb or object of verb. On a third line write the correct form of the pronoun.

EXAMPLE   George told me (who, whom) I could trust.
(who, whom) I could trust
object of verb
whom

1. Mr. MacPherson is a man (who, whom) I will always remember.
2. Janet has a list of the members (who, whom) have paid their dues.
3. You may bring (whoever, whomever) you like.
4. There are three coaches (who, whom) the boys respect.
5. I spoke with some of the boys (who, whom) had seen the game.
6. Can you remember (who, whom) you saw?
7. We need somebody (who, whom) can play the piano.
8. He is one of the men (who, whom), I think, are runing for office.
9. She sells Christmas cards to (whoever, whomever) she can interest in them.
10. I wrote to Mr. Parker, (who, whom), I was sure, would agree with me.

● EXERCISE 15.   Copy on your paper the clause in each sentence, writing (*who, whom*) as you did in the preceding exercise. On the line below the clause, write the use of the pronoun in the clause: subject of verb; predicate nominative; object of verb; object of preposition.

1. I am not sure (who, whom), he said, will attend the meeting.
2. Did you learn (who, whom) the new teacher is?
3. I am not sure (who, whom) she was referring to.
4. When the class president told us (who, whom) he had appointed, we were surprised.
5. Guards were stopping everyone (who, whom), they thought, might cause trouble.
6. I finally found Jane, (who, whom) I had been looking for.
7. You would never guess (who, whom) we saw at the party.
8. Who told you (who, whom) I was going with?

9. Before the election you must know (who, whom) the candidates are.
10. We got a ride with a man (who, whom), we found, was a very poor driver.

● EXERCISE 16.   Number in a column from 1 to 10. Write the correct form of *who* or *whom* for each of the following sentences. After each relative pronoun write how it is used in the clause which it introduces (subject, object of verb, object of preposition, predicate nominative).

EXAMPLE   **I don't know —— is coming.**
            who   subject of clause

1. Do you remember —— borrowed my pen?
2. He is the one —— I remember.
3. He is a plane pilot —— has few equals.
4. The police have never discovered —— the thief was.
5. There is a girl —— I think will be a success.
6. What is the name of the girl —— you introduced me to?
7. The actors —— we saw were professionals.
8. I know —— she went with.
9. We could not find out —— the man was.
10. He is one of those boys —— everyone likes.

● EXERCISE 17.   Supply the correct form of the relative pronoun (*who, whom, whoever, whomever*) to fill the blanks in the following sentences. List them on your paper.

1. I'll wait for —— is late.
2. Everyone —— I invited accepted my invitation.
3. The men —— the President appointed felt highly honored.
4. The President interviewed —— was sent to him.
5. The agency investigates anyone —— is suspected of treason.
6. Anyone —— he disapproves of is in great danger.

7. Jack is the only one —— I told the story to.
8. I am not sure —— he is.
9. That is the boy —— I saw.
10. Did anyone know —— you were talking about?

● REVIEW EXERCISE H. Number on your paper from 1 to 20. After the proper number write how the pronoun in parentheses is used: subject, predicate nominative, object of verb, object of preposition.

On the basis of its use, select the correct pronoun and write it on your paper.

EXAMPLE   **1. I know (who, whom) is coming.**
        1. subject   who

1. She offered to help Jack and (me, I).
2. It was either Henry or (him, he).
3. I haven't heard from either Sid or (she, her).
4. Tell your story to Jim and (me, I).
5. Do you know (who, whom) the winner was?
6. Betty and (she, her) are always arguing.
7. They finished the job without the teacher and (we, us).
8. (He, Him) and (I, me) are brothers.
9. Put Frank and (he, him) on the first team.
10. Was it Sally or (she, her) that told you?
11. I will interview (whoever, whomever) applies.
12. I know (who, whom) you mean.
13. Was the book written by Conrad or (he, him)?
14. We saw you and (he, him) on the corner.
15. You and (me, I) will take turns.
16. After the accident the police took Mr. Cole and (her, she) to the hospital.
17. Did you know (who, whom) Mr. Carlson appointed?
18. Do you think it could have been (they, them)?
19. I have worked for both Mr. Andrews and (him, he).
20. My sister and (me, I) do not always agree.

The two exercises which follow cover all you have so far learned about the correct use of pronouns.

You should make a perfect score on them. If you fall below 90%, you had better review.

● REVIEW EXERCISE I. Number on your paper from 1 to 20. Select the correct one of the two pronouns in parentheses in each sentence, and write it after the proper number on your paper.

1. Have you met Perry and (he, him)?
2. The coach wants you and (me, I).
3. Miss Smith sent for Marie and (her, she).
4. Bill and (I, me) did the homework together.
5. Was it you or (him, he) that did the first problem?
6. I am expecting you and (she, her).
7. (He, Him) and (me, I) took the late bus.
8. I don't know (whom, who) the pitcher was.
9. It was she (who, whom) I told you about.
10. The manager hired both Ellen and (me, I).
11. He will support (whoever, whomever) supports him.
12. Jerry and (they, them) are coming later.
13. I know (who, whom) you were talking to.
14. Please take Ann and (me, I) with you.
15. The fight was between Sanford and (he, him).
16. Mr. Thompson invited (us, we) boys into his office.
17. We'll take (whoever, whomever) comes first.
18. Tell Joan and (me, I) the whole story.
19. (We, Us) girls were sitting on the front porch.
20. He spoke to Sam and (me, I).

● REVIEW EXERCISE J. Number on your paper from 1 to 20. For each correct sentence in which the pronouns are all in the proper case, place a + after the corresponding number on your paper; for each incorrect sentence, place a 0.

1. Will you and he be there?
2. Please ask Jane and her when they will arrive.
3. I remember who came with Pete.
4. The jury gazed intently upon the witness who the attorney was examining.

  5. Hank reached the finish line just ahead of Allan and he.
  6. The postmaster offered jobs to both Tim and I.
  7. The doorman refused Larry and me permission to enter.
  8. She hired Carl and him.
  9. She expected him and me.
 10. This he and I refused to do.
 11. The librarian gave we boys some new books.
 12. Ginger and me decided to share our earnings.
 13. No one but Jessie and him could do the problem.
 14. He and she received the highest marks.
 15. Without you and she the party will be a flop.
 16. Helen and me won the dance contest.
 17. We met your family and them in Chicago.
 18. Mother took Hazel and me home.
 19. When she and I reached the beach, we couldn't resist the water.
 20. Us girls were severely punished.

THE PRONOUN IN AN INCOMPLETE CONSTRUCTION

The following are examples of incomplete constructions. In each one, part of the sentence is omitted and is written in brackets.

My brother is taller than I. [than I am tall]
The new boss paid him more than me. [than he paid me]

From these two examples of an incomplete construction you may notice that you should use the form of the pronoun which you would use if you completed the sentence. Thus in the first sentence *I* is correct because it is the subject of the clause *I am tall.* In the second sentence *me* is correct because it is the object of the verb *paid* in the clause *he paid me.*

Now examine this pair of sentences:

I like Gerald better than he. [than he likes Gerald]
I like Gerald better than him. [than I like him]

As you can see, the case of the pronoun depends on how the sentence is completed. Both the sentences

above are correct, but the sentences are quite different in meaning; they are completed in different ways.

**6f. After *than* and *as* introducing an incomplete
construction, use the form of the pronoun
you would use if the construction were
completed.**

● EXERCISE 18.   Write out each of the following
sentences, supplying the omitted part and using the
correct form of the pronoun. After the sentence write
the use of the pronoun in its clause — as subject,
object of verb, object of preposition, etc.

1. No one worked harder than (I, me).
2. Did you do as well as (she, her)?
3. She did more for Mary than (me, I).
4. I told you more than (he, him).
5. The boys on our team are faster than (they, them).
6. My brothers boasted that they were stronger than
   (we, us).
7. She thought she could swim farther than (me, I).
8. Jane finished earlier than (I, me).
9. Did you study as long as (we, us)?
10. We ate more than (they, them).

● REVIEW EXERCISE K.   Number on your paper
from 1 to 20. Select the correct one of the two pronouns given in parentheses and write it after the
proper number on your paper. Be prepared to give
reasons for your answers.

1. Carol and (me, I) are twins.
2. I know (who, whom) you mean.
3. She played a better game than (I, me).
4. It might have been (they, them).
5. I came in several yards behind Ted and (he, him).
6. My father and (she, her) are listening to the radio.
7. Helen will tell you (who, whom) was absent.

8. Natalie will do the job as well as (she, her).
9. We are expecting Phil and (him, he) on the next train.
10. You and (I, me) ought to talk the matter over.
11. This car was sold to either Mr. Foster or (he, him).
12. I like both Janie and (she, her).
13. The play delighted the children and (we, us).
14. They left Fred and (me, I) alone.
15. The pictures were painted by Mr. Olsen and (she, her).
16. George took longer than (I, me).
17. Elise wants to stay with you and (us, we).
18. You told her more than (he, him).
19. He is a man (who, whom), I think, deserves a great deal of credit.
20. The band played a request number for Sally and (I, me).

● REVIEW EXERCISE L. Fill in the blanks with the proper pronouns, making sure you use a variety of them throughout the exercise. Omit *you* entirely.

1. Phyllis and —— waited for Estelle and ——.
2. I don't remember —— he came with.
3. Perhaps you can tell —— and —— what happened.
4. He is a lot taller than ——.
5. With Geraldine and —— came the two dogs.
6. After closing the car door, Mother and —— went in opposite directions.
7. —— and Mother went shopping, and Elizabeth went with ——.
8. Kent and ——, together with Harry and ——, started a small orchestra.
9. —— and —— practiced faithfully for three weeks.
10. Then Kent and —— thought we were ready to perform.
11. Everybody came to Art and —— for advice.
12. Very freely, —— and —— gave it.
13. Why is Christmas shopping so hard on —— and ——?
14. Paul told Molly and —— not to be frightened.
15. I like desserts better than ——.
16. —— and —— ought to eat more of them.

6f

17. The Fourth of July is fun for our dog and ———.
18. Grandfather met ——— and ——— for tea downtown.
19. Why do Grandmother and ——— live so far away?
20. Was it Bill or ——— who asked that question?

● REVIEW EXERCISE M.   Number on your paper
from 1 to 25. For each sentence in which the pronouns
are correct, place a + after the corresponding number
on your paper; for each incorrect sentence, write
the correct form of the incorrect pronouns.

1. Was it she whom you saw?
2. She and I went to the movies last night.
3. We saw Sally and her as we entered the lobby.
4. Sally and her didn't see us.
5. Was it him who won the award?
6. No, it was she.
7. Luke got a higher mark than me.
8. This is supposed to be a secret between you and I.
9. The team and he are not so confident as us.
10. Ask Jessie whom she knows in Ridgefield.
11. On our last picnic, Mr. Bush and them went with us.
12. He and I ate too many hotdogs.
13. Most of the work was done by Joe and I.
14. Him and me didn't stay very long.
15. No other pitcher has as much control as him.
16. We did not recognize you and her.
17. As we were coming home, Mr. Lean and her saw us.
18. Everyone else arrived earlier than Lucy and I.
19. We told Mr. Lean and her we were sorry to be late.
20. Art and him said they had had a good time.
21. Who was Mr. Walker expecting?
22. Ask Nancy and she where they are going.
23. I don't know who she said was coming.
24. Did you get a message from Helen and me?
25. Whom do you think will be our new principal?

CHAPTER 7

Using Verbs Correctly

In grammar the word *tense* means *time*. It is applied to verbs because verbs indicate time. Study the verbs in the following sentences.

Now she *swims* across the river.   [present tense]
She *swam* across the river yesterday.   [past tense]
She *has swum* across the river often.   [present perfect tense]

You can see that the verbs in these sentences express action happening at different times.

7a. There are four basic forms of a verb. They are the *present*, the *present participle*, the *past*, and the *past participle*.

Study the following list of the six tense (time) forms of a verb. Giving all the forms of a verb in this way is called "conjugating" the verb.

Notice that the six tenses are formed from the first and the last two principal parts.

CONJUGATION OF *TO SWIM*

(Principal Parts: *swim, swimming, swam, swum*)

PRESENT TENSE

Singular	*Plural*
I swim	we swim
you swim	you swim
he swims	they swim

7a

PAST TENSE

Singular	*Plural*
I swam	we swam
you swam	you swam
he swam	they swam

FUTURE TENSE

Singular	*Plural*
I shall swim	we shall swim
you will swim	you will swim
he will swim	they will swim

PRESENT PERFECT TENSE

Singular	*Plural*
I have swum	we have swum
you have swum	you have swum
he has swum	they have swum

PAST PERFECT TENSE

Singular	*Plural*
I had swum	we had swum
you had swum	you had swum
he had swum	they had swum

FUTURE PERFECT TENSE

Singular	*Plural*
I shall have swum	we shall have swum
you will have swum	you will have swum
he will have swum	they will have swum

Regular Verbs

A regular verb is one which forms its past and past participle forms by merely adding *–ed* or *–d* to the present form.

PRESENT	PAST	PAST PARTICIPLE
I walk	I walk*ed*	I have walk*ed*
I believe	I believ*ed*	I have believ*ed*

Irregular Verbs

An irregular verb is one which does not form its past and past participle forms by adding *–ed* or *–d* to the present form. Irregular verbs form their past and past participle forms in various other ways: by changing the vowel, or by changing consonants, or by making no change at all.

PRESENT	PAST	PAST PARTICIPLE
I swim	I swam	I have swum
I see	I saw	I have seen
I beat	I beat	I have beaten
I bid	I bid	I have bid

Since all tenses may be made from the principal parts, it is important for you to know the principal parts of verbs you wish to use.

A glance at the conjugation of *swim* on pages 143–44 will show you how the six tenses are formed from the principal parts. The present and future tenses are formed from the first principal part, *swim;* the past tense is formed from the third principal part, *swam;* and the perfect tenses, those made with *has, have, had,* are formed from the fourth principal part, *swum.*

The regular verbs are easy to use because the past and past participle forms of every regular verb are made in the same way, but in each irregular verb the past and past participle forms are made in a different way, and this fact makes irregular verbs harder to use correctly.

The following irregular verbs are those which are most frequently misused. Most of your everyday errors in using verbs in conversational English can be prevented if you will learn the past and past participle forms of these verbs. The drills which follow will give you practice in their correct use.

When you memorize the principal parts, you will help yourself if you will always include *have* with the past participle. In repeating them to yourself, for instance, say: *go, went,* **have** *gone; see, saw,* **have** *seen*; etc.

The past participle of a verb which takes an object is also used in such expressions as the following, in which the verb acts upon its subject rather than upon an object.[1]

EXAMPLES   Our quarterback **was thrown** for a loss.
The report **had been written** by the secretary.
All the bells **were rung** at one time.
They **have been seen** downtown during school hours.
Two records **were broken** in Saturday's meet.

IRREGULAR VERBS FREQUENTLY MISUSED[2]

PRESENT	PAST	PAST PARTICIPLE
begin	began	(have) begun
blow	blew	(have) blown
break	broke	(have) broken
bring	brought	(have) brought
burst	burst	(have) burst
choose	chose	(have) chosen
come	came	(have) come
do	did	(have) done
drink	drank	(have) drunk
drive	drove	(have) driven
fall	fell	(have) fallen
freeze	froze	(have) frozen
give	gave	(have) given

[1] Verbs which act upon their subject are said to be in the *passive voice*. Verbs which act on an object are in the *active voice*. The whole matter of *voice* has been omitted from these pages as being difficult and of very little importance for young writers.

[2] The especially difficult verbs *lie, lay; sit, set; rise, raise* will be given special attention. See pages 149–156.

go	went	(have) gone
ride	rode	(have) ridden
ring	rang	(have) rung
run	ran	(have) run
see	saw	(have) seen
shrink	shrank	(have) shrunk
speak	spoke	(have) spoken
steal	stole	(have) stolen
swim	swam	(have) swum
take	took	(have) taken
throw	threw	(have) thrown
write	wrote	(have) written

● EXERCISE 1. Your teacher will dictate to you the present tense of these 25 irregular verbs. Write from memory the past and past participle forms for each verb. Place *have* before the past participle.

● EXERCISE 2. Write in a column on your paper the correct form of the verb given at the beginning of each sentence. If necessary, refer to the list given above.

1. *do*   Harold —— his best to win yesterday's match.
2. *come*   He —— in late last night.
3. *begin*   Yesterday everyone —— a new project.
4. *run*   Although we —— after the thief, we did not catch him.
5. *see*   I —— Bob at the game last week.
6. *write*   I have —— the letter.
7. *ring*   The bell had —— before we reached school.
8. *go*   She has —— with him.
9. *give*   Andy —— us our instructions.
10. *drink* He had —— the entire bottle.
11. *break* They've —— out of their cage.
12. *speak* He had —— to no one.
13. *swim*   Then the big fish —— toward us.
14. *throw* Some valuable papers had been —— out.
15. *take*   She has —— more than her share.
16. *ride*   The sheriff had —— to the scene of the crime.
17. *blow*   Last night's storm —— the plane off course.

148   *Using Verbs Correctly*

18. *burst*   As the plane touched the runway, a tire ——.
19. *bring*   Each workman had —— his own tools.
20. *choose*   The coach should have —— you.
21. *fall*   The truck must have —— twenty feet.
22. *drive*   I haven't —— that route for several years.
23. *shrink*   When it was laundered, the dress ——.
24. *steal*   Who had —— the money?
25. *freeze*   The bay has not —— over this winter.

● EXERCISE 3.   Choose the correct one of the two verbs in parentheses. Write the words in a column on your paper. When your paper has been corrected, read each sentence *aloud* several times, using the correct word.

1. After I told her, she (begun, began) to cry.
2. Have you (wrote, written) your theme?
3. You should have (thrown, throwed) the ball to me.
4. The doctors (did, done) all they could.
5. He (drank, drunk) three cups of coffee at breakfast.
6. Who (came, come) home with you?
7. We (seen, saw) the feature picture twice.
8. Have you (rode, ridden) horseback before?
9. She's never (took, taken) any advice from me.
10. The vacant house had been (broken, broke) into.
11. Who (give, gave) you permission to leave?
12. The car (run, ran) well for ten years.
13. Have you (spoken, spoke) to him yet?
14. Who (swum, swam) the channel?
15. Has the bell (rang, rung)?
16. I wish I had (went, gone) with you.
17. Someone had (stolen, stole) the team's mascot.
18. The wallpaper (shrunk, shrank) as it dried.
19. Several TV aerials were (blowed, blown) down.
20. The explorers thought they had (froze, frozen) their feet.
21. We would have (driven, drove) farther if we had not been tired.
22. Three inches of rain had (fell, fallen) during the morning.
23. I wished I had (brung, brought) my parka.

24. When the bag (burst, bursted), the contents spilled on the sidewalk.
25. Has anyone (chose, chosen) his partner?

● EXERCISE 4. **Number in a column on your paper from 1 to 25. Read each of the following sentences *aloud*. If the form of the irregular verb is correct, place a + after the corresponding number on your paper. If it is incorrect, place a 0.**

1. Our bicycles had been ran over.
2. The teacher had spoken sharply to Jane.
3. Both of us run in the quarter-mile relay last week.
4. I seen him go that way!
5. The clock had been broke for years.
6. It seemed as though we swam for miles.
7. Bill had thrown one over home plate.
8. Have you wrote to your aunt yet?
9. They'd went downtown for a soda.
10. It was the longest letter I ever wrote.
11. Who has given the best answer?
12. We have came back earlier than we expected to.
13. Which of you have saw the picture at the Rivoli?
14. We swum in the ocean for the first time yesterday.
15. Who has spoke to you about the dance?
16. We done the best we could.
17. They have taken their places in line.
18. He done the marketing for her.
19. We come to see your brother last night.
20. Has he drunk all the cokes yet?
21. The lions shrunk back from their trainer's whip.
22. A water main had burst beneath the street.
23. She had never before drove the car alone.
24. Several trees had fell across the road.
25. I wished I had brung more money with me.

LIE AND LAY

The verb *lie* means *to recline, to rest or remain in a lying position*. Its principal parts are *lie, lying, lay, (have) lain*.

The verb *lay* means *to put, to place* something. Its principal parts are: *lay, laying, laid, (have) laid.*

Study the following:

PRESENT	PRESENT PARTICIPLE	PAST	PAST PARTICIPLE
lie (to recline)	lying	lay	(have) lain
lay (to put)	laying	laid	(have) laid

The various forms of these two verbs are often confused. Careful thought and drill will help you to distinguish them and to use them correctly.

Lie never has an object.

It may help you to know that *lie (lying, lay, [have] lain)* never has an object, whereas *lay (laying, laid, [have] laid)* may have an object.

EXAMPLES   Please **lie** still.   (no object)
Lay the *child* on the davenport.   (*child* is object of *lay*)

I found my glasses **lying** on the grass.   (no object)
We watched the men **laying** *concrete*.   (*concrete* is the object of *laying*)

● EXERCISE 5.   Study the *lie, lay* forms above until you can write them from memory exactly as given. Be sure you know which verb means *to recline, rest, remain in a lying position* and which means *to put* something.

● EXERCISE 6.   Read over *aloud* several times each of the following sentences, in which the verbs are used correctly. Be able to explain, in the light of the information just given, why the verb is correct. For example: *She **laid** her sewing on the table. Laid* is correct because the sentence means *she **put** her sewing on the table,* and the verb required is *lay,* the past tense of which is *laid.*

1. I *laid* your coat on the chair.
2. We *lay* on the hot sand until we were sunburned.
3. You *lie* here while I get help.
4. For months the machine *lay* untouched.
5. Please *lay* your bundles over there.
6. The men were *laying* a cement foundation.
7. They used the sand which was *lying* about.
8. I had just *lain* down.
9. I had *laid* down my book and rushed to the door.
10. You must *lie* here.

● EXERCISE 7. Supply the correct form of the proper verb (*lie* — *lay*) in the following. List the forms in a column on your paper. Ask yourself whether the action in the sentence is that of resting or placing. Refer to the forms on page 150 if necessary.

1. Where was the dog ——?
2. Who —— this book here?
3. I was —— in bed.
4. He has —— many plans before the school board.
5. John was —— the pictures out to dry.
6. Our ship had —— at anchor all night.
7. Engineers —— a new road through the swamp last year.
8. I grew tired of just —— around the house.
9. We —— under the overturned canoe until the storm had passed.
10. We might have —— there an hour.

● EXERCISE 8. Select from each sentence the correct one of the two words in parentheses and write the words in a column on your paper. Think carefully of the *meaning* of the verb.

1. The vessel (lay, laid) across a sand bar.
2. Fran (lay, laid) down about an hour ago.
3. I'll (lay, lie) here for a while.
4. He (lay, laid) it there.
5. (Lay, Lie) here until we call you.

6. Before noon the men had (laid, lain) a new road.
7. (Laying, Lying) there, we fell asleep.
8. The dog usually (lays, lies) outside his kennel.
9. Horn Mountain (lies, lays) ten miles south of us.
10. After the launching, a new keel was (laid, lain).
11. Had he (laid, lain) there long?
12. Where were you (lying, laying)?
13. The flowers are carefully (lain, laid) in cardboard boxes.
14. (Lying, Laying) there in the rain, I caught a severe cold.
15. The lake (lies, lays) at the foot of a mountain.
16. He (laid, lay) the book open on the desk and began to read.
17. A vast forest (laid, lay) before us.
18. We found fossils which had (lain, laid) there for centuries.
19. He (lay, laid) the white paper over the red.
20. I found it (lying, laying) beside the walk.

● EXERCISE 9. Number in a column on your paper from 1 to 20. Read each of the following sentences and determine whether it is correct or incorrect. If it is correct, place a + after the corresponding number on your paper; if it is incorrect, place a 0. Think of the *meaning* of the verb.

1. After laying on the beach for a while, we took a swim.
2. We saw four fishing boats lying in the small harbor.
3. A piece of candy lay on the table, completely melted.
4. Have you lain in the sun all this time?
5. We had lain our clothes on the river bank.
6. They must have been lying here for an hour.
7. He lay his watch on the balcony railing.
8. The workmen laid the keel last week.
9. I have been laying here waiting for you.
10. Pete and Bob are always laying around the sun porch.
11. I'd get fat if I laid around so much.
12. Our pet hen laid two eggs yesterday.

13. When Betty and Joan come home, they usually lay their books on the table.
14. The books are never left laying around on chairs.
15. Somehow, mine are always lying where they shouldn't be.
16. Laying down to read is a bad but comfortable habit.
17. The crew lay the foundation yesterday.
18. The hounds were laying in wait for the fox.
19. The fox lay in his den, panting.
20. I know I lay them right here, yesterday afternoon.

SIT **AND** *SET*

The verb *sit* means *to rest in an upright, sitting position.* The principal parts of *sit* are *sit, sitting, sat, (have) sat.*

The verb *set* means *to put, to place* something. The principal parts of *set* are *set, setting, set, (have) set.*

Study the following:

PRESENT	PRESENT PARTICIPLE	PAST	PAST PARTICIPLE
sit (to rest)	sitting	sat	(have) sat
set (to put)	setting	set	(have) set

You will have little difficulty using these verbs correctly, if you will remember two facts about them.

1. Like *lie* the verb *sit* means to be in a certain position. It never has an object. Like *lay* the verb *set* means to put something down. It may have an object.

2. *Set* does not change to form the past or the past participle. Whenever the meaning is *to place* or *to put*, you use *set*.[3]

Memorize the principal parts of *sit* and *set* so that you can give them readily from memory.

---

[3] The expressions "the sun sets" and "the setting hen" are exceptions to this rule.

● EXERCISE 10. Read over *aloud* several times each of the following sentences, in which *sit* and *set* are correctly used. Think of the *meaning* of each sentence as you read it.

1. I prefer to *sit* here.
2. *Set* the box down.
3. She had been *setting* out tomato plants.
4. Where have you been *sitting?*
5. Please *sit* down.
6. I *sat* there for an hour.
7. Rover *sat* up and began to bark.
8. He *set* the lamp in the corner.
9. He is content just to *sit* on the porch all day long.
10. You have *sat* there long enough.

● EXERCISE 11. Select from each sentence the correct one of the two words in parentheses and write the words in a column on your paper.

1. Which chair were you (sitting, setting) in?
2. Would you like to (set, sit) here?
3. This is a comfortable place to (sit, set).
4. We found him (setting, sitting) in the living room.
5. I have (sat, set) here too long.
6. The doctor (sat, set) his bag on the table.
7. (Set, Sit) down and relax.
8. I (set, sat) my suitcase down beside me.
9. You may (sit, set) in any seat you wish.
10. (Set, Sit) the packages on the table, please.

● REVIEW EXERCISE A. Number in a column on your paper from 1 to 20. If a sentence is correct, place a + after the corresponding number on your paper; if it is incorrect, place a 0.

1. She prefers to set in the rocking chair.
2. Where should the movers set the piano?
3. Lie as still as you can.
4. Sitting in the grandstand, we were uncomfortable.

 5. I'll lay down right here.
 6. Lay the pillows down first.
 7. Please set them in a row.
 8. Lay down and go to sleep.
 9. Just set there until you are called.
10. Why are you sitting in the principal's office?
11. Who lay his briefcase on my desk?
12. How long have I laid here?
13. We were told to set down and wait our turn.
14. The coach advised us to lie down until we were rested.
15. I lay the mail on your desk an hour ago.
16. From where we were laying we could hear the radio.
17. Father laid out a badminton court on the lawn.
18. Set down a minute, please.
19. I had lain down for a brief nap.
20. We were forced to lay in an uncomfortable position.

RISE AND RAISE

The verb *rise* means *to go in an upward direction.* Its principal parts are *rise, rising, rose, (have) risen.*

The verb *raise* means *to force something to move in an upward direction.* Its principal parts are *raise, raising, raised, (have) raised.*

PRESENT	PRESENT PARTICIPLE	PAST	PAST PARTICIPLE
rise (go up)	rising	rose	(have) risen
raise (force upward)	raising	raised	(have) raised

Like *lie* and *sit*, *rise* never has an object. Like *lay* and *set*, *raise* may have an object.

● EXERCISE 12. Fill the blanks in the following sentences with a correct form of *rise* or *raise*, whichever is required by the meaning.

 1. The thermometer had —— rapidly since morning.
 2. On schedule, plane after plane —— from the field.
 3. Everyone cheered as the balloon —— above the trees.

4. Men stood with tears in their eyes as the flag —— to the top of the pole.
5. By noon, the temperature had —— to 100 degrees.
6. As the river ——, men piled sandbags on the levee.
7. My grades have —— this term.
8. As the barometer ——, our spirits —— with it.
9. At last the clouds —— above the peaks.
10. Prices had —— alarmingly.

● EXERCISE 13.   Number in a column on your paper from 1 to 10. Select from each sentence the correct one of the two words in parentheses and write it after the corresponding number on your paper.

1. When stocks (rise, raise), the broker is happy.
2. His importance has (raised, risen) steadily.
3. Tomorrow the sun will (rise, raise) at six o'clock.
4. Clouds of dust were (raising, rising) skyward.
5. The boats were (rising, raising) and falling on the surf.
6. Spires of several churches could be seen (raising, rising) above the village.
7. The curtain had just (risen, raised) when we found our seats.
8. Swollen streams (raised, rose) until they overflowed their banks.
9. He had (raised, risen) his arm in protest.
10. She (rose, raised) from her chair to greet us.

● REVIEW EXERCISE B.   Number in a column on your paper from 1 to 40. Read each of the following sentences and determine whether it is correct or incorrect. If it is correct, place a + after the corresponding number on your paper; if it is incorrect, place a 0.

1. We found her lost gloves lying in the top drawer.
2. Wouldn't you rather set here?
3. We laid on our sleds, ready for a push.

4. The bird sat on her nest.
5. The doctor advised him to lay still.
6. The men raise the flag to the top of the pole each morning.
7. Judy sets the table every night.
8. Why are you laying around here instead of working?
9. The river has raised six inches since last night!
10. We were just setting there, talking.
11. Quacky laid her first egg yesterday.
12. Shall we sit out this dance?
13. The sun raises at a later hour in winter.
14. Will you rise from your seats, please?
15. We laid out a tennis court on the old baseball diamond.
16. All of us had raised from our chairs.
17. The balloon raised out of sight.
18. It was too hot to lie in bed all night.
19. Please set in that chair, Mrs. Johnson.
20. We laid the light bulbs down carefully.
21. The ducks rose and waddled in a solemn line to the pond.
22. Don't just set there; do something!
23. We got sunburned while laying on the beach.
24. Sit down with us for a while.
25. The whole audience raised up in protest.
26. Buster set there blinking his eyes and wagging his tail.
27. We lay out all the clothes we needed for the trip.
28. The Thompsons raised wonderful tomatoes last year.
29. Their voices rose in a loud shout of approval.
30. Lucky, our dog, laid in wait for the unwary mouse.
31. He was laying there for almost an hour, perfectly still.
32. Finally he raised his head ever so slowly.
33. Being tired, Mary lay down.
34. We set there watching him.
35. We set the pudding there to cool, and the cat ate it.
36. He set there looking very guilty.
37. Then he laid down over in the corner and went to sleep.
38. Lay right down and go to sleep!

39. The price of meat has raised during the past month.
40. Lie down, Rover!

Consistency of Tense

7b. Do not change needlessly from one tense to another.

	Past			Present
WRONG	Henry *spoke* to me about the show and *says* he

WRONG   Henry *spoke* [Past] to me about the show and *says* [Present] he *has* [Present] a part in it for me. [inconsistent tenses]

RIGHT   Henry **spoke** [Past] to me about the show and **said** [Past] he **had** [Past] a part in it for me. [consistent tenses]

Young writers, especially when writing informal essays or narratives, sometimes begin their compositions in one tense and then lapse into another tense. Such lapses are due largely to carelessness, for students usually understand the error when it is pointed out to them. The exercises on the next few pages are intended to make you aware of this kind of error in written English. Let's look at a few isolated examples of sentences in which the writer has been inconsistent in his use of tenses.

WRONG   The gun *went* [Past] off with a bang, and he *runs* [Present] away as fast as his legs *could carry* [Past] him. [tenses inconsistent]

RIGHT   The gun **went** [Past] off with a bang, and he **ran** [Past] away as fast as his legs **could carry** [Past] him. [tenses consistent]

RIGHT   The gun **goes** [Present] off with a bang, and he **runs** [Present] away as fast as his legs **can carry** [Present] him. [tenses consistent]

	Past	Present
WRONG	He *saw* the cause of the trouble, and *decides* to report it. [tenses inconsistent]	

	Past	Past
RIGHT	He **saw** the cause of the trouble and **decided** to report it. [tenses consistent]	

	Present	Present
RIGHT	He **sees** the cause of the trouble and **decides** to report it. [tenses consistent]	

● EXERCISE 14.   Such sentences as those above are, of course, extreme examples. The paragraph below will illustrate a normal case of inconsistency in the use of tenses. List on your paper the verbs which are in the wrong tense. After each write the verb in its proper tense. You must, of course, decide first of all whether the paragraph should be in the present or the past tense throughout.

1. At the age of four I was learning to row a boat. 2. One evening my sister and I are playing in the boat which was tied to the dock.   3. Ruth decides to untie the boat and go exploring.   4. A sudden wind comes up and whitecaps covered the lake.   5. Much to my surprise I found myself in the middle of the lake while my frantic parents stood at the dock anxiously looking for us.   6. I wanted to stand up in the tossing boat and wave to them, but Ruth screams at me to sit still.   7. Our faith in our parents' ability to solve any problem was again strengthened as Dad comes speeding toward us in the launch. 8. He towed us back to shore.

● REVIEW EXERCISE C.   Number on your paper from 1 to 50. After the corresponding number on your paper, write the correct one of the two words in parentheses.

1. How many compositions have you (wrote, written)?
2. His school books (lay, laid) on the table in the hall.
3. We (threw, throwed) out all the old magazines.

7b

4. You must have (taken, took) a long time to do your homework.
5. I couldn't remember where I had (lain, laid) my books.
6. She (swum, swam) beside the boat all the way.
7. Who would have (stolen, stole) anything from him?
8. The dentist expected me to (set, sit) perfectly still.
9. I wish I had (spoke, spoken) less critically.
10. Storm clouds have been (raising, rising) in the west.
11. Improperly laundered, her wool sweater (shrunk, shrank) badly.
12. The bag (burst, bursted) without warning.
13. Do you remember where you (set, sat) the lamp?
14. The dogs had been (laying, lying) in a mud puddle.
15. Then he (ran, run) around to the back door.
16. No one noticed Al (laying, lying) at the edge of the field.
17. We watched the gulls (raising, rising) from the water.
18. When I (seen, saw) Jack, he was going swimming.
19. Have you ever (ridden, rode) this horse?
20. Jerry (brung, brought) some water from the spring.
21. The barometer has (raised, risen) three points.
22. Has he (gone, went) home?
23. The river might have (broke, broken) through the dam.
24. If the bay had (frozen, froze), we'd have been caught in ice.
25. The show (begun, began) exactly on time.
26. The alarm had (rung, rang) an hour early.
27. Several trees were (laying, lying) across the path.
28. If he had (fallen, fell), he would have been killed.
29. The doctors (did, done) everything they could.
30. We (set, sat) waiting for hours.
31. Who (drank, drunk) the coffee?
32. Some boats had been (blowed, blown) ashore.
33. Mr. Larsen (give, gave) me a second chance.
34. The nurse told me to (lay, lie) down.
35. You shouldn't have (drove, driven) without a license.
36. (Laying, Lying) in bed for weeks was boring.
37. When Father (came, come) home, he demanded an explanation.

38. At the good news, our hopes (rose, raised).
39. Harry admitted that he had (chosen, chose) the wrong route.
40. Do you expect me to (sit, set) here all day?
41. You should have (run, ran) faster.
42. She (come, came) back on the afternoon train.
43. The old car (give, gave) us a lot of trouble.
44. I (laid, lay) my book report on your desk yesterday.
45. We (ran, run) until we were exhausted.

From each sentence copy after the proper number on your paper the verbs in the sentence, making the tenses consistent.

46. As the team (came, come) onto the field, the crowd (leap, leaped) to their feet and (start, started) to shout.
47. Jim (got, gets) the ball and (hands, handed) it to Bill, who (fumbles, fumbled) and then (recovers, recovered) it.
48. There (are, were) only twenty seconds left when John (calls, called) for a long pass and (whips, whipped) the ball down the field, where Bob Smith (catches, caught) it and (stepped, steps) across the goal for the winning touchdown.
49. I (explain, explained) to the coach why I missed the ball, but he (looks, looked) pretty angry and (refused, refuses) to put me back into the game.
50. When we (see, saw) Bob's remarkable catch, we (can't, couldn't) believe our eyes, and we (wait, waited) for the announcer to confirm it.

CHAPTER 8

Using Modifiers Correctly

In your study of grammar you learned that a modifier is a word or group of words which modifies (makes more definite) the meaning of another word. You know that there are two parts of speech which are modifiers. One is the adjective, which modifies a noun or pronoun. The other is the adverb, which modifies a verb or an adjective or another adverb. The purpose of this chapter is to help you use modifiers correctly and effectively. If you feel that you need to review adjectives and adverbs, turn to pages 6 and 13 and study them again before beginning work on this chapter. Review also the predicate adjective, page 45.

Adjective or Adverb? — Three Confusing Pairs

You will have little difficulty using most adjectives and adverbs correctly. Almost the only common problems in distinguishing an adverb from an adjective concern the three pairs: *bad — badly, good — well; slow — slowly.* Your problem is to learn when to use the adverb form and when to use the adjective form.

Apply the following rule to the three troublesome pairs.

8a. If a word in the predicate modifies the subject of the verb, choose the adjective form.

162

If it modifies the verb, choose the adverb form.[1]

EXAMPLE   **This *lesson* is easy.** [The adjective *easy* modifies the noun *lesson;* easy lesson.]
You can do this lesson easily. [The adverb *easily* modifies the verb *can do;* can do easily.]

(1) The linking verbs (see page 10) are usually followed by a predicate adjective. The following are the most commonly used linking verbs: *be, become, seem, grow, appear, look, feel, smell, taste, remain, stay, sound.*

▶ NOTE :   In many sentences requiring an adjective after the verb, *is, are, was, were* may be substituted for the verbs without greatly changing the meaning.
EXAMPLE   **She felt happy.** = She **was** happy.

Because many verbs may be used as either a linking verb or an action verb, you must be able to tell which way a verb is used.

LINKING   **The *plants* grew tall.** [verb followed by an adjective modifying the subject; the plants *were* tall]

ACTION   **The plants *grew* rapidly.** [verb modified by an adverb]

LINKING   **She appeared worried.** [verb followed by an adjective modifying the subject; she *was* worried]

ACTION   **She *appeared* suddenly.** [verb modified by an adverb]

LINKING   **He looked heavy.** [verb followed by an adjective modifying the subject; he *was* heavy]

ACTION   **He *looked* sharply in my direction.** [verb modified by an adverb]

[1] Most adjectives become adverbs by adding *–ly:* neat — neatly; strange — strangely; beautiful — beautifully. A few adjectives, however, also end in *–ly* (*lonely, daily, sickly, lovely*) so that you cannot always be sure that an *–ly* word is an adverb.

8a

BAD AND BADLY

Bad is an adjective; in most uses *badly* is an adverb.

EXAMPLES **His *behavior* was bad.** [*bad* behavior]

He *behaved* badly. [adverb modifying verb *behaved*]

The *situation* looks bad. [After the linking verb *looks*, the adjective *bad* modifies the subject *situation*.]

I *played* badly. [The adverb *badly* modifies the verb *played*.]

With linking verbs, the adjective form is used.

WRONG **He looks very badly.**

RIGHT **He looks very bad.** [The adjective *bad* modifies the subject *he*.]

WRONG **This smells badly.**

RIGHT **This smells bad.** [*Smell* is a linking verb here. *Bad* modifies the subject *this*.]

One prominent exception to this rule is the use of *badly* after the sense verb *feel*. In speaking, you may use either *bad* or *badly* after *feel*.

She feels bad about her grades.
She feels badly about her grades.

However, since written English is more exact than spoken English, in writing you should use *bad* after *feel*.

She feels bad about her grades. [*not* badly]

Follow the rules for written English in doing the exercises in this book.

WELL AND GOOD

Well may be used as either an adjective or an adverb. As an adjective, *well* has three meanings.

1. *To be in good health*

EXAMPLES **He is well.**   **He feels well.**

2. *To appear well-dressed or well-groomed*

EXAMPLE   It pays to look **well.**

3. *To be satisfactory*

EXAMPLES   It is **well.**   All is **well.**

As an adverb, *well* means *capably.*

EXAMPLE   He washed the car **well.**

Good is always an adjective. It should not be used to modify a verb.

WRONG   The team played good.
RIGHT   The team *played* **well.**

WRONG   The actors did good.
RIGHT   The actors *did* **well.**

SLOW AND SLOWLY

Slow is used as both an adjective and an adverb. *Slowly* is an adverb.

EXAMPLES   Go **slow.**   [*Slow* is an adverb modifying the verb *go.*]

Go **slowly.**   [*Slowly* is an adverb modifying the verb *go.*]

In most uses (other than *Go slow* and *Drive slow*) it is better practice to use *slowly* as an adverb instead of *slow.*

EXAMPLES   Move as **slowly** as you can.
He walked **slowly** up the stairs.

▶ CAUTION: There are certain words like *loud, hard, deep, fast, tight,* etc., which may be used as adverbs without changing their forms.

EXAMPLES   He played **hard.**
Dig **deep.**
They ran **fast.**
Hold on **tight.**
He spoke **loud** (or **loudly**) and **long.**

● EXERCISE 1.   Number on your paper from 1 to 20. Select the correct one of the two words in parentheses, and write it after the corresponding number on your paper.

1. The children have behaved very (good, well).
2. Your new suit fits (well, good).
3. This plum tastes (bad, badly).
4. He always does his work (well, good).
5. We agreed to proceed as (slow, slowly) as possible.
6. She prides herself on always looking (good, well).
7. That suit doesn't look so (bad, badly) on him.
8. Jane speaks very (slowly, slow).
9. Do you think the team played (good, well)?
10. When the chemistry class finished experimenting, the whole school smelled (badly, bad).
11. Her clothes always fit (good, well).
12. They worked (slow, slowly) but accurately.
13. The eggs smelled (badly, bad).
14. You did very (good, well).
15. The band played (badly, bad).
16. The orchestra didn't play so (good, well) as the band.
17. His voice sounds (badly, bad) on a loudspeaker.
18. If you work too (slow, slowly), you will delay the class.
19. After his long illness he looked (badly, bad).
20. The car was approaching very (slowly, slow).

● EXERCISE 2.   Number on your paper from 1 to 20. If the sentence is correct, place a + after the corresponding number; if it is incorrect, place a 0. Be able to explain your answers.

1. Harry felt pretty bad about losing his match.
2. You're looking well.
3. Go slow on a winding road.
4. The cake tasted well enough.
5. Why are you walking so slow?
6. She felt rather bad all day.
7. I was surprised at how badly the choir sounded.
8. These earrings do not look well on you.

9. By starting slow you can finish fast.
10. No one knew George could sing so good.
11. The time seemed to pass very slow.
12. We thought the soup tasted badly.
13. If you aren't feeling well, you must stay home.
14. I am not doing so good this term as last.
15. She has always gotten along good with other people.
16. There is no reason for you to feel bad.
17. Look the car over good before you buy it.
18. Traffic was moving very slow on all main highways.
19. Driving so slow overheated the motor.
20. I think she looks well in green.

Comparison of Adjectives and Adverbs

COMPARISON OF ADJECTIVES

Adjectives state qualities of nouns or pronouns.

> **tall** building
> **beautiful** day
> **good** dinner

8b. When you wish to *compare the degree or extent* to which one noun has a quality with the degree to which another noun has the same quality, you change the form of the adjective. This change is called *comparison*.

The following examples show how adjective forms change to show comparison.

1. The Empire State Building is **tall.**
   The Empire State Building is **taller** than the Chrysler Building.
   The Empire State Building is the **tallest** building in New York.

2. Today is **beautiful.**
   Today is **more beautiful** than yesterday.
   Today is the **most beautiful** day we have had.

8b

3. The new restaurant served a **good** dinner.
The new restaurant served a **better** dinner than the old restaurant.
The new restaurant served the **best** dinner I have ever eaten.

There are three degrees of comparison: *positive*, *comparative*, and *superlative*.

POSITIVE	COMPARATIVE	SUPERLATIVE
tall	taller	tallest
beautiful	more beautiful	most beautiful
good	better	best

FORMATION OF THE COMPARATIVE AND SUPERLATIVE DEGREES

(1) Adjectives and adverbs of one syllable form their comparative and superlative degrees by adding -er and -est.

POSITIVE	COMPARATIVE	SUPERLATIVE
strong	stronger	strongest
fast	faster	fastest

(2) Some adjectives of two syllables form their comparative and superlative degrees by adding -er or -est; other adjectives of two syllables form their comparative and superlative degrees by means of *more* and *most*.

When you are in doubt as to which way an adjective is compared, consult an unabridged dictionary.

POSITIVE	COMPARATIVE	SUPERLATIVE
happy	happier	happiest
pretty	prettier	prettiest
rapid	more rapid	most rapid
helpful	more helpful	most helpful

(3) Adjectives of more than two syllables and adverbs ending in -ly form their comparative and superlative degrees by means of *more* and *most*.

POSITIVE	COMPARATIVE	SUPERLATIVE
beautiful	more beautiful	most beautiful
industrious	more industrious	most industrious
agreeably	more agreeably	most agreeably

(4) Comparison to indicate *less* or *least* of a quality is accomplished by using the words *less* and *least* before the adjective.

POSITIVE	COMPARATIVE	SUPERLATIVE
gray	less gray	least gray
satisfactory	less satisfactory	least satisfactory

IRREGULAR COMPARISON

Adjectives and adverbs which do not follow the regular methods of forming their comparative and superlative degrees are said to be compared irregularly.

POSITIVE	COMPARATIVE	SUPERLATIVE
bad	worse	worst
good } well	better	best
many } much	more	most

● EXERCISE 3. Write the comparative and superlative forms of the following adjectives. If you are in doubt about the two-syllable words, look them up in an unabridged dictionary.

1. big
2. strange
3. wealthy
4. eager
5. lonely
6. successful
7. capable
8. short
9. difficult
10. certain
11. bad
12. honest
13. well
14. famous
15. good

Use of Comparative and Superlative Forms of Adjectives and Adverbs

Besides knowing how to form the comparative and superlative degrees of adjectives and adverbs, in using them you should follow certain customs which are commonly observed by educated people.

8c. Use the comparative degree when comparing two things, and the superlative degree when comparing more than two.

COMPARISON OF TWO THINGS

RIGHT   We rode **more slowly** than the other party.
RIGHT   Frank is **older** than his sister.

WRONG   Of the two children, the girl is the youngest.
RIGHT   Of the *two* children, the girl is the **younger**.

WRONG   Which of the two spoke most clearly?
RIGHT   Which of the *two* spoke **more clearly**?

COMPARISON OF MORE THAN TWO THINGS

RIGHT   Dr. Jones was the **least excited** man in the crowd.
RIGHT   He is the **most ambitious** student in school.

WRONG   Which of the three books did you like better?
RIGHT   Which of the *three* books did you like **best**?

WRONG   Among the four available routes, we chose the shorter one.
RIGHT   Among the *four* available routes, we chose the **shortest** one.

8d. Do not say, "He is taller than any member of his class," because obviously he too is a member of his class, and he cannot be taller than himself. The sentence should read, "He is taller than any *other* member of his class."

WRONG	George played better than any boy on his team.
RIGHT	George played better than any **other** boy on his team.
WRONG	New York is larger than any city in the Americas.
RIGHT	New York is larger than any **other** city in the Americas.

8e. Avoid the *double comparison*.

A double comparison is one in which the degree is formed incorrectly by both adding *–er* or *–est* and using *more* or *most*.

WRONG	She was more *lovelier* than a movie queen.
RIGHT	She was **lovelier** than a movie queen.
WRONG	I found the city the most loveliest place I had ever visited.
RIGHT	I found the city the **loveliest** place I had ever visited.

● EXERCISE 4. Number in a column on your paper from 1 to 20. If the sentence is correct, place a + after the corresponding number on your paper; if it is incorrect, place a 0, and give the correct usage.

1. Of the three brothers, Jim is the better looking.
2. I saw both *Othello* and *Hamlet*, and I thought *Othello* was the better play.
3. Your story is bad, but mine is badder.
4. In fact, yours is better than any story written in your class.
5. Jane is the most happiest girl I know.
6. Of the three pens I like this one best.
7. We were arguing as to which one of the two writers was best.
8. Of the many suggestions I received, yours was the most helpful.
9. The coach seemed hopefuller than the players.
10. He thinks he can run more faster than I.
11. Shakespeare is more famous than any other English author.

8c-e

12. The policemen seemed more calm than the firemen.
13. I was sick, but he was sicker.
14. The President is better known than any figure in the world.
15. Do you think you're more strong than I?
16. He is regarded as the ablest member of the President's Cabinet.
17. I have never heard anyone sing more beautifully.
18. Who's the honestest merchant in town?
19. I used to think the smallest men were the most conceited.
20. Al seemed to be the most angriest member of the mob.

● EXERCISE 5.   Fill the blanks with the correct comparative forms of the italicized words.

1. This book may be *bad*, but that one is ———.
2. You may be *good*, but she is ———.
3. He is *difficult*, but his brother is ———.
4. This is *pretty*, but that is ———.
5. He is *fat*, but his father is ———.
6. The river is *clear*, but the lake is ———.
7. I am *patient*, but you are ———.
8. I thought I was *efficient*, but you are ———.
9. Helen was *ill* on Monday, but she was ——— on Tuesday.
10. Their argument was *good*, but ours was ———.

Dangling Modifiers

8f. A modifying phrase or clause must clearly and sensibly modify a word in the sentence. A phrase or clause which does not clearly and sensibly modify a word in the sentence is a *dangling modifier*.

WRONG   Looking out the window, every passer-by could be seen.

In this sentence the participial phrase *looking out the window* is a dangling modifier. It seems to modify *passer-by*, but such modification is neither clear nor sensible. The passer-by could not be looking out the window. The sentence should read:

RIGHT *Looking out the window,* **we** *could see every passer-by.*

The following examples show how dangling modifiers may be corrected.

WRONG Waiting in the station, the newsstand attracted me.
RIGHT Waiting in the station, I was attracted by the newsstand.
RIGHT While I was waiting in the station, the newsstand attracted me.

WRONG Recommended by the president, the job was offered to me.
RIGHT Recommended by the president, I was offered the job.
RIGHT Because I was recommended by the president, the job was offered to me.

WRONG After swimming all afternoon, our appetites were tremendous.
RIGHT After swimming all afternoon, we had tremendous appetites.
RIGHT After we had been swimming all afternoon, our appetites were tremendous.

● EXERCISE 6. Study the following sentences containing dangling modifiers. As was done with the preceding examples, rewrite each sentence so that the modifier *clearly* and *sensibly* modifies a word in the sentence. You will have to supply words.

1. Sitting in the last row of the theater, the actors could not be heard.
2. Standing on the river bank, many beautiful fish could be seen.
3. To solve these problems, an answer book should be bought.

8f

4. By working hard and fast, the lawn was soon mowed.
5. While in the army, his wife worked in a factory.
6. Coming across the lake, several mountain peaks can be seen.
7. On the way home from the dance, a thunderstorm drove us to shelter.
8. Convinced of my honesty, I persuaded her to lend me the money.
9. Reading rapidly, the book was soon finished.
10. When at home, the housekeeper spoils him.

● EXERCISE 7. Eliminate the dangling modifiers in the following sentences by rewriting each sentence so that the modifier *clearly* and *sensibly* modifies a word in the sentence. You will have to supply words.

1. After failing to pass the examination, the teacher advised me to try again.
2. Speaking to the entire student body, plans for the celebration were explained by the president of the council.
3. While standing on the corner, an automobile horn startled me.
4. By taking the longer route, many historic sites can be visited.
5. To enjoy traveling, very little luggage should be carried.
6. To play a good game of tennis, new balls must be used.
7. When but a small child, my great-uncle left me his fortune.
8. After firing me, I got some good advice from the boss.
9. To go aboard one of the large aircraft carriers, a permit must be obtained.
10. After being away so long, home seemed good to us.
11. Sailing on the Sound this afternoon, the sun was very hot.
12. When in town, our house is the first place he visits.
13. To understand this process, the third chapter must be mastered.

14. While listening to the radio, the weather report discouraged us in our plans for an outing.
15. Picnicking on the mountain, the red roofs of the college glistened in the distance.

Misplaced Modifiers

In doing the exercises on the preceding pages, you noticed the absurd meaning of the sentences containing dangling modifiers. The modifiers either seemed to modify a word which they could not sensibly modify or they were left without any word to modify at all. Writing just as absurd as dangling modifiers will also result from misplaced modifiers.

8g. **Modifying words, phrases, and clauses should be placed as near as possible to the word they modify.**

MISPLACED SINGLE–WORD MODIFIERS

There are two common words (used as either adjective or adverb) which are often carelessly placed in relation to the word they modify. These words are *only* and *just*. In conversation these words are used carelessly, and yet no confusion results because the tone of the speaker indicates the meaning intended. In written English, which is more exact and lacks the tone of voice to convey meaning, a careful writer will use *only* and *just* with exactness.

(1) To make your meaning clear, place *only* and *just* near to the word they modify and usually before it.

● EXERCISE 8. Explain the difference in meaning between the sentences grouped together in pairs. Show that by modifying a different word in each

8g

sentence the modifier changes the meaning. What word is modified in each sentence?

1. We had *only suggested* having dinner together.
   We had suggested having *only dinner* together.
2. I have *just earned* a dollar.
   I have earned *just a dollar*.
3. We *only argued* for an hour.
   We argued for *only an hour*.
4. We had *only enrolled* the day before.
   We had enrolled *only the day before*.
5. I *just glanced* at the book this morning.
   I glanced at the book *just this morning*.

● EXERCISE 9.   Change the meaning of the following by shifting the position of the modifier in italics.

1. He came in second in *only* the first race.
2. He nodded to me *only* yesterday.
3. She *just* baked a cake.
4. The children *only* looked at their ice cream.
5. The speaker mentioned *only* you.
6. Did you *just* see John?
7. We *only* suggested a senior dance.
8. The wind *just* blew down the elm tree.
9. He *only* talked about what he was going to do.
10. She *only* cried a few minutes.

MISPLACED PHRASE MODIFIERS

(2) Modifying phrases should be placed as near as possible to the words they modify.

The sentences below will indicate the importance of observing this rule.

WRONG   Did you see a boy in the bus with a brown cap?
RIGHT   Did you see a *boy* **with a brown cap** in the bus?
[The phrase *with a brown cap* obviously modifies *boy*. It should be placed next to *boy*. Otherwise

it appears to modify *bus* and gives the impression that it was a bus with a brown cap.]

WRONG   I read your editorial about juvenile delinquents with enthusiasm.

RIGHT   I *read* **with enthusiasm** your editorial about juvenile delinquents.

WRONG   We borrowed an extension ladder from a neighbor 35 feet long.

RIGHT   We borrowed an extension *ladder* **35 feet long** from a neighbor.

BETTER   From a neighbor we borrowed an extension *ladder* **35 feet long.**

WRONG   We came upon a magnificent view rounding the bend.

RIGHT   **Rounding the bend,** we came upon a magnificent view.

WRONG   John asked her to marry him sitting in the moonlight.

RIGHT   **Sitting in the moonlight,** *John* asked her to marry him.

● EXERCISE 10. Read each of the following sentences. Pick out the misplaced phrase, decide what word the phrase should modify, and rewrite the sentence, placing the phrase near this word.

1. We saw a lady talking to a policeman in a green dress and a white coat.
2. He tried to shoot himself after writing a farewell note with a shotgun.
3. He spoke of the need of building new tennis courts in the strongest possible terms.
4. A plane flew over the school building with red wings.
5. Mrs. Stevens went to Florida after her husband had been sent to jail to live with relatives.
6. Parry was stung by a bee hoeing weeds in his garden.
7. I came upon an interesting old bookshop wandering about the narrow streets.
8. The judge sentenced the prisoner to five years in prison with fire in his eyes.

9. The children were offered a piece of chocolate layer cake by a strange lady with white frosting.
10. I told the teacher that I had lost a book on the playground with a red cover.
11. We saw a great deal of farming country riding along in our car.
12. We were told to leave the school building by the principal.
13. A collision occurred in the middle of the block between a delivery car and a fire truck.
14. The telegram was delivered by a messenger boy in a yellow envelope.
15. I had been talking to a lady on the train with three children.
16. We decided to finish trimming the house after we'd had a swim in white paint.
17. A strange-looking dog was led onto the stage by one of the actors with shaggy hair and a stubby tail.
18. We watched plane after plane land and take off sitting in the control tower at the airport.
19. I saw them leave before the sun came up in a long red car.
20. He told us about killing the lion in the auditorium.

MISPLACED CLAUSE MODIFIERS

A thoughtless writer may so place a subordinate clause that it will not come next to the word it modifies. In using modifying clauses, you should follow the rule which applies to phrases.

(3) Place the clause as near as possible to the word it modifies.

These sentences will show you how a misplaced clause may make a sentence ridiculous.

WRONG   She had diamond rings on her fingers which she had bought in Paris.

RIGHT   On her fingers she had diamond rings which she had bought in Paris.

The modifying clause *which she had bought in Paris,* of course, modifies *rings,* not fingers. In the second sentence, by shifting the phrase *on her fingers* to the beginning, the clause has been brought next to the word it modifies. The second sentence is, therefore, clear.

WRONG   I borrowed a book from the library that contained nothing but detective stories.

RIGHT   From the library I borrowed a **book** that contained nothing but detective stories.

WRONG   We caught a dozen fish with the new bait which we fried for supper.

RIGHT   With the new bait we caught a dozen **fish** which we fried for supper.

● EXERCISE 11. Read each of the following sentences. Take out the misplaced clause, decide what word the clause should modify, and rewrite the sentence, placing the clause near this word. If you find a misplaced phrase, correct it.

1. The new bicycle was standing on the porch which we had ordered from Chicago.
2. A large automobile drew up to the curb which was profusely draped with flags.
3. I liked the picture of you on the diving board that you sent me.
4. There are several men selling newspapers that are blind in New York.
5. We strapped the antique chair onto the old truck which was about a hundred years old.
6. He left the hotel in an automobile where he had spent the night.
7. My uncle bought a young terrier who is very fond of animals.
8. Dr. Longstreet cured our pet dog who is our family doctor.

9. An explosion in the refinery awoke everyone in town that had a hundred storage tanks.
10. The fireplace heated the entire cabin which was six feet long.

Phrases and Clauses Which Modify Two Words

Sometimes a writer will place a modifying phrase or clause so that it seems to modify either of two different words. This is not clear writing, because the reader may read the sentence in either of two ways. Naturally, the writer has only one meaning in mind when he writes his sentence. To be sure of being understood, he must place modifiers so that they clearly modify only one word.

NOT CLEAR   He asked me **on the way home** to call him.

Here the phrase *on the way home* may modify either *asked*, meaning that it was while we were on the way home that he asked me; or *to call*, meaning that he wanted me to call him while I was on my way home. Both of the following arrangements of the sentence are correct. Which one the author meant would probably be clear if we had the context from which the sentence was taken. A modifier placed so that it can modify either of two words may mislead the reader.

CLEAR   **On the way home** he asked me to call him.

CLEAR   He asked me to call him **on the way home.**

A modifying *clause* may be similarly misplaced so that the sentence does not make clear which of two words the clause modifies.

NOT CLEAR   I asked Mary **when she reached camp** to send me my mail.

The sentence might mean either:

CLEAR   **When she reached camp,** I asked Mary to send

me my mail.

or

CLEAR   I asked Mary to send me my mail **when she**

reached camp.

● EXERCISE 12.   Rewrite each of the following so that it is clear which word the clause modifies.

1. I thought when he came in I would speak to him.
2. We knew when the bell rang we would be late.
3. I advised Phil after he returned from abroad to go to college.
4. I told him, when we met in New Orleans, we would see the sights together.
5. Mrs. Abbot asked me before I returned to New York to call her.
6. I asked Jerry when he finished mowing the lawn to repair the dog house.
7. He told me when the foot brake failed to use the emergency brake.
8. We expected on Monday to make a trip to town.
9. We found out, after getting home, Jim was sick.
10. Larry promised on the way to school to stop and buy supplies.

● REVIEW EXERCISE.   Sentences 1–15 in the following exercise contain dangling modifiers and misplaced modifiers. Rewrite the sentences so that the meaning is clear.

1. We saw a number of deer driving through the state park.
2. When cooking dinner, the roast was badly burned.
3. To make the trip in two days, all thought of a stopover had to be abandoned.

4. I was hoping when school was out you would go home with me.
5. She went out on a date with Harry dressed in her best clothes.
6. Amy said she would be back by the first of September in her last letter.
7. I saw a box in the post office that was addressed to you.
8. Having given away our position, the enemy attacked at once.
9. She pleaded for a new doll with tears in her eyes.
10. While working in Gover's store, the customers teased her.
11. There is a copy of the speech that I gave in my briefcase.
12. The archaeologists found a skeleton near their camp which, they thought, was a million years old.
13. Expecting an important letter, the postman received a warm welcome from us.
14. I deposited the money in the bank which I had earned during the summer.
15. We had to wait two hours in the hotel lobby for Jim.

Number on your paper from 16 to 25. If a sentence is correct place a + after the proper number. If it is incorrect, place a 0.

16. Drive slow!
17. Which one of the twins is the best dancer?
18. You will look well in this suit.
19. Fran did not play so good as usual.
20. I've never known anyone in my life to work so slow as Bill.
21. Sandra is more industrious than any student in her school.
22. Since his football injury he has not been feeling very well.
23. Tom is the more scientific of the four boys.
24. She is the most crankiest girl I know.
25. Marilyn obviously felt bad about having to break the date.

CHAPTER 9

Sentence Variety

As a writer you cannot express your ideas effectively by way of correct grammar alone, for it is style, not correctness, that marks the difference between dull language and interesting language. To avoid monotony, a skillful writer varies his style by varying the structure and the length of his sentences. This chapter will show you how to increase the effectiveness of your style through sentence variety.

To be sure, working for variety in the structure of your sentences before you have learned to write a sentence would be putting the cart before the horse. But if you have learned the principles taught so far in this book, you should be ready to master one of the finer points of good writing. This chapter will show you how to avoid monotonous writing — how to vary the structure of your sentences.

9a. Vary the beginnings of your sentences.

Beginning every sentence with the subject is a common cause of sentence dullness. Read the following paragraph, in which every sentence begins in the same way — with the subject. Then read the next paragraph. You will see the difference between monotonous style and a style which has some variety.

NOT VARIED

The trial had been scheduled for two o'clock. The audience was noisily settling itself in the courtroom for the coming show. The lawyers were quietly talking and shuffling

9a

183

piles of papers at the polished tables in the front of the
room. The bell in the courthouse tower struck two in resounding tones. Judge Walker, dignified in his long black
gown, walked slowly to his bench. The clerk rasped out,
"Everyone rise." The room seemed suddenly to lift for a
moment; then it settled back into an ominous silence. The
judge opened the case of the People vs. John Strong in a
bored manner which seemed to imply that murder trials
happened every day of his life.

VARIED

The trial had been scheduled for two o'clock. In the
courtroom the audience was noisily settling itself for the
coming show. At the polished tables in the front of the
room, the lawyers were quietly talking and shuffling piles
of papers. When the bell in the courthouse tower struck
two in resounding tones, Judge Walker, dignified in his
long black gown, walked slowly to his bench. "Everyone
rise," rasped the clerk. Suddenly the room seemed to lift
for a moment; then it settled back into an ominous silence.
In a bored manner that implied that murder trials happened
every day of his life, the judge opened the trial of the People
vs. John Strong.

There are, as you may have noticed, several ways
of beginning a sentence. Beginning with the subject is the most natural way. The normal order
of an English sentence is subject first, then predicate;
furthermore, most of our sentences used in conversation begin with the subject. But in order to avoid
writing sentences which begin always in the same
way, you may place a modifying word, a phrase, or
a clause *first* in a sentence.

**(1) You may begin a sentence with a single-word modi-
fier — an adverb, an adjective, or a participle.**

EXAMPLES   **Suddenly** the room seemed to lift for a moment;
then it settled back into an ominous silence.
[adverb]

Cold and hungry, the survivors were brought into town. [adjectives]

Screaming, the frantic child beat her fists against the door. [present participle]

Disgusted, the teacher refused to continue the lesson. [past participle]

● EXERCISE 1. The following sentences, all of which begin with the simple subject, contain a modifier which can be placed at the beginning of the sentence. Find this modifier and rewrite the sentence, placing the modifier first. The sentences in this and the following exercises are good sentences. You are asked to rewrite them so that you will learn a variety of ways of expressing the same idea.

EXAMPLE   **She opened the door cautiously.**
          Cautiously she opened the door.

1. The disappointed crowd filed dejectedly from the gym.
2. He stretched out lazily upon the thick rug.
3. Donald, strong and healthy, showed that his vacation had done him good.
4. The President, grinning, refused to answer the reporter's question.
5. Harold strode confidently toward the principal.
6. The boxer, bruised and beaten, stood swaying in the center of the ring.
7. My paper, illegible and messy, was returned for rewriting.
8. The mechanic expertly removed several pieces of rust from the carburetor.
9. The curtain finally rose.
10. The children, surprised, greeted the announcement enthusiastically.

● EXERCISE 2. Write 5 sentences of your own beginning with single-word modifiers. Include at least one adjective, one adverb, and one participial modifier.

(2) You may begin a sentence with a phrase: a prepositional phrase, a participial phrase, or an infinitive phrase.

EXAMPLES   **At the end of the game,** the crowds swarmed across the playing field.   [prepositional phrases]
Having taken my position behind the wheel, I was ready for my first driving lesson.   [participial phrase]
Angered by the repeated insults, Draper clenched his fists and stepped forward.   [participial phrase]
To avoid the rough detour, they chose a different highway.   [infinitive phrase]

● EXERCISE 3.   The following sentences, all of which begin with the subject, contain phrase modifiers which can be placed at the beginning of the sentence. Rephrase the sentences by placing the modifying phrases at the beginning. Place a comma after each introductory phrase.

1. We borrowed money from our friends to pay for all of the expenses.
2. Everyone finally relaxed on the way home.
3. Joe and I, having seen the picture before, wanted to go to another theater.
4. John's long legs, stretched across the aisle, exerted an upsetting influence on his fellow students.
5. Our team, inspired by the words of the coach, came back in the second half to win.
6. The Bordens had built a beautiful playroom in the basement of their new house.
7. We went to the library to search for more information.
8. Tommy rushed into the house with tears streaming in white streaks through the grime on his face.
9. Mr. Hurley, accompanied by two detectives, returned to the scene of the robbery.

10. We tried, in spite of the bad weather, to celebrate the event in the usual way.

● EXERCISE 4. Rewrite the following sentences so that each begins with either a word or a phrase modifier. In rearranging the sentences, you may wish to drop some of the words or add others; you may do so provided you keep the original meaning. Hints are given to help you with the first 5.

EXAMPLE **We were discouraged and retraced our steps.**
Discouraged, we retraced our steps.

1. We left Perry at the station and went back to school. [Begin with *leaving*.]
2. Every horse looked like a winner at the starting line. [Begin with *at*.]
3. I looked in the latest *World Almanac* to find the information I needed. [Begin with *to find*.]
4. He found himself alone in the big city and began to make inquiries. [Begin with *finding*.]
5. Mr. Kramer, generous and kindly, was soon cheated out of his money. [Begin with *generous*.]
6. Our school is equipped with an excellent pool and always turns out a strong swimming team.
7. The sound of riveters and pneumatic hammers, coming from the building next door, made it impossible for us to work.
8. The crew worked day and night for a week and completed the job earlier than expected.
9. Our science teacher helped us set up the apparatus and then told us to do the experiment by ourselves.
10. We examined the array of instruments on the panel and wondered how anyone could fly a plane like this.

(3) You may begin a sentence with a subordinate clause.

EXAMPLES **Our absence was discovered after we had been gone half the day.**
After we had been gone half the day, our absence was discovered.

> We planned the party in December, and our
> idea was to have a dinner dance.
> **When we planned the party in December,** our
> idea was to have a dinner dance.

● EXERCISE 5.   Rephrase each sentence so that it begins with a subordinate clause instead of the subject. Place a comma after an adverb clause coming first in the sentence.

1. Stuart came to Student Council meeting as though he had been invited.   [As . . .]
2. Mr. Steinberg asked him what he wanted, and he said he wished to present a petition.   [When . . .]
3. The other Council members finally arrived, and the meeting came to order.   [After . . .]
4. President Al Mills was absent from school; hence Billy Thom, the vice-president, conducted the meeting. [Since . . .]
5. This was the first petition the Council had ever re-ceived, and no one knew exactly how to proceed.   [As . . . *or* Since . . .]
6. Billy simply called on Stuart when the time came for new business.
7. Stuart read his petition and kept a perfectly straight face.
8. The Council members tried to preserve their dignity, but they finally broke down.
9. The signers of the petition asked for a free afternoon for every pupil once a week, and the Council sym-pathized with them.
10. Mr. Steinberg pointed out that this was not a matter for the Council and suggested that Stuart carry his petition to the Board of Education.
11. The idea, he thought, would be excellent if it applied to teachers too.

● EXERCISE 6.   Write in the following order: 2 sentences beginning with single-word modifiers, 2 with a prepositional phrase, 2 with a participial phrase, 2 with an infinitive phrase, and 2 with a subordinate clause.

● EXERCISE 7. Change the following sentences in the manner suggested.

1. Mrs. Sweet was agreeable and charming that day, and she treated us with perfect courtesy. [Begin with single-word modifiers.]

2. Towser was feeling unusually vicious, and he nearly succeeded in removing the seat of the stranger's pants. [Begin with a participial phrase.]

3. The workmen finished their work at four o'clock, but they stayed on the job until five. [Begin with a subordinate clause.]

4. I left school early, and I met the attendance officer on the front steps. [Begin with a participial phrase.]

5. The mob surged expectantly down the street. [Begin with a single-word modifier.]

6. We had to work all day Saturday to finish the set for the second act. [Begin with an infinitive phrase.]

7. Our team looked good at the beginning of the game. [Begin with a prepositional phrase.]

8. Lieutenant Hardman was promoted twice during the year and was a major by December. [Begin with a past participial phrase.]

9. The junior high school in this town is in the same building as the high school. [Begin with a prepositional phrase.]

10. Miss Smith was dissatisfied with our dancing and refused to give us a place on the program. [Begin with a past participial phrase.]

11. Detective Harle came in at midnight and told us the case had been solved. [Begin with a subordinate clause.]

12. The campers left their packs at the foot of the mountain and made the ascent in record time. [Begin with a participial phrase.]

13. The librarian told us the book was out of print, and

we gave up all hope of getting it. [Begin with a subordinate clause.]

14. The fish markets are scenes of bustling activity every morning before dawn. [Begin with a prepositional phrase.]

15. She was stubborn and selfish, and she was never very popular. [Begin with single-word modifiers.]

16. The officials called the police to quell the riot. [Begin with an infinitive phrase.]

17. The President finished his address, and every reporter in the room rushed for a telephone. [Begin with a subordinate clause.]

18. Additional election returns kept coming into party headquarters during the day. [Begin with a prepositional phrase.]

19. Tennyson was poet laureate of England from 1850 to 1892, but his best poetry was written before 1850. [Begin with a subordinate clause.]

20. We thought the doors and the windows were locked, and we didn't even try to get in. [Begin with a participial phrase.]

9b. Vary the kinds of sentences.

On page 78 you learned that when classified according to their structure, there are four kinds of sentences: *simple*, *compound*, *complex*, and *compound-complex*. If you are not sure of the characteristics of each of these, you should turn back and refresh your memory before going further.

Just as it is possible to achieve variety in your writing by varying the beginning of your sentences, it is also possible to achieve variety by varying the kinds of sentences you use. Using simple or compound sentences all the time tends to make your style monotonous. For example, read the following paragraph, composed entirely of simple and compound sentences.

1. Nick arrived in class one minute late and was promptly sent to the office for a late permit. 2. He returned a few minutes later and took his seat. 3. I gave him an inquiring look, and he muttered, "Two hours." 4. This meant no touch football for Nick this afternoon; it probably meant the same for me. 5. Nick and I were the backfield, and besides, Nick owned the only football. 6. The teacher droned on in the front of the room, and Nick, tired from his long walk to the office, settled down for a little nap. 7. Mr. Wakeman had noted this further evidence of weakness, and he strode with determination up the aisle. 8. He stood before the sleeping beauty. 9. He rapped lightly on the nodding head and awaited results. 10. There were none. 11. Everyone was watching and snickering — everyone but Nick. 12. He was dreaming of a schoolless world, without classes, teachers, or bells. 13. The bell did it! 14. Nick grabbed his books automatically and leaped with half-closed eyes straight into Mr. Wakeman's arms.

Now read the next paragraph, which tells the same tale but contains 6 complex sentences (the subordinate clauses are italicized). You will see the superiority of this version over the first one.

1. Nick arrived in class one minute late and was promptly sent to the office for a late permit. 2. In a few minutes he returned and took his seat. 3. *When I gave him an inquiring look*, he muttered, "Two hours." 4. This meant no touch football for Nick this afternoon; it probably meant the same for me, *because Nick and I were the backfield and Nick owned the only football.* 5. *As the teacher droned on in the front of the room*, Nick, *who was tired from his long walk to the office*, settled down for a little nap. 6. *When Mr. Wakeman noted this further evidence of weakness*, he strode with determination up the aisle and stood before the sleeping beauty. 7. He rapped lightly on the nodding head and awaited results. 8. There were none. 9. By this time everyone was watching and snickering — everyone but Nick, *who was dreaming of a schoolless world without*

9b

classes, teachers, or bells. 10. The bell did it! 11. Automatically, Nick grabbed his books and leaped with half-closed eyes straight into Mr. Wakeman's arms.

Actually, all that had to be done to break the monotony of the first version was to change some of the less important ideas from main clauses to subordinate clauses. A subordinate clause in a sentence makes the sentence complex.

Using subordinate clauses not only gives variety to your writing but also helps you to show how the ideas in a sentence are related. One idea may be the cause or the result of another idea in the sentence; or it may give the time of another. Study the following pairs of sentences. The first sentence in each pair is compound; the second is complex. Notice that in the second sentence the relationship between ideas is clearer than in the first sentence.

1. The morning was dark and cold, and we wore our heaviest coats.
   Because the morning was dark and cold, we wore our heaviest coats.   [The first idea expresses the *cause* of the second.]
2. I asked Mr. Silvers to explain the homework, and he told me to see him after school.
   When I asked Mr. Silvers to explain the homework, he told me to see him after school.   [One idea gives the *time* of the other.]
3. Jack saves most of his weekly allowance, and then he can buy more photographic equipment.
   Jack saves most of his weekly allowance **so that he can buy more photographic equipment.**   [The idea in the subordinate clause is the *result* of the idea in the main clause.]

The following words, when used at the beginning of a subordinate clause, help to make clear the relationship between the sentence ideas:

CAUSE   because, since, as
RESULT OR REASON   so that, in order that
TIME   when, while, as, since, until, after, before, whenever

● EXERCISE 8.   Change each of the following compound sentences into a complex sentence by expressing one of the ideas in a subordinate clause. Begin each subordinate clause with a word which will show how the ideas in the sentence are related: cause, result or reason, time.

1. We knew the work had to be finished before dark, and we worked as fast as possible.
2. Each speaker wrote his speech down in advance, and then he wouldn't leave out anything.
3. We had heard all the speakers, and we were ready to cast our ballots.
4. Their goalie rushed out from the goal, and our team scored.
5. Keep a record of your expenditures, and you can see how you have wasted your money.
6. Our family lived on a farm, and I did a lot of hunting.
7. Mr. Eaton's son is captain of the team, and Mr. Eaton hasn't missed a game this year.
8. We were walking toward the stadium, and we heard a great shout rise from the crowd.
9. I liked *The Last of the Mohicans*, and I went to the library to get another Cooper book.
10. Several students did not read the directions carefully, and they failed the test.

● EXERCISE 9.   The following paragraphs consist entirely of simple and compound sentences. Rewrite them, varying the style by changing or combining some of the sentences into complex sentences. Naturally you will not try to make all your sentences complex, for your purpose is to get variety.

1. The Frosh Flurry was the first big social event of my high school career. It turned out to be big all right, but

not very social for me. I was chairman of the decorating committee, and I asked most of my friends to be committee members. Everyone likes to be a committeeman, but nobody wants to do any work. I called meeting after meeting, but only the same faithful three would show up. The rest always seemed to have dentist appointments. The dentists around here were certainly busy during the weeks before the Frosh Flurry.

2. We planned our decorations, made a list of necessary things, and completed our shopping on Friday. On Saturday morning I was at the gym right after breakfast. I waited alone. Mr. Jones, the janitor, looked puzzled. About 11 o'clock, the "faithful" trio waltzed in. I thought they'd probably all been to the dentist, and I didn't say anything.

3. Then followed the wildest day of my life. Nothing went right. Colored streamers were arranged in a great panoply on the gym floor. This was raised to the ceiling and fastened there by Jerry. He teetered on a spindly ladder, and I had visions of broken bones and hospital bills. A few hours later we thought the job was nearly done, and we were about to start cleaning up. Suddenly we felt streamers floating down upon us. They fell lightly over everything in the gym. The wire had pulled loose!

4. The lights wouldn't work right either. You can't have much light at a dance, but the chaperones disapproved of dancing in complete darkness. The boys showed themselves to be very poor electricians. They wanted a big *G* in lights over the orchestra, and it took them all afternoon to make it.

5. Jerry called for me at 9 o'clock in the evening. I was asleep. We managed to drag ourselves to school. Everyone was having a good time. The chairman of the decorating committee danced one dance and went home to bed!

● EXERCISE 10.   Write a one-page account of one of your own experiences working with a class committee or preparing for a special event — a school picnic, a family reunion, Christmas, an assembly program, etc. The purpose of your writing is to show that you can avoid a monotonous style by varying the form of your sentences. Before writing, review the three ways of beginning a sentence. Include some complex sentences in your composition.

9c. Vary the length of your sentences.

A composition consisting entirely of short sentences gives the effect of being chopped up. A series of short sentences may sometimes be used to describe exciting action because short sentences give the effect of speed. In general, however, avoid such style as that in which the following paragraphs are written. There are too many sentences for such a short passage; furthermore, the sentences are not varied in their beginnings or their structure.

We moved into our new school building in September. Everyone was enthusiastic about the building. It was entirely finished except for a square hole in the southeast corner. We asked what the hole was for. We were told that it was for the cornerstone. A hollow block of granite was lying a few feet away on the sidewalk. This was the cornerstone. A copper box had been fitted into the cornerstone. The box contained all kinds of documents. This building will be torn down some day in the future. The people at that future time will read the stored documents. They will learn from the documents what life was like in our day.

We learned one day that the cornerstone was to be laid. This was in October. The ceremony was held after school. Town and school officials sat on a platform near the gaping hole in the building. A clergyman offered a prayer. After this the band played the *Star-Spangled Banner*. Officials gave speeches. Meanwhile photographers prepared to take pictures. Workmen were busy getting ready to put the heavy block into place. The president of the Student Council picked up a trowel. He was going to spread some mortar. The big moment finally arrived. The stone would not go

9c

into the opening. It was an inch too long. The cornerstone was finally laid a week after the ceremony.

● EXERCISE 11.   Combine each group of short sentences below into one long sentence. Take special pains to make the long sentences read smoothly. Appositives, introductory expressions, subordinate clauses, and compound subjects and verbs are suggested means.

1. Chet shivered. He stopped writing. He drew his coat closer about him. He decided to speak to the janitor about keeping the heat up.
2. The tree was large and shapely. It was a maple. It stood in the center of the wide lawn. It was the only tree there.
3. Art asked her to go to the movies with him. The date was to be Friday night. She didn't want to go. She accepted.
4. Elinor often watched the doctor rush out late at night. He was on an emergency call. His face was grave and white under the street lamp.
5. The girl across the street always wanted life to be like the movies. She tried to elope one night with an usher from the Royal. Her father stopped them.
6. Tom's opponent hit a beautiful shot down the middle of the fairway. Tom stepped up to drive. All he could think of was another failure under pressure.
7. We had not done our homework. The teacher was angry. She assigned four exercises. This was twice as much as usual.
8. *David Copperfield* was written by Charles Dickens. It is a story of a boy's growing up. Much of it is autobiographical.
9. Red Barnes is president of the Student Council. In assembly today he introduced Myra Atkinson. She asked everyone to support the Red Cross.
10. Nathaniel Hawthorne was an American writer. He wrote short stories. His stories are beautifully written. They are not very exciting.

11. Helen took her first driving lesson yesterday. It lasted half an hour on a deserted highway. She was a nervous wreck after it.
12. Lucerne is a lakeside city. Around it stand the lofty Alps. Their massive shoulders are outlined against the blue sky. They are reflected in the glassy surface of the lake.

● REVIEW EXERCISE. Using any means you wish — compound verbs, appositives, modifying phrases, subordinate clauses, etc. — combine the sentences in the story on page 195 into sentences of greater length. Vary the beginnings of your sentences and the kinds of sentences. Work to avoid monotony. Make the passage read smoothly.

CHAPTER 10

Special Problems In Good Usage

10a. Choosing the Correct Word

The words grouped together in the list below are sometimes misused by persons who do not understand their meaning. Study the meaning of each so that in your speaking and writing you can choose the correct word.

Words whose *spelling* is hard to distinguish (words like *already, all ready; peace, piece; here, hear*) are explained in the spelling chapter. See pages 506–516.

accept, except. *Accept* is a verb; it means *to receive. Except* as a verb means *to leave out;* as a preposition it means *excluding.*

> I *accept* your apology.
> If we *except* the cost of materials, your figures are correct.
> Everyone *except* Dad gave his permission.

advice, advise. *Advice* is a noun; it means a recommendation for a course of action. It rhymes with *nice. Advise* is a verb; it means *to give advice* or *to consult.* It rhymes with *size.*

> I need his *advice.*
> What did he *advise* you to do?

affect, effect. *Affect* is always a verb; it means *to influence*. *Effect* as a verb means *to accomplish*. *Effect* as a noun means the *result* of some action.

> Your story *affected* us deeply.
> The new principal *effected* several changes in the school.
> The *effect* of these changes was good.

If *a*, *an*, or *the* appears before it, the word is *effect*.

> The coach's words had *a* decided *effect* on the team.
> *The effect* of the speech was not foreseen.

This does not mean that *effect* is always preceded by *a*, *an*, or *the*.

> Unusual *effects* are achieved by trick photography.

allusion, illusion. An *allusion* is a *reference* to something. An *illusion* is a *mistaken idea*.

> The speaker's *allusion* to the President was not flattering.
> Boris's ideas were impractical; he lived in a world of *illusions*.

alumnus, alumna; alumni, alumnae. An *alumnus* is a *man or boy graduate*. An *alumna* is a *woman or girl graduate*.

> He is Harvard's most famous *alumnus*.
> Marie is an *alumna* of a distinguished girls' school.

Alumni (pronounced *a* lŭm′nī) is the plural of *alumnus*. *Alumnae* (pronounced *a* lŭm′nē) is the plural of *alumna*. The graduates of a co-educational school are referred to (as a group) as *alumni*.

> The girls were *alumnae* of many different schools.
> Yale has many famous *alumni*.
> The *alumni* of our high school frequently come back to visit us.

10a

beside, besides. *Beside* means *by the side of* someone or something. *Besides* means *in addition to.*

> We will sit *beside* you.
> The school has several musical organizations *besides* the band.

bring, take. *Bring* means to convey something to the person speaking. *Take* means to convey something away from the person speaking. *Bring* is related to *come; take* is related to *go.*

> When you come to school, *bring* your camera with you.
> If you go away this summer, will you *take* your dog?

● EXERCISE 1.   Number on your paper from 1 to 20. Choose the correct one of the two words in parentheses and write it after the proper number.

1. Please (accept, except) my congratulations.
2. His (allusion, illusion) to my brother disturbed me.
3. The Girls' Athletic Association of our school sent invitations to their (alumnae, alumni).
4. When you go shopping, (take, bring) plenty of money with you.
5. The coach has two good pitchers (beside, besides) Carl.
6. Under the (allusion, illusion) that the game was over, Gerald stopped playing.
7. When you come home, (take, bring) your brother.
8. What was her (advice, advise)?
9. The dean refused to (accept, except) my excuse.
10. Everyone was noticeably (effected, affected) by the sudden change in temperature.
11. May I (bring, take) this note to the office?
12. Both men and women among the (alumnae, alumni) contributed to the girls' gymnasium fund.
13. The Student Council (effected, affected) an improvement in student behavior.
14. I was surprised to find my father standing (beside, besides) me.
15. The (effect, affect) of the drug was miraculous.

16. He does not (accept, except) my suggestions willingly.
17. Marilyn is an (alumna, alumnus) of a girls' school in the East.
18. The (effects, affects) of the storm were visible everywhere.
19. (Besides, Beside) her own children, Mrs. Frost takes care of her brother's child.
20. I do not (advise, advice) you to do that.

effect. See **affect, effect.**

emigrate, immigrate. *Emigrate* means *to go from a country* to settle elsewhere. *Immigrate* means *to come into a country* to settle there.

Thousands *emigrated* from Ireland during the years of famine.

Many Europeans *immigrate* to America every year.

except. See **accept, except.**

fewer, less. *Fewer* is used to refer to *number*. It is used with plural words. *Less* is used to refer to *quantity*. It is used with singular words.

There are *fewer* books in the school library than in the public library.

There is *less* carbon in this grade of steel.

formally, formerly. *Formally* means in a *formal manner*. *Formerly* means *in the past* or *once*.

Shall we dress *formally?*

He was *formerly* an actor.

good, well. *Good* is an adjective. Do not use *good* to modify a verb.

WRONG   The boys played good.

RIGHT   The boys played *well*.

Well is an adverb except in three uses: (1) When used to mean *healthy*, (2) when used to mean *neatly groomed* or *attractively dressed*, (3) when used to mean *satisfactory* — in all these instances *well* is an adjective. (See pages 164–165.)

She reads poetry very *well*.   [adverb]
Is your mother *well?*   [adjective]
You look *well* in blue.   [adjective]
All is *well*.   [adjective]

illusion.   See *allusion, illusion.*

immigrate.   See *emigrate, immigrate.*

imply, infer.   *Imply* means *to suggest* something. *Infer* means *to interpret* or *get a certain meaning from* a remark or an action.

In his comments, he *implied* strong opposition to our candidate.

From your comments, I *infer* that you do not approve of my plan.

● EXERCISE 2.   Number on your paper from 1 to 12.   Choose the correct one of the two words in parentheses and write it after the proper number.

1. The Pilgrims (emigrated, immigrated) from England to escape the restrictions on freedom of worship.
2. There are (less, fewer) students in our school than in yours.
3. Jimmy can always be depended upon to play (well, good).
4. The teachers (implied, inferred) that they would excuse us.
5. In the first race, Harry ran (good, well).
6. (Formally, Formerly) he had attended Harvard.
7. Everyone thought you did very (good, well).
8. Most of the people who (immigrated, emigrated) to

the United States in the nineteenth century came from northern Europe.

9. Helen did (good, well) in all her subjects.
10. The Smiths have (less, fewer) children than the Joneses.
11. I cannot help what others (infer, imply) from my remarks.
12. He always does his assignments (good, well).

in, into. Careful speakers use *in* to mean *within a place*, and *into* to mean *movement from the outside to the inside of a place*.

> We waited *in* the lobby.
> I walked *into* the room.

learn, teach. *Learn* means *to acquire knowledge*. *Teach* means *to give out knowledge*.

> At an early age he *learned* to fly.
> I asked my brother to *teach* me how to dive.

leave, let. *Leave* means to go away. *Let* means *to allow* or *permit*.

> *Let* him *leave* when he wishes.

lie, lay. Do not confuse the various forms of these verbs, whose meanings differ. *Lie* means *to recline, to rest, to remain in a lying position*. *Lay* means *to put, to place* something.

Lie never has an object. *Lay* may have an object.

The principal parts of *lie* and *lay* are:

	PRESENT	PRESENT PARTICIPLE	PAST	PAST PARTICIPLE
lie (to recline)	lie	lying	lay	(have) lain
lay (to put)	lay	laying	laid	(have) laid

> I *lay* down for a rest.
> The book *is lying* over there.
> We *had laid* our books down.
> The wounded *had lain* there a long time.

Exercises on the use of *lie* and *lay* will be found on pages 149–150.

like, as. *Like* is a preposition. *As* is usually a conjunction.

> She plays *like* a professional. [prepositional phrase]
> She plays *as* a professional plays. [subordinate clause introduced by a conjunction]

respectfully, respectively. *Respectfully* means *with respect* or *full of respect. Respectively* means *each in the order given.*

> The ambassadors bowed *respectfully* before the king.
> Ruth, Eleanor, and Polly will stand in first, second, and third places *respectively.*

rise, raise. Do not confuse the various forms of these verbs, whose meanings differ. *Rise* means *to go in an upward direction. Raise* means *to force* some object *to move in an upward direction.*

Rise never has an object. *Raise* may have an object.

The principal parts of *rise* and *raise* are:

	PRESENT	PRESENT PARTICIPLE	PAST	PAST PARTICIPLE
rise (to go upward)	rise	rising	rose	(have) risen
raise (to force upward)	raise	raising	raised	(have) raised

> He *rose* from his chair reluctantly.
> The fog *was rising* rapidly.
> Clouds of dust *had risen* from the field.
> He *raised* his hand.

Exercises on the use of *rise* and *raise* will be found on pages 155–156.

sit, set. Do not confuse the various forms of these verbs, whose meanings differ. *Sit* means *to rest in an upright, sitting position*. *Set* means *to put, to place* something.

Sit never has an object. *Set* may have an object.

The principal parts of *sit* and *set* are:

	PRESENT	PRESENT PARTICIPLE	PAST	PAST PARTICIPLE
sit (to rest)	sit	sitting	sat	(have) sat
set (to put)	set	setting	set	(have) set

I *sat* in the fresh paint.
We *were sitting* on the porch.
I *set* the chair in the hall.
I *have sat* in this chair many times.

Exercises on the use of *sit* and *set* will be found on pages 153–154.

take, bring. See **bring, take.**

● EXERCISE 3. Number on your paper from 1 to 20. Choose the correct one of the two words in parentheses and write it after the proper number.

1. At our approach he rushed (in, into) the house.
2. (Leave, Let) us go with you.
3. He (taught, learned) me all I know about riding.
4. With his usual courtesy, he signed the letter (Respectively yours, Respectfully yours).
5. We (lay, laid) the foundation yesterday.
6. "(Leave, Let) us stay a little longer," they pleaded.
7. I always wished I could play the violin (like, as) she does.
8. I crawled (in, into) the room through a small window.
9. The senator expected his audience to listen (respectively, respectfully).
10. Do (like, as) your father does.
11. (Leave, Let) him go when he apologizes.
12. Two dogs are (lying, laying) on the lawn.

13. He (rose, raised) up suddenly.
14. We (set, sat) there for an hour.
15. I (lay, laid) my glasses here an hour ago.
16. We are (sitting, setting) in the last row.
17. The teacher can't (teach, learn) you anything if you won't try.
18. When the fire siren blew, everyone ran (in, into) the street.
19. I offered to (teach, learn) him a few tricks.
20. You learn everything (as, like) I do — the hard way.

● REVIEW EXERCISE A.   Number on your paper from 1 to 25. Choose the correct one of the two words in parentheses and write it after the proper number.

1. Please (leave, let) her do as she wishes.
2. Many Italians have (immigrated, emigrated) to this country since 1900.
3. In school today, Peggy promised to (bring, take) her record player to my house tonight.
4. He reads French (good, well).
5. Go (in, into) the gym determined to win.
6. My father is an (alumna, alumnus) of Princeton.
7. Some artists get remarkable (affects, effects) with water colors.
8. (Besides, Beside) a Christmas party, we're having guests until New Year's.
9. How can anyone (teach, learn) you if you won't study?
10. Do (except, accept) my apologies for being late.
11. Everyone was greatly (affected, effected) by your story.
12. Mr. Brown and Mr. Stevens were (formerly, formally) business partners.
13. I (infer, imply) from your letter that you are not interested in the position.
14. The decorated gymnasium gave one the (illusion, allusion) of being in a garden.
15. Jim refused to go unless he could (take, bring) Betty.
16. Try to do your homework (like, as) your sister does.
17. Where was it (laying, lying)?
18. We listened (respectfully, respectively) to the minister.

19. Bill got (less, fewer) people to vote for him this year.
20. Does he show the (affects, effects) of his illness?
21. Who is (sitting, setting) in the big chair?
22. You should take the doctor's (advice, advise).
23. How long has this been (laying, lying) here?
24. Where do you want to (sit, set)?
25. They have (lain, laid) here for days.

● REVIEW EXERCISE B. Write 20 original sentences correctly using the following words or phrases.

1. the effect
2. had risen
3. was raising
4. not accepting
5. advise
6. beside Jane
7. besides Jane
8. they emigrated
9. bring
10. take
11. formally
12. formerly
13. advice
14. in the lake
15. into the lake
16. leave him
17. let him
18. Ted, Sue, and I respectfully
19. Ted, Sue, and I, respectively
20. hundreds immigrate

● REVIEW EXERCISE C. Number on your paper from 1 to 25. Choose the correct one of the two words in parentheses and write it after the proper number.

1. She said she would (learn, teach) us to make fudge.
2. You will be especially welcome here if you (take, bring) your clarinet.
3. The culprits took their (respectful, respective) places one behind the other.
4. He (sat, set) on the broken chair.
5. Sheila is an (alumnus, alumna) of Girls Commercial School.
6. Bill is under the (allusion, illusion) that he's a star player.
7. (Beside, Besides) going to school, he works at the post office.
8. Who has been (lying, laying) on this bed?
9. Are you (implying, inferring) by your remark that I can't spell properly?

10. Since we couldn't find your gun, we thought you had (taken, brought) it with you.
11. I'm going (in, into) my room now.
12. Prices had (risen, raised) twenty per cent.
13. The soldier's speech (effected, affected) all of us deeply.
14. (Except, Accept) for two girls, the whole class was present.
15. At breakfast, Bob offered to (bring, take) the car to the garage for me.
16. Our ancestors (emigrated, immigrated) from Scotland in 1735.
17. Why are you (setting, sitting) here?
18. These boys are all (alumni, alumnae) of Brown University.
19. May I (take, bring) these books to the library for you?
20. Please (leave, let) me do it my way.
21. The drama shows the (effect, affect) of war on the younger generation.
22. He (lay, laid) his gifts under the tree.
23. What (affect, effect) did this have on you?
24. All the debaters did very (good, well).
25. Storm clouds were (raising, rising) in the west.

10b. Avoiding Common Errors

The words and expressions listed below are common errors in English. Ask yourself whether you ever use any of them. If you do, now is the time to eliminate them from your speech and writing.

ain't. Don't say it!

all the farther, all the faster. Poor English when used to mean *as far as, as fast as.*

> WRONG   This is all the farther you can go.
> RIGHT   This is *as far as* you can go.

and etc. Since *etc.* is an abbreviation of the Latin *et cetera*, which means *and other things*, you are using *and* twice when you write "and etc." The *etc.* is sufficient.

anywheres, everywheres, nowheres. Use these words and others like them without the *s*.

RIGHT *Everywhere* I looked, I saw mountains.

at. Don't use *at* after *where*.

WRONG Where were you at?
RIGHT Where were you?

being as, being that. Poor English. Use *since* or *because*.

WRONG Being that there was no snow, we postponed our sleigh ride.
RIGHT *Since* there was no snow, we postponed our sleigh ride.

WRONG Being as he's the boss, we do what he says.
RIGHT *Because* he's the boss, we do what he says.

bust, busted. Use *broke* or *burst* instead.

WRONG While skiing, he busted his ankle.
RIGHT While skiing, he *broke* his ankle.

WRONG The frozen pipes busted.
RIGHT The frozen pipes *burst*.

bursted. Incorrect past form of *burst*. The principal parts of *burst* are *burst, burst, (has) burst*.

WRONG The gasoline tanks bursted into flame.
RIGHT The gasoline tanks *burst* into flame.

● EXERCISE 4. The following sentences contain the errors just listed. Rewrite each sentence correctly. Practice saying *aloud* the correct sentences.

1. Being as we were tired of rising early, gulping our breakfast, catching the bus, and etc., we were glad to move nearer to school.

10b

2. When I sat on the trunk, it busted wide open, and the contents flew everywheres.
3. Is this all the faster your car will go?
4. In Chicago where did you stay at?
5. A mob of children bursted through the doors.
6. I saw your sister somewheres downtown.
7. Being that the fog was heavy, we didn't know where we were at.
8. The bumper was busted and one of the tires had bursted.
9. Boards, bricks, window frames, and etc., were everywheres around the new house.
10. This is all the farther the road goes.
11. Terry busted his leash and we couldn't find him anywheres.
12. Being that the boiler has a safety valve somewheres on the top, it won't bust.

can't hardly, can't scarcely. See **The Double Negative** (page 214).

can't help but. See **The Double Negative** (page 214).

could of. See **of.**

done. Not the past form of *do. Done* always needs a helping verb: *has* done, *was* done, *will be* done, etc. The past form of *do* is *did*.

WRONG   They done their best.
RIGHT   They *did* their best.
RIGHT   They *have done* their best.

don't. A contraction of *do not, don't* should not be used with a singular noun or the third person singular pronouns (it, he, she). Use *doesn't.*

WRONG   He don't mean what he says.
RIGHT   He *doesn't* mean what he says.

WRONG   It don't make any difference.
RIGHT   It *doesn't* make any difference.

drownded. Incorrect past form of *drown*.

> WRONG   No one was drownded in the flood.
> RIGHT   No one was *drowned* in the flood.

everywheres. See **anywheres.**

had of. See **of.**

had ought. See **ought.**

hardly. See **The Double Negative** (page 214).

he, she, they, etc. Do not use unnecessary pronouns. This error is sometimes called the *double subject*.

> WRONG   My sister she gets better marks than I.
> RIGHT   My sister gets better marks than I.

hisself, theirselves. These words are incorrect substitutes for *himself, themselves.*

> WRONG   He did it all by hisself.
> RIGHT   He did it all by *himself.*

irregardless. Don't say it! The correct word is *regardless.*

kind of a, sort of a. The *a* is unnecessary. Leave it out.

> WRONG   What kind of a book did you read?
> RIGHT   What *kind of* book did you read?

might of, must of. See **of.**

nowheres. See **anywheres.**

of. Do not use *of* for *have*. Writing *of* for *have* (*should of, ought to of, might of, must of*) occurs because of faulty enunciation of *have*. Be careful that you do not *write* it as you sometimes *say* it.

> WRONG   I could of beaten him.
> RIGHT   I could *have* beaten him.

Do not use *of* unnecessarily. Avoid such expressions as *remember of, off of, had of*.

WRONG   I don't remember of reading this before.
RIGHT   I don't remember reading this before.

WRONG   The boxes must have fallen off of the truck.
RIGHT   The boxes must have fallen off the truck.

WRONG   If I had of known, I'd of hurried.
RIGHT   If I had known, I'd have hurried.

off of. See **of.**

ought. The verb *ought* should never be used with *had*.

WRONG   We had ought to have started earlier.
RIGHT   We *ought* to have started earlier.

WRONG   You hadn't ought to work so hard.
RIGHT   You *ought not* to work so hard.

remember of. See **of.**

says. Commonly used for *said*. Avoid this usage.

WRONG   When I saw Arnold he says, "I heard a story about you."
RIGHT   When I saw Arnold, he *said*, "I heard a story about you."

WRONG   I says to him, "Who told you the story?"
RIGHT   I *said* to him, "Who told you the story?"

scarcely. See **The Double Negative** (page 214).

them. *Them* is not an adjective. Use *these* or *those*.

WRONG   She bought one of them plastic handbags.
RIGHT   She bought one of *these* plastic handbags.
RIGHT   She bought one of *those* plastic handbags.

this here, that there. *Here* and *there* are unnecessary Leave them out.

WRONG   This here drawing won first prize.
RIGHT   This drawing won first prize.

try and.   The correct form is *try to*.

> WRONG   I will try and get the tickets for you.
> RIGHT   I will *try to* get the tickets for you.

ways, way.   Use *way* in referring to a distance. Do not use *ways*.

> WRONG   He lives a long ways from here.
> RIGHT   He lives a long *way* from here.

when.   Do not use *when* in writing a definition.

> WRONG   A foul ball is when the ball lands outside the playing field.
> RIGHT   A foul ball is *one that* lands outside the playing field.

where.   Do not use *where* for *that*.

> WRONG   I read where the price of food is going up.
> RIGHT   I read *that* the price of food is going up.

Do not use *where* in writing a definition.

> WRONG   A lab is where a scientist does his experimenting.
> RIGHT   A lab is *a place in which* a scientist does his experimenting.

Where, like *in which*, may be used to introduce a dependent relative clause within a definition.

A lab is a place *where* a scientist does his experimenting.

where . . . at.   See **at.**

which, that, who.   *Which* should be used to refer to *things* only. *That* may be used to refer to *both things and people*. *Who* should be used to refer to *people* only.

> RIGHT   He lived in one of the *houses which* were destroyed.
> There is a *man whom* (not *which*) I admire.
> There is a *man that* I admire.

you was.   Don't say it. Say *you were.*

● EXERCISE 5. The following sentences contain the errors just listed. Rewrite each sentence correctly. Practice saying *aloud* the correct sentences.

1. What sort of a hat do you want?
2. You must of come a long ways.
3. I don't remember of seeing that kind of a car.
4. A revolution is when the citizens rise up against their government.
5. You was going to try and collect some money for me.
6. The people which live on this here street must of lived here for years.
7. That there kind of a boat can go a long ways without refueling.
8. He fell off of one of them high fences.
9. I read where the mayor is going to try and raise taxes.
10. Some of them people which you was watching are wealthy immigrants.
11. I says to Peggy, "Get off of the fender." Then she says to me, "You don't own this here car."
12. I'll try and do them problems without your help.
13. It don't matter why he done it.
14. You hadn't ought to of said he was drownded.
15. My aunt she don't live here.
16. Irregardless of the outcome, I want to try to persuade her to change her mind.
17. Where is your brother at?
18. This here secret they kept to theirselves.
19. Joe he read in the paper where the team could of won.
20. According to them rules, you was wrong.

10c. Avoid the Double Negative

A *double negative* is a construction in which *two negative* words are used where one will do. Avoid using double negatives.

WRONG   There isn't no time left.
RIGHT   There *is* no time left.
RIGHT   There isn't *any* time left.

There are several common double negatives; all are poor English.

can't help but

WRONG   You can't help but like him.
RIGHT   You *can't help liking* him.

WRONG   You couldn't help but doubt such a strange story.
RIGHT   You *couldn't help doubting* such a strange story.

hardly, scarcely, only, or but when it means only, should be used without a negative word.

WRONG   I can't hardly believe you.
RIGHT   I *can hardly* believe you.

WRONG   There weren't scarcely enough dishes for the crowd.
RIGHT   There *were scarcely* enough dishes for the crowd.

WRONG   I haven't but (only) a few more problems to solve.
RIGHT   I *have but* (*only*) a few more problems to solve.

no, nothing, none

WRONG   You hadn't no right to speak for me.
RIGHT   You *had no* right to speak for me.

WRONG   I haven't no excuse.
RIGHT   I *have no* excuse.
RIGHT   I *haven't any* excuse.

WRONG   She hasn't done nothing all year.
RIGHT   She *hasn't done anything* all year.
RIGHT   She *has done nothing* all year.

WRONG   I couldn't find none.
RIGHT   I *couldn't find any.*

● EXERCISE 6. The following sentences contain the errors covered in Exercise 5 and those just listed

10c

under the double negative. Rewrite each sentence correctly. Practice saying *aloud* the correct sentences.

1. It could of been he who was drownded.
2. It don't matter whether I have the original or the copy because you can't hardly tell the difference between them.
3. My father he told me I hadn't ought to use poor English.
4. I can't help but wonder why she don't work harder.
5. My uncle and his family they always drop in when we haven't nothing in the house to eat.
6. If Jack had of been there, he wouldn't of been of no help.
7. It don't make no difference to me.
8. There wasn't scarcely time enough to finish our homework.
9. You hadn't ought to stay out so late.
10. The men drownded because we couldn't do nothing to help them.
11. We couldn't help but wonder where you was at.
12. Although it is a long ways to Houston, we'll try and be there by noon.
13. This here bike is not the kind of a bike I ordered.
14. He says to me, "I done my best."
15. The boys which live on our street formed a ball team, but they didn't win no games.
16. A lateral pass is when the ball is thrown back or across, not up the field.
17. I read in the paper where all them new houses had been sold.
18. They hadn't ought to swim so far out.
19. He done his best, which wasn't hardly good enough.
20. Joe passed the ball hisself.

● REVIEW EXERCISE D. The following sentences contain the common errors you have been studying. Rewrite these sentences correctly.

1. He might of fallen from that there tree, for he can't hardly climb at all.

2. She don't know where she's at.
3. We certainly done our best to try and save her, but she was quite a ways out in the water and we couldn't scarcely see her from where we were.
4. I don't remember of seeing that movie; I must of seen it a long time ago.
5. Here is a boy which needs no introduction to you; you can't help but know him well.
6. Being as Max had a car, Jim and Tom could of gone with him if the fan belt hadn't of busted.
7. Patsy couldn't of thought of anywheres else to go.
8. There wasn't hardly a place around this here town where she hadn't been at.
9. Hand me them shears, will you? I can't hardly reach them.
10. When you got off of the bus, you was nearly home.
11. As he pulled me out, my uncle says, "You might of drownded! You had ought to be more careful."
12. I can't hardly see the fire from here; most of it must be behind that there building.
13. An error is when a player makes a mistake.
14. Books, papers, magazines, and etc., littered the room; there wasn't no place to sit down.
15. If I had of gone with my aunt instead of with my mother, nothing wouldn't of been said.

● REVIEW EXERCISE E. This exercise covers the entire chapter. Rewrite sentences 1–15 correctly.

1. We hadn't only fifty cents, so we shouldn't of started.
2. Our water pipes bursted, and some of the plaster busted off the ceiling.
3. My friends they always phone me before eight o'clock, being that they know I start my homework then.
4. A jackknife dive is when you spring, touch your hands to your knees, and then straighten out.
5. In the paper I saw where we're in for trouble in this here town.
6. Bruce must of gone quite a ways into the woods, since he didn't realize where he was at.

7. We looked everywheres for him; and when we finally found him, we couldn't hardly see him, as it was dark.
8. We done the only thing possible; we hadn't no compass, so we broke a trail to find our way back.
9. I says I didn't remember of doing that.
10. There was a man which we hadn't seen before.
11. Although we hadn't but two gallons of gas, we set out for the beach; we found it wasn't scarcely enough.
12. You hadn't ought to be swimming in this here pond.
13. My pals they said they theirselves hadn't no objection to this here plan.
14. If we'd of been smart, we'd of noticed the rain clouds.
15. It don't matter if the fender is busted.

Number on your paper from 16 to 25. Write after the proper number the correct one of the words in parenthesis. Each sentence has two problems.

16. A few boys and girls, all high school (alumni, alumnae) were unable to (accept, except) our invitation.
17. Did anyone (besides, beside) John and him volunteer to help us (take, bring) the refreshments to the gym?
18. One of the (affects, effects) of this drug is to give a person (illusions, allusions) about himself.
19. Alec played in (less, fewer) games this season because he was not playing so (well, good) as he played last year.
20. If you won't (leave, let) us work for you, will you please (accept, except) our contribution of money?
21. Carol had not (laid, lain) down after lunch (like, as) she had promised the doctor she would do.
22. When I saw you unrigging the boat, I (inferred, implied) that you were going to (take, bring) the sails home.
23. The plane had (raised, risen) to a great height before the crew felt the (affect, effect) of the altitude.
24. He won't (leave, let) me (teach, learn) him anything.
25. In recent years (less, fewer) (immigrants, emigrants) have gone to Australia.

PART THREE

COMPOSITION

CHAPTER 11

Writing the Paragraph

11a. Learning the Structure of a Paragraph

You know what a paragraph looks like. You could point one out on any page of writing. Paragraphs are parts of a composition that are set off by themselves by means of spacing and, generally, by indenting the first line.

You may have seen a long composition written as one paragraph. You know how discouraged you felt as you began to read and how confused you became as you read on. The confusion came because without paragraphs the various divisions of the composition did not stand out. There was no clear indication as to when the author was about to take up another part of his subject. You felt like a traveler who can find no road signs to guide him.

The break between paragraphs is like a road sign. It tells the reader that at this point there is to be a small change in the subject — perhaps a change to a new idea, perhaps a change in time or place, perhaps a change to another argument. In any case, paragraphing makes easier reading.

When you are reading a properly paragraphed story or essay, you know that each paragraph presents one topic. You can see this topic clearly because you know where the discussion of it begins and where it ends.

Strange as it may seem, one of the main weaknesses

of young writers, as any English teacher will tell you, is neglecting to write their compositions in paragraphs at all. Perhaps you have found the familiar sign ¶ on your paper. The sign means, "Begin a new paragraph here." The teacher marking your paper had found that you were introducing a new topic without beginning a new paragraph.

Good planning of your compositions will make paragraphing easier. When you have organized a composition into a number of ideas or topics, you can devote a paragraph to each topic or part of a topic.

(1) A *paragraph* is a series of sentences developing one topic.

The topic is usually, but not necessarily, stated in a sentence somewhere in the paragraph.

(2) The sentence which states the topic of the paragraph is called the *topic sentence*.

The other sentences in the paragraph develop the idea expressed by the topic sentence.

11b. How to Develop a Paragraph

DEVELOPING THE TOPIC SENTENCE

A topic sentence may be developed in many ways, depending on the kind of thing you are writing. In general, you give additional details of information to make clear the meaning of the topic sentence.

The details used in developing a topic sentence may be of several kinds. They may be facts, statistics, examples, reasons, incidents. Whatever their nature, these details must be numerous enough to develop the paragraph idea fully.

In order to see how a topic sentence is developed

into a paragraph, let's take a paragraph from Christopher Morley's famous essay "On Doors." Take the one beginning with the topic sentence, "Also, there are many ways of opening doors." This sentence states the central thought of the paragraph which it introduces. You know at once that Mr. Morley is going to discuss the "many ways of opening doors." He does not disappoint you. Every one of the other sentences in the paragraph describes ways of opening doors. Now read the entire paragraph.

Also, there are many ways of opening doors.   There is the cheery push of elbow with which the waiter shoves open the kitchen door when he bears in your tray of supper. There is the suspicious and tentative withdrawal of a door before the unhappy book agent or peddler. There is the genteel and carefully modulated recession with which footmen swing wide the oaken barriers of the great. There is the sympathetic and awful silence of the dentist's maid who opens the door into the operating room and, without speaking, implies that the doctor is ready for you. There is the brisk cataclysmic opening of a door when the nurse comes in, very early in the morning — "It's a boy." [1]

Notice that the topic sentence makes a general statement about ways to open doors. The method of development is simple: The author supports his topic sentence with specific examples, with particular ways of opening doors.

● EXERCISE 1.   Using Mr. Morley's paragraph as a model, write a paragraph upon one of the topic sentences on page 223. Develop this central idea by giving at least three specific examples in carefully written sentences. The topic sentence that you choose

---

[1] From "On Doors" by Christopher Morley from *Mince Pie*. Reprinted by permission of J. B. Lippincott Company.

will be the first sentence in your paragraph. Your second sentence may well begin with: *For example, . . .*

> There are various ways to spend spare time.
> I would like to visit foreign countries.
> Several shows on television are amusing.
> My dog has quite an assortment of friends.

GIVE SPECIFIC DETAILS

In developing a paragraph, use specific details that support the central idea. Generalizations make dull reading. Compare the following two paragraphs which develop the same topic sentence.

General

Marks are not always a true indication of a student's ability. Some people who make high grades are not so intelligent as other people who make low marks. Able students are sometimes lazy or uninterested. They may spend their time doing other things. A lot of people who make high grades study all of the time. They may not have much ability. Grades are not always accurate in labeling the ability of students.

Specific

Marks are not always a true indication of a student's ability. For example, my friend Harvey Smith makes grades that place him in the top ten per cent of the sophomore class. According to a reliable I.Q. test, however, Harvey is not so intelligent as his sister Ann, whose marks are in the bottom ten per cent of her class. Instead of working on assignments in algebra or general science, Ann often plays tennis or goes swimming. At any time she prefers sleeping to studying. While Ann fritters away her time, Harvey studies at least four hours a day, including Sundays. His efforts and his performances rather than his ability earn high grades. As a not uncommon pair, Harvey and Ann serve to illustrate the fact that grades are not necessarily indicative of ability.

The second paragraph is far more interesting and convincing than the first because it refers to particular people, definite grades, exact activities.

THE OUTLINE OF A PARAGRAPH

Before writing a one-paragraph composition, make a simple outline, a list of the specific details you intend to include in the paragraph. The following is an outline of a paragraph:

TOPIC SENTENCE   People vary a great deal in the conditions they require for efficient study.

Details   1. Some want silence and solitude.
2. Others want noise and company.
3. Some want the radio on.
4. Some want the same conditions day after day.
5. Some can study anywhere.

● EXERCISE 2.   Make a paragraph outline for each of the following topic sentences. The items in the outline need not be in sentence form. Copy the topic sentence first; then list the details you would use in your paragraph.

1. Anyone planning a trip from New York to San Francisco finds several ways of making the journey.
2. There are certain standard types of student in every high school.
3. Luck is often the deciding factor in a football game (or any other kind of game).
4. In every home certain jobs should be delegated to the children.

STICK TO THE TOPIC

Since a paragraph is a series of sentences developing one topic, every sentence in a paragraph must be closely related to the topic of the paragraph. Although usually part of a longer composition, a paragraph is also a complete unit in itself. Any sentence in a paragraph which does not relate to the topic of that paragraph spoils the unity and should be taken out.

The following paragraph contains a sentence which is unrelated to the topic of the paragraph. This sentence is printed in heavy type. Read the paragraph and note how this sentence spoils its unity.

The educational possibilities of television and radio are almost unlimited. Speeches on important social and political subjects are available to everyone who will take the time to listen to them. Educational programs on matters of world interest may be presented with popular appeal through plays and forums. Everyone who can turn a dial can be better informed about world events than he ever could have been before the arrival of broadcasting. Furthermore, the news is interpreted several times a day by competent commentators. More and more people are learning to enjoy good music, which is readily available at almost any hour of the day or night. **Dance music and comedy programs are the most popular.** Finally, the schools are using recordings of good educational programs, and teachers can assign their students to watch important telecasts on literature, science, history, and national and international affairs.

● EXERCISE 3.   In each of the following paragraphs there is one sentence which is not closely related to the topic. Find this sentence and copy it on your paper.

1

Fourth Street is more a playground than a street. It is the place chosen by all the neighborhood children for skating, for bicycle and scooter races, and for games of keepaway and softball. The houses on Fourth Street are small and close together, and they are situated very near to the street. On a summer afternoon the crowd is so great that a motorist who happens to drive his car through the block must think he has missed the street entirely and ended up in a village playground. Cars are generally regarded as bold intruders, and the driver who tries to speed through endangers his

own life as well as those of a dozen children. It was not surprising to find that last week someone had actually painted
a baseball diamond in white on the pavement.

2

The most time-consuming job in painting a house is
painting the trim and the little crosspieces of the windows.
The man who thinks the job is half done when he has merely
painted the walls is in for a surprise. Painting the windows
will take twice as much time as painting the walls. A good
brush and an extension ladder are essential for doing an
efficient job. There are always many unexpected spots on
the sill and sash which have to be scraped and sandpapered
before any painting can be done. Finally there is the exact-
ing task of painting the crosspieces without spreading paint
all over the panes. Count the windows in your house and
multiply by one hour, and you will have a fair idea of how
long this part of the job will take you.

3

There are many things to learn about paddling a canoe.
Since a canoe can be pushed from its course by a slight
breeze, the paddler must sit in such a way that the bow will
not be forced too high out of the water where it will catch
too much wind. In calm weather, the canoeist should sit
in the stern, but in windy weather he should kneel just aft
of the middle, for in this position he can control his craft
with less effort. He should paddle on the side opposite the
direction of the wind because the wind then actually helps
him to hold to a straight course. A canoe should never be
loaded with stones for ballast because the stones will sink
the canoe should it capsize. Steering is done by a twist of
the paddle at the end of each stroke, the extent of the twist
depending upon the force of the stroke and the strength of
the wind against the bow.

4

Many a poor boy has risen to high position. Abraham
Lincoln was born in a humble log cabin, spent part of his

life as a rail splitter, and later became the emancipator of the slaves and President of the United States. Louis Pasteur was born of poor parents, but through great struggle became world-renowned for his pasteurization process. Giuseppe Verdi was born poor in a small Italian village, and as a youth played an organ for the community church. In his later years, he wrote the unforgettable opera *Aïda*. In the present day, Eddie Cantor is a man who was born in the New York slums, and today he is a favorite actor. Both Theodore Roosevelt and Franklin D. Roosevelt were sons of wealthy parents, but they had to overcome handicaps in their rise to the Presidency. Indeed, there are many people in this world who were born of poor parentage, but as men or women made for themselves high positions in life.

5

Walking is more than an everyday necessity — it can be used for all kinds of reasons. As a recreation it serves to pass your leisure time. When you are feeling lonely and depressed, a long walk in the crisp air does heaps of good toward cheering you up. Then again, if you're filled with the glorious feeling that everything is perfect, you enjoy a walk outdoors where everything in nature seems to be happy with you. On hikes through wild country campers make many wonderful and surprising discoveries. A nervous businessman, waiting to hear whether the stock market has gone down another point, puts his hands behind him and paces impatiently up and down the room. Riding in a car everywhere you go is faster but not so good for you as walking. Next time you're bored or happy or unhappy or worried, take a walk.

THE CLINCHER SENTENCE

It is a good plan, in descriptive and explanatory writing especially, to add a concluding sentence to a paragraph. This sentence sometimes repeats the idea expressed in the topic sentence. Its purpose is to sum up, to "clinch" the central thought. Teachers of composition call it the "clincher" sentence. Read the two paragraphs which are given below. Notice that the final sentence in each is a "clincher."

The reading habits and tastes of the people of the United States have been roundly condemned and highly praised. Some writers find a degradation of our national tastes in the large number of tabloid newspapers, the rise of the comic books and strips, and the tremendous output of the pulp magazines. The newspaper with the largest circulation in the country (the *News* of New York, with an approximate daily circulation of 3,000,000 and a Sunday circulation of 5,000,000) is a tabloid, as are many other large newspapers. Comic books are now sold at the rate of nearly a quarter of a billion a year. Their readers include an estimated one out of every five United States adults. There may be unnecessary alarm over the influence of the comics, but it seems true that some of the comic books, more than newspaper strips, which are regulated by the newspaper's need of public approval, violate many standards of decency and good taste. There are about ten million pulp magazines published monthly in the United States, with an average of four or five readers each. These are the *Dream Romances*, *Snappy Stories* sort of thing, which usually have no literary merit and bear no resemblance to ordinary living. **In terms of interests and tastes, then, reading habits may be said to be in need of improvement.**

One of the reasons for the low level of current general tastes in reading may be the lack of accessibility to good books. The American public library has had a long and honorable history dating back at least to Benjamin Franklin's time, and the United States was the first country to institute libraries supported by municipal taxes; but many portions of the country still do not have public-library service. Nearly 92 per cent of rural people and about 8 per cent of urban people have no libraries they can reach easily. The American Library Association estimated that a library should have a minimum of one and one-half to three books and should spend about one dollar a year for each person in the community it serves. Actually, fifteen states spend less than ten cents per capita per year for library service. While other factors, such as economic ability to pay, influence the picture, lack of libraries and books may be one reason for the general popularity of the pulps and the comics.[2]

● EXERCISE 4. Write a paragraph on any topic you wish. Make the first sentence a topic sentence. Develop it with a number of specific details. Make the last sentence a "clincher" sentence. You may write one of the paragraphs you outlined in Exercise 2 on page 224.

● EXERCISE 5. Choose one of the topic sentences below and write a well-knit paragraph. Make an outline before you write. Begin with the topic sentence. Be sure that every sentence deals with the subject introduced by the topic sentence. All the sentences lend themselves to development by examples.

1. Teachers may be classified in four types.
2. To me most of my sister's girl friends seem crazy.
3. There are many beautiful buildings in this city.
4. There are five days in every year that I always look forward to.
5. He can find more ingenious excuses for not doing his homework than anyone else I know.

SUMMARY

(1) A composition should be divided into paragraphs. Correct paragraphing helps the reader.

(2) A paragraph is a series of sentences developing one topic.

(3) The topic of a paragraph is usually stated in a sentence which is called the *topic sentence*. This sentence

[2] From *Children Learn to Read* by David H. Russell. Reprinted by permission of Ginn and Company.

is usually the first one in the paragraph, although it
may come at some other point.

(4) Every sentence in a paragraph must be closely related to the topic.

(5) In general, a paragraph is developed by means of
examples, *facts*, *statistics*, *reasons*, or *incidents* supporting the topic sentence.

11c. The Descriptive Paragraph

A descriptive paragraph is usually developed by
means of a series of *descriptive facts* which together
make up the picture the writer is trying to describe.

In the paragraph below about the tropical night,
the author gives details which "paint" the picture
introduced in the topic sentence. To the story writer
this is a common way of building a paragraph.

It was a beautiful night, dewy and still and fresh, with a
full moon rising above the palm trees on the Taravao isthmus.
The road wound this way and that around the shoulders
of the hills, now skirting the sea, now crossing the mouths
of broad valleys where the *hupe* — the night breeze from
the interior — blew cool and refreshing. I had glimpses
through the trees of lofty precipices festooned with the
silvery smoke of waterfalls and, on the left hand, of the
lagoon bordered by the barrier reef where great combers,
rising to break on the coral, caught the moonlight in lines
of white fire. From native houses along the road came
snatches of song, a strange mixture of airs, part French,
part Tahitian, to the accompaniment of guitars, accor-
dions, and mouth organs. On verandas here and there
women were busy with their ironing, sitting crosslegged
on the floor with a lamp beside them, and far out on the
lagoon the lights of the fishermen were already beginning
to appear.[3]

[3] From "Sing a Song of Sixpence" by James Norman Hall. Reprinted by permission of *The Atlantic Monthly*.

THE ORDER OF DETAILS
IN A DESCRIPTIVE PARAGRAPH

When you have planned what you are to include in a paragraph and have written a topic sentence, you must decide in what order you will give the various details. The natural order in a descriptive paragraph is the order in which the various parts of the picture appeared to you. You may, of course, for the sake of clearness, describe your scene from left to right, foreground to background, top to bottom. On the other hand, you may go from picture to picture in whatever order you think most effective, provided you keep the reader informed as to where you are going. The use of "connecting" words and phrases will help the reader to follow you. Observe the use of the "connecting" words in heavy type in the following paragraph.

Football practice presents a lively and colorful picture. As I hurry down the gravel path toward the practice field, I can smell the crisp autumn air with its faint tinge of burning leaves. I hear **in the distance** the harsh cries of the coaches mingled with the high-pitched voices of the younger boys. I approach the field, and the scene, as I stop to take it in, presents a pageant of color and movement against a background of green grass and the orange glow of the setting November sun. **On my left** are the lightweights, scampering about, their shrill voices shrieking louder and louder. Leaping into position, they prepare for the play. One stout little fellow seems momentarily lost and stands bolt upright hesitating before he finds his place. In a sudden blur of colors the play swings **toward the right** and ends abruptly in a splash of maroon and gray jerseys, a milling pile bristling with legs and kicking feet. I hear the insistent wail of the whistle and watch the referee dive hard down into the wriggling mass to find the ball.

11c

USE OF CONNECTIVES
IN A DESCRIPTIVE PARAGRAPH

The following words and phrases will prove useful in making clear to the reader the location of each thing you are describing:

here, beyond, on my left, on my right, near by, opposite to, adjacent to, on the opposite side, in the distance, above, below

● EXERCISE 6. Below are the skeletons of two descriptive paragraphs. Write the paragraphs, filling in the descriptive details suggested. Use connectives to make the order of details clear. Connectives may be placed either at the beginning of a sentence or within the sentence. Your ability to select vivid words will determine the effectiveness of your paragraphs.

1

Most American high school classrooms are alike. A row of windows............... The chalkboards.......... ..... A bulletin board............... The teacher's desk............... Pupils' desks and chairs.......... ..... The American flag............... This plan and these furnishings are repeated thousands of times in schools throughout the United States.

2

The village pond on a January afternoon presents many entertaining sights. The little tots "just learning"...... .... Their older brothers and sisters............ ..... At the far end, within a roped-off space, the hockey players............... Of course, weaving in and out and around are the lovesick couples who...............

● EXERCISE 7. Select one of the following topic sentences and, by supplying descriptive details, build a descriptive paragraph presenting in full the picture introduced by the topic sentence. Use connectives to make the picture clear. Choose the best words you know to make the picture vivid.

1. If I had my choice of places I'd prefer to be at this moment, I'd choose . . .
2. As I entered the room, I could tell that it belonged to a typical teen-age girl (boy).
3. In my travels the sight that thrilled me most was . . . .
4. The new Ford (any car) is good-looking.
5. The crowded beach was a confusion of sound and color.
6. The results of the storm were shocking.
7. The decorating committee had transformed the gym.
8. She presented a picture of complete misery.
9. The monkey house at the zoo presented a fascinating picture at feeding time.
10. One look at the house and yard told me that small children lived there.

11d. The Explanatory Paragraph

Creating a paragraph by giving details of information in support of the topic sentence is a technique which may also be used when you are *explaining* something. In the following paragraph John Muir is explaining the construction and operation of a large thermometer which he built when he was a young man. Read it carefully. Note the topic sentence at the beginning and how it is developed by additional details of information.

1

One of my inventions was a large thermometer made of an iron rod, about three feet long and five-eighth of an inch in diameter, that had formed part of a wagon-box. The expansion and contraction of this rod was multiplied by a series of levers made of strips of hoop-iron. The pressure of the rod against the levers was kept constant by a small counterweight, so that the slightest change in the length of the rod was instantly shown on a dial about three feet wide, multi-

11d

plied about thirty-two thousand times. The zero point was gained by packing the rod in wet snow. The scale was so large that the big black hand on the white painted dial could be seen distinctly, and the temperature read, while we were ploughing in the field below the house. The extremes of heat and cold caused the hand to make several revolutions. The number of these revolutions was indicated on a small dial marked on the larger one. This thermometer was fastened on the side of the house, and was so sensitive that when anyone approached it within four or five feet the heat radiated from the observer's body caused the hand of the dial to move so fast that the motion was plainly visible, and when he stepped back, the hand moved slowly back to its normal position. It was regarded as a great wonder by the neighbors, and even by my own all-Bible father.[4]

There is often no difference at all in method between a paragraph developed by examples and a paragraph developed by explanatory pieces of information. The paragraph which follows is explanatory; as you will see, it is developed by examples.

2

A study of the penmanship of your friends will reveal some interesting things. Women are usually neater with the pen than are men — perhaps because their sense of beauty is often higher and their patience greater. The age of a person, his condition of health, his tidiness, carefulness, determination, nervousness, and various other traits of his character are all more or less clearly revealed by penmanship. No two persons write alike. The letters which are written with the greatest variety of form are *F*, *S*, *T*, *H*, *I*, *M*, *L* and *r*, *s*, *t*, *e*, *o*, *a*, *d*, *p*, and *n*. You will be interested in comparing the ways in which you and your friends form these particular letters.[5]

[4] From *Story of My Boyhood and Youth* by John Muir. Reprinted by permission of Houghton Mifflin Company.
[5] From "Are You Handy with the Pen?" by Julia W. Wolfe. Reprinted by permission of *Scholastic Magazines*.

The following paragraph is developed by giving details of information.

3

The simplest and most practical type of bridge for spanning a wide river is the suspension bridge. A suspension bridge is constructed on the simple theory that if you can string cables across a space, you can hang a bridge on them. The bridge consists of steel cables of great strength passing over high towers and anchored in the ground at each end. The platform for the roadway is suspended from the dipping cables by means of vertical cables. In order to keep the bridge from swaying, stiffening girders are installed under the roadway. Because a suspension bridge is not likely to be so stable as some other kinds, it has not always been practical for railways, whose rails must be kept in strict alignment; but modern suspension bridges are so firm that they can carry as many as eight railway tracks. The length limit of the main span of a suspension bridge, according to engineering theory, is about 7,000 feet. The George Washington Bridge across the Hudson River in New York has a main span of 3,500 feet.

THE ORDER OF DETAILS
IN AN EXPLANATORY PARAGRAPH

Details in an explanatory paragraph should be arranged so that the reader can follow the explanation clearly from beginning to end. In general, one of two arrangements is used

1. From the *familiar to the unfamiliar* or from the *easy-to-understand to the hard-to-understand*. This method is especially important when you are handling new and difficult subject matter or vocabulary — making a scientific explanation, for instance. This is generally the order used by the authors of the preceding paragraphs 2 and 3.

2. *Chronological order*. This is time order and is especially useful in explaining a process or an operation consisting of a series of actions.

CONNECTIVES IN THE
EXPLANATORY PARAGRAPH

Connective words or phrases are especially useful in writing the explanatory paragraph which follows a chronological order. The following words will be helpful in keeping the time order clear:

first, second, third, finally, next, at the same time, similarly, likewise, for this purpose, then, thereupon

Observe the connective words in heavy type in the following *chronologically* arranged paragraph.

In building a brick wall, the builder must **first** prepare a bed which is perfectly horizontal. **At the same time** he must be sure that the bed is firm enough to hold a wall without sinking. **For this purpose** cement or cement blocks may be used. On this foundation the bricklayer **next** builds up the ends or corners several layers high. **After** he has got these absolutely true, he stretches a line between the corners at the exact height of his first layer of bricks, and **then** lays the entire row to fit this line. He lays only a few layers of brick at a time all around the building or the full length of his wall because bricks are liable to settle and so carry the work out of plumb. **Finally,** when his day's work is finished, the bricklayer covers his wall to protect it from excessive weathering during the drying process.

● EXERCISE 8.   The following topic sentences are the kind that must be developed by additional explanatory details of information. Select one that you think you know enough about and write an explanatory paragraph. Use connectives to keep the explanation clear.

1. In making a dress you should follow several distinct steps.
2. Buying photographic equipment and supplies requires experience and judgment.

3. Air pressure makes it possible for an airplane to fly.
4. Mother taught me some important things about making a cake.
5. The editor of a school newspaper has a great many responsibilities.
6. The typical camp day keeps everyone busy almost every minute.
7. There are many things to think about when you drive a golf ball (shoot a rifle, plow a field, water ski, etc.).
8. Sailing a boat is not so simple as it looks.
9. Organizing a club turned out to be more complicated than we had thought.
10. A quarterback has a difficult job.

11e. The Narrative Paragraph

Much of the writing that you do is devoted to telling what happened. This is narrative or story writing, and you divide it into paragraphs to make it clear and interesting to the reader. A narrative paragraph, however, does not need to be so carefully constructed as paragraphs in other kinds of writing. It is not always possible to have a topic sentence in every paragraph when you are relating an experience or telling a story. You change paragraphs when the action of your story shifts to a different scene, when you bring in a new character, when you wish to insert a descriptive passage, or when you change to a different time.

Nevertheless, even in story writing, you can often use the topic sentence and additional details effectively. The following are narrative paragraphs of this kind. Notice how the authors have begun their paragraphs with a general statement — like a topic sentence — and then have gone on to explain by giving further details.

11e

1

About this time I found out the use of a key. One morning
I locked my mother up in the pantry, where she was obliged
to remain three hours, as the servants were in a detached
part of the house. She kept pounding on the door, while
I sat outside on the porch steps and laughed with glee as
I felt the jar of the pounding. This most naughty prank
of mine convinced my parents that I must be taught as
soon as possible. After my teacher, Miss Sullivan, came
to me, I sought an early opportunity to lock her in her
room. I went upstairs with something which my mother
made me understand I was to give to Miss Sullivan; but
no sooner had I given it to her than I slammed the door
to, locked it, and hid the key under the wardrobe in the
hall. I could not be induced to tell where the key was. My
father was obliged to get a ladder and take Miss Sullivan
out through the window — much to my delight. Months after
I produced the key.[6]

2

**But the trick that set the town talking was her bowing to
anyone I spoke to.** "Lennie Steffens' horse bows to you,"
people said, and she did. I never told how it was done; by
accident. Dogs used to run out at us and the colt enjoyed
it; she kicked at them sometimes with both hind hoofs. I
joined her in the game, and being able to look behind more
conveniently than she could, I watched the dogs until they
were in range, then gave the colt a signal to kick. "Kick,
gal," I'd say, and tap her ribs with my heel. Anyway, she
dropped her head and kicked — not much; there was no
dog near, so she had responded to my unexpected signal
by what looked like a bow. I caught the idea and kept her
at it. Whenever I wanted to bow to a girl or anyone else,
instead of saying "Good day," I muttered "Kick, gal,"
spurred her lightly, and — the whole centaur bowed and
was covered with glory and conceit.[7]

[6] From: *The Story of My Life* by Helen Keller. Reprinted by permission of Doubleday & Company, Inc.

[7] Reprinted from *Autobiography of Lincoln Steffens*, by permission
of Harcourt, Brace and Company.

A narrative paragraph is almost always written in chronological order because, by its very nature, a story moves in the time order in which its events happen. The following words are commonly used in narrative writing to make the order of events clear:

first, second, third, finally, next, hence, therefore, consequently, as a result, meanwhile, at length, immediately, soon, afterward, after a few days, in the meantime, later, now.

Observe the connectives in heavy type in the following narrative paragraph.

3

Now we all had leisure to notice two things. **First,** the movement had not been of the whole jam, as we had at first supposed, but only of a block or section of it twenty rods or so in extent. **Thus** between the part that had moved and the greater bulk that had not stirred lay a hundred feet of open water in which floated a number of loose logs. **The second fact** was, that Dickey Darrell had fallen into that open stretch of water and was in the act of swimming toward one of the floating logs. That much we were given just time to appreciate thoroughly. **Then** the other section of the jam rumbled and began to break. Roaring Dick was caught between two gigantic millstones moving to crush him out of sight.[8]

● EXERCISE 9. Write a good narrative paragraph developing one of the following topic sentences or one of your own creation.

1. Herb held the advantage throughout the first four rounds.
2. The blaze was nearly under control when we discovered that sparks had set the barn afire.

[8] From "The Riverman," in *Blazed Trail Stories*, by Stewart Edward White. Reprinted by permission of Doubleday & Company, Inc.

3. It looked for a minute as though our heroic efforts to rescue the animals were going to fail.
4. Bewildered as I was by the confusion of the county fair, I grew frantic when I realized that I had become separated from my father.
5. Anger in every line of his face, Mr. Strong strode into the auditorium.
6. All of a sudden I felt my ski strap break.
7. Down the hill came the driverless Ford, careening from side to side.
8. There I was, on my first date, facing a barrage of questions from Elsie's father.
9. We had a lot of fun that night.
10. My first day in the new school was unforgettable.

11f. The Argumentative Paragraph

Writing which expresses the author's opinions and argues in favor of them is argumentative writing. Newspaper editorials and the talks of some television and radio commentators are often of this kind. You yourself occasionally use this type of writing in your class tests when you are asked to give an opinion and to support it with facts learned in the course. The purpose of argumentative writing is usually to convince the reader that the author is right. You must present your arguments clearly if you wish them to be convincing.

The argumentative paragraph usually begins with a statement of the opinion to be supported in the rest of the paragraph. This statement is the topic sentence. There are several ways of supporting opinion. Perhaps the way most commonly used is the listing of facts or examples (evidence) in support of the opinion. A writer may also prove his point by giving reasonable arguments arrived at through logical thinking. A combination of evidence and reasonable arguments is probably the most effective. At the end of the paragraph you may wish to add a summarizing sentence to clinch your point.

The paragraph which follows is an argumentative paragraph. Notice how the author begins by announcing his opinion and then gives facts and examples in support of his argument.

If Claiborn High School is to be the best kind of high school, it will have to have a strong injection of school spirit now. The need for school spirit has been shown by the fact that the recent campaign to sell General Organization tickets barely reached its goal even after being extended two weeks and after every kind of argument had been brought out and shined up. Of course, you should buy G. O. tickets because they will admit you to all school functions at a real saving. But it ought not to be necessary to base this sales campaign on dollars and cents considerations. You ought to buy a G. O. ticket for one reason and only one — because your school needs this money and it is asking you to give it. Students should have enough school spirit to want to support their school in whatever it undertakes. It's easy enough to support a winning football team or a school dance because those things are fun, but the quieter, less spectacular support of the whole school's General Organization is still more important even though it isn't fun. A dose of school spirit injected into the bloodstream of every student in C. H. S. is what Dr. Commonsense recommends, and we hope he'll inject it.

THE ORDER OF IDEAS
IN AN ARGUMENTATIVE PARAGRAPH

The order in which your examples, details, and arguments should be arranged in an argumentative paragraph will be determined by their importance. Usually, you should begin with the least important and work through to the most important, saving your most powerful argument or your most convincing evidence until the last, when you may present it as a kind of climax. Observe the arrangement of ideas *in order of importance* in the following paragraph.

I have very little use for the man who takes pride in his ability to keep himself aloof from other people and hides his talents from the world. Such a man not only exhibits a distastefully self-centered character but is a piece of useless timber in the social structure. For example, this hermit shows himself unwilling to pay for what he gets. I do not mean that he doesn't pay his bills. He must do that to avoid the law. I mean that all the things in civilization which make it possible for him to enjoy his comforts he owes to the efforts of others; yet he himself contributes nothing to others. He does not interest himself in the problems of society — in the poor, the suffering, the struggling. He does not strive to make the world any better. He creates nothing. As a result, he is of little good in the world or to the world. Therefore, I neither approve of him nor respect him.

CONNECTIVES IN THE ARGUMENTATIVE PARAGRAPH

The following words will be helpful in carrying the thought smoothly from one idea to the next in an argumentative paragraph:

moreover, first, second, third, finally, furthermore, in addition, then too, equally important, on the contrary, at the same time, hence, therefore, accordingly, thus, in fact.

Observe the use of connectives in the following argumentative paragraph.

There are several reasons why homework should not be assigned over the week end. First, five days out of seven devoted to school are enough for teen-agers, who really do have other things to do besides study. For instance, when are we going to work on the lawn for Dad, clean house or run errands for Mother, go shopping, get outdoors, see a show, or just read that book we have been waiting to get into? **Second,** week-end homework must be left until Sunday night unless you're one of those rare souls who, after five days of school, can settle down to the books on a Friday night in spite of the movies, the games, and the dates which Friday seems to inspire. **Then, too,** week-end homework is so often either not done at all or so poorly done that teachers have nervous breakdowns all day Monday trying to work with students who don't have the vaguest idea what the lesson is all about. **In fact,** it would be easier on everyone if the assignment had never been given at all. **Finally,** you come back to school on Monday fresher, more willing to start in again, if you have had a clean break from school for two days. A change is good for everyone, and anyone knows what all work and no play does to Jack.

● EXERCISE 10. Each of the following topic sentences can be developed into an argumentative paragraph. Choose one which interests you and write a paragraph. Use connectives to make your point of view clear.

1. To become a famous athlete can be very bad for a boy.
2. Seeing a moving picture of a great book is not a substitute for reading the book.
3. Personality is more important than beauty.
4. Every boy should be required to participate in at least one sport.
5. The legal driving age should be eighteen.
6. Eighteen-year-olds should be allowed to vote.
7. All public transportation should be run by the Federal Government.
8. A small college is preferable to a large state university.
9. I am against co-education.
10. We need a new school building.

● EXERCISE 11. From an old copy of a newspaper or magazine, cut out three paragraphs which you consider good examples of what a paragraph should be. Underline the topic sentence (it need not be the first sentence) and underline the summarizing sentence at the end if there is one. Paste the clippings on a piece of notebook paper. Under each tell what kind of paragraph it is — descriptive, explanatory, narrative, argumentative — and tell how it is developed, whether by examples, details, facts, or arguments.

● REVIEW EXERCISE A.   Select one of the topic sentences given below and expand it into a paragraph, underlining the connective words you use.[9]

1. Procrastination is my greatest fault.
2. I have a favorite daydream.
3. Our daily school schedule should be changed.
4. I enjoy (do not enjoy) eating in our school cafeteria.
5. Certain traits characterize the good school citizen.
6. I should like to be an athletic coach (any other occupation).
7. Our home is never normal during one of Grandmother's visits.
8. Conditions in our locker room should be improved.
9. It was the new secret play that won the game.
10. The study of chemistry (any subject) is valuable.
11. I have been trying to increase my vocabulary.
12. The teacher of a course is often more important than the subject matter.
13. You should have seen the kitchen the first time I prepared dinner.
14. There are several reasons why I like our school paper.
15. Our school offers a complete course in home economics.
16. I have my own system for reading the daily paper.
17. Joan gasped with delight when she saw her first evening dress.
18. An astonishing sight greeted our eyes as we turned the corner.

[9] Additional instruction and practice in paragraphing will be found on pages 260–263. There you will learn how to divide a composition into paragraphs and how to join paragraphs in a composition by using linking or transition words and phrases.

19. The amusement park at night is a thrilling sight.
20. Each season of the year has its advantages.

● REVIEW EXERCISE B. The paragraphs which follow are included for study and analysis. Although they vary somewhat in quality, they are fairly good paragraphs. They were written by high school sophomores. Your teacher may direct you to:

1. Copy on your paper the topic sentence from each paragraph.

2. Decide which one of the four types each paragraph is: descriptive, explanatory, narrative, argumentative.

3. Explain by what kind of details each paragraph is developed: examples, facts, statistics, reasons, or incidents.

4. Select what you consider to be the best paragraph and the poorest paragraph. Be prepared to defend your selections.

1

Lightning is sometimes disastrous. I remember one humid summer day when it really gave us something to worry about. A clear flash and a clap of thunder heralded the storm. The shutters on our old clapboard house rattled, and wind and rain beat on the windows for hours. Suddenly a terrific blast of lightning struck near us. The rafters shook, and our hair stood on end. A little while after the storm we heard a heavy crash outside. Going out to investigate, we found that the lightning had struck our chimney, which had chosen this moment to fall. Since then, whenever we have had a severe lightning storm, I always go out and look at the chimney.

2

It was a restless crowd that eagerly awaited the express that would carry them to the annual Army-Navy football game. There were men and women from all walks of life milling about in the smoke-filled atmosphere of the station concourse. From the shabby newsboy to the well-dressed businessman, the humble rubbed elbows with the mighty;

and whether old or young, rich or poor, they all had the same feeling of expectancy. College boys, hatless and wearing topcoats, chatted with attractive girls in colorful autumn hats and coats. A little boy, pulling at his father's hand, kept repeating, "Pop, when's the train gonna come?" His father, none too calm himself, told his son that they had not long to wait. Over in a dim corner a talkative woman kept asking questions of her unfortunate victim and followed every question with a silly grin. At last, with a short blast of its whistle, the train came slowly into the station. Conversation increased in volume and rapidity as the people pushed forward toward the gates.

3

My Aunt Myra is strangely like a thunderstorm when she's angry. Like a bright, sunny day that is usually the prelude to a storm, Aunt Myra's normal disposition suddenly begins to cloud. As the day darkens and a few thunderclaps roll out, so Aunt Myra darkens and begins to explode. The bolts get more and more frequent until finally the rain begins. With Aunt Myra, however, it is a torrent of words punctuated with frequent roars of thunder. The end of her wrath, like the end of a storm, is usually sudden. The words end abruptly; the clouds linger for a while; then the sky clears.

4

As long ago as 1951 our school men warned the country about the large increase in school enrollment that was coming. All they had to do was compare the birth statistics for the years 1946 to 1950 with those of the five years before 1946. The average birth rate per thousand of the population in 1941 to 1945 was 20.1. The average rate for the next five years was 24.1. In other words, between 1946 and 1950, the birth rate was four points higher than during the preceding five years. In actual numbers almost four million more children were born during this period. As anyone could see, it would require a great many more teachers and schools to take care of four million additional pupils. The nation's failure to prepare properly for this increase has resulted in terribly overcrowded conditions.

5

Many persons are afraid of freedom of speech. They do not trust the people to reject the false but attractive ideas that may be offered to them. They believe that certain things should never be discussed or questioned because they are sacred. I believe that freedom to express one's views is a right which should not be denied to anyone. No matter how dangerous or absurd an idea sounds today, perhaps in a few years it will have proved itself to be correct. Men were once imprisoned for expressing their beliefs that the earth is round and moves around the sun. Had these beliefs been false, what possible harm could have resulted from talking about them? If they had been false, the more they were discussed the sooner they would have been discarded. Since they were true, the most cruel and extreme measures of silencing the source of the ideas could not keep the truth hidden. We need not fear false ideas if they can be discussed and studied freely.

6

In one-design racing the first boat to cross the finish line wins, but not so in the handicap class. The handicap and one-design classes start the same way, but there the resemblance ends because the winner is not always the first boat to finish. The faster boats have to give the slower boats "time." For example, we will say that *Boat A* has given *Boat B* an allowance of five minutes. Suppose *Boat A* finishes first; if *Boat B* can finish within five minutes after *Boat A*, it wins. This system keeps the local math wizards busy all week figuring handicaps for a Sunday race. It isn't as much fun racing in the handicaps division because of the fact that the first boat over is not necessarily the winner. In one race last summer the winning boat came in forty minutes after the first boat to finish. Needless to say, the owner of the boat which finished first was very bad company for several days afterward.

7

The audience is as amusing as the film. For instance, the heroine is praying in church and the hero is trying to slip her a note of warning that the villain is the organ pumper in disguise. The audience rises in a body, frantically pointing to the hero and screaming, "Look! Right in back of you!" If, on the contrary, the hero is being bested by the villain, there are protests of, "Foul, foul!" The audience, which is always two jumps ahead of the story, sees the hero about to be killed, and all laugh unsympathetically. They know the bullet will be stopped by a bag of gold in the right place, a medal of valor, or some such trinket. The tale ends satisfactorily to everyone except a few callous souls like myself who would like to see our curly-headed boy left for buzzard-fodder for a change.

8

As for the romantic picturesqueness of ranch life — that comes in the evening. The cowboy with his guitar (you'll seldom find one without some musical instrument) stations himself at some point not far from the ranch house and starts to play and sing. Pretty soon the ladies, just out of curiosity, wander out to investigate and, as a rule, stay out there for at least two hours. There is a special appeal in a cowboy song, mostly in the way it is sung. The songs are usually about ill-fated love and the "gal who was untrue to me." The cowboy invariably glances up at each member of his audience in turn, singing the words as though that particular part were meant for her alone; and when the ladies finally retire, slightly chilled and bitten but very satisfied, each one feels that he was singing to her and no one else and that this is going to be a nice summer after all. The cowboy retires, smiling to himself and wondering idly whether it will rain tomorrow so that he won't have to work.

CHAPTER 12

Planning
a Composition

The purpose of all your work in this book is improvement of your writing and speaking. Understanding sentences and how to make them clear, correct, and interesting is an important help, but being able to write good *sentences* is not enough. Nor is it enough to know how to organize a paragraph. You must be able *to plan a whole composition*, to *organize* your ideas for writing. Study of the suggestions made in this chapter should make it easier for you to write good compositions.

Selecting a Subject

12a. Choose a subject you know something about.

Really good writing is possible only when you know well the subject you are writing about. If you choose to write on a subject about which you have only a small amount of information or in which you are not interested, the result of your work will be of little value even though the writing is technically correct.

When your teacher gives you a choice, choose a subject about which you know more than the average

12a

student knows. If you are expected to look up information on a subject before writing, don't be satisfied
until you have gathered enough information to make
an interesting composition.[1] In other words, you can
always write better if you are convinced that what
you are saying is going to be worth reading. Avoid
saying over again the same old things that everyone
always says about the subject. No matter how *correctly*
you write, your work will be unsatisfactory if what
you say is commonplace.

POOR PARAGRAPH — CORRECTLY WRITTEN
BUT COMMONPLACE IN CONTENT

Everyone with normal ability should have a high school
education. In high school you learn how to make a living,
and since you are going to have to do some kind of work
after you leave school, it is important that you have
enough education to get a job. The first thing any employer asks you when you apply for a job is how much
education you have had. Then, too, you live in a very
complex civilization. To understand the world and to
live properly in it, you must be able to understand what
you read in the papers and see and hear on television and
over the radio. Furthermore, you cannot be a good citizen unless you know enough to vote wisely. Finally, a
high school education will increase your enjoyment of life.
Appreciation of good books and good music makes your
life more enjoyable and makes you a better person. Certainly everyone should have the benefits of a high school
education.

12b. Limit the subject.

Another way to make sure that your compositions
are worth writing is to limit the subject enough so
that you can cover it in the space and time allowed.

---

[1] For an explanation of useful library sources of information,
see pages 311–319.

For essays of two or three pages, you do not need a big subject. In fact, you should learn to choose a *part* of a subject to write about. Before choosing a subject to write on ask yourself first, *Do I know enough about this subject to write a worthwhile composition on it?* Second, *Is the subject narrow enough for a short theme? If not, how can I limit it?*

Notice how the following general topics may be subdivided into more limited topics.

GENERAL TOPIC: HIGH SCHOOL ATHLETICS
 Specific Topics
   The Value of High School Football
   Dangers of Interscholastic Contests
   How to Succeed in Track

GENERAL TOPIC: GOOD HOUSEKEEPING
 Specific Topics
   Spring Cleaning
   The Care of Rugs
   An Efficient Kitchen
   Three Time-Saving Aids in Housekeeping

GENERAL TOPIC: CITY GOVERNMENT
 Specific Topics
   Are We Paying Enough for Our Schools?
   Is Our City Government Democratic?
   A Needed Change in Our City Government
   The Duties of the Mayor

12c. Determine the purpose of your composition.

When you set about narrowing a broad subject, you must usually decide exactly what is to be your purpose in writing. The topic "High School Athletics" is not a good topic because it does not indicate the purpose of the writer. "Values of High School Football" is a better topic because it does indicate the

**12
b-c**

writer's purpose. The writer has taken a particular attitude toward his subject. He has a purpose. In this case the purpose is to show in what ways football in high school is valuable. The writer may even state his purpose at the beginning of his composition: "High school students learn many valuable things from playing football."

● EXERCISE 1.   Below are 10 composition subjects. Of these, 5 are too general; 5 are properly limited. Decide which of these subjects could be discussed in a short paper. For each of the 5 general subjects write out 3 narrower topics which show clearly your purpose in writing and can be covered adequately in a few pages. The following are subjects or topics, not titles.

1. Pioneer life in America
2. Necessary instruments in a small dance orchestra
3. Popular music today
4. The qualities of a good umpire
5. Advice to a jaywalker
6. Modern education
7. Study habits I have developed
8. Fishing
9. Recent contributions of science
10. Why I like the *Post* (or any other magazine)

How Outlining Helps

12d. Plan your composition before writing.

(1) List your ideas.

The first step in planning a composition is to list on paper all the ideas you have on the subject you have chosen. Write them down as they come to you as rapidly as you can, without worrying too much at this time about the value of the ideas or where you would include them in your composition. Later, when you are organizing, you can cut out those which you decide not to use. The important thing is to see what material you have to work with.

FIRST LIST OF IDEAS
FOR A COMPOSITION ON "OCTOBER"

Purpose: to tell why October is the best month of the year.

football	the welcome change from
soccer	summer heat
the county fair	clear and crisp days
big football games	invigorating air
the colorful outdoors	first-of-term hopefulness
school again	new subjects and teachers
new acquaintances	hiking
old friends	Halloween

(2) Group related ideas under headings.

The second step is to group related ideas in this list so that your plan will gradually develop into a few larger divisions. When you have grouped your ideas together according to the phase of the subject they deal with, you will be able to decide on the principal headings in your composition.

IDEAS FOR THE COMPOSITION ON "OCTOBER"
GROUPED UNDER HEADINGS

I. fall sports
    football
    soccer
    hiking
II. events
    county fair
    big football games
    Halloween
III. school again
    new acquaintances
    old friends
    new subjects and new teachers
    first-of-term hopefulness

12d

IV. weather
        welcome change from summer heat
        clear and crisp days
        invigorating air
        colorful outdoors

(3) Arrange ideas in order; make an outline.

The third step is to arrange the ideas in the order in which you will discuss them in your composition. Some subjects will require a certain order. If your composition contains happenings which follow one another in story form, you will have to follow a chronological order. If the various headings are of varying importance, you may arrange them with the most important coming last and the least important first. The material under one heading may be necessary for understanding the material under one of the other headings. Then you will have to put that first heading before the one which depends upon it.

If the ideas themselves do not determine the order in which they should come, you may decide yourself upon the most interesting and clearest arrangement.

Arranging your ideas in a definite order is the first step in making an outline. Besides showing the order in which the ideas come, an outline shows their relative importance. You will have main headings and subheadings under them. If you acquire the habit of making an outline *before* you write a composition, you will find the writing much easier and the result much clearer. *It is always a good thing to have a plan. Your outline is your plan.*

For most of the compositions you will write, a *topical* outline will be satisfactory. A *topical* outline is one in which the various items are *topics*, not complete sentences.

TOPICAL OUTLINE

OCTOBER

(The title is not included within the outline.)

Purpose: to tell why October is the best month of the year.

I. Weather
   A. Clear and crisp days
      1. Welcome change from summer heat
      2. Invigorating air
   B. Colorful outdoors
II. School again
   A. First-of-term hopefulness
   B. New acquaintances
   C. Old friends
   D. New subjects and new teachers
III. Fall sports
   A. Football
   B. Soccer
   C. Hiking
IV. Events
   A. County fair
   B. Big football games
   C. Halloween

12e. Observe rules for form in making an outline.

(1) **Place the title above the outline. It is not one of the numbered or lettered parts of the outline.**

(2) **Use Roman numerals for the main topics. Subtopics are given capital letters, then Arabic numerals, then small letters, then Arabic numerals in parentheses, then small letters in parentheses. Study the outline form on page 256.**

(3) **Indent subtopics. Indentions should be made so that all letters or numbers of the same kind will come directly under one another in a vertical line.**

(4) **There must always be more than one subtopic because subtopics are divisions of the topic above**

12e

them. When you *divide* you must have at least two resulting parts, because you cannot divide anything into less than two divisions.

CORRECT OUTLINE FORM

I.
  A.
  B.
    1.
    2.
      a.
      b.
        (1)
        (2)
          (a)
          (b)
II. etc.

If you find yourself wanting to use a single subtopic, rewrite the topic above it so that this "sub idea" is included in the main topic.

WRONG   D. New subjects
                1. New teachers

RIGHT   D. New subjects and new teachers

(5) For each number or letter in an outline there must be a topic. Never place an *A*, for instance, next to *I* or *1* like this: *IA* or *A1*.

(6) A subtopic must *belong* under the main topic beneath which it is placed. It must be closely related to the topic above it.

(7) Begin each topic with a capital letter. You may place a period after each topic or you may not, as you wish. But be consistent. If you use a period after one topic, use a period after all of them.

(8) The terms *Introduction*, *Body*, and *Conclusion* should not be included in the outline. Of course, you may have an introduction and a conclusion in your composi-

tion, but the terms are not topics you intend to discuss.
Hence they should not be listed as topics in the outline.

● EXERCISE 2. Copy carefully the skeleton outline
given at the right below and place each of the topics
in the list at the left in its proper position in the
outline. The title is included among the topics.

	(TITLE)
Working indoors	I. . . . .
Mowing lawns	A. . . . .
Delivering newspapers	B. . . . .
Baby-sitting	C. . . . .
Working outdoors	D. . . . .
Clerking in a store	E. . . . .
Ways to earn spending money	II. . . . .
Delivering groceries	A. . . . .
Clerking in an office	B. . . . .
Waiting on table	C. . . . .
Washing cars	D. . . . .
Shoveling snow	

● EXERCISE 3. Follow the directions given for the
preceding exercise.

	(TITLE)
Raise hand before speaking	I. . . . .
Don't push	A. . . . .
In the cafeteria	B. . . . .
Good manners in school	C. . . . .
Leave table clean	D. . . . .
Obey the teacher	II. . . . .
In the classroom	A. . . . .
Let others have a chance to recite	B. . . . .
	C. . . . .
Don't block traffic	III. . . . .
Respect others' opinions	A. . . . .
Don't yell	B. . . . .
Wait in line for your turn	C. . . . .
Display good table manners	
In the corridors	

● EXERCISE 4. The unsorted list of ideas below can be grouped under the 4 main headings given before the list. On your paper write these main headings; under each, list the topics which belong there. Number, letter, and arrange in a correct outline.

CHARACTERISTICS OF A GOOD DRIVER

Main Headings

    maintains a courteous attitude
    obeys the law
    keeps his car in good condition
    drives carefully

Unsorted List

    stops at red lights
    is courteous to other drivers
    keeps brakes in good condition
    keeps tires in good condition
    drives at moderate speed
    is courteous to pedestrians
    signals clearly
    keeps lights in good condition
    parks only where parking is permitted

● EXERCISE 5. The following topics can be arranged in an outline under the title "My Taste in Television Programs." Find the three main topics and place the subtopics under them according to your own taste. Write the outline neatly.

MY TASTE IN TELEVISION PROGRAMS

soap opera serials
programs I don't like
news programs
old movies
comedy shows
crime dramas
quiz programs
programs I like very much
family-situation serials
give-away shows
programs I like mildly
musical shows
panels on current events

● EXERCISE 6.   Select a subject of interest to you
and write a complete outline of a composition you
could write on this subject. Mix up the topics in
your outline and arrange them in a list. Bring this
list to class for one of your classmates to rewrite in
outline form.

Introduction, Body, and Conclusion

**12f. Every composition has a beginning, a middle,
and an end.**

This simple fact is called to your attention so that
you will plan your composition with an introduction
(the beginning), a body (middle), and a conclusion
(end). Although they are not topics in your outline,
you should always have these three parts of an essay
in mind as you plan your work.

The *introduction* is always important. Although brief,
it must be interesting enough to make the reader
want to read more. It must state clearly the purpose
of your composition. It should include any facts or
pieces of information which you think the reader will
have to know in order to understand your composition.

The *body* is really the composition itself. It must
fulfill the purpose you have set out to accomplish.
The body will usually be about three-fourths or more
of your paper.

The *conclusion* may summarize what you have said.
A summary should not, as a rule, be a listing of the
main points. It should be a concise restatement of the
main idea of your paper and should leave the reader
with a feeling of completeness, as of a job now
finished.

Very often in a short article one paragraph for the

12f

introduction and one paragraph for the conclusion will be enough.

● EXERCISE 7.   Read the composition "Eating in Bed" on page 264. Be able to show that the composition fulfills the requirements just given regarding the introduction, body, and conclusion of a composition.

12g. Divide your composition into paragraphs.

In Chapter 11 you can learn how to write a paragraph, but there the paragraph is considered as a unit by itself. Usually, however, a paragraph is part of a larger composition. Now is the time to consider the paragraph used in this way.

It may be that in the body of your composition you can devote one paragraph to each main heading in the outline. If so, the problem of dividing your work into paragraphs will be solved as soon as you have made an outline. On the other hand, you may have more paragraphs than main headings, if your paper is long enough, or you may have fewer paragraphs than main headings. In any case, *each of your paragraphs must be built around one idea*. Every time you take up a new idea, begin a new paragraph. *Do not start a new paragraph without having a good reason for doing so.*

12h. Use *linking* expressions to bridge the gap between paragraphs.

One problem which arises in a composition of several paragraphs is the problem of bridging the gap between paragraphs. *The thought of your composition should flow steadily from paragraph to paragraph.* It should not be so abruptly shifted at the beginning of a new paragraph that the reader cannot see the connection between the idea in the paragraph he has just read and the one he is just beginning.

Writers frequently use *linking words*, therefore, to link paragraphs.

Familiarize yourself with this list of linking words. Using one of them in the opening sentence of a paragraph will show the reader the relationship between the paragraph he is starting and the one that he has just finished.

LINKING EXPRESSIONS

therefore	furthermore
in spite of this	in the next place
consequently	however
accordingly	as might be expected
as a result of this	an example of this
similarly	finally
besides	lastly
nevertheless	also
on the contrary	meanwhile
on the other hand	soon
after all	in other words
such	in addition
likewise	

Read the four paragraphs which follow, and note how the author has used linking words to bridge the space between the ideas in one paragraph and the ideas in the next.

1

Through the friendly aid of Harold Bixby, of St. Louis, a businessman much interested in aviation, a number of St. Louis citizens supplemented the fund that Lindbergh had saved from his earnings and thus enabled him to set about the purchase of a plane. He investigated various types of machines and decided that the one best suited for his purpose was a monoplane with a single motor. The monoplane he considered more serviceable than the

12
g-h

biplane because of the lack of interference between the wings, which enabled it to carry a greater load for each square foot of surface at a higher speed. The single-motored machine had much less head resistance and therefore possessed a greater cruising range.

2

Lindbergh **therefore** placed an order for **such a machine** with the Ryan Airlines, of San Diego, California. The plane was to be equipped with a Wright Whirlwind 200 horsepower radial air-cooled motor. It also was to have a small cabin to protect the pilot from storms, with a periscope for vision ahead and side windows for looking right and left. He watched the building of the plane and when it was completed found that it flew perfectly on its first test flight. In compliment to the men who had helped him to buy the plane he christened it the *Spirit of St. Louis.*

3

A number of accidents occurred **during this time** to aviators who were planning to compete for the Orteig prize. In April Lieutenant-Commander Noel Davis and Lieutenant S. H. Wooster were killed when their biplane *American Legion* crashed to earth in Virginia. The Fokker monoplane *America*, built specially for the flight across the Atlantic, was wrecked in New Jersey and its captain, Lieutenant-Commander Richard E. Byrd, and its pilot, Floyd Bennett, together with two others of the crew, were injured. In May, Lindbergh heard that the celebrated French war ace, Captain Charles Nungesser, and Major François Coli were preparing at Le Bourget Flying Field, outside Paris, to take off for New York. On May seventh the two French aviators started; storms were encountered; and although search was made of their route across the water and of lands where they might have landed, no trace was discovered of them or their plane.

4

Meantime at Long Island Clarence D. Chamberlin was waiting for news of the French aviators before making his start. Richard E. Byrd was also working on his plane in preparation for the transatlantic flight. Then arrived Lindbergh in the *Spirit of St. Louis.* He had made the journey from San Diego to St. Louis in a single flight and from there had sped to Roosevelt Field. He reached that place on the afternoon of May twelfth. Little was known about him as an aviator; he was said to be a skilled and daring western air-mail pilot. To those who greeted him he said he intended to try to fly from Roosevelt Field to Paris.[2]

12i. In the first sentence of a new paragraph, you may refer to the thought in the preceding paragraph.

A common method of bridging the gap between paragraphs is to refer in the beginning of a paragraph to what you have just said in the paragraph before. You may do this by using a pronoun — *this, these, that, those, such, it, them,* etc. — which reminds the reader of what he has just read. Suppose, for instance, that you have been writing about the accomplishments of a prominent athlete. You have said that he was a star in football. Then you begin your next paragraph by saying, "But *this* was not Bill's only sport. He was as fast and skillful on the basketball court as on the football field." The pronoun *this* refers to *football,* a key word in the preceding paragraph.

An even surer way of making the change to another idea in a new paragraph is to refer directly to the preceding paragraph, not by a pronoun but by mentioning again the principal idea in the preceding paragraph. In the case of Bill, you might say, "But outstanding as he was in football, Bill played basketball even better."

[2] Adapted from *Historic Airships* by Rupert **Sargent Holland.** Used by permission of the publishers, Grosset & Dunlap, **Inc.**

12i

● EXERCISE 8. Read the following informal essay written by a high school sophomore.

1. Select the sentence in the first paragraph which states the purpose of the essay.

2. Select the topic sentence of each paragraph.

3. Select the expression (word or phrase) at the beginning of each paragraph which links the thought with the paragraph above it.

4. What does the final paragraph accomplish?

EATING IN BED

There is no doubt that eating your meals from a tray is your greatest problem when you are sick in bed. Unless you have a table especially constructed to hold the tray, you encounter the greatest difficulty in putting yourself and your tray in a position which is comfortable yet practical for eating. During your illness you try all sorts of ways to hold your tray, none of which ever seem successful.

The first way you try is sitting up straight with your back held up by pillows and the tray lying on your lap, but there are numerous drawbacks to this position. For instance, if you have a cold, and during the meal you feel that irritation in your air passages which foretells a cough, your whole body involuntarily shakes. This turbulent eruption forces the milk and soup upward against the force of gravity, forming a display equal to that of Old Faithful at Yellowstone. During the following seconds you get the sensation of being under a waterfall. First you feel the burning soup splashing over your body, streaming down your neck, and running over your stomach. Accompanying this scalding spray are small droplets of milk which tingle and tickle your skin. By this time your anger has reached its zenith. You jump out of bed, throwing back the soaked covers, which carry the tray, food, and dishes to their destruction.

Another objectionable feature of this method of eating is that your back is not perpendicular to your legs but slants backward. In order to see your food, you must press your chin into your neck. Moreover, when you finally manage to adjust your body to this position, you discover that there is a great distance between your mouth and your food. However, you gamely try to transport your food to your chewer. This is not so difficult until you make a sad attempt to convey a spoon of soup over the vast area. No one can realize how unsteady his hands really are until he has tried this. When the bowl of soup is empty, you find that one-third of it has entered your mouth. The rest has been absorbed by that towel which you had so cautiously placed over you. If you are a frugal person, you can wring out the towel over your mouth and thus enjoy all your soup.

Another slight disadvantage of placing your tray on your body is that, during your meal, you will undoubtedly have that uneasy sensation in the skin which makes you want to scratch the affected spot. It is always impossible to reach this irritated part because of your awkward position. Thus you begin that tiring process of carefully removing the tray and gently placing it on some firm surface. By the time you have satisfactorily scratched yourself and again placed your tray back on your lap, your food is cold and your itching begins again.

Other ways of posing yourself on the bed for eating usually make you dependent upon your elbows for support. You may lie on your side supporting yourself with one elbow and shoveling your food with the other arm. Or you may be flat on your abdomen, raising yourself with both elbows. When in this position you carry the food upward as far as your wrists will stretch and then lower your head to meet the food. However, these methods also inflict torture. Your elbows and neck muscles become sore. When your right hand tires, you must clumsily eat with your left. When eating with your left hand, you encounter great difficulty in making the fork hit its target squarely.

These are some of the ways in which I have suffered in trying to discover a satisfactory manner of eating in bed. I hope others may profit by my experience.

— ED BUSH

● EXERCISE 9. Examine a magazine or newspaper article. Mark any linking words or expressions which serve to connect paragraphs. Bring the article to class.

● EXERCISE 10.   Examine one of your reading assignments in history or some other subject and find the topic sentence in each paragraph.[3] Note how it helps you to grasp the thought of the paragraph. Topic sentences in your own paragraphs will help your readers too.

● EXERCISE 11. Choose one of the following topics and write a three- to five-paragraph composition on it. Be sure that each paragraph contains a topic sentence. Include a linking word or expression in the opening sentence of all paragraphs except the first.

1. On Never Knowing What Time It Is
2. Breakfast at Our House
3. The Tricks of Advertisers
4. My Favorite Comic-Book Characters
5. On Passing a Lifesaving Test
6. Juvenile Fiction
7. On Taking Care of Children
8. Our Neighbors
9. Getting Out the School Newspaper
10. On Being a Junior Counselor
11. If Advertisements Came True
12. The Traits of a Good Citizen
13. Classical vs. Popular Music
14. The Values of Being a 4-H Club Member
15. My Favorite Elementary School Teacher
16. On Learning to Dance
17. Me
18. On Being Lucky (or Unlucky)

[3] For discussion of topic sentences, see pages 221–23.

Composition Materials

The way to learn to write is to write. Before you write, you must have something to write about. The following six assignments will suggest subjects.

The check list below is for use *before* and *after* you write. Use it *before* to remind you of the *techniques* of good writing. Use it *afterward*, before you write the final copy of your composition, to help you detect *weaknesses* in your writing.

COMPOSITION CHECK LIST

1. Logical organization?
2. Proper division into paragraphs?
3. Complete sentences?
4. Clear sentences?
5. Varied sentences?
6. Correct punctuation?
7. Topic sentences?
8. Choice of words?
9. Spelling?
10. Interesting and appropriate title?

1. A Character from Life

The fact that you like to talk about others doesn't mean that you are a gossip. Everyone knows that there is nothing more interesting in the world than people; it's human nature to think about their peculiarities, their beauty or homeliness, the strange things they do. Maybe you don't talk about the people you know. If you don't, then you're different, and not talking about others is certainly one of *your* own peculiarities.

But have you tried your hand at *writing* about someone, putting him down on paper exactly as he is, and then taking a good look at him? You'll find it an entertaining experience, sometimes a very helpful one, for afterward you'll be sure to understand him better.

Remember Aunt Jane, who for forty years refused to eat breakfast? She said breakfast didn't agree with her. But after having lunch with her a few times, you discovered how she made up for the meal she missed. You know Mr. Timeline, the social studies teacher? He's always in a fog, you say. Well, is he really? Maybe he's thinking about that new development in Europe or what Lincoln said to McClellan. You know how much fun his classes are, too. Remember the time he got so excited pointing out local geography that he nearly fell out the window?

Of course, if you think it's safe, you can write a word picture of Joe Blair. He's a pretty good friend, but he surely does bother you sometimes. That voice that always seems to be changing, that crew haircut, that grammar!

Somebody you know will make a good subject for a sketch. Try your hand at writing one. Can you make your reader know the subject of your sketch as you know him? Can you make your subject as interesting to others as he is to you?

SUGGESTIONS

1. You can show what a person is like in several ways:
    a. By telling what he says and how he says it
    b. By describing typical actions
    c. By describing the person's appearance

2. Include some incidents (actual happenings) in your sketch. Select incidents which will show the character traits you want to show. Your reader will be much more interested in reading of actual occurrences in which your character had a part than he will be in a formal description of your character's personality.

3. Begin with an incident, or, if you wish, with an arresting fact. Above all, do not begin by saying, "The person

I am going to write about is . . ." The following beginnings would be good:

    a. "Duck, everybody! Here comes Self-Importance."

    b. Two hundred pounds of pure fat may not appeal to you, but it is the physical structure of the best-natured man that ever forgave an icy snowball.

    c. She's pretty, she's graceful, she's charming, she's smooth!

2. *A Character from Literature*

In the same way that most of us spend a good part of our conversational hours learning *about* our friends *from* our friends, so we spend a good part of our reading hours reading about other people in books. Indeed, the characters we read about are often more vivid than the people we actually know. Very often we know so much more about the novelist's or the biographer's characters because the writer has told us more things about them than we know even about the members of our own family.

In your memory you cherish the acquaintance of many people whom you have read about. Some you admire; some you hate; some you love; some you can't understand. How many of the following do you *know?*

PEOPLE FROM FICTION

Winnie the Pooh	Jody Baxter
Sue Barton	Long John Silver
David Copperfield	Penrod
Scrooge	Captain Bligh

Sidney Carton

PEOPLE FROM REAL LIFE

Orville Wright	Theodore Roosevelt
Richard Byrd	Robert E. Lee
Dwight Eisenhower	Louis Pasteur

Perhaps you have recently read about a character who made a deep impression upon you. Maybe he was a fictional character; maybe he was a hero of World War II, or a hero of science or medicine. Plan a sketch of this character. Lift him right out of the book. Make him appear to be as real to others as he is to you.

SUGGESTIONS

1. Summarize by giving your general impressions. Don't try to write the whole book over again. Determine the two or three main qualities, or even only the one main quality, of the person. Build your composition around these qualities. Was your character brave, clever, ruthless, cruel, selfish, funny, brilliant, strong? Make your character's *outstanding* quality *stand out.*

2. Tell incidents in your character's life which will illustrate the truth of what you are saying about him. You will be able to include only three or four such incidents; therefore, select them carefully. Make the reader see why this person interested you so much that you chose to write about him.

3. Do not write a book report. Leave out the *whole* life story. Never mind all the interesting things you found in the book unless they are important to the points you are making about this one person.

4. Don't begin by saying, "Robert E. Lee was born at Stratford, Virginia, on January 19, 1807."

Better: "A noble gentleman first, a skillful general second — that was Robert E. Lee."

5. Polish up your adjectives. One well-chosen adjective is worth ten poorly chosen ones. This composition will test your fund of adjectives.

Now, let's hear about your hero — or your favorite villain!

3. Explaining How To Do Something

Explaining is a common activity, but there is a vast difference between a clear explanation and a confusing one. Careful planning before you write is of utmost importance.

Undoubtedly you have had more than average experience in some activity (a job or a hobby) which will make a good subject for a "how to do" essay. Possibly you have developed your own special techniques for doing something that nearly everyone has to do occasionally. Your techniques will be helpful to others. Perhaps you have had experience in doing something that the other members of your class do not know how to do. Select an activity and write an essay on it. Your purpose is to explain clearly how to proceed in this activity.

The following suggested topics may prove helpful.

How to train a dog	How to care for tropical fish
How to wash a car	How to sketch a portrait
How to clean a house	How to get along on your
How to change a tire	allowance
How to plan a party	How to prepare a dinner
How to water ski	How to study
How to take flash pictures	How to judge a movie
How to care for your hair,	How to ride a horse
nails, or complexion	How to rig a sailboat

SUGGESTIONS

1. Follow a chronological order. An essay of this kind consists of a series of carefully explained steps. Be especially sure to get these steps in the correct order; otherwise you will only confuse your reader.

2. Include in your explanation such things as special precautions, "tricks of the trade" that you have learned, short-cuts you use, and special equipment which you recommend.

3. You will help your reader if you include things not to do, common mistakes to avoid.

4. List in advance the tools and equipment necessary in the activity so that you won't omit any important ones.

Plan where in your essay you can use diagrams and illustrations effectively. A good diagram will be clearer than a lot of explanation.

5. Make an outline before you write.

6. Make your beginning a general introduction. Don't begin, for instance, with a sentence like this: "The first thing to do when you plan a party is . . . ." Leave that for the second paragraph. A better beginning would be: "Are you going to give a party in your home? If you are, you had better do some careful planning. As everyone knows, one party can be fun and another can be deadly even in the same surroundings and with the same crowd. The difference between a successful party and an unsuccessful one lies in the kind of preparation the host or hostess makes beforehand."

4. What's Your Idea?

Every thinking person has a head full of ideas. Some of them aren't worth much; some of them are very good. You probably have a few pet ideas that, at times when you're alone, you think about and develop and criticize. Take out one of these ideas and write it down for this composition.

Be serious about it. Don't waste your time on a trifling notion, but try seriously to explain the idea you really believe in. Do you think the marking system is fair? That's an old chestnut, but you may have strong feelings about it. Do you approve of TV commercials? Granted that business concerns give us good entertainment in return for a chance to advertise, have you a better idea for their commercials? Maybe you think school should be held in July and August and the usual vacation time distributed evenly through the year. Could you suggest something to make Sunday School or church more attractive to young people? What's the greatest need of the world today? What's *your* idea?

In case your head may not be bursting at present with an important theory, you may find material in the daily newspaper, in a magazine, or on the radio or television. Wherever you go, whatever you read, you are always forming opinions. These opinions can often be developed into really important ideas which you can easily sign, seal, and deliver as an English composition.

SUGGESTIONS

1. Before you begin to write, plan in detail what you are going to say.
   a. Define your purpose.
   b. List the ideas or arguments that will support your purpose.
   c. Organize these ideas into a brief outline.

2. Convince your reader that your idea is a good one. You can judge your success by the reactions of your classmates to your composition.

3. Don't be entirely critical. Spend most of your composition building up your theory. If you are proposing a better way for the city to keep its young people off the streets and out of trouble, devote most of your composition to explaining this better way — not to criticizing the present unsatisfactory method.

5. Telling a Story [4]

The preceding composition assignments were essays. They required you to plan carefully, list and arrange your ideas in an outline, and write with careful consideration of paragraphing, topic sentences, connectives, introduction and conclusion, etc. For a little relief from that kind of writing, try your hand at telling a story.

[4] For a fuller treatment of story telling, see Chapter 14, "Narrative Writing," pages 323–340.

A very large part of your daily conversation is devoted to telling what happened — either to you or to someone you know. Story telling has always been a natural human activity. When, therefore, you are asked to write a story, you are being asked to do only "what comes naturally."

Because people write best when they write what they know from firsthand experience, you will do well to base your story on a personal experience. Of course, you may fictionize the experience as much as you want to. This is one situation in which you are not expected to tell the exact truth.

Telling a story in writing is different from telling it orally. You must plan in advance so that you won't just ramble on aimlessly. You have neither the space nor the energy to write as much as you would say orally. It is harder to hold the interest of a reader than of a listener.

Think back over your experiences of the past year or two. Can you find one that you can make into an interesting story? Perhaps the following suggestions will help you:

An experience which taught you a lesson
　　　　　　　in which you were frightened
　　　　　　　that was costly
　　　　　　　that excited or thrilled you
　　　　　　　in which you lost your temper
　　　　　　　in which you made a mistake
　　　　　　　in which you made an enemy (a friend)
　　　　　　　in which your family played an impor-
　　　　　　　　　tant part
　　　　　　　in which an accident or a coincidence
　　　　　　　　　played a part

SUGGESTIONS

1. Begin your planning by selecting the point of highest interest in your story. Everything in your story should lead

up to this point. Plan to end your story very soon after this point.

2. Plan to begin your story as near to the point of highest interest as you can and still have a story to tell. If this point comes at five o'clock in the afternoon during a boat race, don't begin by telling about how hard it was to get up that morning and what you had for breakfast and why it took you so long to get to the lake. Begin with the race itself.

3. Begin the story in such a way that it will arouse your reader's interest. Here are a few suggestions as to how to begin.

A snatch of dialogue

"Don't bother to bring the canteen," Fred had said. "It's heavy, and besides, there are lots of springs along the way."

The setting

The heavy cabin door slammed behind me as I followed Bill into the night. The wind made me gasp for breath; the driven snow stung my face. Immediately I lost sight of Bill.

Action

Bob stepped on the gas, and we shot out into the heavy holiday traffic.

Don't begin with "One day" or "One morning" etc. Such beginnings are too much like the old "Once upon a time" opening of children's fables.

4. *Show* the action of your story; don't just summarize it. *Showing* takes longer and requires more effort, but it makes the story interesting. Think of yourself as a moving picture cameraman catching the story in a series of pictures, not as an old man wandering idly through his memories.

Summarizing

Everyone was in high spirits as our little picnic party started out for the State Park. Even Jeanie White's worries about snakes couldn't dampen our fun.

Showing

As we joined the other picnickers at the edge of town, I saw Pete waiting for me with a broad grin on his face. "Come on, slow poke," he called. "Let's get this picnic on the road." Betty, Jill, and I were laughing at the hiking costume in which Miss Seeley, our teacher, was leading us down the road. She was wearing a pair of too-tight dungarees and a mammoth straw hat which flopped wing-like as she bounced along.

"Are there any snakes where we're going?" asked Jeanie White.

"Don't be silly, Jeanie," Betty said. "Who's afraid of a few little snakes?"

6. A Look at Ourselves

How good is your sense of humor? Can you laugh at yourself? Can you see some of the crazy things you and your crowd do, as your parents or your teachers may see them? How well do you know the modern adolescent? After all, you are one.

Put yourself and your friends into writing. Take a good look at *all* of you as you really are. Do you think the television programs about boys and girls your age are true to life? Are the movies doing wrong by our high school students? What *are* you like, anyway?

This is not an assignment requiring you to write a serious essay about teen-agers. Rather it is an assignment to give a word picture of them in action. *Show*, don't *tell*, what they do, how they talk, where they go, what they look like.

To do this you must decide two things first of all.

(1) What is the *scene* of your picture to be? The locker room? the soda fountain? the study hall? the lunchroom? the movies? a dance? a pajama party? Pick a place where your characters will be seen just as they are, talking as they really do talk — pull no punches here — looking as they actually do look.

(2) You must have a chain of actions for your characters to perform. Maybe the best way would be to look around you today. Watch them with an author's eye. What exactly do they do?

SUGGESTIONS

1. Don't have too many characters. Three or four will be enough for a short composition. Identify your characters early by giving a distinguishing characteristic of each. Betty has blonde hair and big blue eyes. Jack thinks he's funny. (He certainly wasn't funny the afternoon he tried to make his own soda. Mr. Krip's mirror still has spots on it!)

2. Make the setting clear in the beginning.

3. Start out with the action, not with a general description.

Poor Beginning: I am going to describe some of the things I saw in the cafeteria the other day.

Better Beginning: "Hi, Mary!" Sam Ingalls dropped from nowhere into the chair beside me. The mouthful of potato salad I had just taken in nearly exploded on my tray. "What's up?" he beamed.

4. The dialogue may very well make or break your composition. Make it natural. Perhaps you'd better look over pages 475–78 before you write any conversation, just to get the punctuation and paragraphing right.

Get busy on adolescents in action, as they really are!

7. *How They Do Talk*

Yes, how *do* they talk? Who are *they?* Anybody you want them to be — that couple that sat in the seat ahead of you in the bus the other day, for instance. You weren't eavesdropping. You just couldn't help hearing them. Yes, they certainly "had it bad." Try, if you wish, to reproduce their conversation. Maybe you and your family trying to get started in the morning, or the fateful hour when you met *her* parents on that first big date, would provide a more interesting dialogue. The purpose of this assignment is to give you practice in writing *dialogue* — conversation — which will reveal the personalities of people who do the talking.

Did you listen in when your mother had callers a little while ago? Could you tell what each woman was like from what she said and the way she said it? Did you hear your father chatting about politics with the neighbor the time Dad got so excited? Maybe you can imagine two seniors talking about their boy friends or two freshmen talking about whatever two freshmen talk about. Did you ever think that two of your teachers might talk about *you?* Your task is to show, through what your characters say and how they say it, what kind of people they are.

SUGGESTIONS

1. Choose characters whose manner of talking you really do know — people that have distinct personalities — people that are "characters."

2. Let the dialogue carry the whole composition. The less you have to describe, the better. Most people describe themselves when they talk.

3. Make your dialogue natural. Let your people interrupt each other occasionally. Let them speak in words and phrases. We seldom use complete sentences in conversation.

4. You needn't use *said*, *replied*, *added*, etc., after every speech. Occasionally, give the speaker's action.

    a. "So I says to her, I says, 'You've got a lot of nerve.' " *Mamie's eyes burned with the memory.*

    b. "Look here, Al, I don't know where you get such crazy ideas." *Mr. Martin emphasized the remark by crushing in his fist the tomato he had just proudly picked in his garden.*

    c. "Well, if *he* isn't a fresh customer!" *Arlene snapped her gum a little to show her indignation, and leaned over the showcase.*

d. "Where did you get that hat?" *Father dropped his newspaper.*
"Don't you love it, Carl? I just bought . . ."
"You just *bought* it? You mean you paid money for . . ."
"Now, Carl, you know I needed a hat." *Mother began her defense.*

5. Begin by setting the scene. Your first sentences may be dialogue and also give the *time* and *place*.
"Look, Helen, here are two seats." I was startled out of the first scene of the second feature by a high-pitched voice at my elbow.
6. Review the rules for punctuating and paragraphing dialogue on pages 475–78.

TOPICS FOR COMPOSITION

The topics collected in this list are intended as suggestions. If you find one that you could write on if it were changed a little, change it to suit your wishes. Word your own title.

People

1. The man (woman) I admire most
2. Our school custodian
3. A little friend
4. Our druggist
5. My crowd
6. My doctor
7. Our postman
8. Mother's friends
9. Father remembers when he was a boy
10. A champion
11. If I were a parent
12. Our school bus driver
13. Midge learns to skate
14. My favorite movie star
15. My favorite TV entertainer
16. A teacher I'll never forget
17. My interesting relatives
18. The kind of girl boys (girls) like
19. The kind of boy girls (boys) like
20. My little brother (sister)
21. A hero I know
22. The typical baseball fan
23. The neighbors

24. Student types
25. My favorite character from fiction

Personal

1. My Saturday job
2. My kid brother's hard life
3. Prejudices
4. Traits I inherited
5. Helping out at home
6. Alibis
7. My greatest success
8. On being unprepared
9. My preference among the armed services
10. Hairdos
11. By their hats shall ye know them
12. How to be unpopular
13. They called it initiation
14. On being too busy
15. An embarrassing experience
16. Earning spending money
17. My favorite meal
18. Breakfast at our house
19. My moods
20. Daydreaming
21. A chapter from my autobiography
22. My parents' criticisms of me
23. Our family customs (traditions)
24. Complexion care
25. Dieting

26. Traveling with the family
27. How to be a good friend
28. How to keep healthy
29. On trying to be glamorous
30. A person I'd like to know
31. My happiest surprise
32. My troublesome conscience
33. Me — ten years hence
34. Why I want to be a nurse (any vocation)
35. My fluctuating bank account
36. How to be a good hostess
37. I'd rather live in the country (city)
38. On being bashful
39. My struggles with my diary
40. On being a big sister (brother)
41. On being a twin

Occasions

1. The best party we ever had
2. My favorite holiday
3. The best day of the week
4. My first home permanent
5. An afternoon in the beauty parlor

6. And I came in dungarees!
7. *There* was a pillow fight!
8. My sister learns to drive
9. Sunday morning at our house
10. Spring housecleaning
11. Moving day
12. I misread the time table
13. The day I kept house
14. I take up bowling
15. A surprise party
16. My first big fight
17. My first experience on the varsity
18. I repair the plumbing
19. My first date
20. A date I did not enjoy
21. I learn something about cooking
22. I learn not to gamble
23. Driving in a storm
24. I learn how to milk a cow
25. The hurricane
26. My first public appearance

School

1. The world in the microscope
2. The grading system
3. Systematic vs. random reading
4. How a barometer works

5. How to prepare for college
6. My struggle with authority
7. Basic books for a high school student's library
8. On spelling
9. Planning an assembly program
10. How to study lines for a play
11. What vitamins do for you
12. Once I tried to bluff
13. How to study for a test
14. We see a Shakespearean play
15. Why we study mathematics
16. The most important school subject
17. Fraternities and sororities
18. Getting a club out of the red
19. On homework in general
20. Stage lighting
21. Stage make-up
22. How to make a poster
23. Teachers are funny
24. Father helps me with homework
25. **Building a vocabulary**
26. **A system for doing homework**
27. My opinion of poetry
28. Our school newspaper
29. Lunch period

30. The dictionary — a remarkable tool
31. Teachers I have had
32. Why read?
33. The typical student in our school
34. Petty thievery in school
35. My science project
36. Sportsmanship in our school
37. School spirit
38. Overemphasis on sports
39. The football season — an evaluation
40. On being a second-string player
41. Needs of this school
42. School politics
43. Good student government
44. School manners
45. Appropriate school dress

Places

1. Motels
2. My favorite resort
3. The record shop
4. The church I attend
5. The supermarket
6. The lake at night
7. Our trip to Washington
8. The kitchen on Saturday morning
9. My favorite room
10. The view from our cabin
11. Dad's study — the Den of Dollars

12. Al's Snack Bar
13. A road I love
14. Bargain basement sale
15. The five-and-ten
16. Our town
17. The airport
18. A room with a view
19. Where I'd like to spend a vacation
20. The drive-in theater
21. A new building
22. Our recreation room
23. The drugstore at 4:30 in the afternoon
24. The doctor's waiting room

Hobbies

1. Raising hamsters
2. The do-it-yourself fad
3. On being an amateur magician
4. Snakes are interesting
5. We made our own canoe
6. On collecting things
7. How to care for tropical fish
8. Knitting
9. On learning to play an instrument
10. An educational hobby
11. Tips for stamp collectors
12. Hot rodding
13. Mr. Fix-it
14. How to take interesting pictures

15. Model hobbies (rail-roading, airplanes, etc.)
16. Flower arrangements

Out of Doors

1. On having a garden
2. On horseback riding
3. How to sail
4. Outdoor Christmas decorations
5. Camp life
6. An overnight hike
7. My first try at ice-skating
8. My favorite sport
9. Life on a ranch
10. Campfire time at camp
11. Caught in a blizzard
12. The values of Scouting
13. On being a tenderfoot
14. My first hunt
15. Outdoor games in our neighborhood
16. Lost in the woods
17. On mountain climbing
18. The art of trout fishing
19. Advice to a young camper
20. The outdoor type

Miscellaneous Subjects

1. Telephone manners
2. Teen-agers and the telephone
3. Rainy-day fun
4. The county fair

5. The slang we use
6. On making friends
7. Privileges that must be earned
8. If I were the President (anyone else)
9. Comic books
10. What's wrong with the movies?
11. TV programs for children
12. TV commercials
13. Safe driving
14. "Apple polishing"
15. Corresponding overseas
16. Importance of good manners
17. Southern customs
18. Virtue is rewarded
19. Superstitions and their effects on us
20. The most important news story of the week
21. The most important event of the year
22. How to enjoy an illness
23. On losing things
24. On borrowing and lending
25. On judging others
26. On avoiding work
27. Fads in clothes
28. On wearing a cast
29. Hospital life
30. Fame vs. reputation
31. Happiness vs. pleasure
32. This I believe
33. The conquest of space
34. Western movies

CHAPTER 13

Finding Information

USING DICTIONARIES AND THE LIBRARY

Few of the things you learn in school will be of more value to you than learning how to use the dictionary and to locate information in the library. An educated person, someone has said, is a person who knows where and how to find out what he wants to know. If this is true, a thorough acquaintance with both the dictionary and the library is an important part of your education, for they contain the information you want to know. This chapter will help you to make the best and most efficient use of these important tools.

13a. What the Dictionary Tells

The dictionary of the English language is probably the most useful of all the reference books you will encounter in either your classroom or library. The chances are you will have one or more at home, too. So common is the dictionary and so much is it a part of the daily work of high school students that you should know it in detail. You may regard a dictionary as nothing more than a big book which gives the meaning and spelling of all the words in the language. It is, however, much more than that. You may be surprised to know all the various kinds of information the dictionary contains.

Webster's New International Dictionary is the best-known of the *unabridged* dictionaries. Your library undoubtedly has one or more copies. The unabridged — complete — dictionary contains all the words in the language and gives more detailed information about them than does the abridged — or shortened — dictionary which you are accustomed to use. For most purposes your smaller dictionary is adequate.

There are several popular dictionaries. The one you own or have been provided with for class study may be arranged in a way different from certain others, but it probably contains essentially the same information as all the others. What these differences among dictionaries are will be clearer to you as you gain experience in using various dictionaries. Eventually, you will be able to tell at a glance how the dictionary you are using is arranged; you will be able to use any dictionary efficiently.

WHAT THE DICTIONARY TELLS ABOUT A WORD [1]

As you study the following pages, keep the excerpt on page 287 from *Webster's Students Dictionary* before you so that you can refer to it easily.

1. *Spelling*

The dictionary is the authority on correct spelling. If there are two spellings for a word, the Webster dictionaries give the preferred spelling first (*judgment, judgement*).

[1] To the teacher: The dictionary on which this section is based is *Webster's Students Dictionary* (1953). The material will be found to apply to any good student dictionary, but the teacher will do well to check the drills and tests with the book his students are using. The most noticeable differences among dictionaries are the differences in indicating pronunciation of words. The work in this book is based on the Webster system, since the Webster unabridged is the most frequently used in schools.

13a

If there might be some question as to the spelling or formation of the plural of a noun, the dictionary shows you how to spell the plural. *Gas*, for instance (see sample page), is spelled *gases* in the plural, not *gasses*. If the word is a verb, the past forms may offer a spelling problem. The past form of the verb *gas* is given, therefore. It is *gassed*, with two *s*'s.

2. *Capital Letters*

If you are in doubt as to whether a word is capitalized, the dictionary will help you. In the sample on page 287, the word *Gascon* is defined as "One of the natives of Gascony, in France, who were noted for boasting; hence [*not cap.*], a boaster." The [*not cap.*] means that when the word is used merely to mean a boaster, it should not be capitalized. "For what he said about his own successes, he was called a *gascon.*" But, when used to mean a native of Gascony, the word is capitalized as the dictionary shows.

3. *Syllables*

Sometimes, for purposes of dividing a word at the end of a line, you may wish to know how to split it up into syllables, for words should be divided only between syllables. The dictionary divides all words into syllables: *garrulous*, for instance (see sample page) is divided into three syllables — *gar ru lous.*

Between syllables the dictionary places a dot or a small dash unless there is an accent mark between the syllables. Do not confuse the dot (·) or small dash (-) which shows the syllables with the longer, heavier dash (–) which indicates a hyphen. The noun *go-between*, for instance, is hyphenated as indicated by the long dash. Between the second and third syllables only a dot is used to show the syllables: *go'–be·tween'.*

gar'ri·son (găr'ĭ·sŭn; -s'n), *n.* [OF. *garison*, fr. *garir;* see GARRET.] *Mil.* **a** A fortified place in which troops are quartered. **b** A body of troops stationed in a fort. — *v. t. Mil.* **a** To furnish with soldiers, as a fort. **b** To secure with fortresses, as a frontier.

gar·rote' (gă·rōt'; -rŏt') *or* **gar·rotte'** (-rŏt'), *n.* [Sp. *garrote*.] **1.** A Spanish method of execution by strangulation with an iron collar tightened by a screw; also, the collarlike device. **2.** Throttling as if with the garrote, esp. for robbery. — *v. t.;* -ROT'ED *or* -ROT'TED; -ROT'ING *or* -ROT'TING. To strangle with a garrote; hence, to throttle and rob.

gar·ru'li·ty (gă·rōō'lĭ·tĭ), *n.* Talkativeness.

gar'ru·lous (găr'ŭ·lŭs; -ōō·lŭs), *adj.* [L. *garrulus*, fr. *garrire* to chatter, talk.] Talking much, esp. about trifles; wordy. — **Syn.** See TALKATIVE. — **gar'ru·lous·ly**, *adv.* — **gar'ru·lous·ness**, *n.*

gar'ter (gär'tẽr), *n.* [ONF. *gartier*, fr. *garet* bend of the knee.] **1.** A band or strap worn to hold up a stocking. **2.** [*usually cap.*] The blue badge of the **Order of the Garter**, the highest order of British knighthood; also, this order or membership in it. — *v. t.* To bind or support with a garter.

garter snake. A harmless agile American snake with yellow stripes along the back.

gas (găs), *n.; pl.* GASES (-ĕz; -ĭz). [invented by the chemist Van Helmont of Brussels (d. 1644); — suggested by L. *chaos*, Gr. *chaos*, chaos.] **1.** An airlike fluid, having neither independent shape nor volume, but tending to expand indefinitely. **2.** In popular usage, any gaseous mixture except air; specif.: **a** Any gas used as an anesthetic. **b** Any combustible mixture of gases for illuminating or fuel. **3.** Any substance used to produce a poisonous atmosphere, as in warfare. **4.** *Slang.* Empty, boasting, or humbugging talk. **5.** *Colloq.* Gasoline. — *v. t.;* GASSED (găst); GAS'SING. **1.** To affect or treat with gas; as, to *gas* lime with chlorine in making bleaching powder; to poison with gas, esp. in warfare. **2.** To supply with gas. — *v. i.* **1.** To give off gas. **2.** *Slang.* To indulge in idle or empty talk.

Gas'con (găs'kŏn), *n.* [F.] One of the natives of Gascony, in France, who were noted for boasting; hence [*not cap.*], a boaster. — **Gas'con**, *adj.*

gas'con·ade' (găs'kŏn·ād'), *n.* [F. *gasconnade*.] A boast or boasting; bravado. — *v. i.* To boast.

gas'e·ous (găs'ē·ŭs; *Brit. usually* gā'zē·ŭs *or* gā'sē·ŭs), *adj.* **1.** In the form of, like, or relating to, gas. **2.** Lacking substance or solidity.

gas fitter. A workman who installs or repairs gas pipes.

gash (găsh), *v. t.* [fr. OF. *garser*, *jarser*, to scarify.] To make a long deep cut in. — *n.* A deep and long cut, esp. in flesh.

By permission. From Webster's Students Dictionary
Copyright, 1938, 1943, 1945, 1950, 1953
by G. & C. Merriam Co.

4. *Pronunciation*

The dictionary shows the correct pronunciation of a word. In order to show how a word is pronounced the dictionary uses markings, called *diacritical markings*, which indicate the sound of vowels, and it respells the word using certain consonants to mean certain sounds. Time and experience are required to master the dictionary's method of showing the correct pronunciation of a word. A pronunciation *key* is usually given at the bottom, or the top, of each page. Dictionaries differ somewhat in the marking system they use, but if you understand one system, you will probably be able to understand all of them. In the front part of some dictionaries there is a chapter on the whole subject of pronunciation, but this is usually too detailed to be of interest to the average person.

Your teacher may wish to have you learn the common pronunciation markings now so that in your dictionary practice you will be able to understand how to pronounce a word you have looked up. At your teacher's direction, you should turn to pages 294–97, where you will find a more detailed account of this subject and exercises to give you practice.

5. *The part of speech*

After each word listed in the dictionary, an abbreviation tells what part of speech the word is. These abbreviations are:

noun	*n.*	adverb	*adv.*	adjective	*adj.*
verb	*v.*	pronoun	*pron.*	preposition	*prep.*
		conjunction	*conj.*		
		interjection	*interj.*		

Since many words may be used as more than one part of speech, you will find the part of speech given before the definitions. Referring again to the sample page from a dictionary, you will see that *gas* is given first as a noun (*n.*). Then it is given as a transitive verb (*v.t.*) and then as an intransitive verb (*v.i.*)

6. *Derivation*

The derivation of a word is, briefly, the history of the word. The dictionary tells you either the origin of a word or the language from which a word has come. To indicate the languages, abbreviations are used. For instance, *L* means Latin; *F*, French; *AS*, Anglo-Saxon, etc. The meaning of other abbreviations can be found by consulting the page of "Abbreviations Used in This Dictionary," which appears usually in the front of the book.

A glance at *garrulous* on the sample page will show you how derivation is indicated. There you see that the word is derived from the Latin adjective *garrulus*, which in turn is formed from the Latin verb *garrire*, meaning *to chatter, to talk*. Hence the meaning of *garrulous* is "Talking much, especially about trifles; wordy."

The dictionary gives other types of information about the origin of words. The word *gas*, you are informed, was "invented by the chemist Von Helmont of Brussels," who died in 1644. It was suggested to him by the Latin word *chaos*, which in turn was based on the Greek word *chaos*.

7. *Meaning*

The basic purpose of a dictionary is to give the meanings of words. You understand this well enough. You should realize, however, that most words have many different meanings; and since the dictionary gives them all, you must seek out the particular definition you are looking for. *Gas*, as a noun, has five meanings. These are indicated by number. The verb *gas* has two meanings. The dictionary from which the excerpt on page 287 is taken usually places the oldest meaning first. Because this old meaning is not necessarily the meaning you are looking for, you will have to run your eye over the many definitions until you find the one that fits the sentence in which you have found the word. Some dictionaries list the meanings in the order of their use, the most common meaning being given first.

8. *Slang, Colloquial, Obsolete, etc.*

Gas in its fourth meaning is labeled *slang*. The word may be used to mean "empty, boasting, or humbugging talk." People do use it this way commonly, but the dictionary tells you that the word, used in this sense, is not considered good usage. It is slang.

Used to mean gasoline (fifth meaning) *gas* is *colloquial*, which means that the word is used this way in conversation and informal writing, but not in formal speech or writing.

A word marked *obs.* is no longer in common use; it is *obsolete*.

There are many other special classes of words; for example: *archaic* (old-fashioned), *Mil.* (military meaning limited to military use), *Gram.* (grammar), *Bib.* (Biblical), *Dial.* (dialect), etc.

9. *Synonyms and Antonyms*

For some entries in the dictionary synonyms or antonyms, or both, are given. A synonym is a word having nearly the same meaning as the word being defined: *brave — courageous*. An antonym is a word having the opposite meaning: *brave — cowardly*.

Sometimes when there is only a slight difference in meaning among several words, the dictionary explains these shades of meaning, as shown in the sample dictionary entry that follows:

Syn. Gaze, gape, stare, glare, glower, peer, gloat. **Gaze** implies prolonged attention, esp. as in wonder. **Gape** implies stupid and openmouthed wonder; **stare**, esp. insolence or vacant fixedness; **glare**, fierceness or anger; **glower**, scowling ill temper. To **peer** is to look curiously, esp. through or from behind something. To **gloat** is to gaze with profound, often malignant, satisfaction.

10. *Illustrations*

If the meaning of a word can best be shown by a picture, the dictionary may give an illustration. While you, of course, cannot depend on finding a picture of the thing you may be looking up, there is a chance that you might find one, especially if the object cannot be easily described.

WHAT THE DICTIONARY TELLS ABOUT FAMOUS PERSONS

Who was Clara Barton? When did Edison die? What was Chopin's nationality? What were the dates of Queen Elizabeth's reign? For what is Anthony Van Dyck famous? What was George Eliot's real name? How do you pronounce Hippocrates? The answers to such simple fact questions about famous persons can probably be found in your dictionary.

Some dictionaries devote a special section to famous persons. It is called a *Biographical Dictionary*. Others give names of persons and places in a section called *Proper Names*. Sometimes these names are included in the body of the book. You can easily discover which method your dictionary uses.

The following common pieces of biographical information are usually given in a dictionary:

1. *Name:* spelling, pronunciation, first name.
2. *Dates:* of birth and death and of reign if a king or queen, or term of office if head of a government.
3. *Nationality*
4. *Why famous*

The following is a typical dictionary entry for a famous person.

> **Byrd** (bûrd), Richard Evelyn, 1888–   .
> American rear admiral and explorer. Airplane flights over North Pole (1926), South Pole (1929).

By permission. From Webster's Students Dictionary
Copyright, 1938, 1943, 1945, 1950, 1953
by G. & C. Merriam Co.

Mythological and Biblical, as well as some literary characters, are usually listed in the body of the dictionary: *Odysseus, Lancelot, Naomi, Romeo, etc.*

WHAT THE DICTIONARY TELLS
ABOUT PLACES

Like the biographical entries in the dictionary, the geographical entries are sometimes given in the body of the book and sometimes in a special section. This section may be called a gazetteer — a geographical dictionary.

In general the following information is given about a place:

1. *Name:* spelling, pronunciation.
2. *Identification:* whether a city, country, lake, mountain, river, etc.
3. *Location.*
4. *Size:* population, if a city or country (usually given in thousands — 225 = 225,000); area in square miles, if a country or territory or body of water; length, if a river; height, if a mountain, etc.
5. *Importance:* If a city is the capital of a state or country,

this will be indicated by a star or an asterisk. The capital city of a country or state will also be given under the name of the country or state.

6. *Historical or other interesting information of importance:* Thus for Hampton Roads, Virginia . . . "battle of *Merrimac* and *Monitor,* March 9, 1862." For Lake Mead, formed by Hoover Dam in the Colorado River, the dictionary says "the largest man-made lake in the world."

7. *Governed or controlled by what country:* For Wake Island, the dictionary says "belongs to U.S.A."

OTHER INFORMATION IN THE DICTIONARY

Most good dictionaries include the following kinds of information, either in separate sections or in the body of the dictionary itself.

1. *Foreign words and phrases:* spelling, pronunciation, meaning.

2. *Abbreviations:* a list of abbreviations of all kinds, giving the words in full.

An unabridged dictionary and some of the larger student dictionaries include:

3. *Signs and symbols:* Not all dictionaries include a section of this kind, but some do, and if yours does, you should study the section to familiarize yourself with its contents.

4. *Spelling rules*
5. *Punctuation rules*
6. *New words*

● SPEED AND ACCURACY TEST A. When your teacher gives the signal, look up the answers to the following questions in the dictionary you have. Write the answers on your paper. Accuracy is more important than speed, but speed *is* important. Your speed will show to some extent your knowledge of the dictionary.

1. Who was Nebuchadnezzar? (Biblical)
2. When did Shakespeare live?

3. Give the meaning of the abbreviation B. P. O. E.
4. Write out the pronunciation and the meaning of the Latin phrase *carpe diem.*
5. Who was Arachne? (mythology)
6. What is the derivation of *curfew?*
7. What is the height of Mt. McKinley? Where is it?
8. What is the area of Lake Michigan?
9. What is the capital of Albania?
10. What country owns the Azores?

● SPEED AND ACCURACY TEST B.   At the direction of your teacher look up in your dictionary the answers to the following questions.

1. Give the pronunciation and meaning of *laissez faire.*
2. Who was Persephone? (mythology)
3. Give the preferred pronunciation of *ration.*
4. Of what country is Bangkok the capital?
5. What is the population of Buenos Aires?
6. What is the length of the Danube River?
7. What is the derivation of *calculate?*
8. What country governs Sicily?
9. Who was Sir John Falstaff? (literature)
10. What is the meaning of the abbreviation *ms.?*

13b. Diacritical Marks and How to Read Them

VOWEL SOUNDS

The two commonest vowel sounds are indicated in the dictionary by the markings known as the *macron* and the *breve*.

The *macron* (⁻), the long, straight mark over a vowel, indicates that the vowel is pronounced as it is named. For instance, the name of the letter *a* is the sound of that letter when it is written ā as in *mācron* itself. Pronounce the following: ā, ē, ī, ō, ū. The sound of *u* is *yew* as in *cūbe*, not o͞o as in *co͞ol*.

The dotted macron (⁺) means that the sound is still that of the name of the letter, but in pronouncing the letter you speak somewhat more rapidly. The dot "shortens" the long sound a little: *ĕvent′*, *ôbey′*.

The *breve* (ˇ), pronounced *brēve*, is the curved mark over a vowel, and it indicates that the sound is "shortened." Study the sounds shown by the breve:

ă	ădd	ĭ	ĭll
ĕ	ĕnd	ŏ	ŏdd
	ŭ	ŭp	

While understanding the meaning of the macron and the breve will help you considerably to get the correct pronunciation of a word from the dictionary, you will need to know the markings used for other vowel sounds. To interpret these markings, all you need do is refer to the key which is printed at the bottom (sometimes at the top) of each page of the dictionary. This key is given below. Read aloud the key words, noting the markings as you do so.

āle, chăotic, câre, ădd, ȧccount, ärm, ȧsk, sofȧ; ēve, hẽre, ĕvent, ĕnd, silĕnt, makẽr; īce, ĭll, charĭty; ōld, ôbey, ôrb, ŏdd, sŏft, cŏnnect; fōōd, fŏŏt; out, oil; cūbe, ūnite, ûrn, ŭp, circŭs; menü;

By permission. From Webster's Students Dictionary
Copyright, 1938, 1943, 1945, 1950, 1953
by G. & C. Merriam Co.

CONSONANT SOUNDS

Whereas there are only five vowels in the language, there are twenty-one consonants. Most of these are pronounced just as they are named. A few, however, do present special difficulties, such as the sound of *th* in *th*en and in *th*in. Notice how these two sounds are shown in the key below.

chair; go; sing; then, thin; natŭre, verdŭre; K = ch in G. ich, ach; F. boꜰ; yet; zh = z in azure.

By permission. From Webster's Students Dictionary
Copyright, 1938, 1943, 1945, 1950, 1953
by G. & C. Merriam Co.

13b

Pronunciation markings not given in this key may be looked up in the "Guide to Pronunciation" in the front of the dictionary.

The dictionary uses respelling to indicate the sounds of some consonants. How does the dictionary show the difference in sound between *c* in **c**an and *c* in **c**ertain; between *g* in **g**erm and *g* in **g**ood; between *ch* in **ch**ain and *ch* in **ch**aracter; between *s* in loo**s**e and *s* in lo**s**e?

ACCENT

In words of several syllables, one syllable is accented or stressed more than the others. This accented syllable is shown by an accent mark (′) placed immediately after and above it. For instance, *be lieve′*, *de cide′*, *un doubt′ed ly*, etc. In long words there may be two accented syllables, one of which receives greater stress than the other. The accents of these two syllables are shown in the words *man′u fac′ture*, *gen′er a′tion*. The main, heavier accent is shown by the heavier accent mark. The secondary, lighter accent is indicated by the lighter accent mark. Some dictionaries use a double accent mark in light type (″) for the secondary accent: generation, *jĕn″ ĕr ā′ shŭn*.

Sometimes the same word may be accented in different ways, depending upon how the word is used. The listed words are examples of how the accent shifts when the words are used as different parts of speech.

com′pact (noun)	com pact′ (adjective)
con′duct (noun)	con duct′ (verb)
con′tent (noun)	con tent′ (adjective)
pro′test (noun)	pro test′ (verb)

The meaning may change completely with a change in accent: *ref'use, re fuse'*.

● EXERCISE 1. Using the key on page 295, write the vowel markings above the vowels in these common words. Place accent marks in the words of more than one syllable. Final silent *e*, of course, cannot be marked.

1. stop	11. un til
2. old	12. de cide
3. lame	13. re make
4. like	14. mo lest
5. rib	15. rob in
6. peek	16. al i bi
7. send	17. a long
8. use	18. sum mer
9. us	19. trop i cal
10. doom	20. look ing

● EXERCISE 2. Using the key, rewrite with diacritical markings, respelling, accents, etc., the following words as you think the dictionary might rewrite them to show their pronunciation. When you have finished, check your work with the dictionary.

1. guide	6. ac tive
2. Cu pid	7. mi crobe
3. rul er	8. pep per mint
4. pan cake	9. in ten tion
5. cir cus	10. book mark

● EXERCISE 3. The words on page 298 are frequently mispronounced. Look up the pronunciation of each in a dictionary and copy each word onto your paper with the diacritical markings as shown in the dictionary.

Practice pronouncing the word yourself. Your teacher will tell you whether you have read the

markings correctly. Note the meaning of any unfamiliar words.

A

1. arctic	6. coupon
2. bade	7. grimy
3. cache	8. often
4. café	9. ogre
5. chasm	10. via

B

1. admirable	6. mischievous
2. condolence	7. municipal
3. gigantic	8. museum
4. height	9. preferable
5. infamous	10. theater

C

1. athlete	6. diphtheria
2. bicycle	7. genuine
3. biography	8. government
4. blackguard	9. Italian
5. culinary	10. stomach

● EXERCISE 4. Ability to understand the pronunciation markings will be valuable to you. Through
no other means will you be able to learn from the
dictionary how to pronounce a word. The following
exercise will test your ability to read dictionary
markings. The exercise assumes that you know the
correct pronunciation of the words; it is designed
merely to test your ability to interpret the markings.

Of the pronunciations written after each word,
one is correct. Try pronouncing each as it is marked.
Decide which is correctly marked.

1. because	bē kŭz′	bē kôz′	bē′kôz
2. hundred	hŭn′dĕrd	hŭn′drĕd	hŭn′dĕr ĕd
3. diploma	dĭp lō′má	dī plō′má	dĭ plō′má
4. pretty	pĕrt′ĭ	prĭt′ĭ	prĕt′ĭ

5. faucet	fä′sĕt	fä′sĕt	fô′sĕt
6. bicycle	bī′sĭk·'l	bī′sĭk·'l	bĭs′ĭk·'l
7. orchestra	ôr kĕs′trà	ôr′kĕs trĭ	ôr′kĕs trà
8. champion	chăm pē′ŭn	chăm pēn′	chăm′pĭ ŭn
9. perspiration	pûr′spĭ rā′shŭn		prĕs′pĭ rā′shŭn
10. experiment	ĕks pĕr′ĭ mĕnt		ĕks pûr′ĭ mănt

WORDS COMMONLY MISPRONOUNCED

The words in the following list are commonly mispronounced. The correct pronunciation of each is given here. By means of the diacritical markings, figure out how the word should be pronounced. Practice saying the word aloud, correctly.

Many of the words in the list below are included because, in pronouncing them, many persons enunciate poorly. *Enunciation means pronouncing with distinctness.* Such errors as "jography" and "jometry" for *jē·ŏg′rà·fĭ* and *jē·ŏm′ē·trĭ* are errors in enunciation rather than in pronunciation. As you know, pronunciation refers to letter sounds and accent. Study the meaning of any unfamiliar words.

across à·krŏs′
alias ā′lĭ·ăs
almond ä′mŭnd
alumnae à·lŭm′nē
alumni à·lŭm′nī
architect är′kĭ·tĕkt
arctic ärk′tĭk
athlete ăth′lēt
attacked ă·tăkt′
auxiliary ôg·zĭl′yà·rĭ

bade băd
because bē·kôz′
blackguard blăg′ärd
cabaret kăb′à·rā′
cache kăsh

café kă·fā′
calliope kă·lī′ō·pē
cello chĕl′ō
cement sē·mĕnt′
champion chăm′pĭ·ŭn

chasm kăz'm
column kŏl′ŭm
combatant kŏm′bà·tănt
communiqué kŏ·mū′nĭ·kā′
comparable kŏm′pà·rà·b'l
coupon koo′pŏn
creek krēk
culinary kū′lĭ·nĕr′ĭ
deaf dĕf
diphtheria dĭf·thēr′ĭ·à

discretion dĭs·krĕsh′ŭn

docile dŏs′ĭl

drowned dround

elm ĕlm

extraordinary ĕks·trôr′dĭ-
nĕr′ĭ

faucet fô′sĕt

film fĭlm

futile fū′tĭl

genuine jĕn′ū·ĭn

geography jē·ŏg′rȧ·fĭ

geometry jē·ŏm′ē·trĭ

gesture jĕs′tūr

gibberish jĭb′ĕr·ĭsh

gigantic jī·găn′tĭk

grimy grīm′ĭ

handkerchief hăng′kĕr-
chĭf

height hīt

impious ĭm′pĭ·ŭs

incomparable ĭn·kŏm′pȧ-
rȧ·b'l

indicted ĭn·dīt′ĕd

infamous ĭn′fȧ·mŭs

influence ĭn′flŏŏ·ĕns

Italian ĭ·tăl′yȧn

italics ĭ·tăl′ĭks

just jŭst

length lĕngth

library lī′brĕr·ĭ

mischievous mĭs′chĭ·vŭs

mortgage môr′gĭj

municipal mū·nĭs′ĭ·pȧl

museum mū·zē′ŭm

pathos pā′thŏs

perhaps pĕr·hăps′

perspiration pûr·spĭ·rā′-
shŭn

poem pō′ĕm

preferable prĕf′ĕr·ȧ·b'l

probably prŏb′ȧ·blĭ

raspberry răz′bĕr·ĭ

recognize rĕk′ŏg·nīz

scion sī′ŭn

solace sŏl′ĭs

stipend stī′pĕnd

strength strĕngth

suite swēt

superfluous sū·pûr′flŏŏ·ŭs

telegraphy tē·lĕg′rȧ·fĭ

theater thē′ȧ·tĕr

wrestle rĕs″l

● EXERCISE 5. *Oral Drill.* Practice reading the following sentences aloud, correctly pronouncing the italicized words.

1. Turning off the *faucet*, I *futilely* tried to understand the *gibberish* of the *mischievous* child.

2. *Across* the street under an *elm* tree stood an *infamous wrestler;* he made foolish *gestures* with a *grimy handkerchief.*

3. *Just* as the *architect* arrived at the *theatre* to see the *film*, I *recognized* him.

4. The *incomparable poem* was of *extraordinary length;* many words were in *italics.*

5. *Perhaps* the *deaf* and *impious blackguard drowned* in the *creek,* but he was *probably* a victim of the *diphtheria* epidemic.

6. *Solace* is *preferable* to *strength.*

7. In the first *column* is an account of the *influence* of the *champion's superfluous* remarks upon the *Italian's* decision.

8. I have an *idea* that he went to the *library* to study *geography* and *geometry.*

9. Covered with *perspiration,* he continued to *wrestle.*

10. The *architect* was not *interested* in *telegraphy.*

13c. How a Library Is Organized

Since a library is a collection of books on all sorts of subjects, there must be a method of organizing or arranging these books so that it will be easy to find any volume you want.

FICTION

In most libraries fiction books (novels and stories) are arranged alphabetically by the authors' names, and the books are placed on the shelves in this alphabetical order. If you wish to find a novel by John Tunis, you will find out first on which shelves the fiction books are standing. Then you will locate the books whose authors' names begin with T, and among these you will find the books by Tunis.

NONFICTION: THE DEWEY DECIMAL SYSTEM

But books of fiction are only a part of the total quantity of books in a library, and the other books (nonfiction) are arranged according to a number system. Most libraries today arrange their books according to the Dewey system, a system developed by Melvil Dewey, an American librarian. Anyone

13c

who wishes to find his way around a library using the Dewey system of classifying books should be familiar with the general nature of that system. Whenever a new book is added to the library, the librarian writes on the back of the book its proper number. As a result, all books on the same subject will be placed together, making it easy for you, once you have found the proper number of the subject you are looking up, to find all the books the library owns on this subject. For example, all books about aviation are given the number 629.1.

According to the Dewey system, all books are grouped in ten subject classes. The classifications with the numbers that stand for them are as follows:

000–099	General Works (includes encyclopedias, periodicals, etc.)
100–199	Philosophy (includes psychology, conduct, etc.)
200–299	Religion (includes mythology)
300–399	Social Sciences (includes economics, government, law, etc.)
400–499	Language (includes dictionaries, grammars, etc.)
500–599	Science (includes mathematics, chemistry, physics, etc.)
600–699	Useful Arts (includes agriculture, engineering, aviation, etc.)
700–799	Fine Arts (includes sculpture, painting, music, etc.)
800–899	Literature (includes poetry, plays, orations, etc.)
900–909 930–999 }	History
910–919	Travel
920–929	Biography

The Subdivisions

Within each of these classifications there is an unlimited number of subdivisions. As an example of how the numbering is done, let's take a book of poetry by the American poet, Robert Frost, and see how it would be classified. Poetry falls in the 800 (literature) classification. Since the numbers 810–819 are reserved for American literature, the book's number will begin with the two digits 81. The third digit in the number indicates the classification of the book — in this case, poetry. The number for poetry is the number 1, and so with this added to the number 81, the classification number becomes 811. (Small libraries class American and English poetry together under 821, the classification number for English poetry.) Added to this is the letter F, for Frost. Your librarian can explain further details of this remarkable, but complex, system of classifying books; the principal facts given here are enough to show you how the system works.

The Call Number

The number by which the book is classified is known as the *call number*. To find the call number of a book you look up the book in the card catalog. The call number is located in the upper left hand corner of the catalog card.

The call number is useful to you in two ways.

1. You can find out where on the library shelves the books of any particular number classification are located. By going at once to the shelves containing books with the number of the one you want, you can, in a few moments of looking along the shelves, find your book.

2. In a large library where books are kept in the "stacks" so that you cannot look for the book yourself, you tell the librarian the call number of the book you want, and he will send for it.

13d. How to Locate a Book in the Library: The Card Catalog

In every library there is a chest of small drawers containing cards. These cards represent the books in the library. In the average well-indexed library there are usually three cards for each book. They are the *author card*, the *title card*, and the *subject card*.

THE AUTHOR CARD

The author card, as its name suggests, has the author's name at the top. You may find any book by looking it up under the author's name, and this way of locating the book has the added advantage of leading to all the books the library owns by this author. For instance, if you have read one book by Robert Louis Stevenson and you would like to know what other books of his the library owns, you will find cards for all of them arranged in alphabetical order of their titles, all with "Stevenson, Robert Louis" at the top of the card.

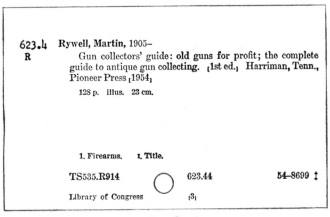

623.4	Rywell, Martin, 1905–
R	Gun collectors' guide: old guns for profit; the complete guide to antique gun collecting. ₁1st ed.₁ Harriman, Tenn., Pioneer Press ₁1954₁
	128 p. illus. 23 cm.

1. Firearms.   ɪ. Title.

TS535.R914   623.44   54–8699 ‡

Library of Congress   ₁3₁

Author Card

Biographies are arranged on the shelves according to the person they are written about. Cards for books *about* an author are placed in the catalog *behind* the cards for books written *by* this author.

THE TITLE CARD

At the top of the title card is the title of the book. If you wish to find out whether a certain book is in your library and what its call number is, you may thumb through the card catalog in which title cards are alphabetically placed. In its proper alphabetical position as determined by the first word of the title, you will find the card. (If the first word of the title should be *the*, *an*, or *a*, the book will be listed under the second word in the title.)

Much useful information is given on a card in the card catalog. Not only can you find the call number and the author's name, but sometimes the date of his birth (and death), and occasionally a very brief statement about what is in the book. Often the card will also tell you the number of pages in the book

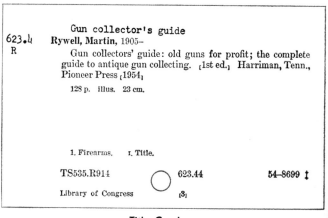

Title Card

and the illustrator, if the book is illustrated. You can also find the name of the publisher and the date the book was published.

THE SUBJECT CARD

Books are also catalogued according to the subjects they deal with. If you want to find out what books your library has on model railroads, you could look up "Model Railroads" in the card catalog. There you will find in one place a card for each book in the library on this subject.

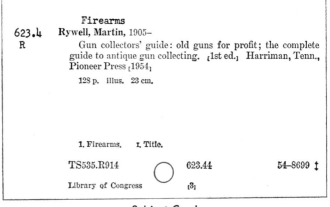

	Firearms
623.4	Rywell, Martin, 1905–
R	Gun collectors' guide: old guns for profit; the complete guide to antique gun collecting. ₁1st ed.₁ Harriman, Tenn., Pioneer Press ₁1954₁
	128 p. illus. 23 cm.

1. Firearms.   ɪ. Title.

TS535.R914   623.44   54–8699 ‡

Library of Congress   ₁3₁

Subject Card

"SEE" AND "SEE ALSO" CARDS

Occasionally when using the card catalog you will find what is known as a "see" card or a "see also" card. A "see" card is one which refers you to another part of the catalog for the information you are seeking. For instance, suppose that you are looking up material on various vocations. You look for a subject card marked "Vocations." Perhaps the card will say "see *Occupations.*" This means that books in your library on the subject of vocations are catalogued under the subject heading "Occupations."

A "see also" card refers you to other subjects closely related to the one you are looking up. If, for example, you should be looking up "radar," you might find a card saying "see also *Electronics*." Looking under electronics, which is a subject to which radar is closely related, you would quite possibly find more books of help to you.

SUMMARY

The card catalog, then, is the place to find out what books the library owns. Since books are catalogued in three ways (by title, author, and subject) you can use the catalog as follows:

1. To find out whether a certain book is in the library.

2. To look up the call number of a book whose title you know.

3. To look up the call number of a book whose author you know.

4. To look up call numbers or titles of other books by an author one of whose books you have enjoyed.

5. To find out what books on a certain subject the library owns.

6. To find the publisher, date of publication, and a general idea of the contents of a book, provided, of course, the book is in the library.

● EXERCISE 6.   Remembering that books are catalogued by title, author, and subject, answer the following questions by using the card catalog in your library.

1. Does the library have these books?
   Life with Father
   A Tale of Two Cities
   Life on the Mississippi
   Robinson Crusoe

2. Does your library have any books written by Eugene O'Neill, Pearl Buck, Charles Lamb, James Fenimore Cooper? If so, write the title of one book by each author.
3. Look up one of your favorite books of fiction. Give the title and the author, the publisher, and the date of publication.
4. List three books the library owns on aviation. Give the call numbers.
5. List two books in the library about Abraham Lincoln. Give titles, authors, and call numbers.

13e. How to Find Magazine Articles: *The Readers' Guide to Periodical Literature*

To locate a magazine article on any subject, you use a most valuable book known as the *Readers' Guide to Periodical Literature*. The *Readers' Guide* indexes all the articles, poems, and stories in more than 100 magazines. A list of these magazines is given in the front of the *Readers' Guide*. The *Readers' Guide* is kept so closely up to date that every two weeks your librarian receives copies of the *Readers' Guide* for magazines published only a few weeks before. Furthermore, the *Readers' Guide* has been published since 1900, so that by using back volumes of it, you can find what articles have been published on a subject over a period of many years. It is published every two weeks from September through June, and monthly in July and August. Every year the numbers are combined into one volume, and every three years into a larger volume.

The *Readers' Guide* lists magazine articles by subjects and authors. It gives information about each magazine article listed, using abbreviations which are easy to read. A key to these abbreviations is given in the front of the *Readers' Guide*.

Study the sample entries on page 310 taken

from the *Readers' Guide*. Can you "read" the abbreviations? Stories are listed in the *Readers' Guide* by title as well as by author. Poems are listed by title under the general heading POEMS, and by authors.

"See" and "see also" references are used in the *Readers' Guide*, just as they are used in the card catalog. See page 306.

Of course, finding out what articles have been published on a certain topic will be of little help to you unless you can get the magazine in which the articles appeared. Whether you can do so depends upon whether your library takes the magazine and whether it keeps back numbers of it. Usually you will find on or near the *Readers' Guide* table in your library a list of the magazines which the library takes. The list will tell you, too, whether back numbers are available and if they are, exactly which ones.

● EXERCISE 7. Using the *Readers' Guide* in your school or town library, look up the answers to the following questions.

1. Choose one of these topics and look up in the *Readers' Guide* three recent articles on it. Give complete information: title and author (if given), magazine, date, page numbers.

   The U.S. Armed Forces   Atomic Power   Cookery
   Medical Research   The U.N.   Sports

2. List the titles and authors of those articles you found in Question 1 which can be found in your library.
3. Select a prominent government figure — the President, Vice-President, Secretary of State, Ambassador to England, etc., and find in the *Readers' Guide* an article about him. On your paper copy the listing from the *Readers' Guide*.
4. Suppose you are writing an essay on Dwight Eisenhower. How many articles about him were published

13e

Sample Excerpt from Readers' Guide [2]

JACK, Homer A.
  Bandung in perspective. For Policy Bul 34:
  189-92 S 1 '55
JACKS
  How's your pioneer instinct? wagon jack. B.
  Bridges. il Sat Eve Post 228:128 O 22 '55
JACKSON, Janet
  Crucial year in school. Parents Mag 30:40+
  N '55
JACKSON, William Harding
  People of the week. U S News 39:16 O 14 '55
JACOBS, Elijah L.
  Word to Emily; poem. Sat Eve Post 228:125
  O 22 '55
JACOBSON, Ethel
  First man doesn't have a chance; poem. Look
  19:136 N 1 '55
  Hunters of the dusk; poem. Sat R 38:21 O 22
  '55
JAFFRAY, Norman R.
  Routine; poem. Sat Eve Post 228:40 O 22 '55
JAGUAR hunting
  Tigre of Momotombo. F. C. Hibben. il Out-
  door Life 116:48-9+ N '55
JAI-alai. See Pelota (game)
JAMES, Lewis
  Favorite pioneer recording artists. J. Walsh.
  il pors Hobbies 60:30-2+ O '55
JAMES, Selwyn
  I.Q. test for babies. McCalls 83:8-10 N '55
JAPAN
                Foreign relations
                  United States
  Japan and the h-bomb. H. Passin. Bul Atomic
  Sci 11:289-92 O '55
JAPAN and the United States
  Interim report on the maidens. N. Cousins.
  Sat R 38:22-3 O 15 '55
  Japan and the h-bomb. H. Passin. Bul Atomic
  Sci 11:289-92 O '55
  Thoughts on the new Asia. T. Aikawa. Chris-
  tian Cent 72:1172-4 O 12 '55
  Young ladies of Japan; Hiroshima maidens.
  il Time 66:53 O 24 '55
JARMAN, Rufus
  Big business is stage-struck. Sat Eve Post
  228:18-19+ O 22 '55
JARRELL, Randall
  Recent poetry. Yale R 45 no 1:122-32 [S] '55
JAZZ music
  Few false notes at Newport. R. Maren. il Re-
  porter 13:41-4 S 8 '55; Discussion. 13:7 O 20
  '55
JEFFERSON, Thomas
  Feast days at Monticello. M. Kimball. il por
  McCalls 83:42-7+ N '55

[2] Reproduced by permission of the H. W. Wilson Company.

last year? List them and give the information from the *Readers' Guide.*

5. How many articles on fishing are listed in the volume of the *Readers' Guide* you are using?

13f. Reference Books in the Library

In every library there is a section known as the reference section. Here the librarian keeps together those ready reference volumes which are designed to help you look up brief articles giving various kinds of information. You will find acquaintance with certain of these reference books to be very valuable.

SPECIAL DICTIONARIES

Belonging to the reference section of a library are various dictionaries of the English language such as those described on pages 285–293. In addition, there are many special dictionaries written to help you with specific problems of word choice, correct usage, etc. Very often a writer has some trouble thinking of the exact word with which to express his meaning. Often, too, he has used the same word so many times in a composition that he wishes to find a synonym for it to avoid repeating. The two books listed here, as their names suggest, will help a writer to find the words he needs.

Roget's *Thesaurus of English Words and Phrases*

A *thesaurus* is a collection. The word is derived from a Latin word meaning *treasure*, so that literally a thesaurus is a treasury or storehouse. Roget's *Thesaurus* is a book of synonyms. The latest edition is arranged in alphabetical order

13f

Webster's *Dictionary of Synonyms*

This book is especially valuable in explaining the fine differences in meaning between words whose meanings are somewhat, though not exactly, alike.

ENCYCLOPEDIAS

As you have already discovered, an encyclopedia is a collection of articles, arranged in alphabetical order, on almost all subjects in the many fields of knowledge. It is useful to you especially in looking up information for history, science, and English classes. Biographies of great men of the past, historical events, information on countries, cities, etc., industrial and scientific processes — these are only a few of the subjects for which the encyclopedia is usually consulted.

Finding a Reference in the Encyclopedia

Use the guide letters and the index to find an encyclopedia article. You may find an article in an encyclopedia in much the same way that you find a word in the dictionary; that is, by looking it up in its alphabetical position, using the guide words at the top of the page. Since encyclopedias consist of many volumes, guide letters are printed on the back of each volume. However, there may be several articles in an encyclopedia which would be of use to you in your search for material on a certain subject. Arranged alphabetically, these articles would appear under different subject headings at different places in the various volumes. In the index of the *Encyclopedia Americana*, for example, you will find that there are articles on rockets in eleven of the thirty volumes. You probably would not have found all of these, if you had merely looked under "Rockets" in the R volume. But using the index, you found them listed all together. To do a thorough job and to save time, use the index of an encyclopedia. If an encyclopedia has an index, you will find it in the last volume or at the back of each volume.

How Encyclopedias Are Kept Up to Date

Most encyclopedias, like dictionaries, are rewritten and revised continuously. Probably, however, the encyclopedias in your library were published several years ago. This does not mean that you cannot find up-to-date information in an encyclopedia, for some encyclopedias publish each year an *Annual* or *Yearbook* containing articles in all fields of knowledge on important events which occurred during the past year. If your library buys any of these yearbooks, you will find them useful additions to the wealth of information in the encyclopedia itself.

The following encyclopedias are the best-known:

GENERAL ENCYCLOPEDIAS

Encyclopedia Americana
    30 volumes
    Index in Volume 30
    Publishes the *Americana Annual*

Encyclopædia Britannica
    24 volumes
    Index and atlas in Volume 24
    Publishes *Britannica Book of the Year*

Collier's Encyclopedia
    20 volumes
    Bibliography and index in Volume 20
    Publishes *Collier's Yearbook*

Compton's Pictured Encyclopedia

15 volumes

One third of space is devoted to pictures

Fact index (an index which itself gives information) at
end of each volume

Yearbook and annual supplement

World Book Encyclopedia

19 volumes

Reading and Study Guide in Volume 19

Publishes an *Annual*

BIOGRAPHICAL REFERENCE BOOKS

There are many reference books, besides the
standard encyclopedias, which will give biographies
of important persons.

Dictionary of American Biography

This twenty-volume set contains excellent lives of
famous Americans no longer living.

Current Biography

Published monthly in pamphlet form, *Current
Biography* is the best source of information about
persons prominent in the news. The monthly pamphlets are bound into a book each year. By using the
cumulative index in each issue, you can locate
biographies of persons in the news in previous months.
There are frequently pictures of the persons whose
lives are given.

Who's Who and *Who's Who in America*

These are important volumes giving only the main
facts about famous *living* persons. *Who's Who* contains
information about famous Englishmen and some
world figures from countries other than England.

Who's Who in America contains information about famous Americans. Parentage, dates, positions held, principal achievements, books written, names of members of family, and present address are the sort of information given about a man or woman in the *Who's Who* volumes. Remember that these particular books contain information on *living* persons only and that they give only the essential facts of a person's life. *Who's Who* is published annually; *Who's Who in America* is published every two years.

REFERENCE BOOKS ABOUT AUTHORS

If your library has any of the "authors" books by Kunitz, you will find them valuable sources of "human-interest" information about authors. So far as possible, these books contain a picture of each author.

Authors Today and Yesterday, by Stanley J. Kunitz
The Junior Book of Authors, by Stanley J. Kunitz and Howard Haycraft [About authors of juvenile literature.]
British Authors of the Nineteenth Century, by Kunitz and Haycraft
American Authors 1600–1900, by Kunitz and Haycraft
Twentieth Century Authors, by Kunitz and Haycraft
Twentieth Century Authors; First Supplement, by Kunitz and Haycraft

ATLASES

You should know where in the library the atlases are kept, and you should take time to familiarize yourself with at least one good atlas. An atlas is much more than just a book of maps. It contains a vast amount of information about the cities and countries of the world. Population, resources, industries, natural wonders, climate, exports and imports, history, and many other kinds of information are easily found in an atlas. One or more of the following atlases are commonly found in high school libraries.

Collier's World Atlas and Gazetteer
Goode's World Atlas
Hammond's Standard World Atlas
Rand McNally–Cosmopolitan World Atlas
The Britannica Atlas

ALMANACS

For factual information on the world today, the most useful of all reference books in your library are almanacs, such as *The World Almanac and Book of Facts* and *Information Please Almanac.*

Published annually, these books are full of information and statistics on current events. They contain much of historical interest, too: historical facts, dates, statistics, prominent people, sports records, etc. A principal feature of both is an account of the major events of the past year. The *World Almanac* has an index in the front; the *Information Please Almanac* has an index in the back. You should become well acquainted with one or the other of these handy volumes.

LITERATURE REFERENCE BOOKS

Bartlett's *Familiar Quotations*

Most famous of all "quotation books," Bartlett's *Familiar Quotations* is useful when you wish the following information: (1) the author of a quotation; (2) the source or literary work in which a quotation appeared; (3) the complete quotation of which you know only a part; (4) a few famous lines from any author.

This book is arranged chronologically by authors and contains alphabetical indexes of authors and quotations. To find a number of quotations from an author, you look up his name in the alphabetically arranged author index in the front of the book, then turn to the page where quotations from this author are given. If you know the quotation or a part of it and wish to find its author or the full quotation, you will use the index in the back of the book. This index is arranged alphabetically by the first word of the quotation. For instance, if you wish to find out who said

> "The night has a thousand eyes,
> The day but one . . ."

you would look under the word *night*.

Stevenson's *Home Book of Quotations*

Used for somewhat the same purpose as Bartlett's book, Stevenson's *Home Book of Quotations* is, however, arranged differently. The quotations in this book are arranged by subjects. You can also find the author of a quotation, although, since the book is not arranged by authors, you will find the book less efficient for this purpose than Bartlett's. Stevenson's book is especially helpful if you want a quotation on a certain subject. For instance, if you want one on *love* or *happiness* or *Christmas*, you will find many listed under each of those topics.

Granger's *Index to Poetry and Recitations*

Granger's *Index* contains no poems or recitations. It tells you in what books you can find almost any poem or recitation (popular prose passage) you wish. If you know the title of a poem or its author, yet do not know in what books you will find the poem, look it up in Granger's. There you will find a list of books in which the poem can be found. By checking this list with the books in your library (use the card catalog), you will probably find that one or more of these books are available in your library. Since the titles of the books containing the poem you want are not written out in Granger's *Index* but are abbreviated to save space, you will have to refer to the list of abbreviations in the front of the book to find the title. Thus you might find that a poem you want is in a book entitled *Best Loved Poems of the American People*. Granger's refers to this book by the abbreviation BLPA. Granger's *Index* also contains listings of poems according to subjects. Since most poems and poets are listed in Granger's *Index*, the book is also a good place to find out who wrote a certain poem. Remember that Granger's *Index* will help you find a poem, but it does not itself contain any poems.

Stevenson's *Home Book of Verse* and Stevenson's *Home Book of Modern Verse*

These books contain well-known poems. Since the volumes are so large, you stand a fairly good chance of finding in them the poem you wish. At any rate you may save yourself time, when you are hunting for a poem, by looking in Stevenson first. The books are indexed in three ways: by author, by title, and by first line. The poems are classified under general headings; for instance, Poems of Youth and Age, Love Poems, Poems of Nature, Familiar Verse, and Poems, Humorous and Satiric. This classification helps you when you want a poem on a certain subject, but have no single poem or author in mind.

● EXERCISE 8. Your teacher may assign you to give a brief description of those books in the following list with which he thinks you should be familiar.

Tell what sort of material the book contains, how the
material is arranged, and how to use the book.

SPECIAL DICTIONARIES

Roget's Thesaurus of English Words and Phrases
Webster's Dictionary of Synonyms

ENCYCLOPEDIAS

Collier's Encyclopedia
Compton's Pictured Encyclopedia
Encyclopedia Americana
Encyclopædia Britannica
World Book Encyclopedia

BIOGRAPHICAL REFERENCE BOOKS

GENERAL

Dictionary of American Biography
Current Biography
Who's Who
Who's Who in America

ABOUT AUTHORS

Authors Today and Yesterday
Junior Book of Authors
British Authors of the Nineteenth Century
American Authors 1600–1900
Twentieth Century Authors
Twentieth Century Authors; First Supplement

ATLASES

Hammond's Standard World Atlas
Goode's World Atlas
Britannica Atlas
Collier's World Atlas and Gazetteer
Rand McNally–Cosmopolitan World Atlas

ALMANACS

World Almanac and Book of Facts
Information Please Almanac

LITERATURE REFERENCE BOOKS

Bartlett's *Familiar Quotations*
Stevenson's *Home Book of Quotations*
Granger's *Index to Poetry and Recitations*
Stevenson's *Home Book of Verse*
Stevenson's *Home Book of Modern Verse*

● EXERCISE 9.   Disregarding dictionaries and encyclopedias, decide what reference book would be the best in which to look up the following. Number on your paper from 1 to 10 and after the corresponding number write the title of the reference book. It is not necessary to use the same answer twice.

1. A picture of the modern author Carl Sandburg
2. The national tennis champion in 1940
3. A biography of someone recently risen to prominence in the news
4. Facts about the president of a college in which you are interested
5. The poem "A Visit from St. Nicholas"
6. Several quotations from Shakespeare
7. A number of quotations about courage
8. The title of a book containing Vachel Lindsay's poem "The Congo"
9. A good, brief biography of Benjamin Franklin
10. The poem "Birches" by Robert Frost, a modern poet

● EXERCISE 10.   Disregarding dictionaries and encyclopedias, decide what reference book would be the best in which to look up the following. Number on your paper from 1 to 10 and after the corresponding number write the title of the reference book. It is not necessary to use the same answer twice.

1. An authoritative, brief biography of Stonewall Jackson
2. A list of the principal rivers of the world
3. Facts about the career of the British Prime Minister

4. Some interesting information about the modern author Sinclair Lewis
5. The rest of the quotation beginning "All the world's a stage . . ."
6. The author of the poem "The Charge of the Light Brigade"
7. A picture and biographical sketch of Walt Whitman, nineteenth-century American poet
8. The name of the Chief Justice of the United States Supreme Court
9. Other important positions that the Chief Justice has held
10. The titles of several books in which the poem beginning "The boy stood on the burning deck . . ." appears

● EXERCISE 11. Name the reference book *best suited* for use in getting the following information. You may include the dictionary and encyclopedia. Be prepared to explain your choices.

1. A list of words meaning *cold*
2. An authoritative description of the open-hearth method of making steel
3. A good brief account of the life of William Jennings Bryan
4. A *complete* explanation of the differences in meaning among these words commonly used interchangeably: *desire, wish, want, crave*
5. A list of Senators and Representatives
6. A number of pictures of Chicago
7. The year Bobby Jones was both National Open and National Amateur golf champion
8. A brief biography of Charles Dickens
9. The title of a poem in which these lines appear:

> "And what is so rare as a day in June?
> Then, if ever, come perfect days . . ."

10. The date of publication of Carl Sandburg's biography of Abraham Lincoln
11. The winner of the World Series in 1933

12. The height of Mt. Everest
13. The principal cities of Iran
14. The title of a book containing the poem "Casey at the Bat"
15. The meaning of the French phrase *raison d'être*
16. The capital of Vermont
17. Information about a man or woman prominent in the news recently
18. The titles of several books containing the poem "The Battle of Blenheim"
19. The source of the quotation "A little learning is a dangerous thing"
20. A number of humorous poems

CHAPTER 14

Narrative Writing

If you can tell lively stories about everyday experiences, then your daily conversation is probably interesting, worth listening to. These stories that your friends enjoy hearing can also make your written work interesting, worth reading. If you learn to write good stories, you can use entertaining, true narratives not only for informal friendly letters but also for convincing illustrations of main points in your compositions. Most important, by writing stories you can develop your talent for storytelling.

STEPS IN PLANNING AND WRITING A BRIEF NARRATIVE
1. Find a story to tell.
2. Decide upon a purpose.
3. Decide upon a few characters and present them realistically.
4. Consider the importance of the scene and the time of the action.
5. Organize the story.
6. Write an appropriate title.
7. Write the first draft.
8. Carefully revise the first draft.

14a. Find incidents that are suitable for narrative writing.

Many happenings are more suitable for novels than for brief narratives. For example, it would be absurd

14a

to try to write a complete account of the adventures of the baseball team at your school because to do so would require volumes, not pages. To reduce the subject so that you can cover it in a few pages, you would have to change your plan to concentrate on only one player and one important event. By selecting one incident with a central character — a game-winning double play or a game-losing strike-out with the bases full — you could treat the subject in a short narrative, the kind you will write during your study of this chapter. *Remember that a story must be brief: the action is necessarily limited to a small part of experience, a quick series of happenings, often to only a single crisis.*

In addition to being brief, a story must also present conflict; that is, the characters are involved in a struggle or a predicament of some kind. The struggle springs from the character's attempt to cope with or to overcome an obstacle, which may be physical or mental. The obstacle may be real or imaginary, external or internal — a boulder in one's path, a fantasy of the mind, or a guilty conscience. If you should write about a plain girl's efforts to be glamorous, about a boy who struggles to overcome a physical handicap, about a student who must pass an important test, then you would be presenting characters with problems that make for conflict in narrative.

In conversations at school, you often exchange stories about everyday occurrences. When a friend tells you of the trouble he has keeping his pet alligator in the family bathtub, you are reminded of the time you experimented with keeping a parakeet and a canary in the same cage. Your own experiences provide the best sources for good stories. Each day, if you will make original use of what you see, hear, and do, you can find many ideas for interesting narratives. Once you get an idea for a suitable story, set your imagination to work as you fill in important details and limit the scope of the action.

● EXERCISE 1.   Below are 10 general subjects for long narratives. Make each subject specific so that the action will be suitable for a short story.

EXAMPLE   **1. Family troubles**

        1. The day my brother disappeared

1. Life on a farm.
2. Last-minute touchdowns.
3. The story of my life.
4. An imaginary voyage around the world.
5. Memories of a happy childhood.
6. Unsolved mysteries.
7. Misfortunes of a sophomore.
8. The life and times of my grandfather.
9. Adventures at camp.
10. An autobiography of a hot rod.

● EXERCISE 2.   Find in newspapers at least 3 items about persons your age or about experiences you are familiar with that you think you could use as basic material for short narratives. Paste these clippings on a piece of paper, and bring them to class for discussion. Be prepared to explain (1) how you would limit the action, if necessary, (2) what details not in the news story you would supply, (3) how you would change the telling of the story to make it more interesting, and (4) what the central problem or conflict in your story would be.

● EXERCISE 3.   Before continuing in your study of this chapter, try your hand at writing a brief narrative. Select an interesting incident from your own experience or that of someone you know or have heard about. Limit your subject so that you can tell the story in 200 words or less. Writing this incident will help you to understand better the advice given on the following pages.

14b. Decide upon a definite purpose for telling your story.

Whenever you select a story to tell, ask yourself: *What single total effect do I want my story to have upon the reader?* Do I wish to amuse him? terrify him? Shall I arouse his sympathy? With a clear purpose in mind, you can not only select vivid details to produce the desired effect but can also establish a consistent tone or feeling to emphasize the one dominant impression that you want the story to make upon the reader.

● EXERCISE 4. On page 327 are incomplete summaries of four incidents, each of which could be used as the basis for a short story. Assume that you are to make a story out of each incident. In a sentence or two for each, state what your story purpose would be, what dominant impression you would want to make on the reader. In another sentence tell how you would end the story.

EXAMPLE   As a babysitter, Irene had to care for three unruly children. The baby cried for hours. The five-year-old girl, concerned about the health of her imaginary doll, insisted on telephoning the family doctor. The oldest child busied himself with taking the furniture apart to see if he could put it together again.

PURPOSE: To entertain the reader by showing how amusing babysitting can be. Make sure that the reader does not sympathize with Irene.

ENDING: The father and mother return and pay the babysitter, who tells them the children behaved perfectly; but before she leaves, the father sits in a chair which collapses under him, and the doctor arrives.

1. For the first time of the season, Jimmie, a second-string quarterback, has a chance to make a touchdown for the Eagles. The final minutes of the game are running out. On a fourth-down try, Jimmie fumbles the ball inches short of the goal line, and the Tigers recover.

2. On an all-night fishing trip with friends, Ned couldn't sleep because of singing mosquitoes. About midnight he arose and went down to the canoe, hoping to surprise everyone by catching a lot of fish. When he reached into the open bucket tied over the side of the canoe, he felt something very large splashing about among the minnows. Believing it to be a big fish, he tried unsuccessfully to catch it with his hands. Then he searched for a flashlight so that he could see better. Upon his return he saw a water moccasin coiled around the edge of the minnow bucket.

3. Legend has it that a horrible monster stalks the swamps of a certain area in Louisiana. One stormy night in that vicinity, two girls find shelter in an upstairs room of an old vacant mansion. Soon they hear a series of strange noises downstairs; next they hear something slowly making its way up the stairs. Suddenly a flash of lightning reveals a hairy, three-fingered hand upon the facing of the door.

4. After telling a Scotsman about how severe the drought was and about how badly the cattle needed water, a rancher tossed a dime down a dried-up crawfish hole. The Scotsman frantically started digging for it, and kept on digging.

14c. Decide upon a few characters and present them realistically.

(1) Each character should have a function in the story.

Too many characters in a narrative confuse the reader. As you choose your characters, make sure that each one has a reason for being in the story. Like the murderer in Poe's "Tell-Tale Heart," a character may act as the narrator of the action; or like Dr. Watson in Doyle's stories of Sherlock Holmes, he may be a listener so that the main character, through con-

14 b-c

versation, can set forth a problem and unravel a mystery. A character may also advance the action of the story by serving as an obstacle, or he may be in the story merely to help provide atmosphere. Whatever the function, be sure that you have a reason for each character.

(2) Describe characters vividly.

Real people think and act as individuals, each one having his own peculiarities and distinctive characteristics. As a writer, you should create a clear visual image of each individual in your story. Instead of merely talking *about* a personality, you should make the reader *see* him.

One way to make a character come alive is to describe him vividly. If your descriptions are sometimes dull, you may be using too many adjectives or trite comparisons.

DULL

Nell's hair is red, her eyes are blue, and her complexion is fair. She is attractive and popular. Her only bad habit is telling jokes as old as the hills.

The weak adjectives in this description do not make us see Nell. The comparison "as old as the hills" is lifeless; the writer ought to use more original similes, such as "as old as the pointed toes on great-grandmother's shoes."

As you read the following description, taken from *Oliver Twist* by Charles Dickens, notice how the comparison helps to make the reader see the character in action.

VIVID

As he glided stealthily along, creeping beneath the shelter of the walls and doorways, the hideous old man seemed like some loathsome reptile, engendered in the slime and darkness through which he moved: crawling forth, by night, in search of some rich offal for a meal.

This description creates a visual image. Although adjectives like *hideous* and *loathsome* are exact and full of meaning, it is verbs like *glided* and *crawling* that give the picture its vitality. The strongest words in the sentence are *reptile, slime, darkness,* all nouns. To write vivid description and to make your characters lifelike, use original comparisons and many nouns and verbs.

By telling what a person *does*, you can frequently *show* what he is. Notice in the following how actions can often tell as much about a character as descriptive statements can.

Description	*Action*
She is indeed a flirt.	At parties she winks and smiles at every boy who looks her way.
He was self-conscious and hesitant.	He ran his fingers through his hair and bit his lip nervously.
The frisky puppy was a very friendly animal.	Bouncing about the room, the puppy wagged his tail and barked for attention.

If you let the action speak for itself, the reader can not only see the events as they happen but can also become acquainted with a character as he lives.

Conversation also reveals character. Before you attempt to write natural dialogue, however, spend some time listening to people in real life as they carry on conversations. Notice how they say things and what they do while they are talking. Observe their expressions and habits of speech. As you start writing conversations, keep in mind the following requirements of natural dialogue.

(1) *The words should fit the character.* Let each character sound like himself. Should you quote your six-
year-old brother, do not give him the vocabulary and
the attitudes of a high school sophomore. If a messenger boy is talking, let him sound like a messenger boy,
not like a taxicab driver, a cowhand, or an English
teacher.

(2) *Long speeches are unnatural.* Orations are for political conventions or for conversational bores. In real life,
most persons make brief comments; they say what they
have to say in a few sentences, or pieces of sentences.
Even then, they are often interrupted by an impatient
listener. To write natural conversation, be brief.

If you attempt to report all of the conversation of a
character, your story will lose its focus and become
boring. Always remember to edit the conversation so
that it will (1) advance the action of your story and
(2) reveal the personality of the speaker. For instance,
if you are writing about an athlete trying to become a
good blocker, do not waste space by having him talk
about his girl friends or his desire to get a summer job.
Instead, let him talk enthusiastically about football
plays involving skillful blocking.[1]

● EXERCISE 5. Write a paragraph describing a
classmate. Make your characterization so lifelike that
the class can identify the person without your having
to use his name in your description.

● EXERCISE 6. Select a character and write a story
involving him in a predicament of some kind. You
may wish to build a story around someone you know —
a close friend, a favorite teacher, or an interesting
neighbor.

[1] For further work on characterization and dialogue, turn to "A
Character from Life" and "How They Do Talk" in the chapter
Planning a Composition, pages 267 and 277.

● EXERCISE 7. Listed below are groups of characters in specific situations. After choosing 1 out of the 7, write a conversation (about 150 words) that reveals the personality of each speaker. For this exercise, use dialogue only, not description.

1. Two girls have been shopping. One describes a new dress she has bought on sale; the other girl discovers that she has one just like it.

2. Two football fans talk about an exciting game.

3. A policeman has difficulty trying to tell a woman driver how to make turns in heavy traffic.

4. Two strangers discuss the weather. One is a Missourian and the other a Texan.

5. A boy argues with his girl friend on the telephone.

6. Two sophomores talk about the fish they have caught.

7. A sophisticated junior tries to get a date with a shy freshman.

● EXERCISE 8. Select 5 of the following actions and characterize two individuals (ones that you know) as they perform the actions in different ways. Limit each description to two sentences.

EXAMPLE   1. **riding an airplane**

1. After a glance at his watch, Mr. Fowler settled back comfortably in his seat and closed his eyes for a long nap.

Putting her forehead against the window, Florence chattered happily as she watched the clouds hurrying by.

1. Posing for a picture.
2. Counting money.
3. Looking into a mirror.
4. Waiting for an elevator.
5. Answering the telephone.
6. Walking to class.
7. Standing in line at the cafeteria.
8. Holding a baby.

9. Saying a prayer.
10. Baiting a fishhook.

14d. Consider the importance of the scene and the time of the story.

By using a definite time and an exact setting for your story, you can not only present a very clear picture for the reader but can also establish a mood or create an atmosphere. For many kinds of narratives — for example, outdoor adventures or ghost stories — the scene of the action is important. Sometimes, as in Poe's "The Pit and the Pendulum," the setting is especially important because it actually shapes the direction of the events. In other narratives, such as *A Christmas Carol* by Dickens, the time of the action is very significant.

For many stories about your experiences, you can make a quick reference to the time and place with a short sentence such as: "Yesterday after band practice, Bob Loomis and I helped decorate the gymnasium for a school dance." Other stories, however, may need to stress the time and setting more. As you decide upon the emphasis needed, be sure to take into account the total effect that you want your story to have upon the reader.

● EXERCISE 9.   Using a sentence or two, set a time and a place for each type of story listed below.

1. A love story.
2. A ghost story.
3. A tall tale.
4. An amusing experience.
5. An unforgettable experience.
6. A true adventure story.
7. An autobiographical incident.
8. A biographical incident.

9. A sports story.
10. An anecdote about a well-known person.

14e. Organize the story.

Every story presents its own problem of organization. For one story, you may organize the action by relating events in chronological order; for another story, you may decide to plunge into the middle of the action and then give the previous happenings by way of a flashback. For any story, however, you must answer two simple questions: Where shall I begin? When shall I stop?

(1) Determine the end of the story first.

In order to plan a trip, you need to know your destination, and in order to plan a story, you must know where you are going to stop. Every story builds up to a climax, which is a point of highest interest. Until you know what this is, you cannot plan the beginning or the middle. Your story should stop as soon as the climax is developed; and your conclusion should grow logically out of the events preceding it.

Suppose, for example, that you must decide upon a plan for the following incident. Where should the story end?

Last week my friend Hildegard found a beautiful turquoise and purple feather. She was puzzled because she had never seen one like it before. To satisfy her curiosity, she decided to find out about the feather. She took it to Mr. Hooten, a neighbor, and then to Mr. Morris, her science teacher. Neither could solve the riddle. Hoping that someone else might see and identify the feather, she attached it to her favorite fishing cap. The next day, when Hildegard was buying some hooks and sinkers at the five and ten, a salesgirl recognized the feather as she laughingly

**14
d-e**

spoke of "such a darling idea." She then pointed to a counter of dust mops made of feathers exactly like the one on Hildegard's cap; they were ordinary turkey feathers attractively dyed to catch the customer's eye. Hildegard did not tell anyone about her discovery for several days. Yesterday she turned down an invitation to join a club of bird watchers because she has lost interest in birds and feathers.

If you stop this story when the salesgirl identifies the feather, then you will not run the risk of losing the reader's interest. After deciding upon that conclusion, you could plan every preceding event so that it would lead logically to the salesgirl's revelation.

(2) Begin the story as near the end as possible.

After you have determined the ending, ask yourself: "Where is the latest point that I can begin — and still have a story to tell?" Begin with action, and make the reader interested in the situation and the characters. The beginning should *not* contain rambling details or dull descriptions, nor should it tell too much about the climax or the end of the story. Below are two beginnings for the story of Hildegard:

POOR

This story is about my friend Hildegard, who goes to school at Madison High. She has a wonderful personality, especially after you get to know her. Ordinarily she is not very observant. Her sister Martha usually notices everything, but not Hildegard. Well, anyway, one day Hildegard did see a feather lying in the driveway. She grew curious because she had never seen a bird having a feather like that one. Before she learned that she really had found a dyed turkey feather from a neighbor's dust mop, she had quite a time trying to figure out what kind of bird the feather belonged to. She began by showing it to Mr. Hooten, the man who lived next door.

BETTER

"Where did that come from?" Hildegard asked in astonishment as she saw a beautiful turquoise and purple feather lying in the driveway. "I've never seen a bird of that color! Look, Martha, at the odd purple tip. Can you guess where it came from?"

"No, I can't," replied her sister. "Why don't you go next door and ask Mr. Hooten?"

The second introduction is better narrative than the first because it *shows* the action as it happens. The first introduction merely talks *about* what happens; it also lacks direction as it rambles and gives away the end of the story in the beginning.

● EXERCISE 10. Carefully plan an original short narrative. As you write the summary, remember to begin the story as near the end as possible, to lead up to and develop the highest point of interest, and to stop with the climax. Write an interesting beginning, about 100 words, for the story.

14f. Write an appropriate title.

Like the beginning, the title of a story should be closely related to the main happenings, but it should not reveal too much about the climax or final outcome. For example, "Who Killed Louise?" or "The Case of the Black Cat" is a better title for a mystery story than "Alan Blake, Murderer" or "The Black Cat Finds a Killer." The title should also be original, specific, interesting. "An Amusing Experience" and "My Most Embarrassing Moment" are dull, trite, general; whereas "Hypnotizing Uncle Charlie" and "Three Men on Base" are more interesting because

14f

they are more specific. Always seek an original title that will catch the reader's attention.

● EXERCISE 11.   Many of the following titles are general, trite, or tell too much about the story. Find and change these titles, writing your revisions beside the corresponding numbers. Be able to give reasons for your changes.

1. A Terrifying Experience
2. Aunt Inez Takes Up Magic
3. A Joke That Backfired
4. A Dog That Played Baseball
5. Jones Makes a Touchdown
6. The Missing Diary
7. One Foot in the Grave
8. The Time I Almost Drowned
9. My First Date
10. Twenty Seconds to Live

14g. Write a first draft.

No matter how carefully planned, a summary is not narrative. It does not become narrative until you add concrete details. The following story — which could be summarized in a few sentences — was based upon short snatches of conversation about how girls were in the old days. After listening to her great grandparents talk, the writer used her imagination to supply abundant details to make a true incident interesting narrative. As you read the story, point out these accompanying details.

ELLY AND THE ABORIGINES

The 1850 Australian night was hot, dry, clear, as the buggy left the farm door and clattered away. The children crowded in the doorway went grudgingly inside, with a few decisive pushes from Elly, the oldest, who was fifteen. Elly had wanted so badly to go to the dance celebration in town, but not for another year would she be able to "put her hair up" and be officially recognized as a young lady. So, with a toss of long, blonde hair, Elly shut the door on the night and turned the wick up on the lamp.

It was dark outside, although clear, and a dingo on a distant hill began to howl, but this was a common sound and did not even deserve notice. The fact that she was alone at night with the responsibility of five children did not worry Elly. She was a strong, capable girl who could ride a horse as well as any boy around.

The little farmhouse was roughly made of corrugated iron, and from a distance looked as if it hung together by leaning up against the large trees which crowded over it. There wasn't another house to be seen, but about a mile and a half from the homestead, some workmen's shacks huddled near a gully. Except for the howls of the dingo, everything was quiet.

It was nearing midnight when Elly heard the sound, and even then she didn't take much notice. She guessed it was a tree knocking against the iron — it did all the time. She knew her parents would not be home before 1:00 A.M. as it was a long ride from the town. She checked on the two youngest children to see if they were still asleep and then went back to the front room to finish the game she was playing with the older children.

The second time she heard the rattle from the kitchen, Elly stopped suddenly and wondered. Unafraid, she went to the doorway of the dark kitchen. Then Elly froze with horror. Standing in the moonlight in the window was a black aborigine with his long spear in his hand, and behind him Elly saw another. At the end window stood another one. In her terror, Elly screamed silently. She shrank back into the hall and into the front room, where the other children waited. Her throat was parched and dry, and her hands dripped with perspiration. Sick with fear, she tried to collect her thoughts and noted that all the windows in the house were locked, even though they were easy to break into. Her parents would not be back for an hour at least; the nearest neighbors were miles away. What to do! What to do!

14g

Leaving the children again, she went into the side bedroom and edged along the wall until she could see through the window. Now at least ten were on that side of the house —some moving around with their spears catching the moonlight and with their black, naked bodies shining with the grease they had rubbed on to evade capture. Returning to the front room, she turned off the lamp and said to the children, "Let's sing 'Waltzing Matilda.' Just for fun!" After they had all started singing, Elly chose other noisy songs. She left the singing and went back to the bedroom and, just as she had hoped, the aborigines had gone to the front of the house to listen to the noise, dragging their spears along the corrugated iron wall as they went.

Elly grabbed a black shawl and tied it over her head. After looking through the window again, she quietly and slowly opened it while her heart pounded. She knew that straight south from the window would take her to the gully and the workmen. Quickly, she slipped out of the window and ran with her feet hardly touching the ground down the well-worn track to the gully. The noise of the children's singing floated after her, and she prayed that it would cover her flight. At last, she fell on the door of the shack, and soon all the men were out and running up to the house. The children's singing had turned to screams because the aborigines were shaking the flimsy walls before breaking in. When the men reached the house, spears flew in the night and clashed to the ground in the struggle. One aborigine was captured, but the well-greased bodies of the others made escape easy.

Next day, a very pretty young lady was seen riding her horse across the fields. "That looks like Elly," said one of the workmen to a friend. "But this young lady has her hair 'put up' and — you know — Elly's not sixteen yet."

— Carmel Fleming Coleman

As you write your first draft, the important thing is getting the story down on paper according to plan, adding as you go along concrete details that will make the action interesting narration. You can polish your style and correct sentence structure as you make revisions.

14h. Revise the first draft.

As you revise the first draft, use the following check list:

1. Is the title appropriate?
2. Does the first sentence create interest?
3. Does the beginning clearly introduce main characters?
4. Can any character be omitted?
5. Is every character lifelike?
6. Is the situation clear?
7. Have I been definite regarding the time and the place of the action?
8. Have I carried out my purpose?
9. Are the conversations natural? Is there a new paragraph for each change of speaker?
10. Do I have errors in grammar, punctuation, or spelling?

SUGGESTIONS FOR WRITING STORIES

Follow your teacher's instructions regarding the suggestions below.

1. Build a finished story around the plan that you used for Exercise 10.
2. Write a story based upon a newspaper clipping that you submitted for Exercise 2.
3. Select an exciting incident from your life, and present it as a chapter from an autobiography.
4. Retell a favorite anecdote or a well-known parable in your own style.
5. Plan and write a short story based upon any of the following situations:
   a. being afraid during a storm
   b. losing confidence in a friend
   c. fighting a fire

14h

       d. losing a contest

       e. striving to make a good impression

       f. eavesdropping

       g. being a good Samaritan

       h. playing a practical joke

6. Write brief narratives to illustrate the truth of each of the following statements:

       a. A liar needs a good memory.

       b. He who hesitates is lost.

       c. A girl often changes her mind.

       d. What matters is how you play the game.

       e. It pays to be courteous.

       f. Barking dogs do bite.

       g. A man reaps what he sows.

CHAPTER 15

Letter Writing

When you hear the term "letter writing" you probably think of a friendly letter because most of your experience to date has been with that type of correspondence. This chapter provides you with a review of things to remember when writing a friendly letter and includes in addition instructions for writing the social note and the business letter.

Letter Writing in General

Before you write any letter, plan what you are going to say and how you are going to say it. Remember that when your letter is read, you will not be there to explain what you mean. The letter must be clear. Furthermore, a letter represents *you*. Many times, especially in business, letters are received from people whom the reader has never met and never will meet. The writer is judged entirely by his letter. If you send a neat, correctly and clearly written letter, you will naturally be taken for an intelligent, educated person. If you send a letter which is not neat, which is filled with misspelled words and errors in writing, and which shows you do not know how to write a letter, the reader's opinion of you will drop accordingly. Be sure your letter makes a good impression.

In friendly letters, as in all your personal relationships, *be yourself*. Don't try to write like Jim because

341

you think Jim is clever, or like Sally because she is so smart in everything. Write the way *you* can write. An original is always better than a poor imitation, and there are few better ways of reflecting your personality than a letter written by *you*, in *your own style*, saying what *you* want to say. If you write naturally, if your letter "sounds like you," it will be a much better product than if you try to mimic somebody else.

15a. The Friendly Letter

This is the kind of letter with which you already have had a good deal of experience. It is a casual, informal sort of letter, the kind you write to your family and friends. The form of a friendly letter is rather elastic, but there are a few customs which you should follow.

APPEARANCE

Take pride in the appearance of your letter. Use letter stationery, preferably white or lightly tinted, and always write in ink. Never write a letter of any kind on lined paper or in pencil. A typewritten letter is perfectly proper, but don't subject your friends to inaccurate and messy typing.

Arrange your letter so that it looks well on the page. Keep the margins as even as possible; try to have equal margins on either side. Have at least three lines on the last page; never finish your letter on one page and put the closing and signature alone on the next page. If you use folded stationery and your letter is more than two pages long, use the page order of a book. Write page two on the back of page one. If your letter is only two pages long, write the second page on the third page of your stationery.

1. *Heading*

It is customary to write your complete address (unless you are sure the receiver knows it) and the date in three lines at the top right-hand corner of the page, with a comma between the town (after the zone number) and the state, and a comma between the day of the month and the year. Begin the heading at least a half-inch below the top of the page. The heading should not look crowded.

BLOCK STYLE	INDENTED STYLE
14 Brixton Road	12 Brixton Road
Dayton 3, Ohio	Dayton 3, Ohio
September 17, 19—	September 17, 19—

In general, it is better not to use abbreviations, but if you do use them, be consistent — abbreviate the word "street" as well as the state. An abbreviation is always followed by a period.

You may, if you prefer, put your address and the date at the end of the letter, in the lower left-hand corner, instead of at the top.

2. *Salutation*

The salutation of a friendly letter is easy to learn. The usual form is "Dear . . ." followed by a comma. Begin the salutation at the left-hand margin about a half-inch below the heading.

Dear Dad,
Dear Dr. Riley,
Dear Bruce,

3. *Body*

The body is the letter itself. Don't forget to divide it into paragraphs.

15a

206 Elm Street
Haverford, Pennsylvania,
November 6, 19 — —

Dear Nancy,

Last night at the fall dance Joe Smith asked me whether I had heard from you. I told him I still owed you a letter. Joe took Betty Calder to the dance, but I think he was wishing it was last summer and you were around. I went with Jack. He usually gives me a big pain, but he asked me first — nobody asked me second — and I decided a date with Jack would be better than no date at all. The dance was pretty good. Joan and Fred went with us. You know how crazy they are!

Sally, Becky and I went bowling yesterday after school. What a riot! You've probably bowled a lot, being the athletic type, but this was my first time. I made 36 the first game, and Becky and Sally weren't much better. I got all the way up to 50 in my third game. Some boys from South High kept trying to help us and show us how to hold the ball and how to score and everything(!). They were sort of cute, too. One of them asked for my telephone number. I didn't give it to him, but now I almost wish I had. We bowled at Johnson's. It's a barn-like place out near Five Corners. My wrist is sore and my pocket book is flat. I spent $1.50 just to roll that ball — it weighs a ton — down the gutter. At least, it wasn't always the same gutter.

Pam came over Saturday and stayed all night. We got to sleep about one o'clock. Dad and Mom were out. Pam's going to New York for Thanksgiving. Maybe she'll look you up. I gave her your address. I wish I were going with her. Now you owe me a letter! Remember, Joe's waiting!

Love,
Jean

4. *Closing*

In a friendly letter there are many appropriate closings. Among these are *Sincerely yours, Sincerely, Cordially, With love, Affectionately,* etc., each of which is followed by a comma.

Avoid "clever" closings such as "Yours till Niagara Falls." They don't ever look as well as you think they will, and they are usually trite and in very poor taste.

Capitalize only the first letter of the closing. Do not use a business letter closing such as *Very truly yours* on a friendly letter.

5. *Signature*

Below the closing, write your name. Even when your letter is typewritten, the signature is always handwritten.

THE ENVELOPE

Place the name and address on the lower half of the envelope about midway between the ends. Always write Mr., Mrs., or Miss before the person's

Jean White
206 Elm Street
Haverford, Pennsylvania

Miss Nancy Brownlow
85 East Forty-ninth Street
New York 17
New York

name unless you are using some other title like Reverend, Dr., President, or Professor.

Do not abbreviate the name of the state; the Post Office prefers to have the state written on a separate line.

Your own name and address should be written in the upper left-hand corner of the envelope.

THE CONTENT OF A FRIENDLY LETTER

A friendly letter is like a conversation. An English textbook can no more tell you exactly what to say in a letter than it can tell you what you and your friends should talk about. The most important thing, of course, is to make your letter lively and interesting to the person who receives it. Naturally you would not write to your Aunt Mary the same things in the same way that you would write to Bill or Helen, friends of your own age. Remember that telling in detail about a recent experience is more interesting than simply telling in general that everybody is well at home and you are enjoying school this year. Something interesting about mutual friends is always appropriate, but avoid malicious gossip.

Beginning your letter with a series of questions may show your interest in the person to whom you are writing, but it can also be very dull and commonplace. (How are you? Did you have a good time at the dance? What did your mother say?) The receiver wants a *letter* from you, not a questionnaire.

Ending a letter with such awkward statements as "I have to go now" and "Well, I can't think of anything else to say" is neither original nor graceful. If you are writing a friend whom you haven't seen in some time, perhaps you can suggest a visit to you. If the letter is going to someone to whom you have long owed a letter, you might assure him you will try to do better next time. Make your closing appropriate to the person to whom you are writing as well as to the situation.

Always remember that in friendly letters the most important things for you to think of are *to be interesting* and *to be yourself*.

● EXERCISE 1. Each of the following parts of a friendly letter is incorrectly written. On your paper rewrite each correctly.

1. Heading: October 3, 19—
              Santa Barbara California.
              411 Beach Ave.
2. Salutation: Dear Jill:
3. Salutation: Dear uncle George
4. Closing: Sincerely Yours
5. Envelope: Marian Higgins
              Huntting Lane
              East Hampton, N.Y.

● EXERCISE 2. On a piece of regular letter stationery (your personal stationery if you have any) write a letter to your English teacher. This is, of course, an artificial situation, but it will serve to let your teacher know whether you have learned all the matters of correct form and good taste which are involved in letter writing. It will also afford a good opportunity for you to tell something about yourself which your teacher may not know.

Make your letter interesting. Don't bore your teacher even if you think teachers sometimes bore you. The following suggestions may help you decide what to write about: your home and family; your activities outside of school — club, church, sports, music, social; a recent experience — a trip, a party, a school experience; comment on your English course or your English class or your school program in general; your "crowd"; what you usually do on week-ends; where you spend your vacations; analysis of yourself — personality, likes and dislikes, faults, strong qualities, worries.

Place your letter, properly folded, in an envelope and address it correctly. Do not seal it.

15b. The Social Note

The social note is a short letter usually written for one of the following purposes: (1) to extend an informal invitation; (2) to accept or decline an informal invitation; (3) to thank someone for a gift or for entertaining you.

The form of the social note is very much like that of a friendly letter, with the address and the date either in the top right-hand corner or the lower left-hand corner, the salutation *Dear . . .,* and the informal closing.

The social note may be written on regular note paper, on correspondence cards if the note is a short one, or on personal note paper. White is preferred, although a pastel shade may be used. You may be proud of your violent-colored paper, and you may like to use white, brown, or green ink on it, but don't use that kind of thing for social notes. It's likely to brand you as a person who doesn't know the proper thing to do.

THE INFORMAL INVITATION

Although the form and content of an invitation are very similar to those of a friendly letter, you do have to be careful to include the following:

1. Your full address.
2. The date, time, and place (if other than your home).
3. Any necessary explanation regarding the kind of affair it is to be.

Informal Invitation

> *14 Woods Road*
> *Highland Park, Illinois*
> *May 5, 19—*

Dear Ann,

   How about a week-end in the country? It's time you gave your old friends a look at you. I'd love to have you come for the week-end of May 16. If you can come, I'm going to schedule a slumber party for the old crowd Saturday night. I think I won't tell them you're coming; that will be a wonderful surprise.

   You can get a 4:30 train on Friday which will get you here in time for dinner. Bring some old clothes — no party dresses. Tell your family you will be back late Sunday afternoon.

> *Sincerely,*
> *Alice*

REPLYING TO THE INFORMAL INVITATION

Still another kind of social note is the one you write when accepting or declining an invitation that is informal. Perhaps a friend of yours has invited you to his summer home for the day, or he and his sister have planned a party in your honor. If the invitation is a written one, your acceptance or refusal should be written. Don't forget that it should be a gracious acceptance or a regretful refusal. Always remember the importance of politeness, even more particularly when you write than when you speak. Experience in writing letters will enable you either to accept an invitation gracefully or to decline one courteously.

15b

Informal Invitation

418 Bay Avenue
Riverhead, New York
April 7, 19—

Dear Sam,

Bill Mercer came over the other night, and we started talking about last summer at camp. That reminded us of canoeing. I remembered how much you like canoeing, and Bill and I wondered whether you could go on a trip with us the last week end of the month — the 28th and 29th.

We could leave here before noon on Saturday, camp out somewhere along the shore of the bay that night (I've managed to get an extra bed roll for you), and paddle back on Sunday. Bill is already bragging about what a good chef he is, and I guess I can stand his cooking if you can.

Try to get the 4 o'clock train from Penn Station Friday afternoon. You can go back on Sunday at 5:00. We hope you can come.

Sincerely,
Bob

THE THANK-YOU NOTE

Most of the social notes you have had to write so far are thank-you notes for a gift you have received. A gift should never go unacknowledged, as it represents a thoughtful gesture on the part of the person who gave it to you. Your thank-you notes should always be prompt, courteous, and appreciative. Always mention the gift by name. Do not say merely, "Thank you for the birthday present." Go out of your

Note of Acceptance

> *876 Lake Road*
> *Chicago 21, Illinois*
> *May 8, 19—*

Dear Alice,

Your invitation for the week end of the 16th sounds like more fun than I've had all year. Mother said O. K. at once, and I'm counting the days. Dad will take me to the 4:30 train and will meet me at 6:30 on Sunday. The news can wait until I see you and the gang.

> *Sincerely,*
> *Ann*

Note of Regret

> *23 Morningside Drive*
> *New York 27, New York*
> *April 10, 19—*

Dear Bob,

Your invitation came in yesterday's mail, and how I hate to have to turn it down! I already have a big date with Linda for that Saturday. A bunch of us are going to the spring play at school.

A first-of-the-season canoe trip sounds great. You and Bill have fun. Give me another try sometime, will you?

> *Sincerely,*
> *Sam*

way to make certain that the giver feels that you enjoy the gift and will make use of it.

THE "BREAD-AND-BUTTER" NOTE

Another type of social note is the thank-you letter you write after you have been entertained at someone's home. Commonly called a "bread-and-butter" letter, this kind of social note is sent to your hostess, thanking her for her hospitality and saying what a good time you had. If you have been visiting a friend of your own age at his home, you should write your "bread-and-butter" letter to his mother (or whoever your hostess happened to be).

Thank-you Note

---

29 Kimberly Road
Glen Oaks, Wisconsin
June 22, 19—

Dear Jane,

You are a dear to remember my birthday! The beautiful white scarf you made arrived this morning, and it is already dated up with me for a trip tomorrow, when I'll show off your handiwork to some of my friends. How did you ever find time to do it? I particularly love the long fringe and the tiny hemstitching that only you can do.

Today is really going to be celebrated in a grand way — Daddy is taking us to town for dinner and the movies. I can hardly wait for three o'clock.

Thanks again, Jane, for your marvelous scarf.

Love,
Sue

"Bread-and-Butter" Note

---

44 Appleton Road
Long Beach, California
August 2, 19—

Dear Mrs. Fairben,

Thank you a lot for having me at your home over the week end. You know what a good time Bruce and I had, and I hope I didn't make too much extra work for you. (Sometime would you tell my mother how you make apple pie?) It was swell of you to invite me, and I enjoyed every minute of the week end.

Tell Bruce I'll write him soon.

Sincerely yours,
Larry

● EXERCISE 3. Write a social note covering the following situation: You have received an unusual gift for Christmas. Thank the person who gave it to you and explain why you are glad to have it.

● EXERCISE 4. You have been entertained for a week end at the cottage of your best friend. On Saturday it rained all day, but you all had a good time learning new card games and toasting marshmallows. Sunday the weather was perfect and you were in the water almost all day. Write your friend's mother a "bread-and-butter" letter, thanking her for her hospitality and also for having been resourceful about what to do to keep you entertained during the bad weather.

● EXERCISE 5. Write a note to an out-of-town friend, asking him to spend the day with you during

Easter vacation. Give him a choice of either of two days. Tell him what you plan to do (a bicycle trip, a baseball game, fishing — these are suggestions), and suggest a train or bus for him to take.

● EXERCISE 6. Answer the preceding invitation, either accepting or declining it. If you decline it, be sure to explain why you can't go.

15c. The Business Letter

A business letter is written usually to a firm or an individual in a firm. It must be a combination of clearness, brevity, and courtesy.

APPEARANCE AND STATIONERY

Proper stationery is the first important consideration in a business letter. Businessmen much prefer that you type your letter if possible, on the usual $8\frac{1}{2} \times 11$ plain white paper. The typewritten letter is more legible and therefore more quickly read than a handwritten one. Business firms know that time is money to them; they do not want to have to decipher or decode your letter. If you write the letter by hand, use the same stationery as for a typewritten letter, if you have it; if not, any good-sized white writing paper will do. Also, remember to write carefully; your best penmanship is a courtesy you owe to anyone to whom you are writing.

FORM

The form of a business letter follows a certain pattern. Whether your letter is typewritten or handwritten, the pattern is the same. The semi-block form is used in the illustrations which you will find later in this chapter; however, the pure block form is also acceptable, and an illustration of that form is also given.

THE LETTER PICTURE

Two commonly used forms for the business letter are the pure block and the semi-block style.

Pure Block	Semi-block

In this chapter the semi-block style is used for both friendly and business letters; that is, except for the beginning of each paragraph, no lines are indented. In the pure block form, no lines are indented.

Before beginning your letter, judge the amount of space it will occupy on the page you are using. Center it as nearly as possible by making sure you have approximately the same margin at the top of your page as at the bottom, and the same margin on both the left- and right-hand sides. *Never* run your letter off the page at the right-hand side, and never finish the body of your letter at the end of a page so that you have nothing left for the second page except the complimentary close and your signature, or worse still, just your signature. For a model letter, see page 359.

15c

1. *Heading*

To begin your business letter, always put your *complete* address and the full date in the upper right-hand corner beginning no less than one inch from the top of the page. It is better to write this heading without abbreviations.

EXAMPLES

49 Surrey Lane		R. F. D. 4
Clinton, Iowa	*or*	Cross Corners, Pennsylvania
June 4, 19—		September 27, 19—

2. *Inside Address*

The inside address should be placed at the left-hand side of the page, flush with the margin and several spaces (at least four, if the letter is typewritten) lower on the page than the heading. It should include the full name of the company to which you are writing, as well as its full address. If you are writing to an individual in the firm, use his full name and title, with a comma between the two if they are on the same line; if the name and title are too long to be put on one line, put the title on the next line.

The James Mills Company
220–224 Center Street
Waukegan, Illinois

Mr. James R. Joy, Vice-President
Newland and Company
40 Fifth Avenue
Dallas 8, Texas

Mr. Reginald B. MacPherson
Secretary to the President
Wilbur Field and Sons
218 South Street
Fort Hamilton, Virginia

Principal
Lakeview High School
Lakeview, Michigan

3. *Salutation*

The salutation is placed two spaces below the last line of the inside address and flush with the margin. The proper salutation for a letter written to a firm is *Gentlemen* followed by a colon. *Dear Sirs* is also used. When writing to an individual within the firm, the correct salutation is *Dear Mr. . . .* (or *Mrs.* or *Miss*) followed by a colon. If you are writing to a professional man or woman, use his title instead of *Mr.*

EXAMPLES   Gentlemen:
              Dear Mr. Bowne:
              Dear Dr. Grayce:
              Dear President Tyson:

Sometimes you may be writing to an officer in a firm without knowing his name. You may have just "Principal," "President," or "Secretary" on the first line of the inside address. The proper salutation then is *Dear Sir* followed by a colon.

4. *Body*

The form of the body of a business letter is the form followed in the body of any letter. A double space is used between paragraphs of a typed letter. If your typewritten letter is short (7 lines or less), you may either put it on a smaller sheet of stationery or double-space the entire body of the letter on $8\frac{1}{2} \times 11$ stationery.

5. *Closing*

The closing of a letter comes between the body of the letter and the signature. In business letters, appropriate closings are limited, and the same ones you use in friendly letters will not do. *Very truly yours*, *Yours truly*, and *Yours very truly* are the ones most frequently used. *Sincerely yours* and *Yours sincerely* are also correct. The closing is placed just to the right of the center of the page, two spaces below the last line of the body of your letter. It is followed by a comma.

Avoid ending your letter with an outmoded phrase such as "I beg to remain," "Hoping to hear from you soon, I am," or "Thanking you in advance, I am . . ." End the body of your letter with a *period*, and then begin your closing.

EXAMPLES   Very truly yours,
            Yours truly,
            Sincerely yours,

6. *Signature*

Sign your full name to your letter. Do *not* put "*Miss*" or "*Mr.*" before your name. An unmarried woman writing to a stranger should put *Miss* in parentheses before her signature.

EXAMPLE   (*Miss*) *Margaret Hoyt*

A married woman signs her full name (*Elise M. Rhoad*), and if she wishes, she may put in parentheses and directly below her signature (*Mrs. Robert L. Rhoad*).

EXAMPLE   *Elise M. Rhoad*
           (*Mrs. Robert L. Rhoad*)

A signature should always be handwritten. If your letter is typewritten, type your name below your written signature, flush with the first letter of the complimentary close and far enough below to allow room for your signature.

Heading	1112 Rose Boulevard
	Salt Lake City 2, Utah
	June 1, 19 _ _

Inside
address

Mr. George R. West, Director
Camp Winona
Sunrise Lake
Waban, Montana

Saluta-
tion

Dear Mr. West:

Body

    Will you please send me the booklet
about your summer camp? I have heard about
your camp from several of my friends and it
sounds like just what I want.

    If the booklet does not contain spe-
cific information about rates, will you
send me that also?

Closing

                        Very truly yours,

Signature

                        Gregory Jones

                        Gregory Jones

7. *Envelope*

For a letter on small stationery, use a small envelope
(be sure the letter fits it). A letter on small single-
sheet stationery is usually folded twice unless it fits
into the envelope without any folding. The folds are
made in this way: up from the bottom about a third
of the way, then down from the top, so that when it
is unfolded it will be right side up for the reader.
Note paper or personal stationery is usually folded
in half and inserted with the fold at the bottom of the
envelope.

Either a small or a large envelope may be used
for a letter on large single-sheet stationery. If a
large envelope is used, the folding is the same as that
of a small sheet for a small envelope. If the envelope

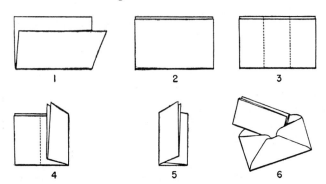

is small, fold your letter up from the bottom to within a quarter of an inch of the top; then fold the right side over a third of the way; finally, fold the left side over. Insert in the envelope with the fold at the bottom of the envelope.

Your envelope should carry the same inside address as is on the letter and also your own name and full address. You may put your return address on the back of the letter, but the Post Office prefers that you put the return address in the upper left-hand corner of the envelope on the same side as the address to which it is going. Unless the address to which a letter is being

```
Gregory Jones
1112 Rose Boulevard
Salt Lake City 2, Utah


            Mr. George R. West, Director
            Camp Winona
            Sunrise Lake
            Waban, Montana
```

sent is very long, you should start it about halfway down the envelope and place it midway between the ends.

15d. Types of Business Letters

THE REQUEST LETTER

This kind of letter is one in which you usually ask for information from the firm or individual to whom you write. Make your request simple and clear; one or two paragraphs will be sufficient for this type of letter.

● EXERCISE 7. Write to a college, asking for their catalog. If you think the catalog may not include all the information you need, ask specifically for whatever you wish to know.

Another type of request letter is the kind you write when you ask a firm to send a representative to your school for some purpose or other. This kind of letter is a little more complicated to write, because it is *you* who have to give the company information before they reply. Remember to include all the details necessary for the company's complete understanding of the situation.

EXERCISE 8. Copy in proper form the business letter given below.

420 Jackson Avenue, Far Hills, Texas, January 8, 19—. Mr. R. F. Hawkins, Business Manager, Perry and Company, 480–96 Dallas Street, Dallas 14, Texas. Dear Mr. Hawkins: Our junior class of 170 pupils in Far Hills High School is to decide this month on our class rings and pins. We expect to have representatives from several companies here on Monday, January 21, to show us samples of the rings and pins their firms make, together with price lists. We'd like very much to have someone from your company

15d

here on that date, if possible. Your representative should come to Room 31, any time after 2:45. Very truly yours, Sarah Porter, Secretary of the Junior Class, Far Hills High School.

Model Request Letter

```
                                    76 Brixton Place
                                    Phoenix 8, Arizona
                                    July 8, 19—


Model Airways, Inc.
410-12 Second Avenue
Flagstaff 4, Arizona

Gentlemen:

     Will you please send me a copy of your
latest catalog on model planes?  I have
three of your models and would like to add
some of the later ones to my collection.

                         Very truly yours
                         Frank Tyndall
                         Frank Tyndall
```

● EXERCISE 9. Using the following information, set up this material in the form of a business letter. You must compose the letter.

Miss Elsie Dowing of 222 Twin Oaks Road, Carlsburg, Ohio, writes on April 6, 19—, to the George C. Buckeye

Company, 240 Lexington Avenue, Cleveland 2, Ohio, stating that while shopping there the week before, she lost a valuable gold ring. It contained a diamond and two pearls in an old-fashioned setting. She would like to know if it has been found and if so, where she may call for it.

● EXERCISE 10.   As student assembly-program chairman, you wish to have a neighboring high school send their glee club to perform in one of your assembly periods. Give the time, date, place, length of program, type of song selection (if you wish), details about transportation to your school, and any other information you think is necessary.

● EXERCISE 11.   You are interested in art. There is an exhibit to be given in the high school auditorium of a near-by city. Write to the art department of the high school requesting information. Ask specific questions about what you want to know — time, admission price, dates the exhibit will be displayed, etc.

● EXERCISE 12.   You have failed your English course. Your principal has just told you that if you study through the summer you may be given a make-up examination in the fall. Your English teacher has already gone for the summer. Write to your teacher, explaining the circumstances and asking him to recommend an English textbook for you and perhaps suggest specific chapters in it which would help you most.

THE ORDER LETTER

If you are writing an order letter, you should list the items you wish, one below the other, with complete information (catalog number, style, size, price, etc.) about each item. The price should be put at the right-hand side (flush with the right-hand margin) and each amount should be placed directly under the one above, to make it easier to add the prices. List the cost of shipping, if you know it, and include it in the total, unless you know the firm pays for it.

Model Order Letter

```
                                    58 Crane Street
                                    Canton, Iowa
                                    December 1, 19—


Webb and Sons
140—156 Seventh Avenue
Des Moines 11, Iowa

Gentlemen:

        I should like to order the following
articles, as advertised in the Des Moines
Press of November 29.

2 white silk scarves, fringed, one with
  black initials A. J., the other with red
  initials M. W., @ $2.98               $5.96
1 size 15—34 Supercron white
  shirt, collar attached                 6.50
                          Postage         .20
                          Total        $12.66

        I am enclosing a check for $12.66 to
cover the total amount.

                     Very truly yours,

                     Amy Ladd
                     Amy Ladd
```

Also, in an order letter, be sure to specify how the articles you are ordering are to be paid for — check, money order, C.O.D., etc.

● EXERCISE 13.　Write a business letter to Marshall Field and Company, Chicago, ordering 2 size 14, long-sleeved cotton blouses, 1 plain white, the other French blue, at $4.98, 1 green "Betty Gaye" dress, size 13, at $11.95. Have them sent C.O.D.

● EXERCISE 14.　Write to Ritz Camera Center, 1147A Sixth Avenue, New York 36, N.Y., an order letter ordering the following: 1 Star D Model D–18 tripod, price $9.75; 3 rolls 35 mm. Kodachrome film at $1.75 a roll. Include $.25 postage. You are enclosing a money order for the amount.

THE ADJUSTMENT LETTER

An adjustment or complaint letter is one which you write after an error has been made, either on your part or on that of the firm to which you have written.

Perhaps the wrong catalog has been sent to you, or you did not receive all the materials you ordered. Since this kind of situation is often a delicate one to handle, it calls for all the tact and diplomacy you can command. Even though it is a "complaint" letter, the tone need not necessarily be complaining. A courteous request to clear up the misunderstanding is more likely to meet with a courteous and prompt response than is a curt letter saying, "*This* time send me what I ordered in the first place!" Try to put yourself in the other person's place — the Golden Rule is still applicable — and let that be your guide in writing your adjustment letter. Be sure you give all information needed to clear up the situation.

● EXERCISE 15.   In response to an order you sent on December 1 to the Nestor Johnson Manufacturing Company, 1906 Springfield Avenue, Chicago 47, Illinois, you have received a pair of North Star ice skates and shoes, but they are not the size you ordered. Write a letter to the company explaining the situation and asking them to send the correct size in exchange for the skates and shoes that you are mailing back to them. Be courteous.

THE LETTER OF APPLICATION

Model Letter of Application

> 98 Oxford Street
> Clayton, Illinois
> April 2, 19—
>
> Mr. O. A. Lester, Director
> Camp Carlson
> Oneidaga Lake
> Bloomfield, Illinois
>
> Dear Mr. Lester:
>
>   Ben Nichols, one of your regular campers, told me this week that you have a vacancy for a swimming counselor on your camp staff this summer, and I should like to apply for the position.
>
>   I am a senior at Clayton High School and am eighteen years old. For the last two years I have been the junior swimming counselor at Camp Winnebega, Cauhoga Falls, Wisconsin. I have just received my Examiner's badge in lifesaving and am now certified for the position of senior swimming

counselor. If you have junior or senior lifesaving classes, I am also qualified to direct them. Although I must admit I haven't had much experience in teaching lifesaving as yet, I feel right now as though I had been 'worked on' plenty, both at camp and in our 'Y' here at home.

The following men have given me permission to use their names as references:

Mr. J. B. Morse, Director, Camp Winnebega, Cauhoga Falls, Wisconsin.

Mr. Alexander B. Davis, Secretary, Y.M.C.A., Clayton, Illinois.

Mr. Chester Roberts, Principal, High School, Clayton, Illinois.

I shall be glad to come for a personal interview at your convenience.

Sincerely yours,

Frank Larson

Frank Larson

The letter of application is one with which you have no doubt had very little experience to date. However, you soon may find that it is one of the most important types of business letter, for it is in the application letter that you try to *sell yourself*.

When you apply for a position, your letter of application comes before your personal interview with your prospective employer. It is the first contact you have with him. Therefore, you must "put yourself across" in a way which will make him feel confident that you can do the job called for. You will also have an added advantage if you can put some original, personal touch into your letter (but only if it comes naturally to you), to distinguish you, favorably, from the rest of the applicants this employer may be considering.

There are certain things which should be included in every letter of application.

(1) Include a statement of the position you are applying for, and how you learned about it.

(2) Show that you know what qualifications are needed and that you believe you can fill them. State your age, experience, and education.

(3) Give references as to your character and ability.

(4) Request an interview at the employer's convenience.

● EXERCISE 16.   You have learned from a friend that a woman she knows in another city is looking for a high school girl to spend the summer with her family at their summer home. She wants the girl to take care of her three children, ages two, four, and six. Write to the woman (make up a name and address) and apply for this job. State your qualifications. Try to make your letter interesting as well as informative.

● EXERCISE 17.   A drugstore in a neighboring town needs a delivery boy from 4:00 to 6:00 after school and all day on Saturdays. Write your letter of application. Convince the druggist that you are the best one for the job.

PART FOUR

SPEAKING

AND

LISTENING

CHAPTER 16

Social Conversation

You spend a great deal of your time every day in conversation. You exchange information, opinions, and experiences with friends and acquaintances. You chat about ordinary things — school affairs, movies, sports, dances, and similar matters.

Would you like to improve your conversational skill? With study and practice you can learn how to converse with greater satisfaction to yourself and others. A person who converses easily and pleasantly is popular, and rightly so.

Making Social Introductions

The purpose of introducing one person to another is to make them acquainted so they may enjoy each other's company.

The etiquette of introductions is simple. No set expressions are used. You may simply mention the persons' names. However, be sure to pronounce each name distinctly.

EXAMPLES   **Edna, Joe Everett.**

Mother, this is Neil Smith.

Miss Brown, Mr. Philips.

370

Or you may say something like this:

> Edna, may I introduce Joe Everett.
> Mother, I'd like you to meet my friend Neil Smith.
> Miss Brown, I'd like to present Mr. Philips.

It is desirable to add a remark that will help start a conversation.

EXAMPLES   Edna, may I introduce Joe Everett, who captained our tennis team this season.

> How are you, Joe? I've seen you play many times. That was a close match with South Side High, wasn't it?

> Mother, I'd like you to meet my friend Neil Smith. Neil is editor of our school yearbook.

> How do you do, Neil? Editing a yearbook must take a lot of your time. Have you decided on the theme of this year's book?

16a. Introduce a man to a woman.

Mention the woman's name first. A man is always introduced to a woman even if he is older. The woman need not rise and she need not extend her hand unless she wishes to.

EXAMPLES   Sue, this is my Dad.

> Sis, I'd like you to meet Charlie Hyams. Charlie, this is my sister Kate.

> Miss Teen, may I present Mr. Well-Known.

> Miss Middle-Age, this is my classmate Ed Thomas.

16b. Introduce a young person to an older person of the same sex.

When introducing one man to another, it does not matter which name is mentioned first unless there is a great difference in their ages. In such a case, introduce the younger man to the older. The young person

16 a-b

should not call the older man by his first name unless invited to do so.

EXAMPLES   **Dad, this is Ed Bourke.**

               Mr. Ancient, Mr. Youngman.

               Mr. Principal, this is my brother Bob.

               Bill, this is my son Jack. Jack, this is Mr. Butler.

Similarly, a young woman is introduced to an older woman. Mention the older woman's name first.

EXAMPLES   **Mother, I'd like you to meet Susie Blair.**

               Miss Grayhair, this is Mrs. Honeymooner.
               (Marriage makes no difference in introductions. A young married woman is presented to an older single woman.)

               Miss Elder, may I present Miss Young.

At social gatherings young people generally use first names and disregard the titles *Mr.*, *Miss*, and *Mrs.*

EXAMPLES   **Dorothy Keaton, Tom Fielding.**

               Marion, this is Katherine Hayden.

               Esther, I'd like you to meet Joe and Estelle Metz.

When introducing groups of persons, the simplest procedure is to mention the names of those in one group and then the names of those in the other.

EXAMPLES   **Ella and Sue, Grace and Loretta.**

               Eileen, Kate, and Sally, may I introduce Joe Smith and Tom Fitzpatrick.

Acknowledging an Introduction

16c. Respond to an introduction courteously and properly.

Respond to an introduction in such a way that the new acquaintance feels you are really pleased to know him.

In formal situations the usual reply is, "How do you do?" Add the person's name to fix it in your mind.

In informal situations there is no fixed reply. Any sincere and pleasant acknowledgment will do. If you can think of nothing better, "How are you, Mr. Jones?" or "Good afternoon, Mr. Jones" may be used. Avoid shopworn expressions like "Pleased to meet you" and "Glad to know you."

● EXERCISE 1.   In groups of two or three, one person acting as host and the other two as the persons indicated below, demonstrate good form in the following introduction situations.

1. A teen-age boy and a teen-age girl.
2. A teen-age boy and a city official.
3. A young girl and an older woman.
4. Two older men.
5. Two young men.
6. A young married woman and an older married woman.
7. A young married woman and an older single woman.
8. A young woman (seated) and a young man (standing).
9. A young woman (seated) and an older man (standing).
10. An older woman (seated) and a young woman (standing).
11. A young man (seated) and an older man (standing).
12. Two young girls.

● EXERCISE 2.   With one person acting as host and others as members of the following groups, perform these introductions.

1. Two boys to a group of three girls.
2. Two girls to a group of three girls.
3. One of your friends to your father and mother.
4. Your father and mother to your teacher.

16c

Topics of Conversation

The weather is a favorite opening topic, but its possibilities for conversation are soon exhausted. Among other topics which might be used to get a conversation started are the surroundings in which you find yourself or a current happening which has aroused widespread attention.

16d. Talk about the other person's interests rather than your own.

Find out what he is interested in and encourage him to talk about it. No one is at a loss for words when he is talking about his hobby, activities, ambition, family, or job. Unless your companion shares your interests, it is well to avoid talking about your own ideas, plans, and experiences.

16e. Listen attentively.

If you want to be considered a good conversationalist, you must be a good listener. Look at the person who is talking and pay attention to what he is saying even when it may not be particularly interesting to you. Your attitude should be friendly and considerate. Interrupt rarely. If you do have to break in on the other person's remarks, apologize.

Exercise self-control. Immature listeners fidget, become bored or distracted quickly, interrupt without cause, ask irrelevant questions, or make comments which show that they have not listened closely. Give a speaker your complete and undivided attention. Gradually your attention span will become longer, a sign of increasing maturity.

16f. Cultivate conversational topics.

To participate intelligently in conversations, know at least a few topics thoroughly and have a general knowledge of many more. By wide reading of books, magazines, and newspapers, by participating in community affairs, by attending sports events, motion pictures and plays, by listening to worthwhile broadcasts and viewing good TV programs, by travel, and by education you can build up a store of conversational topics.

16g. Learn to tell stories and personal experiences effectively.

A conversation that lasts more than a few minutes is almost bound to include a personal experience, story, or joke. To improve conversational skill, therefore, you must know some of the principles underlying good storytelling.

Every experience you have had or read about is not worth retelling. Only surprising occurrences or those filled with suspense arouse interest in your audience.

Maintain suspense when relating an anecdote or personal experience. Every detail should lead to the final outcome.

EXAMPLE   An elementary school teacher prepared a little play for a PTA meeting at Christmas time. Four little girls, each bearing a large letter, were trained to march upon the stage and form the word S-T-A-R.

On the day of the performance the children, to the amusement of the parents and the consternation of the teacher, marched on the stage in reverse order!

16
d-g

Be brief. An unnecessarily long story is boring. Shakespeare pointed out that brevity is the soul of wit.

Some *don'ts* when relating an anecdote or personal experience are:

(1) **Don't tell a story that may give offense. If you are in doubt, don't tell it.**

(2) **Don't tell a story that ridicules any group.**

(3) **Don't tell a story that puts someone else in a bad light.** (It is all right, however, "to tell one on yourself.")

(4) **Don't tell a story that makes you seem important.** (Your listeners will label you a show-off.)

16h. Avoid improper conversational topics.

Some topics are out of place in social conversation. Gossip, complaints, religion, race, personal illness, and partisan politics are usually taboo subjects. Engage in shoptalk only when all the other members of the group are of the same trade or profession and are interested in discussing it.

● EXERCISE 3.   Suggest topics that would be suitable for conversation in each of the following situations.

1. You and a community leader who is visiting the school
2. You, your classmate, and your mother
3. You and an exchange student from England
4. You, your parents, and your teacher
5. You and a speaker who has been invited to address a school assembly

● EXERCISE 4.   Relate an unusual personal experience to the class. If you can, select an incident that illustrates a point. Arouse and maintain suspense. Be brief.

When you have finished, your classmates will comment on your choice of experience, your manner of relating it, and its appropriateness in emphasizing or clarifying an idea.

● EXERCISE 5.   Relate an experience to illustrate a proverb. The following list is suggestive.

A stitch in time saves nine.
A rolling stone gathers no moss.
Waste not, want not.
An empty barrel makes the most noise.
A fool and his money are soon parted.
A watched kettle never boils.
Easy come, easy go.
Pride goeth before a fall.
Spare the rod and spoil the child.
A cat may look at a king.

● EXERCISE 6.   Tell a tall story. Compose one of your own or narrate an incident attributed to Paul Bunyan, Pecos Bill, or John Henry. The humor of such stories lies in their ridiculous exaggeration.

Leave-taking

16i. When leaving a conversational group, express regret and explain briefly your reason for leaving.

No extended explanation or apology is necessary. Leave as unobtrusively as you can.

EXAMPLES   I'm sorry I must leave now. I promised Dad I'd have the car back by eight-thirty. Excuse me.

Will you excuse me, please? I have a dentist's appointment at four o'clock. Goodbye, everybody.

16 h-i

16j. When leaving a social affair, thank the host and hostess. At a school party, say goodbye to the chaperones.

Be sure to tell your host or hostess how much you have enjoyed yourself. Leave without lingering.

EXAMPLES Thank you for inviting me to your party, Jane.
I had a wonderful time. Good night!

When taking your leave from adults, say *Goodbye*, *Good night*, or *Good afternoon* rather than the more colloquial *So long* or the slang *See you some more*, which you would use only with your own crowd. After you have made your farewell, leave promptly.

● EXERCISE 7. Form groups of three, four, or five and take your leave in each of the following situations.

1. A boy or girl leaves a conversational group before the others.
2. A boy leaves a party before it is ended, says goodbye to his friend's parents and to his hostess.
3. A girl and her escort stop to say goodbye to the chaperones before leaving a school dance.
4. A girl who has been visiting her friend takes her leave early.
5. A boy who has been chatting with his friend's parents takes his leave before the conversation is completed.

Some additional suggestions for good conversation are:

(1) Speak briefly each time you talk. Allow others to speak before you talk again.
(2) Welcome new arrivals and tell them what you were talking about before they arrived. ("*We're glad to see you, Ed. We were just talking about the movie at the Palace this week. Have you seen it?*")
(3) Praise others when you sincerely can. Avoid saying anything that makes you seem important. Don't blow your own horn.

● EXERCISE 8.   Form groups of five or six with a host or hostess designated for each group. Arrange seating in a circular or semicircular pattern.

After introducing the members of the group to one another, each host or hostess starts a conversation on a topic of interest to all, and the members try to keep the ball rolling. At the end of 15 minutes the groups are re-arranged and the same procedure repeated. When the second 15-minute period is ended, the class re-assembles to analyze the conversations, considering such matters as the choice of topics, conversational courtesy, the extent to which everyone participated, and the skill of the host or hostess. If a tape recorder is available, record a conversation for class analysis.

● EXERCISE 9.   A group of five or six students seated in a semicircle at the front of the room carries on a conversation while the rest of the class listens. At the end of 15 minutes the conversation is ended. The class then comments on the merits of the conversation and the skill of the participants, and offers suggestions for improvement.

● EXERCISE 10.   Enact the following situations before the class. At the conclusion of each, the class will suggest ways of improvement.

1. You and a friend disagree on the merits of a movie you have just seen. Another friend of yours comes along. Introduce him to the first participant and continue the conversation.
2. Introduce your mother to your teacher. The three of you carry on a conversation.
3. You visit your father at his office. He introduces you to his partner and the three of you converse on a topic of mutual interest.

● EXERCISE 11.   Prepare a list of conversational *Do's* and *Don'ts*. Discuss them with the class, pointing

16j

out the reason for each and inviting the class to offer
additional suggestions.

Expressing Disagreements

You may disagree with a speaker in the course of a
conversation. This is a healthy sign, for it shows that
you are alert and have the courage of your convic-
tions.

16k. Learn to disagree without being disagree-
able.

You can be forthright and pleasant at the same time.
Differences of opinion can be expressed in reasonable
terms. Express contrary opinions calmly and firmly,
but always in a friendly manner.

There is no need to raise your voice. An idea is not
stronger because it is shouted.

Statements such as, "You're wrong," "That's not
true," and "You don't understand the problem"
arouse antagonism. The person with whom you are
conversing feels that he must save face by defending
his viewpoints. No difference of opinion is settled when
emotion takes the place of reason.

● EXERCISE 12.   While the rest of the class listens,
converse with a group of students on a controversial
topic about which several of you disagree. At the conclusion of the conversation your classmates will comment upon the manner in which disagreements were
expressed and settled.

Giving Travel Directions

If a friend or stranger asks you for travel directions,
answer only if you are certain of your information. Do

not hesitate to admit ignorance, for it is better to confess you do not know than to guess.

161. Make travel directions simple.

If two routes are possible, describe the one that is easier to follow even though it may be longer.

Sketch a rough diagram if the directions are complicated.

Use the terms *north, south, east,* and *west,* but first be sure your questioner knows the direction he is facing. If the directions of the compass confuse rather than clarify, use such expressions as *straight ahead, turn right,* and *turn left.*

Mention some easily observed landmark so that the questioner may check his progress en route. Give an approximate notion of the distance. For example: "A mile from here" or "Fifteen minutes' walking distance from this spot."

● EXERCISE 13.　Relate from your own experience an incident in which you were misdirected. Describe the results. Explain how the would-be informant should have directed you.

● EXERCISE 14.　Form teams of two, one member of the team to ask and the other to give directions. Devise situations of your own. The following list is only suggestive.

1. A stranger asks the way to the railroad station.
2. A motorist asks directions to the next town.
3. A new student asks the way to the school library.
4. A new acquaintance asks the way to your home.
5. A visitor to your town asks where some points of interest are located.

16 k-l

Extending Thanks, Congratulations, Apologies, and Sympathy.

16m. Express with sincerity, brevity, and simplicity every statement of thanks, congratulations, apology, and sympathy.

Saying thanks is easy yet often neglected or overlooked. Form the habit of expressing appreciation for kindnesses and courtesies extended to you. "Thank you" followed by the person's name is more courteous than just "Thanks."

When a friend or acquaintance attains success — for example, if he wins a scholarship, distinguishes himself in a game, or receives an award — congratulate him on his achievement. Let him know your pride and pleasure in his attainment.

Congratulate warmly and genuinely but without exaggeration. Be specific: mention why the success is deserved.

EXAMPLES   Congratulations, Joe! That ninth inning catch saved the game for us.

Helen, your characterization of the leading role was excellent! You seemed to get inside the character. We're all proud of you.

Ed, I just heard the news that you have won a scholarship to State Tech. Congratulations!

It is enough to say "Thank you" simply and sincerely if you are the recipient of congratulations. You may add that you were lucky if such was the case, but beware of false modesty — that may be worse than boastfulness.

When an apology is required, speak to the offended person as soon as possible. The apology should be offered in a face-to-face meeting, but use the telephone rather than delay.

If the incident for which you are apologizing was unintentional on your part, no lengthy apology is necessary. A simple "Excuse me" or "I'm sorry" is enough. If the incident could be interpreted as intentional, an explanation is necessary. Shoulder the blame if you are at fault.

Accept an apology immediately and graciously if one is tendered to you. Make light of the incident that made the apology necessary, and as soon as possible change the subject.

EXAMPLES   Sorry to keep you waiting, Edith. I misjudged the time needed to get here.

That's all right, Bob. We can still get to the theatre on time.

I'm sorry that I lost my temper this afternoon, Sonia.

Thank you, Phil, but I was wrong, too. Let's forget it.

I want to apologize for being so thoughtless yesterday. I hope you'll forgive me.

All right, Jerry. I know that you didn't mean anything by what you said. Did you see the ball game today?

If a friend suffers some misfortune, let him know that you share his disappointment or sorrow. Be encouraging if you can. Your expression of sympathy should be sincere and simple.

EXAMPLES   I was sorry, Frank, to hear you'd been ill. I hope it won't be long before you are feeling better again.

I just wanted to tell you, Edith, that I sympathize with you.

Too bad the match didn't go your way, Ronnie. Better luck next time.

16m

● EXERCISE 15. Acting in groups of two, extend and accept congratulations in situations such as the following. (You may devise additional situations of your own.)

1. Winning a medal for excellence in scholarship.
2. Winning first place in a track event.
3. Election as class president.
4. Obtaining an important position.
5. Performance on a radio or TV program.

● EXERCISE 16. Acting in groups of two, extend and accept apologies in situations such as the following. (As in the previous exercise, this list is only suggestive. Think of additional situations.)

1. Misconduct in class.
2. Breaking a school regulation.
3. Forgetting an appointment.
4. Spilling coffee on a tablecloth.
5. Accidentally scratching a piece of furniture.

● EXERCISE 17. Tell orally how you would express sympathy in each of the following situations.

1. To a close friend on the death of his sister.
2. To a neighbor who is convalescing from a serious illness.
3. To a classmate who has failed an important examination.
4. To a storekeeper who is going out of business.
5. To a friend who has lost a valuable watch.

Asking for a Date

16n. Be considerate and specific when asking for a date.

A boy who is considerate asks a girl for a date several days in advance of the event. The invitation should be phrased to make the invited person feel that you are happy to be with her, and should include the date, time, place, and event.

Don't say, "Are you doing anything Saturday evening?" Say instead: "Our fraternity is holding its annual dance next Saturday evening in the Hotel Essex. It's an informal affair. Fred Humphrey's swing band is going to play — and you know that's one of the best in town. Will you come with me? Irma, Dotty, Neil, and Ernie are going to be there and we'll have a lot of fun together."

The girl should accept or decline the invitation immediately. It is discourteous to merely say, "I'll let you know" with no explanation. Whether she accepts or declines, she should express appreciation for the invitation.

● EXERCISE 18.   Read and report orally to the class on any of the following books on teen-age manners. All of them were written expressly for high school students.

Allen, Betty, and Briggs, M. P. *Behave Yourself*
Betz, Betty. *Your Manners Are Showing*
Boykin, Eleanor. *This Way, Please*
Heal, Edith. *The Teen-Age Manual*
Jonathan, Norton H. *Gentlemen Aren't Sissies*
Stratton, D. C., and Schleman, H. B. *Your Best Foot Forward*

● EXERCISE 19.   Submit in writing to your teacher questions on dating that puzzle you. Your teacher will select those of general interest, read them aloud to the class, and conduct a discussion on them.

16n

CHAPTER **17**

Listening

Why should you learn how to listen? "I've been listening all my life," you may say. "I don't need any instruction." But you do. Intelligent listening is difficult. Sometimes it is more difficult to listen than to read, write, or speak.

Everyone can improve his listening ability with a little study and practice. With improvement in listening will come more individual satisfaction, progress, and pleasure.

Purposeful Listening

When you approach a listening situation, you should have clearly in mind what you wish to gain from your listening. For example, your purpose may be to obtain information, to analyze and evaluate arguments, to get answers to specific questions, or to understand directions. A listening experience is most valuable when you are prepared for it.

17a. Listen to acquire information.

You usually listen more carefully when you are interested in the subject under discussion and want to increase your knowledge of it. You pay close attention when you expect to use what you hear, and you will

386

often ask questions to clear up points about which you are doubtful.

If someone is talking about one of your hobbies or interests, listen to refresh your knowledge of it, fill in gaps in your background, and extend what you already know. The speaker may have a point of view which you have never thought about and which may be valuable as well as novel.

● EXERCISE 1.　Listen while your teacher or a member of your class reads aloud an informational article from a digest magazine. Write several questions based on what you hear. At the conclusion of the oral reading, ask your questions and call on other members of the class to answer them.

● EXERCISE 2.　Listen while one of your classmates discusses a subject about which you know a great deal. When he has finished, tell what you learned that you did not know before, explain how the speaker refreshed your knowledge, or ask questions to clear up doubtful points.

● EXERCISE 3.　Compose a paragraph that contains a contradiction or absurdity. Read it aloud and call upon your classmates to discover what is wrong.

EXAMPLE　Commercial airplanes fly non-stop from New York to San Francisco every hour. New flights will be added when rates are lowered. These planes cross the continent in twelve hours, not including a half hour spent in refueling at Kansas City.

● EXERCISE 4.　With your teacher's permission make a tape recording of a pupil's oral report. Play back the recording in another class and call upon the listeners to summarize it.

17a

● EXERCISE 5.   Conduct a class discussion on a topic of general interest; for example, comic books, teen-age drivers, strict vs. easy teachers, coeducation, radio and television programs. At the conclusion of the discussion call upon a pupil to summarize the main points presented.

17b. Listen to judge arguments on controversial subjects.

Intelligent people do not make up their minds on debatable questions until they have heard both sides and have enough information on which to base an opinion. Untrained listeners leap to conclusions before hearing both the pro and con of disputed issues.

Before forming an opinion on a controversial subject, ask yourself:

1. Have I heard both sides of the question?
2. Have I obtained enough information to reach a conclusion? If not, on what points do I need additional information? Where can I obtain it?

17c. Listen to find answers to your questions.

You listen attentively when you want answers to questions that trouble you. If you know beforehand the topic which a speaker is going to discuss, you can think of questions about it that you would like to have answered. For example, if a speaker at a coming assembly is going to talk about choosing a career, you might prepare to listen by considering such questions as: Are there any tests that will help me decide the type of work for which I am best fitted? Can I delay my choice of career until I finish my college education?

● EXERCISE 6.   Find out the subject which a guest speaker is going to discuss at the next assembly or which a classmate is going to discuss before the class. Write three questions that you would like to have answered. After the speech tell the class:

1. Whether the speaker answered your questions in his presentation.
2. Whether you found it easier to pay attention because you were listening with a definite purpose.

17d. Listen to understand directions.

If you do not listen carefully to directions, you will not be able to follow them no matter how clear they may be.

When you are given instructions about doing or making something, visualize each step of the process. Remember the order in which you should perform each operation. If you are confused or in doubt, ask for clarification. Get the directions straight before you attempt to carry them out.

When you are told the route to a certain destination, repeat the directions aloud to be sure you remember and understand them.

● EXERCISE 7.   Listen to directions given by your teacher or a classmate and, without further instruction, carry them out in proper sequence.

EXAMPLE   **Enter the room quietly, go to your seat, put your English textbook on the desk and all other texts in the desk, and start to copy in your notebook the material on the side blackboard.**

● EXERCISE 8.   Listen while your teacher reads aloud instructions for fire drills or air raid drills. Repeat these instructions as completely and accurately as you can.

**17
b-d**

● EXERCISE 9. Listen while one of your classmates gives directions for doing or making something. The following list is suggestive.

Baking a pie	Building a dog house
Dancing a waltz	Starting a car
Caring for African violets	Playing girls' basketball
Swimming the crawl stroke	Wiring a lamp
Operating a mimeograph machine	Pitching a tent

Repeat the directions aloud to show that you understand.

Accurate Listening

Spoken language is sometimes difficult to follow. If you do not listen closely, you may misinterpret what is said or fail to hear important information.

Accurate listeners notice how a speaker organizes and develops his thoughts. They perceive and remember his central ideas.

17e. Listen for main ideas.

At the beginning of a talk a speaker often signals the important ideas he is going to discuss.

EXAMPLE   Boys and girls, I want to thank your principal for permitting me to talk to you today about an essay contest which our Rotary Club is sponsoring. I want to tell you about the subject of the contest, the rules which govern it, and the prizes which will be given to the winners.

In the foregoing example, to help you follow the thread of the discussion, the speaker has signalled the three main ideas he is going to discuss: the topic, rules, and prizes of a Rotary Club essay contest.

Another way of discovering main ideas is to listen

for transitional words and phrases. A speaker indicates that he is advancing from one important idea to another by using bridging words and expressions. For example:

Also	Moreover
Besides	Next
Furthermore	On the other hand
In conclusion	Thirdly
In the second place	Still another

You can perceive main ideas more easily if you know how to distinguish between generalizations and examples. A *generalization* is a broad statement or principle. An *example* is a specific case which illustrates the statement or principle.

Thus, a speaker may want to show that boys may learn a useful civilian occupation while serving in the armed forces. He may give examples of boys who learned to operate business machines, repair automobiles, service radios, make electrical installations, or type while serving in the Army, Navy, or Air Force. A listener need only remember:

> A young man may learn a civilian occupation in the armed forces.

Still another way of finding a speaker's main ideas is to listen to his summary. Before concluding a speaker often lists the important ideas he wants you to remember.

EXAMPLE In bringing my remarks to a close, I want to stress once more the importance of good grooming for girls and boys of high school age. Dress appropriately for school. Your appearance affects you and those about you. If you are neatly dressed, you have increased self-respect, you behave better, and you are regarded more highly by others. The way pupils dress affects the tone of the school.

17e

You may have trouble in following main ideas in a
group discussion because of digressions, that is, not
keeping on the subject. Some participants may wander
down by-ways which are interesting but not closely
related to the subject at hand. Intelligent listeners
keep the goal of a discussion always in mind and
recognize the difference between fruitless digressions
and the main thread of an argument. If they are
also participants, they lead the discussion back to the
main issues when they can do so without offense. If
they are not participants but only listeners, they make
a mental distinction between relevant and irrelevant
comments.

● EXERCISE 10.   Your teacher or a classmate will
read aloud the introductory paragraphs of a speech.
Raise your hand when you can predict what the
speaker's main points are going to be. (For usable
speeches, consult the magazine *Vital Speeches* in your
library.)

● EXERCISE 11.   Make a tape recording of a news
broadcast or short talk. Your classmates will jot down
the main ideas in correct order as you play it to them.
Re-play to check.

● EXERCISE 12.   Conduct a class discussion on one
of the following topics. After a number of pupils have
expressed their opinions, call on someone to summarize. Consider whether the summary is complete and
accurate.

   Ways of improving our school
   Traffic accidents
   Teen-age manners
   School clubs and teams
   Our school lunchroom
   An eleven-month school year

Why go to college?
Why I prefer to live in a small town (or large city)
Should 18-year-olds have the right to vote?

● EXERCISE 13.   The familiar game of "In Grandma's Attic" is an exercise in accurate listening. One pupil starts by saying, "In Grandma's attic there was an apron." Another pupil repeats what he said and adds another item. Each subsequent pupil repeats the items in proper order and adds another.

17f. Listen and take notes.

By taking notes you can see the sequence of ideas, prevent your attention from wandering, and recall what was said.

Note-taking is not easy. Many college students fail, particularly during their freshman year, because they do not know how to take notes of lectures. As they learn how to record what they hear, they have less difficulty.

Observe the following procedures in taking notes:

(1) *Record only important ideas.* Do not attempt to jot down everything that is said. With experience you will learn to differentiate between important and relatively unimportant ideas.
(2) *Use abbreviations.* Unless you know shorthand, you cannot write as fast as a lecturer speaks. Develop your own abbreviations.
(3) *Record your notes in running form.* Number each new idea. As you become more proficient in note-taking, you may take notes in outline form if you wish. An outline shows you at a glance the relationship of one idea to another, but it is a more difficult form of note-taking and in the beginning may confuse rather than help you.

17f

An example of running notes:

APPLYING FOR A JOB

1. Learn about job opportunities from friends, ads, agencies. 2. Make appt. for interview. 3. Prepare résumé. Include: name, age, tel. no., educ., exper., previous empl. 4. Dress neatly — hair, clothing, skin, shoes, fingernails. 5. Arrive punctually. 6. Answer questions completely, truthfully. 7. Ask questions if nec. 8. Leaving — thank empl. for priv. of interview.

(4) *Review your notes.* To refresh your memory look over your notes shortly after taking them. If necessary, complete them and check to be sure they are legible. Notes quickly grow "cold" and may lose some of their value to you if you do not look them over from time to time.

Critical Listening

In a democracy everyone has the right to express his opinions whether they are right or wrong, true or false. Freedom of speech is necessary and desirable, but it involves certain responsibilities. As speakers, we have the responsibility of saying only what we know or believe to be true. As listeners, we have the responsibility of weighing what someone says and judging its worth.

17g. Be aware of your own feelings that may predispose you to accept or reject a speaker's arguments.

Some people listen just to refute arguments with which they disagree. Others listen to find additional arguments in favor of opinions they already hold. Such listeners are neither open-minded nor critical.

A speaker's words may influence you more than they should because you were inclined beforehand to give him favorable consideration. His reputation, appearance, achievements, or previous speeches may have impressed you.

On the other hand, you may underestimate what a speaker says because you were prejudiced against him even before he started to speak.

A critical listener is aware of such biased feelings. He may not be able to rid himself of them entirely, but he takes them into consideration when evaluating what he hears.

● EXERCISE 14.   From radio or television programs published in a newspaper, select a well-known personality scheduled to speak on a topic of general interest. Analyze your feelings toward him. Are you favorably or unfavorably inclined to heed his message. Why?

Listen to his talk and evaluate it. To what extent, if any, did your earlier feelings affect your evaluation?

17h. If a speaker has an axe to grind, you should be aware of it.

A critical listener recognizes bias in a speaker and makes allowances for it.

For example, a salesman may recommend a product out of all proportion to its true worth. He is sincere, but his judgment is affected because he is a paid employee of the manufacturer. In evaluating his claims, take this understandable bias into consideration. This does not mean that you should reject out of hand the arguments of anyone who stands to gain personally from your support. It means, rather, that you should be conscious of his prejudice when weighing his statements.

17 g-h

● EXERCISE 15.   Why should you be particularly careful in listening to each of the following speakers?

1. The president of a college fraternity speaking about the advantages of fraternity life.
2. A movie actress advertising a cold cream.
3. A candidate of a political party speaking about his party's platform.
4. A radio announcer delivering a commercial.
5. A parent of a failing student criticizing a school.

17i. Look for and weigh evidence for every important statement.

Assertion is not proof. A speaker should support his arguments by facts, figures, examples, and statements of competent authorities. If he offers no evidence, ask for it.

When two speakers present contradictory opinions, reserve judgment until all facts are in and you have had a chance to mull over them.

If you do not understand what is said, do not hesitate to ask questions. Some listeners remain silent because they are afraid to appear ignorant. This attitude is unintelligent.

● EXERCISE 16.   Before listening to a class discussion of a controversial subject, divide a sheet of paper into two columns headed "Arguments for" and "Arguments against." As the discussion progresses list each argument in the appropriate column and beneath it indicate the evidence offered to substantiate it in the form of facts, figures, examples, or quotations from authoritative sources.

● EXERCISE 17.   Before reading aloud an actual speech or a magazine article which advocates a course of action, list on the board the arguments which the speaker or writer is going to develop. During the reading the listeners will jot down the evidence for each of the arguments listed.

17j. Distinguish between words that report and words which are emotionally loaded.

Some words report a fact objectively. They have few emotional overtones, if any. Others are loaded with emotion.

Compare the following pairs of words. Notice how one member of each pair is relatively colorless, while the other arouses feelings.

house	shack	dwelling	mansion
car	jalopy	defeat	rout
book	tome	recline	sprawl
reply	rebuke	failure	fiasco
verse	doggerel	evening	gloaming
farmer	peasant	dog	mongrel
work	drudgery	boy	rascal

Loaded words carry positive or negative charges. A positively charged word creates a favorable reaction; a negatively charged word, an unfavorable one. Propagandists make use of loaded words to influence listeners. They employ positively charged words to sway you to their way of thinking and negatively charged words to make you reject what they oppose.

On a separate sheet of paper indicate by plus and minus signs which of the following words affect you positively or negatively.

1. adorable	7. democracy
2. skinny	8. dictatorship
3. glamorous	9. noise
4. communism	10. music
5. fabulous	11. reactionary
6. fascism	12. glutton

17 i-j

13. miserly
14. generous
15. crude
16. rebellious

17. sympathy
18. sentimentality
19. horse opera
20. screech

Be suspicious of loaded words. They may stir your emotions so strongly that you will fail to reason soundly.

● EXERCISE 18.   Make a list of loaded words used in radio and television commercials.

● EXERCISE 19.   Besides using emotive words, what other psychological appeals do advertisers use?

● EXERCISE 20.   Record two news broadcasts of the same date. Choose one that gives you only a factual report and another that includes comment and analysis. Contrast the language used in both when the same item is discussed.

17k. Listen in a courteous way.

Not every speaker, musical program, play, or assembly presentation is entertaining. Some are dull. But whether a program bores or entertains you, you have an obligation to listen politely. Your attitude affects a speaker or performer. You can help or hinder him by your behavior.

The task of an actor or speaker is always hard. You owe him a courteous audience.

Good listening manners require that you:
(1) Listen — and do nothing else. If you take notes, take them unobtrusively. Do not read, doodle, converse, or in any other way create a distraction.
(2) Be patient and quiet if a speaker experiences difficulty.

(3) Remain in your seat until the speaker has finished. If you must leave ahead of time, slip out quietly.

(4) Applaud with your hands only. Whistling and shouting are objectionable.

171. Sit comfortably alert. Do not slump or sprawl.

When you are listening to a speaker or watching a television broadcast, watch your posture. It is important to your health. Also, a person with good posture gives a better appearance and creates a more favorable impression on others.

● EXERCISE 21.   What are some discourteous listening habits which are common in your school?

● EXERCISE 22.   Draw up a code of good manners for listeners. After class discussion forward it to your student council for school-wide action.

17
k-l

CHAPTER 18

Parliamentary Procedure

All organizations, except those which are very small and informal, conduct their meetings according to a code known as rules of order or parliamentary procedure.

Parliamentary procedure protects the rights of all and enables individuals to work together efficiently. It is a means of determining the will of the majority and at the same time safeguarding the rights of the minority.

To participate intelligently in meetings of clubs, labor unions, social and religious societies, political and civic organizations, and other groups, a person must know parliamentary procedure.

18a. A constitution is a document which sets forth the aims of an organization and the fundamental rules by which it operates.

A constitution should include the following:

(1) Name of the organization
(2) Purpose
(3) Duties of officers, length of term, method of election
(4) Qualifications of membership
(5) Minimum number of meetings
(6) Method of amending the constitution

18b. By-laws are less important rules than those found in a constitution.

By-laws deal with such matters as dues, penalties for nonpayment of dues, time of meetings, order of business, and quorum. They are usually placed at the end of a constitution.

18c. Officers are elected according to the method prescribed in an organization's constitution.

Officers may be nominated in two ways. A nominating committee may submit a slate of officers to the membership, or members may make nominations from the floor. To make a nomination, a member rises and says, "Mr. Chairman, I nominate John Jones for the office of president." Nominations need not be seconded.

Elections are usually held immediately after nominations are closed unless a by-law directs that they be held at a following meeting.

Voting is by secret ballot. Slips of paper are distributed to all members; these slips should be large enough to fold so that what a member writes cannot be seen by those near him. The chairman appoints tellers who collect and count the ballots. They report the result to the chairman who announces it to the members.

A majority vote is usually required for election unless a by-law states otherwise. If no one receives a majority, a new vote must be taken, limited to the two candidates who received the highest number of votes on the first ballot.

When there is only one candidate for an office, a motion for a unanimous ballot is in order. "I move that the secretary cast one ballot for . . ." If the motion is seconded and carried, the secretary goes through

18 a-c

the form of writing the candidate's name on a slip of paper and handing it to the chairman who formally announces that the candidate has been elected.

DUTIES OF OFFICERS

The president presides over meetings, appoints committees, calls special meetings if necessary, and sees that the organization's constitution and by-laws are observed.

The vice-president acts in place of the president if the latter is absent. He may have other duties specified in the constitution.

The secretary notifies members of meetings, takes the minutes, keeps a record of attendance, and answers letters as the president directs.

The treasurer receives dues and other income, and keeps a record of all receipts and disbursements. At every meeting he gives a report of the organization's current financial status.

18d. Committees are of two kinds: standing and special.

Standing committees are permanent. Their terms end with the term of the president who appointed them. Membership and finance committees are usually standing committees.

Special committees are those appointed for a particular purpose. When the purpose is accomplished, the committee ceases to exist. A committee appointed to conduct a dance is a special committee.

18e. The minimum number of members necessary to hold a meeting is called a quorum.

The number is usually specified in the by-laws. If the by-laws do not mention the number, a majority of the total membership constitutes a quorum.

If a quorum is lacking, the only business that may be transacted is to set the time for the next meeting, take a recess, or adjourn.

18f. The regular procedure at meetings is called the order of business.

The following is a typical order of business:

(1) Call to order
(2) Roll call
(3) Reading of minutes of previous meeting
(4) Treasurer's report
(5) Committee reports
(6) Unfinished business
(7) New business
(8) Adjournment

18g. A motion is a proposal offered to the membership for discussion and action.

EXAMPLES   I move that we purchase new uniforms for the basketball team.
I move that we publish a monthly bulletin.
I move that this question be referred to a committee of three appointed by the chair.
I move we adjourn.

An organization transacts all its business at meetings through motions.

STEPS IN MAKING A MOTION

(1) A member requests and receives recognition by the chair. If two or more members rise at the same time, the chair recognizes the one who addressed him first.

Member: "Mr. Chairman."
Chair: "Mr. Jones."

18 d-g

(2) The member states his motion.

Member: "I move that our club hold a skating party."

(3) Another member seconds the motion. All motions must be seconded before they can be considered. The purpose of a second is to show that more than one person is interested.

Another member: "I second the motion."

(4) The chair repeats the motion using the original words.

Chair: "It is moved and seconded that our club hold a skating party."

(5) The members discuss the motion.
(6) When the discussion is finished, the chair repeats the motion.
(7) The chair puts the motion to a vote.

Chair: "All those in favor say 'aye.' Those opposed, 'nay.'"

(8) The chair announces the result.

Chair: "The motion is carried."

If the vote is taken by a show of hands or by ballot, the chair may announce the exact count.

Chair: "By a vote of 25–8, the motion is carried."

● EXERCISE 1. Practice the steps in making a motion. With one class member acting as chairman, the others will offer various main motions. Suggested subjects for motions:

Abolition of homework
Class picnic
Purchase of books
Petition to principal
Field trip
Publication of class newspaper

18h. Motions are of two kinds: main motions and procedural motions

A main motion brings new business before a meeting. It has to do with matters of substance. Motions to run a bazaar, stage a show, or purchase equipment are main motions. Main motions can be debated and amended. Only one main motion can be considered at a time.

A procedural motion concerns the procedure of a meeting or ways of handling main motions. Motions to postpone consideration of a question or to adjourn are examples of procedural motions. Most procedural motions cannot be amended. There may be several procedural motions before a meeting at one time. The most important procedural motions are:

(1) Adjourn
(2) Lay on the table
(3) Close debate
(4) Refer to committee

AMENDING A MAIN MOTION

Main motions may be amended. Not more than one amendment can be considered at a time. If desired, another amendment may be proposed when the first has been disposed of.

18i. A main motion may be amended by adding, striking out, or substituting words.

EXAMPLES   I move to amend the original motion by adding the word "monthly" before "dance."

I move to amend the original motion by striking out the word "new."

I move to amend the original motion by substituting the word "semi-annual" in place of "annual."

**18
h-i**

● EXERCISE 2. Practice making and amending main motions using the topics listed in Exercise 1 or others of your own devising.

PROCEDURAL MOTIONS

Motion to adjourn. The purpose of this motion is to bring the meeting to an end. It cannot be debated or amended and must be put to a vote as soon as seconded.

> I move we adjourn.
> I move that this meeting adjourn.
> I move that this meeting do now adjourn.

Motion to lay on the table. The purpose of this motion is to stop consideration of a main motion at least for the time being. If a motion to lay on the table is passed, the main motion is put aside indefinitely. It may be reconsidered at some future time if a motion "to take from the table" is passed. A motion to lay on the table cannot be debated or amended.

> I move to lay this motion on the table.
> I move that this motion be tabled.

Motion to close debate. The purpose of this motion is to cut off discussion and bring a question to a vote. This motion used to be called the Previous Question, but because the term was confusing it is now called the motion to close debate.

The motion to close debate may not be debated or amended. It requires a *two-thirds* vote for adoption. (Notice that any motion which restricts freedom of speech requires a two-thirds vote in order to protect minority rights.)

> I move that debate on the pending motion be closed and that we vote at once.
> I move to close debate and vote on this question at once.

Motion to refer to a committee. The purpose of this motion is to assign a question to a committee for study and report. Unlike the foregoing procedural motions, the motion to refer to committee can be debated and amended.

MOTION: I move that this question be referred to committee.
AMENDMENT: I move that the motion be amended by adding the words "and that the committee report its findings at our next meeting."

18j. A point of order is an objection to a violation of parliamentary procedure.

Its purpose is to require members to comply with the rules of order.

Since a point of order is not a motion, it requires no second and no vote. Typical points of order are: absence of a quorum, irrelevant remarks by a speaker, motion which violates club's constitution.

Member: Mr. Chairman, I rise to a point of order.
Chair: State your point of order.
Member: I make the point of order that the meeting is so noisy the speaker cannot be heard.
Chair: The point is well taken and the meeting will come to order.

● EXERCISE 3. Practice the following procedures in class.

Proposing, discussing, and voting on a main motion.
Rising to a point of order.
Adjourning a meeting.
Nominating and electing officers.
Proposing a procedural motion.

● EXERCISE 4. With one class member acting as chairman, other members of the class will propose,

18j

discuss, and vote upon humorous motions. For example:

> That the members purchase a yacht for the custodian-engineer.
> That students be allowed to arrive late without penalty.
> That examinations be abolished.
> That the teacher invite the class to a party.
> That ice skating be permitted on the school roof.

● EXERCISE 5. Attend a meeting of a club, fraternity, or association, and report orally on the way the meeting was conducted. What did you learn about parliamentary procedure that you did not previously know?

● EXERCISE 6. Organize the class as a club. Elect officers, draw up a constitution, appoint committees, and transact business. Rotate officers and committee memberships so that everyone has an opportunity to exercise leadership.

● EXERCISE 7. Read and report on one of the following references. Explain a topic not taken up in this chapter so clearly that everyone understands. (Some suggested topics: duties and rights of members, reading and approving minutes, the motion to postpone, the motion to reconsider.)

> Cushing's *Manual of Parliamentary Practice*
> Eliot's *Basic Rules of Order*
> Robert's *Rules of Order*
> Sturgis' *Standard Code of Parliamentary Procedure*

● EXERCISE 8. Two features of parliamentary procedure are freedom of discussion and majority rule. Of the two, which is the more important? Why?

PART FIVE

MECHANICS

CHAPTER 19

Capital Letters

The use of capital letters is a matter of habit and carefulness as well as of knowing the rules. Always read over your written work to check it for capitals.

● TRY-OUT TEST. If you can make 100% on the following quiz, you may work through this chapter very rapidly. If you make a lower score, you should learn the uses of capital letters and do the exercises so that you will be able henceforth to use capital letters correctly.

Number on your paper from 1 to 25. In each of the following items you are to choose the correct one of two forms. After the proper number on your paper write the letter of the correct form (a or b).

1. a. We spent the summer in Maine.
   b. We spent the Summer in Maine.

2. a. the Mississippi River
   b. the Mississippi river

3. a. the Empire State building
   b. the Empire State Building

4. a. He lives on Pine Street.
   b. He lives on Pine street.

5. a. Lafayette college is in Easton.
   b. Lafayette College is in Easton.

6. a. Are you going to the Senior Prom?
   b. Are you going to the senior prom?

7. a. He will be a senior next year.
   b. He will be a Senior next year.

8. a. Amherst was his college.
   b. Amherst was his College.

9. a. I am taking Latin and Geometry.
   b. I am taking Latin and geometry.

10. a. the Atlantic ocean
    b. the Atlantic Ocean

11. a. our High School
    b. our high school

12. a. a package of Wrigley's gum
    b. a package of Wrigley's Gum

13. a. The President spoke from the White House.
    b. The president spoke from the White House.

14. a. Mr. Lewis, superintendent of schools
    b. Mr. Lewis, Superintendent of Schools

15. a. They worshiped god in their own way.
    b. They worshiped God in their own way.

16. a. the Rivoli Theater
    b. the Rivoli theater

17. a. Zeus was a Greek god.
    b. Zeus was a Greek God.

18. a. Is he a Frenchman?
    b. Is he a frenchman?

19. a. We admired the cathedrals of europe.
    b. We admired the cathedrals of Europe.

20. a. Harold owns a cocker spaniel pup.
    b. Harold owns a Cocker Spaniel pup.

21. a. Thirty-fourth Street
    b. Thirty-Fourth Street

22. a. We spent our vacation in the North.
    b. We spent our vacation in the north.

23. a. They drove South for ten miles.
    b. They drove south for ten miles.

24. a. the General Electric Company
    b. the General Electric company

25. a. Everyone feared a civil war.
    b. Everyone feared a Civil War.

19a. Capitalize the pronoun *I*, the interjection *O*.

WRONG   "o boy!" i cried.
RIGHT   "**O** boy!" **I** cried.

19b. Capitalize the first word in any sentence.[1]

WRONG   Jefferson was an early champion of states' rights. on the other hand, Hamilton believed in a strong central government. it was a good thing to have these two views represented in the early days of our country.

RIGHT   Jefferson was an early champion of states' rights. **O**n the other hand, Hamilton believed in a strong central government. **I**t was a good thing to have these two views represented in the early days of our country.

19c. Capitalize proper nouns and proper adjectives.

A proper noun is the name of a particular person, place, or thing.

How a proper noun differs from an ordinary, common noun, which is not capitalized, can be seen from the following lists.

COMMON NOUN	PROPER NOUN
city	Chicago
boy	George
lake	Crater Lake

Do not confuse proper nouns, which are *names*, with nouns which merely state kind or type. For instance, *terrier* is not a proper noun because it is not the name of a particular dog; it is merely a kind

[1] Failure to use a capital letter at the beginning of a sentence is almost always the result of failure to recognize the beginning of a sentence. For exercises in recognizing the beginning of a sentence see pages 93–95.

or type of dog; similarly, *truck* is not the name of a particular automobile (like Chevrolet, Plymouth, etc.) but tells only the type of automobile.

RIGHT   **Helen's dog is a cocker spaniel.**

RIGHT   **His name is Blackie**

WRONG   **Jerry's ambition is to own a Ford Convertible.**

RIGHT   **Jerry's ambition is to own a Ford convertible.**

A proper adjective is an adjective formed from a proper noun.

PROPER NOUN	PROPER ADJECTIVE
Spain	*Spanish* town
America	*American* citizen
Democrat	*Democratic* leader

Careful study of the classifications which follow will help you to recognize the most frequently used proper nouns.

(1) Capitalize geographical names.

CITIES AND TOWNS   Meadville, Kansas City

COUNTIES AND TOWNSHIPS   Nassau County, Sherman Township

STATES   Arkansas, New Mexico

COUNTRIES   Union of Soviet Socialist Republics, United States of America, Great Britain

CONTINENTS   Europe, Asia

ISLANDS   Fire Island

BODIES OF WATER   Columbia River, Great Salt Lake, Lake Erie, Pacific Ocean, Red Sea

MOUNTAINS   Appalachian Mountains, Bear Mountain

STREETS   Main Street, Fairmount Boulevard, Dover Parkway, Twenty-third Street. [In a hyphenated *number*, the second word begins with a small letter.]

PARKS   Yellowstone National Park, Deerfield State Forest

SECTIONS OF THE COUNTRY   the East, the Middle West

19
a-c

(2) Do not capitalize *east, west, north,* **and** *south* **when they indicate merely directions. Do capitalize them when they refer to commonly recognized sections of the country.**

RIGHT Go west for two miles and turn south.
We enjoyed our winter in the South.

(3) Do not capitalize a common noun modified by a proper adjective unless the common noun is part of a proper name.

RIGHT a Mediterranean country
a Pacific island
Catalina Island [*Island* is part of a name.]

● EXERCISE 1. Copy the following, using capital letters wherever they are required.

1. anderson park
2. the arctic ocean
3. washington avenue
4. a french village
5. glen lake
6. savannah river
7. staten island
8. bergen county
9. the kansas wheatfields
10. an indian reservation
11. a mile west of here
12. an american industry
13. birmingham, alabama
14. twenty-first street
15. in south america
16. living in the east
17. the west side of twelfth street
18. the ural mountains
19. some montana copper mines
20. a lake michigan steamer

● EXERCISE 2. Copy the following sentences, inserting capitals wherever needed.

1. Heading west from new york, we drove across thirty-fourth street, through the lincoln tunnel under the hudson river, and onto the new jersey turnpike.

2. Outside philadelphia we entered another superhighway, which spans the great state of pennsylvania, crossing the allegheny mountains, which separate the east from the middle west.

3. At pittsburgh the allegheny river and the monongahela river come together to form the ohio.

4. After continuing our drive across ohio to buckeye lake and columbus, we headed west to visit our friends on an indiana farm near indianapolis.

5. Father wanted us to see chicago, which lies in cook county, illinois, at the foot of lake michigan.

6. We visited municipal pier, where we boarded a large lake steamer which had just arrived from mackinac island and a northern cruise into lake superior.

7. The meeting place of the great railroads of the east with those of the west, chicago has always been the greatest inland city of north america.

8. As there were no mountains on our route between the appalachians and the rockies, we had to wait until we reached denver, where we saw pikes peak towering to the south.

9. We spent a week in rocky mountain national park before continuing our westward journey toward california.

10. In salt lake city we saw the mormon temple; after crossing the salt flats to nevada, we made our way toward the northwest and the pacific ocean.

● EXERCISE 3. Read the following paragraphs and list in a column all words requiring capitals. When two capitalized words belong together list them together: *West Main Street, Memorial Park,* etc. Before each word write the number of the sentence in which it appears. Do not list words already capitalized.

1. We moved recently from west main street to park boulevard.   2. Our new home looked out on memorial park and morgan's creek.

1. West Main Street
   Park Boulevard
2. Memorial Park
   Morgan's Creek

1. Our school is a consolidated school on the shores of greenwood lake in macy county. 2. The students come from farms and towns as far away as somerset to the west and bordenville to the east. 3. Yesterday our assembly speaker was a professor of economics from Western Reserve University in cleveland.

4. He was explaining to us our dependence upon all parts of the united states for products we use every day. 5. To her embarrassment, he called Betty, a junior from storm corners, to the platform and asked her where she thought her sweater had come from. 6. Betty told him her mother had bought it for her at Boyd's Department Store on franklin avenue, and this gave the speaker his chance.

7. He pointed out that the wool may have come from a farm in the middle west and been knitted by a machine in a new england factory, perhaps on the shores of the merrimack river in new hampshire. 8. He thought the sweater may have been designed on thirty-first street in new york city. 9. Dyes for the wool may have come from germany, but probably were manufactured in the east. 10. As for Betty's blouse, made of nylon, there was little doubt that its source was coal mined in pennsylvania or west virginia.

11. The speaker thought that the leather for Betty's loafers may have once roamed a ranch in wyoming. 12. He said that it could have come from argentina, by ship through the atlantic ocean, into the caribbean sea

and via new orleans up the mississippi river to st. louis, shoe-manufacturing capital of north america.

13. Noticing the textbook in Betty's hand, the speaker told of seeing trees growing along nipigon bay and nipigon river in ontario, canada, on the northern shore of lake superior, which were destined to be shipped as pulpwood down through lake huron to paper mills in michigan.

(4) Capitalize names of organizations, business firms, institutions, government bodies, ships, planes, brand names of business products, special events, items on the calendar, races, and religions.

ORGANIZATIONS AND CLUBS Independent Order of Odd Fellows, Masquers Club, North Shore Country Club

BUSINESS FIRMS Harcourt, Brace and Company; Sperry Gyroscope Company; Hostage Book Stores, Inc.

GOVERNMENT BODIES the Senate, Securities and Exchange Commission, Congress, the Supreme Court [Usage is divided on the capitalization of *post office, court house,* etc. You may have them either way, unless the full name is given, when they must be capitalized: *Utica Post Office, Omar County Court House.*]

INSTITUTIONS Mercy Hospital, Woolworth Building, Waldorf-Astoria Hotel, Fantasy Theater, Harvard University, Belmont High School, Montclair Academy

▶ NOTE. Do not capitalize such words as *hotel, theater, college, high school* unless they are part of a proper name.

Williams College	a college in Massachusetts
Commodore Hotel	a hotel in New York
Lakewood High School	a high school in Ohio

SHIPS, PLANES, BUSINESS PRODUCTS, AND OTHER THINGS HAVING PARTICULAR NAMES the *Britannic* (ship), a Constellation (plane), the Congressional Medal of Honor

▶ NOTE: Do not capitalize the noun which often follows a brand name: Treat potato chips, Bazooka bubble gum, Chevrolet convertible.

EVENTS National Horse Show, National Tennis Championships, Senior Prom

HISTORICAL EVENTS AND PERIODS Dark Ages, Battle of El Alamein, Reconstruction Period, World War II

CALENDAR ITEMS Monday, January, Thanksgiving, Memorial Day [2]

RACES AND RELIGIOUS GROUPS Negro, Presbyterian

(5) Do not capitalize the names of seasons.

RIGHT summer, winter, spring, fall [Some newspapers do not follow this practice.]

(6) Do not capitalize *senior, sophomore, junior, freshman*, unless part of a proper noun.

RIGHT A sophomore may go to the Senior Prom if escorted by a senior.

19d. Do not capitalize the names of school subjects, except the languages. Course names followed by a number are usually capitalized.

RIGHT English, French, Spanish, Latin, German, Italian
algebra, art, chemistry, domestic science, history
Algebra II, History III

● List all words requiring capitals. When two capitalized words belong together, list them together. Before each item write the number of its paragraph. Do not list words already capitalized.

1. Dr. James Moore, Sr., has been the leading physician in Riverton as long as most residents can remember. His

[2] Some authorities recommend that *day* be capitalized when it is a part of the name; otherwise, it is written with a small letter: Memorial Day, but Christmas day. This distinction, however, is not always observed.

office in the Riverton medical center on main street is the best equipped in calhoun county.

2. Dr. Moore is head surgeon at Riverton memorial hospital, a new hospital which was dedicated on veterans day last year in memory of Riverton men who fought in world war II and the korean war. He is also on the staff of university hospital in the south end of town.

3. Dr. Moore is a charter member of the rotary club, president of the calhoun county medical association, and one of the directors of the summerfield country club. He lives on Circle drive in Edgemere acres, a real estate development in which he is a stockholder.

4. Equally prominent in the community is Dr. Moore's son, James Moore, Jr., who belongs to the same clubs as his father and is the youngest member of the Riverton board of education. His red lincoln convertible is as familiar to residents of Main street as his father's black cadillac coupe.

5. James, Jr., is a different kind of doctor. He owns the woodlawn animal hospital on woodlawn boulevard out near the Curtis dairy and the Roosevelt race track.

6. While a student at Riverton high school, he had a Saturday job at the dairy and spent his summers working on a farm in the western part of the state. Between high school and college, he worked on a ranch in the west. These experiences gave him an absorbing interest in animals, especially in horses and cattle.

7. While in high school, he had looked forward to becoming a doctor. He excelled in biology and took advanced courses in science, like chemistry II and physics II, as well as Latin and german, which, he thought, would help him in medicine.

8. When he was a sophomore in college, he told his father that he had decided to become a veterinary rather than a doctor. Although disappointed, his father took the news philosophically, after pointing out the difference in income and prestige between the two professions.

9. It has become standard in Riverton to think of the name *Moore* whenever illness strikes, whether the patient be

19d

someone's pet persian cat, a prize hereford bull, or a member of the family. Unfortunately, residents do not always get the right Dr. Moore. You can imagine how Dr. Moore, Sr., enjoys being called on a sunday afternoon or on new year's day to attend a sick bull and how his son feels when he is called from bed at 4 o'clock on a winter morning because somebody's child has a pain in his side.

● EXERCISE 5.   Follow directions for Exercise 3, page 415.

1. On the fourth of July, the tri-state industrial exposition will open in the Chicago coliseum.
2. Is he a member of either the local masonic lodge or the elks club?
3. The american legion will have charge of the parade on veterans day.
4. The parade will form at the gate of the shelley electric company and march past the johnson memorial hospital and the sherman building to the united presbyterian church.
5. Jerry, whom I knew when we were in high school, resigned from his position with the general electric company in order to enroll at cornell university.
6. Although I don't do so well in social studies, mathematics, and chemistry, I enjoy them as much as english and french, which are my best subjects.
7. The stamp club, which meets at the community building once a week, probably has quieter meetings than any other club in our high school.
8. The park theater, which stands next to the new hayesbelmont hotel, shows pictures made by metro-goldwynmayer, damon brothers, and paramount.
9. On the morning of thanksgiving day the family went to municipal stadium for the game between madison high and southwestern.
10. Because he had studied only two years of latin in high school, he had to take latin I during his freshman year in college.

11. The juniors were invited to attend the senior prom the night before commencement, but freshmen and sophomores had to be escorted by a junior or senior.

12. Fred's description of costumes worn during the stone age was naturally much shorter than Helen's account of dresses worn during the victorian era.

13. Because he failed both algebra and history last spring, my brother went to the freeport summer high school this summer.

14. The dramatic club meets every friday afternoon from december to march, but only on every other friday during the fall and spring.

15. The posters made by seniors in their art classes this fall, picturing the work of the red cross, were displayed from thanksgiving to christmas in the store windows of the C. G. Longmans company.

● EXERCISE 6. As you did in Exercise 3, list all words requiring capitals in the following sentences. Do not list words already capitalized.

1. Mary Ann was a stranger here last october. 2. On memorial day, she had landed in detroit from dayton, but she had gone to dayton from washington and to washington from texas. 3. All this she had done in one year because she was the daughter of an Army officer who was apparently getting new orders about once a month.

4. Her first view of the city was from an airplane. 5. The penobscot building, she said, was clearly distinguishable, as were such places as cadillac square, grand boulevard, and briggs stadium.

6. So far as high schools are concerned, Mary Ann has seen all kinds. 7. Although she prefers smaller schools, she says she likes highland park high. 8. The trip downtown on a woodward avenue bus seems long to her, but any ride on land seems long to Mary Ann, who is used to flying her own aircoupé at the wayne county airport.

9. Her father, Colonel Bryan, taught her to fly last year in arizona. 10. Furthermore, she seems to be rather used to swimming in the pacific ocean one day and in the atlantic

ocean the next. 11. Perhaps now that she's living in the north she'll be having her summer swims in the detroit river at belle isle and her winter ones in our school pool. 12. She plans to fly to florida for Christmas and get acquainted with the gulf of mexico.

13. Mary Ann is taking english, social studies, trigonometry, chemistry, and commercial work. 14. She's had to give up her spanish because her frequent moves interrupted her work. 15. She says you have to keep at a foreign language to learn it at all and that when you know as little about spanish as she does you forget between moves. 16. She had the same trouble with french and latin last year. 17. With all the traveling around she seems to do, though, she'll probably end up in france or spain and learn her french and spanish that way.

18. I think Mary Ann is lucky to have seen so much, but she says to give her a home in either the north, south, east, or west, but not in all four at once.

● REVIEW EXERCISE A. Copy the sentences below, using capital letters wherever they are required.

1. The old school building at the corner of twenty-first street and carlton avenue has been sold by the greenville board of education.
2. The church street junior high school was built by the wagner construction company during the spring and summer of last year.
3. In junior high school I had better grades in english than in social studies and math.
4. The drama club tried to rent the peabody auditorium for its play, but the woman's club had reserved it for a concert by the minneapolis symphony orchestra.
5. His ship, the *Flying Gull*, sailed from lake michigan to the gulf of mexico via the mississippi river.
6. New factories in the south rival the industrial plants of the north.
7. On the west side of town lies coolidge park, and on the east side lies burnham park.
8. Some of the countries of europe have been uncertain

whether to turn their faces west toward the americas or east toward asia.

9. The great smoky mountains are the principal mountains in tennessee and north carolina.

10. Both seniors and juniors have been invited to the sophomore carnival in the gym on the eve of christmas vacation.

11. During the victorian age the british empire expanded into all corners of the world.

12. The american history classes of the three city high schools produced a pageant on memorial day honoring american soldiers and sailors.

13. A dodge coupé belonging to the gulf oil corporation was parked at foster's garage in the mechanical trades building.

14. On the north side of the street several indian and mexican villagers formed a small crowd.

15. The paramount theater was showing a french film with english subtitles.

19e. Capitalize titles.

(1) Capitalize titles of persons: General Marshall, Superintendent Jones, President Marks.

Do not capitalize titles used alone or after the person's name unless they are titles of important government figures or titles of persons to whom you wish to show special respect.

RIGHT   The President addressed Congress today.
Mr. Harper is president of this company.
Mr. Anderson, the superintendent of schools, introduced Captain Armstrong.

Names of official positions, such as *senator, representative, admiral,* etc. are not capitalized unless used with a name or to refer to a particular person.

RIGHT   Although he wanted to be a senator from his state, he ran first for the office of representative.
The Senator will be glad to help you.

19e

Words of family relationship (*mother*, *cousin*, *aunt*, etc.) are capitalized when used with a person's name.

RIGHT   **Uncle** George, **Cousin** Martha

Words of family relationship may be capitalized or not when used in place of a person's name.

RIGHT   "Hello, **Father**." [*Father* is used in place of the man's name.]
         "Hello, *father*."

When preceded by a possessive noun or pronoun, words of family relationship are not capitalized.

RIGHT   The boy's *father* sent him to a private school.
         I visited my *uncle* in Denver.

▶ EXCEPTION: When family-relationship words like *uncle*, *aunt*, and *grandmother* are *customarily* used before a name, capitalize them even after a possessive noun or pronoun.

    RIGHT   My **G**randmother Wharton sent me a birthday gift.
             I am fond of Joe's **U**ncle Bill. [You customarily call these people *Grandmother Wharton* and *Uncle Bill*.]
    RIGHT   I am fond of my **b**rother Bill. [You do not customarily call him *Brother Bill*.]

(2) Capitalize the first word and all important words in the titles of books, magazines, newspapers, articles, historical documents, works of art: *Atlantic Monthly*, *Madonna of the Chair*, *The Last of the Mohicans*, *Treaty of Paris*, *Mutiny on the Bounty*.

The words *a*, *an*, and *the* written before a title are capitalized only when they are a part of the title. Before the names of magazines and newspapers, they are usually not capitalized in a composition.

Unimportant words in a title are *a, an, the,* and short prepositions and conjunctions.

RIGHT   *A Tale of Two Cities*
          The End of the Trail
          I read the *Saturday Evening Post* and the *Philadelphia Evening Bulletin.*

(3) Capitalize words referring to the Deity: God, Father, His will, etc.

The word *god,* when used to refer to the pagan deities of the ancients, is not capitalized.

RIGHT   The Greek *gods* had human traits.

● EXERCISE 7. List all words requiring capitals. Before each word place the number of the group in which it appears. Do not list words already capitalized.

1. A novel, *lost horizon,* by the English writer, James Hilton, was recommended by Betty Swan, president of the Book Club.
2. The movie version of the play *ten little indians* was called *and then there were none.*
3. Mr. Briggs, principal of the high school, enjoys good biographies. He told me to read Carl Sandburg's life of Lincoln, which is called *abraham lincoln: the prairie years.*
4. We asked professor Barclay, head of the art department in Burton College, to tell us about Leonardo's painting, *the last supper.*
5. My aunt Jane, who is my mother's sister, lives with grandfather Whiting in Nebraska.
6. Anderson's play, *the eve of st. mark,* describes the hardships of our soldiers before the loss of Bataan, but his best-known war play, *what price glory?,* was written about World War I.
7. The statue, *the returning warrior,* by professor Hall, is a better work of art than Miss Long's painting, *the veteran returns.*

8. The French painter Millet, who painted *the angelus*, should not be confused with the English artist Millais, who painted *the boyhood of raleigh*.

9. The reverend John Boardman, pastor of our church, urged his congregation to do the will of god and to pray for his blessing.

10. After reading the *Saturday evening post* from cover to cover, dr. Bowles read the current issue of *reader's digest*.

11. Whenever I ask mother for money, she says, "Ask your father."

12. Marilyn, who has read *gone with the wind* five times, never has time to read *the history of the United States*, her history textbook.

● REVIEW EXERCISE B.   Follow directions for Review Exercise A on page 422.

1. "Learning to use capital letters," said professor quiz at his lecture in byrne hall, "is as important as it is easy."

2. They put in a call for dr. carter, the only doctor in geopolis, whose office on main street and maple avenue occupies the back part of the commercial building.

3. Although the united states is bounded on the east by the atlantic ocean, on the south by the gulf of mexico, and on the west by the pacific ocean, the state with the longest coast line is not florida or california, but michigan, which is bounded on three sides by the great lakes.

4. "Languages taught in american high schools are latin, which is a classical language, and german, spanish, french, and italian, which are modern languages," explained mr. bright of woodview high school in addressing the meadville chapter of the league of women voters last monday.

5. "Their native language, english," added the teacher, "often seems more foreign, even to juniors and seniors,

than do some of the other modern languages they learn in high school.''

6. Around garden city, nassau county is very flat, but north of there, in the region of great neck and roslyn, there are hills which look out upon long island sound.

7. My friend peter blakely, president of the american cycle company, has an office in the empire state building, a home in the suburbs, and a summer home on the delaware river in the pocono mountains of pennsylvania.

8. The smith shoe company has factories in new england and in the south, but the main offices are in the smith building overlooking the hudson river in new york city.

9. The *great charter*, which was signed by king john at runnymede on june 15, 1215, is one of the great documents in english history.

10. The president closed his address before congress on memorial day with a request to god for his guidance.

11. Having read *a tale of two cities* by the famous english novelist charles dickens, I read *the old curiosity shop* and *bleak house*, and then turned to some of the other victorian writers.

12. Velasquez' paintings, *the forge of vulcan* and *portrait of the child don carlos*, which are hung in the prado museum in madrid, were moved to geneva, switzerland, during the spanish civil war.

● REVIEW EXERCISE C. Copy the following sentences, inserting capital letters wherever needed. In this exercise apply all the capital letter rules you have learned.

1. Fred Martin graduated from lincoln high school in seattle, washington, in june, and he entered washington state college the following fall.

2. In high school he was captain of the football team and majored in science and math, but in college he went out for cross country and majored in english and european history.

3. Since all school teams follow the rules of the american football association, the football played in the west is exactly like the football played in the east.

4. Our seats in bryce stadium were on the east side of the field, so that we had to look west directly into the sun.

5. Between albany and buffalo the new york central railroad follows the mohawk valley, running alongside the mohawk river and the new york state barge canal.

6. On labor day we hurried back from baker lodge in the white mountains, where we had spent the summer.

7. The american holiday, the fourth of july, commemorates the signing of the declaration of independence at independence hall in philadelphia in 1776.

8. My mother and I went to father's office where we met uncle bill and my aunt.

9. My first book report this fall was on *the carolinian,* Sabatini's story of the south in the american revolution.

10. The board of directors elected mr. thomas marshall to the presidency of the eagle aircraft corporation, makers of the *cloudbreaker* and the *hi-flyer.*

11. A class in french for juniors was scheduled this fall at mayer high school for students who had not taken a foreign language in their freshman and sophomore years.

12. The minister prayed, "o god, teach us to do thy will at all times."

13. On saturday, december 3, we took off from newark airport in new jersey, in an american airlines plane.

14. It was principal Marks of the grove street school who objected to mayor walker's forcing the board of education to hold school on the friday after thanksgiving day.

SUMMARY STYLE SHEET

GEOGRAPHICAL NAMES

Dodge *City*	a *city* in Kansas
Chippewa *State Park*	a *state park*
Bear *Mountain*	a *mountain* stream

Arctic *Ocean*	an *ocean* liner
Main *Street*	a wide *street*
Missouri *River*	a navigable *river*
living in the *West*	facing *west*, the *west* side of the road
a *Western* cowboy	the *western* slope
the Mediterranean *Sea*	a Mediterranean *country*

ORGANIZATIONS, INSTITUTIONS, BUSINESS PRODUCTS, SPECIAL EVENTS, CALENDAR ITEMS, RACES, AND RELIGIOUS GROUPS

Varsity *Club*	a *club* for athletes
Elco *Electric Company*	an *electric company*
the Bijou *Theater*	a modern *theater*
Garfield *High School*	a large *high school*
Roosevelt *Hotel*	the newest *hotel*
the *Civil War*	a *civil war*
the *Middle Ages*	in *medieval* times
Labor Day	*Christmas* day
English, French, Latin, German, Spanish, Italian, Algebra II	algebra, art, domestic science, science, history, math
the *Senior Prom*	a *senior* [*junior, sophomore, freshman*] in high school
	summer, winter, fall, spring
Negro	
Roman Catholic	
Hershey's *chocolate*	

TITLES

Superintendent Jones	Mr. Jones, the *superintendent*
the *President* [the *Senator*, the *Congressman*, etc. — high government officials]	a *senator's* power, the *president* of the class
A Tale of Two Cities, The Casting Away of Mrs. Lecks and Mrs. Aleshine	
God made *His* will known.	the *gods* of the Greeks
Aunt Sarah	my *aunt*
I'll tell *Mother*.	my *mother*

CHAPTER 20

Punctuation

END MARKS

Punctuation for Clearness

The various marks of punctuation exist for the single purpose of making meaning clear. What this means may be seen in the following sentences, where punctuation marks are necessary to make the sentence understandable.

CONFUSING Into the stew she dropped the onions and Mary stirred them with a spoon.

My uncle Captain Leslie said James is a poor sailor.

The children munched happily on the various courses: soup vegetables and meat salad rolls and butter pie and ice cream.

He settled wearily onto the first chair which was not strong enough to hold him.

When in Doubt Leave It Out

Modern writers use punctuation as much as is necessary to make clear what they want to say, but they use it only when it *is* necessary. Have a reason (either a definite rule or a matter of meaning) for every mark of punctuation you use. When there is no rule requiring a mark of punctuation and the meaning of the sentence is clear, do not insert any punctuation mark. This is a general principle which applies to most situations, though not to all; it does not mean that you can argue in favor of careless punctuation by insisting to the reader, "You know what I mean!" It's your business to punctuate so clearly that your sentences can have only one meaning.

The various punctuation marks are listed on the following pages, and rules are given for the use of each. Learn the rules; do the exercises. *Above all, apply what you learn to everything you write.*

Period, Question Mark, Exclamation Point

20a. A declarative sentence is followed by a period.[1]

RIGHT   I went to South America by plane.

Mr. Shafer left a fortune to his daughter.

20b. An interrogative sentence is followed by a question mark.

RIGHT   Where have you been?

▶ NOTE: Distinguish between a declarative sentence containing an indirect question and an interrogative sentence which asks a question directly.

EXAMPLES   *I asked him* where he had been. [declarative]

Did you know where he had been? [interrogative]

20c. An exclamation is followed by an exclamation point.

RIGHT   What a game!

My heavens!

[1] For explanation of the kinds of sentences see page 36. For the position of end marks with quotation marks, see Rule 24e, p. 476.

20 a-c

20d. An imperative sentence may be followed by either a period or an exclamation point, depending upon the purpose of the sentence.

RIGHT   Hand me the hammer, please.
         Get out!

If you keep your wits about you, you will have little difficulty using the question mark and the exclamation point correctly. Failure to use a period at the end of a sentence, however, is a common error with writers who do not know what a sentence is and therefore do not know where a sentence ends. If you have studied Chapters 1–4 of this book, you should have learned what a sentence is; and knowing a sentence when you write it or see it, you will know where to place a period.

● EXERCISE 1.   In this exercise write on your paper only the final word of each sentence followed by the proper end mark. Add the first word of the sentence which follows.

EXAMPLE   He went home during the fifth period did you see him leave he looked rather worried . . . etc.

period.   Did
leave?   He

1. What a day we were late to school because the icy roads slowed down the school bus my English teacher called on me because I was whispering to Betty what do you think he asked me he wanted me to tell the whole class what I had whispered to her was I embarrassed what could I do I just looked foolish and said nothing
2. In social studies Jane tried to pass me a note Miss Lang saw her and took the note she read it aloud did Jane and I blush everybody teased us after class how we suffered

3. Do you think this is all that went wrong today no, indeed lunch hour was terrible I had forgotten to bring any money, and I couldn't borrow any talk about starving they had hot roast beef sandwiches, too it was awful

4. What luck Jimmie Clark offered to buy me a sandwich if I'd let him copy my math homework of course, I knew better, but I was so hungry Mr. Taylor quickly discovered the copied lesson he sent both Jimmie and me to the office did you ever hear of such a bad day

● EXERCISE 2. Copy the following sentences, inserting the proper end marks — period, question mark, exclamation point. Begin each sentence with a capital letter. Whenever an end mark and quotation marks come together *in this exercise,* place the end mark inside the quotation marks.

1. When Helen gets on the telephone, the rest of us give up Helen is my seventeen-year-old sister what a girl do you think she can talk less than half an hour every evening she settles down at the phone, which is in the back hall she doesn't seem to care whether anyone overhears her perhaps she knows that no one would listen twice to her silly patter the calls begin coming in about seven o'clock Josie is usually first, but Josie isn't very long-winded she lasts only about twenty minutes then Sally takes over an hour later, when the conversation has passed through the low-tone stage and the giggles have worn everyone out, Dad emerges from his paper

2. "Good heavens" he explodes "Doesn't that girl have anything else to do"

3. Mother lays down her sewing and leaves the room we can hear her telling Helen the time is up

4. Helen is indignant "Oh, Mother, we've hardly said anything yet listen, Sally, shall I call you back later g'by"

5. "Come here, young lady" Dad exclaims as Helen waltzes in "Do you know you have been on that phone for nearly two hours do you know that I had a letter from

20d

the telephone company yesterday asking me to shorten
our calls a fine situation"

6. "Why, Dad" exclaims injured innocence "we were
talking over our homework all the time"

7. At this point I let out one big howl

● EXERCISE 3.   Write a paragraph one page in
length which calls for the use several times of *all
three* end marks. Make a copy without any end marks
and bring this copy to class. In class exchange papers
with someone and put the end marks on the paper
you receive.

● EXERCISE 4.   For further practice in the use
of end marks turn to Exercises 7–9 on pages 93–95
in Chapter 4, "Writing Complete Sentences."

20e. An abbreviation is followed by a period.

Abbreviations are capitalized only if the words
they stand for are capitalized.

    adv. adverb
    Col. Colonel
    Colo. Colorado
    Fla. Florida
    etc. et cetera (Latin)
    N.S.P.C.A. National Society for the Prevention of
              Cruelty to Animals

▶ NOTE: Abbreviations of government agencies are often
    written without periods.

      AEC Atomic Energy Commission
      ICC Interstate Commerce Commission

CHAPTER 21

Punctuation

THE COMMA

21a. Use commas to separate words, phrases, and subordinate clauses written in series.

WORDS IN SERIES   Books, pamphlets, magazines, and newspapers cluttered the teacher's desk. [nouns]
We played, swam, ate, sang, and danced.
[verbs]
He was a short, fat, good-natured man. [adjectives]

PHRASES IN SERIES   Examinations will be given at the beginning of the term, at midterm, and at the end of the term.

SUBORDINATE CLAUSES IN SERIES   He declared that the roof leaked, that the windows leaked, and that the plumbing leaked.

(1) When the last two items in a series are joined by *and*, you may omit the comma before the *and* if the comma is not necessary to make the meaning clear.   Some publishers, however, insist on this comma, whether or not it is necessary. Follow your teacher's instructions on this point.

CLEAR WITH COMMA OMITTED   Telegrams, letters and gifts poured in upon him.

NOT CLEAR WITH COMMA OMITTED   The following courses will be offered by the art department this term: figure sketching, fashion design, interior decoration,

20e
21a

435

advertising and commercial art. [How many courses will be offered, four or five? Is *advertising and commercial art* one course, or are there two courses, *advertising* and *commercial art*?]

CLEAR WITH COMMA INCLUDED   The following courses will be offered by the art department this term: figure sketching, fashion design, interior decoration, advertising, and commercial art.

> ▶ NOTE: Some words usually appear in pairs and may be set off as one item in a series: *hat and coat, bread and butter, pork and beans,* etc.
>
> RIGHT   The meal consisted of soup, bread and butter, pork and beans, and crackers and cheese.

(2) If all items in a series are joined by *and* or *or*, do not use commas.

RIGHT   Father and Chester and Jerry and I went to the movies together.
Harry or Bill or Joe will take us.

(3) When the last adjective in a series is thought of as part of the noun, the comma before the adjective is omitted.

RIGHT   He was a clever, fearless *little man.*
He was a fearless *little man.*

Consider *little man* as one word, like *policeman.* Then *fearless* does not modify *man;* it modifies *little man.* The comma is omitted before *little.*

RIGHT   I got the information from a polite, helpful *young man* at the hotel desk.
The stranger was a funny *little fellow.*

(4) Main clauses in series are usually separated by semicolons. Short main clauses, however, may be separated by a comma.

RIGHT   The huge ship rose slowly to the top of each mountainous wave; it poised there for a moment; it plunged sickeningly into the flowing valley of green water below.

Dogs barked**,** children shouted**,** adults applauded.

Occasionally within a series of main clauses separated by semicolons, commas are used to indicate omission of words.

Jane was elected president; Maude**,** vice-president; Ann**,** secretary; and Joan**,** treasurer.

● EXERCISE 1. Copy the following sentences, inserting commas where needed.

1. Frances Jane Alice and I organized a spinster club.
2. Mother had planned to serve frankfurters baked beans salad and ice cream and cake.
3. The clinic will be open this afternoon tonight and tomorrow morning.
4. We traveled by car bus train and plane.
5. The boys were expected to play and study and work in equal amounts every day.
6. Father snapped the switch tightened the plug tried a new bulb and finally called an electrician.
7. I had expected a tall handsome young man.
8. He handed me the paper thrust a pen into my hand and told me to sign on the dotted line.
9. He stopped he looked and he listened.
10. The following groups will be formed: freshmen sophomores juniors and seniors.
11. Diplomats Congressmen and reporters mobbed the President's office.
12. The winner will probably be Bayside or Rockville or Freeport.

● EXERCISE 2. Copy on your paper each series in the following sentences; punctuate it correctly. Before each series write the number of the sentence in which it appears. (Remember that commas always go *inside*

quotation marks; for example, *Three well-known poems
are "The Raven," "If," and "Trees."*)

EXAMPLE 1. **Singing in a quartet teaches you concentration
accuracy and cooperation.**

1. **concentration, accuracy, and cooperation.**

1. Mary Carolyn Jane and I have been singing together
for a year. 2. We have sung at school assemblies church
socials and school parties. 3. Our quartet was formed one
boring lazy fall afternoon at Jane's house. 4. We discovered that our voices had a wide range — two sopranos
a mezzo-soprano and a contralto. 5. Jane's radio record
player and piano were at once brought into use to help us.
6. We began on such old favorites as "Who" "Sweet Sue"
"Tea for Two" and "I Been Workin' on de Railroad."
7. Mary and Jane and Carolyn have solo voices, but I
stick to harmonizing. 8. Through September October
and November we practiced on Friday afternoons Sundays
after our young people's meeting at the church and occasionally during lunch hour at school. 9. Mr. Sorrell,
director of our school chorus, asked us to sing at the fall
concert. 10. We found we liked to sing classical religious
and popular selections equally well. 11. We sang some
beautiful old French songs for our French class some Eliza-
bethan madrigals for English and some ballads and folk
songs for Miss Martin's history class. 12. All this took
our week ends free periods and lunch hours, but we had
so much fun getting together and practicing and perform-
ing that we didn't mind.

● EXERCISE 3. Write 5 sentences, each sentence
illustrating one of the following uses of the comma.

1. Adjectives in a series.
2. Nouns in a series requiring a comma before the *and*
between the last two items.
3. Phrases in a series.
4. Short main clauses in a series.
5. A series joined by conjunctions, requiring no commas.

21b. Use commas to set off expressions which interrupt the sentence.

There are seven kinds of "interrupters" which you should be able to recognize.

(1) Appositives with their modifiers are set off by commas.

An appositive is a word or group of words which follows a noun or pronoun and means the same thing. An appositive usually gives information about the noun or pronoun that precedes it.

EXAMPLES Bergen**,** *the* **fullback,** played a good defensive game.
Mr. Salt**, owner** *of the ranch***,** offered me his own horse.
I sent for Joe**,** *the school's* **plumber.**

In these sentences *fullback, owner,* and *plumber* are appositives.

▶ NOTE: When you set off an appositive you include with it all words which modify it.

EXAMPLES Mike Casella, *the* **custodian** *at our school* is always good-natured.
Arnold Wilcox, *the* **boy** *I met at the convention,* gave me some inside information.

Sometimes an appositive is so closely related to the word preceding it that it should not be set off by commas. Such an appositive is called a "restrictive appositive." It is usually a single word.

EXAMPLES My brother Bill
The composer Beethoven
Her old friend Betty

21b

● EXERCISE 4. Copy the following sentences containing appositives, inserting commas where needed.

1. Helen the leader of the group conducted the meeting a membership rally.
2. My sister Jean a sophomore at Briarcliff will be home for the holidays.
3. His new car a streamlined model attracted much attention.
4. My friend Joan has a new bicycle a Rollfast.
5. The dog a mongrel was purchased by Mr. Sayles mayor of the village.
6. We enjoyed the meals a combination of French and Italian dishes.
7. The stream a cataract of ice and debris gradually rose to flood height.
8. My younger brother Bill is working for Mr. Henry owner of a local drug store.
9. Our pastor the Reverend John Brooks works hardest on Sunday the "day of rest."
10. Joe Green the best guide in Maine was hired to take us on our canoe trip a 200-mile voyage.
11. The poet Longfellow enjoyed great popularity at home and abroad.
12. The book a novel about the Revolution was written by Kenneth Roberts an American author.

(2) Words used in direct address are set off by commas.

RIGHT   Please give us a hand**,** *Frank.*
         Yes**,** *my friend***,** you are probably right.
         *Mr. Chairman***,** I rise to a point of order.

(3) Parenthetical expressions are set off by commas.

These expressions are often used parenthetically: *I believe* (*think, suppose, hope,* etc.)*, on the contrary, on the other hand, of course, in my opinion, for example, however, to tell the truth, nevertheless, in fact.*

RIGHT   You have, *on the other hand,* nothing to lose.
         The speech, *in my opinion,* was a failure.

▶ NOTE: These expressions, of course, are not *always* used as interrupters.

> NOT USED AS AN INTERRUPTER **You must try *to tell the truth.***
>
> USED AS AN INTERRUPTER **He is, *to tell the truth,* dangerous.**
>
> NOT USED AS AN INTERRUPTER **I think these are the best students.**
>
> USED AS AN INTERRUPTER **These are, *I think,* the best students.**

▶ NOTE: A contrasting expression introduced by *not* is parenthetical and must be set off by commas.

> RIGHT It is character, *not money,* that makes the man.

(4) Certain words, when used at the beginning of a sentence or remark, are followed by a comma. These words are *well, yes, no, why,* etc.

RIGHT *Yes,* your answers are correct.
Well, we were certainly taken by surprise.
Why, you little rascal!

● EXERCISE 5. Copy the following sentences, using commas where they are needed to set off the interrupting expressions. Be prepared to give the rule for each comma.

1. One of the boys Joe Withers took his sister Mary to the dance.
2. No Janet I haven't met Mrs. Williams our new adviser.
3. My friend Raymond lives in Columbus the capital of Ohio.
4. Well it was Bill I believe who bought the decorations.
5. The answers on the other hand are incorrect.
6. Yes we should offer our services to Betty the president.
7. Come here Sally. Mother I think is looking for you.
8. Well when this liquid a salt solution touches the ice, the freezing point drops.

9. Yes these are in my opinion very good criticisms of this book *Silas Marner*.
10. Experience shows however that students do in general enjoy the book.
11. Well this class is I am sure a superior group.
12. There is according to our teacher another book by the author Daly that we should read.

(5) In dates and addresses every item after the first is enclosed by commas.

"Enclosed" means having a comma before and after.

RIGHT   Since September 1, 1955, we have lived at 345 Hill Street, Ann Arbor, Michigan.

RIGHT   My new address will be 70 Fifth Avenue, New York 11, New York, until Christmas.

My year in St. Louis, Missouri, was very successful.

Write to John Mills, 450 Madison Avenue, New York 17, New York.

Friday, December 13, was my lucky day.

● EXERCISE 6.   Copy the following exercise, inserting commas wherever needed.

1. We are staying at 41 Meadbrook Road Summerville Alabama.
2. On June 20 1955 the office at 31 Main Street Mount Pleasant Michigan was closed.
3. Please change my address from 18 Broad Street Newark New Jersey to 421 Springfield Avenue South Orange New Jersey.
4. He arrived on September 1 1955 and left on April 1 1956.
5. After several years in Columbus Georgia we moved to Orlando Florida on March 1 1956.
6. The letter came from Boulder Colorado and was addressed to Mr. Harry Moore 231 Fifth Avenue New York 10 New York.

7. The United Nations Charter was completed on June 26 1945 and came into effect on October 24 1945 when the necessary ratifications were obtained.
8. Brownsville Texas is a winter resort across the Rio Grande River from Matamoros Mexico 400 miles from New Orleans Louisiana.

● EXERCISE 7.   Below are parenthetical expressions or interrupting elements. Use each one, correctly punctuated, in sentences of your own.

EXAMPLE   1. a dog with personality
          1. Pluto, a dog with personality, won the hearts of the judges at the show.

1. the owner of the car
2. not a long novel
3. my friend
4. on the other hand
5. 1957

6. Alabama
7. I believe
8. my favorite writer
9. for example
10. he replied

● EXERCISE 8.   Write 5 sentences of your own, each of which illustrates the punctuation of a different one of the 5 types of interrupting expressions you have learned.

(6) A nonrestrictive clause is set off by commas.

A *nonrestrictive* clause is a subordinate clause which merely adds an idea to the sentence but is not necessary to the meaning of the sentence. The opposite of a nonrestrictive clause is a *restrictive* clause, which *is* necessary to the meaning of the sentence.

NONRESTRICTIVE   Fred Bates, *who is a sophomore,* played all season on the varsity.

Since you know without the clause who it was that played all season on the varsity, the clause is not necessary to identify Fred, but adds information about Fred. It is a nonrestrictive clause and should be set off by commas. *Most adjective clauses which modify proper names* are nonrestrictive and require commas.

RESTRICTIVE   Boys **who skip school** must be punished.

The subordinate clause *who skip school* serves to identify the boys. It is necessary to limit the meaning of *boys*. If the clause is omitted, the sentence has a very different meaning. The clause is restrictive and does not require commas.

RESTRICTIVE   The book **that I want** is not in the library.

The clause *that I want* tells which book is not in the library; it identifies *book;* it is restrictive. A helpful guide to follow is that adjective clauses introduced by *that* are almost always restrictive. Hence, if you can substitute *that* for *who* or *which* at the beginning of a clause, you may usually assume that the clause is restrictive.

Study these examples of restrictive (no commas) and nonrestrictive (commas) clauses. Can you explain the punctuation?

EXAMPLES   The girl *whom you met this morning* is my sister.
Marilyn, *whom you met this morning,* is my sister.
George Washington and Abraham Lincoln, *who were born in February,* were our greatest Presidents.
The Presidents *who were born in February* were George Washington and Abraham Lincoln.
A Tale of Two Cities, *which we read last term,* was written by Charles Dickens.
The Dickens book *which we read last term* was *A Tale of Two Cities.*

Sometimes the writer of a sentence is the only one who knows whether the clause he uses is nonrestrictive (commas) or restrictive (no commas). This is true because he has a definite meaning in mind for his sentence. For example, the clauses in the following sentences may be either nonrestrictive (commas) or restrictive (no commas), depending upon the meaning intended by the writer.

NONRESTRICTIVE **My older brother, *who goes to Cornell,* will be home for the holidays.** [I have only one older brother. The clause is not needed to identify him. It is unnecessary, nonrestrictive, and requires commas.]

RESTRICTIVE **My older brother *who goes to Cornell* will be home for the holidays.** [I have two older brothers. Only one goes to Cornell; the other goes to Dartmouth. The clause is necessary to tell which brother I am talking about. It is restrictive and does not require commas.]

● EXERCISE 9. Punctuate the following sentences. Be able to explain orally the reasons for your punctuation. Some of the sentences could be interpreted in two ways.

1. Jean who is blonde always looks best in blue.
2. Of my three sisters the one who is blonde looks best in blue.
3. Philip who enjoys winter sports prefers to live in the North.
4. A man who enjoys winter sports prefers to live in the North.
5. The movie that we saw last night is a thriller.
6. I picked up the magazine which Harold had been reading.
7. The copy of *Life* magazine which Harold had been reading was all marked up.
8. The *Saturday Evening Post* which comes to us weekly is a large magazine.
9. The police caught the thief who had broken into the school building.
10. The thief who was a stranger in town confessed his crime.

(7) A nonrestrictive participial phrase is set off by commas.

A participial phrase (see page 60) is a group of words containing a participle. When nonrestrictive — not necessary to the sentence — the phrase is set off by commas. Present participles end in *–ing*. Most past participles end in *–ed*.

NONRESTRICTIVE PRESENT PARTICIPLE   Jimmy**,** *leaning lazily against the door***,** fell into the room when the door opened.

RESTRICTIVE PRESENT PARTICIPLE   We carefully watched the stranger *leaning lazily against the door.*

NONRESTRICTIVE PAST PARTICIPLE   Bart and I**,** *deserted by our companions***,** found our way home alone.

RESTRICTIVE PAST PARTICIPLE   Anyone *deserted by his companions* should sound a distress signal.

● EXERCISE 10.   Punctuate the following sentences. Be able to explain orally the reasons for your punctuation.

1. Will the people standing in the back of the room please come forward?
2. The referee who is wearing a striped shirt is very strict. (How many referees are there?)
3. No one liked the records which John brought.
4. Coffee which is a stimulant is not usually served to children who are very young.
5. The dinner which Mother served on Thanksgiving was the best that I have ever eaten.
6. Jack who is usually late didn't know how to set the alarm clock which he received for Christmas.
7. This clock which is a new type got him up an hour too early.
8. Mr. Olds seated in the front row was able to hear every word.
9. The brunette whom George took to the dance was too popular with the other boys.

10. Helen Boyd whom George took to the dance is the most popular girl in school.
11. Planes which are built for military purposes are different from those which are built for commercial use.
12. The people waiting for the bus grew impatient.

● EXERCISE 11. Write 5 sentences containing a nonrestrictive clause (commas) and 5 sentences containing a restrictive clause (no commas).

● EXERCISE 12. Copy the following sentences, inserting commas where needed. Be prepared to give the reason for each comma. This exercise covers the use of commas with expressions which interrupt the sentence (**21b**).

1. Buenos Aires which has a population of more than two million is I believe the largest city in South America.
2. Situated on the south bank of La Plata River which is formed by the Paraná and Uruguay rivers Buenos Aires is the capital of Argentina the second largest South American country.
3. The pampas large treeless plains in the center of the country provide good grazing for cattle raising a major industry.
4. Most of the meat which is produced in Argentina is exported to England which does not produce enough for its own needs.
5. Argentina a largely agricultural country must on the other hand import manufactured goods from Europe and our own country the United States.
6. Its climate which is temperate differs very little according to the atlas from that of the United States.
7. Henry bring me the atlas which is on my desk and turn to the page which gives a map of South America.
8. There is I believe no map of Argentina in the atlas which you have brought, but this map a physical map of the continent will do.

9. My friend Esteban who lives in Buenos Aires sent me his address which is if I remember correctly 423 Avenida de Mayo Buenos Aires Argentina.

10. Well Esteban urged my brother Jim and me to go to Argentina this summer, but Father on the contrary advised us to wait until we are older.

11. My Spanish teacher Mr. Guera sailed for Buenos Aires on June 21 1957 and returned to New Orleans Louisiana on September 5.

12. He brought me a fine pair of rancher's boots which he had bought in Argentina and several books large illustrated volumes describing the country.

13. Mr. Guera having nothing to do one day called on my friend Esteban who showed him some parts of the city which a foreigner usually doesn't see.

14. The teacher pleased by such kindness entertained Esteban at a party given by Americans.

15. No Don I have never been abroad, but I hope to go to South America after graduation.

21c. Use a comma before *and, but, or, nor, for,* when they join main clauses.

RIGHT   In the morning the custodian cleans the walks in front of our apartment house, and his wife straightens up the lobby.

There are few islands in the Eastern Pacific Ocean, but there are thousands of them in the Western Pacific Ocean.

I had to wait a long time at the airport, for the weather did not clear until noon.

I'll go and I will not return.   [clauses too short to require commas]

Do not be misled by compound verbs which often make a sentence look as though it contained two main clauses.

COMPOUND SENTENCE **They toured Colonial Williamsburg, and they visited historic William and Mary College.** [main clauses requiring commas]

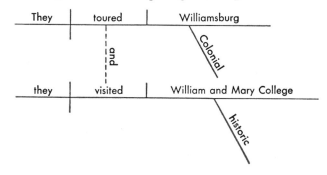

COMPOUND VERB **They toured Colonial Williamsburg and visited historic William and Mary College.** [no clauses, no comma]

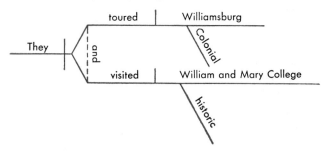

● EXERCISE 13. The sentences in this exercise contain main clauses joined by the conjunctions *and, but, or, nor, for.* Do not copy the sentences. Number on your paper from 1–20. Decide where the commas should come, and write on your paper after the proper number the word preceding each comma; add the comma and the conjunction following it. Do not be misled by compound verbs.

21c

EXAMPLE   Williams got a two-base hit but Bernstein hesitated
at third and the throw beat him to the plate.

hit, but
third, and

1. The audience was composed of hundreds of formidable-looking thugs and Commissioner Wright felt that these men would appreciate his strongest language.
2. Carol bought a new dress for her mother would not let her wear the old one.
3. For Friday's dance I made a date with Jane and Jim made a date with Belle.
4. Janie got a bad cold and Belle sprained her ankle playing hockey; we all stayed home and felt glum.
5. Our golf team had consistently bad luck this spring. They would be rained out of their matches or one of the best players would be unable to play on the scheduled day.
6. We came early and we left early.
7. Do your homework conscientiously every day or I shall have to keep you after school until it is done.
8. The women served and the men ate.
9. No one could figure out the answer to the fifth problem and the teacher had to admit that either the problem was given incorrectly in the book or the answer given there was wrong.
10. Allan studied his history lesson and finished his English theme before going to bed but did not do his math.
11. The noon train was an hour late but the passengers had been warned beforehand that they wouldn't get into Denver until one o'clock.
12. Dinner was served on the plane and it was the best meal we had eaten in weeks.
13. The boys couldn't figure out why Beth was laughing at them so hard nor did they realize that several other girls had just gone around the corner, holding their sides at the ludicrous picture the boys presented.

14. We spent the day fishing for my father would rather fish than eat.
15. The farmer's wife banged on a big kettle and shouted in her loudest tones but the men were late to dinner.
16. She said the dinner would be cold but it was steaming hot.
17. Sarah Wilkins had her youngest son run all the errands for the family and she often said she did that because his legs were newer and hadn't had a chance to get tired.
18. Keith and Sally couldn't decide whether to go to the movies or stay home; if they went to a movie, they'd have to walk a mile each way and they were in a lazy mood that night.
19. The wave rose menacingly as it approached the shore and it spilled over a hundred sand castles on the beach.
20. The motor sputtered and died and left an ominous stillness but our driver leaped out and began to make repairs.

21d. Use a comma after an introductory adverb clause, an introductory participial phrase, or a succession of introductory prepositional phrases.

An introductory clause or phrase is a clause or phrase coming first in a sentence or preceding a main clause.

INTRODUCTORY ADVERB CLAUSE *Whenever Mother sees the telegraph boy approaching the house,* she assumes that bad news is coming.
As soon as you finish, your dinner will be ready.

INTRODUCTORY PARTICIPIAL PHRASE *Leaving the dishes for me to do,* my sister Helen dashed gaily out.

A SUCCESSION OF INTRODUCTORY PREPOSITIONAL PHRASES *On the morning after graduation,* Jack began looking for a job.

21d

A short introductory phrase does not require a comma unless it is necessary to make the meaning clear.

RIGHT   **At the movies we forgot our troubles.**
In this school, teachers are highly respected. [Comma is necessary to avoid reading *school teachers*.]

● EXERCISE 14. The sentences in this exercise contain introductory clauses and phrases. Decide where a comma should be used. Copy on your paper the word preceding each comma and place the comma after it. Number your answers to accord with the numbers of the sentences.

EXAMPLE   **With a clatter of hoofs and a blare of trumpets the white charger galloped into the center ring.**

trumpets,

1. When the people realized that the hurricane was headed in their direction they had little time left to prepare for it.
2. After the warning had been passed by word of mouth to all who could be reached preparations were made to withstand the storm.
3. Since the Everglades are low and hold a great deal of water high winds and rain bring floods.
4. For most of a day, while people huddled in the few strong buildings available the storm tore down their houses and carried off their possessions.
5. Although the center of a lake would seem to be a very dangerous spot in a hurricane a large barge anchored there rode out the storm, carrying 211 persons safely through.
6. While the hurricane lasted many acts of great courage were performed.
7. By midnight the storm had reached its height.
8. On the morning following the storm several rescue crews made their way through a ruined world.
9. After a thorough inspection of the area had been made

the country realized that it had suffered one of its greatest tragedies.

10. Receiving news of the disaster the Red Cross rushed help to the scene.

11. Although thousands had lost everything the people of the Everglades bravely set about their heart-rending job of restoration.

12. For years signs of the destruction caused by the high wind could be seen.

13. At last the land was made productive, and at the present time it is second to none in the entire country.

14. Traveling through the region today one would never suspect how devastated it had once been.

● EXERCISE 15.   Write compound sentences using each of the following conjunctions and requiring a comma before the conjunction: *and, or, but, nor, for.*

Write 5 sentences, each introduced by an adverb clause followed by a comma.

● EXERCISE 16.   Decide where commas should be used in these sentences. Copy on your paper the word preceding the comma in each sentence. Place the comma after the word. Be on the alert for commas in all uses and for sentences which do not require commas. Number your answers to accord with the numbers of the sentences.

EXAMPLE   **If he insists on an immediate decision have him call me.**

decision,

1. As long as you and he are such good friends you ought to be able to tell him the truth.

2. Since the pay was small and the hours very long the workmen quit the job.

3. As the flag was carried past the reviewing stand the mayor and his party removed their hats.

4. Standing in the arched doorway two guards held their guns stiffly.

5. At last we had won the big game of the year.
6. Although we begged them to leave the boys hung around for hours.
7. When he is left alone in the house Laddie usually curls up on the best furniture.
8. Production has been stepped up rapidly but it has not been able to meet the demand.
9. Although water forms between the threads of the weave it does not soak into the thread and the ground does not really get wet.
10. The fiber was combed and spun into yarn and the yarn was woven into cloth.
11. If a crime is considered to have national importance it is briefly reported in the *Times*.
12. When he had looked over the housing situation rather thoroughly Mr. Banks decided the house on Fernwood Terrace was the best buy.
13. After the school census had been taken the census-taker discovered that twenty-four new families had moved into the town.
14. By noon we had all our work done.
15. Although we wanted desperately to go on a skiing trip we realized there was not enough snow on the mountain to make it safe for us beginners.
16. Leaving the house so early in the morning I never see my neighbors.

Summary of Uses of the Comma

21a. Use commas to separate words, phrases, and subordinate clauses written in series.

21b. Use commas to set off expressions which interrupt the sentence.

(1) Appositives

(2) Words in direct address

(3) Parenthetical expressions

(4) The words *well, yes, no, why,* etc., when used at the beginning of a sentence

(5) Items in dates and addresses

(6) Nonrestrictive clauses

(7) Nonrestrictive participial phrases

21c. Use commas to separate main clauses joined by *and, but, or, nor, for,* unless the clauses are very short.

21d. Use a comma after an introductory adverb clause, an introductory participial phrase, or a succession of introductory prepositional phrases.

● REVIEW EXERCISE A. *Comma Rules* 21a–21d. Select from the following sentences all words which should be followed by a comma. List these words on your paper, placing a comma after each. Number your answers to accord with the numbers of the sentences.

EXAMPLE   Yes the boys did a good job but the girls did a better one.

yes,
job,

1. We could we believed make it in an hour.
2. As long as we could see the liner from the pier we frantically waved our handkerchiefs.
3. Bayne ran across the deserted field and stooped so low on the other side of it that Sam couldn't see him at all.
4. Mother will you please pass the fruit?
5. At 212 Front Street Emporia stands an ancient jalopy advertised for $25.
6. Steve Mary and I were on the prom committee.

7. As we quickly backed out of the garage we heard an ominous sound and we were afraid to get out to view the damage we knew we had done to Dad's car.

8. Although we realized we'd have to pay for it out of our allowances the prospect of ever borrowing the car again looked dim.

9. Mastering our courage and timidly peering around the rear wheel we were delighted to find it was only the garbage pail caught on the bumper.

10. In a second our worries had disappeared.

11. You can imagine however how scared we'd been.

12. Betsy and Charlie and Tom and I ceremoniously carried the pail back to where it belonged.

13. After a thorough search to make certain the driveway yielded no more hazards we pulled out again.

14. Miss Jones this letter goes to Mr. A. R. Morton 113 Lake Shore Drive Chicago Illinois.

15. Doubleday and Company is a publishing concern in Garden City Long Island New York.

● REVIEW EXERCISE B. *Comma Rules* **21a–21d.** Copy each of the following sentences, inserting commas. After each copied sentence, write the numbers of the comma rules you have followed. There are at least two rules (for commas or the omission of commas) involved in each sentence.

EXAMPLE   **Yes, your mail has arrived, Abner. 21b (4), 21b (2)**

1. When Arden came home from school her friends met her at the door and they led her into her own surprise birthday party.

2. Since everyone enjoys being fooled a magician I believe provides excellent entertainment.

3. A tall gaunt gentleman in black a scarecrow met us at the door.

4. No you will not be permitted to leave the house tonight nor can you stay up late.

5. Maps charts paintings and photographs covered the

walls and in my opinion gave the classroom an interesting appearance.

6. He was born on January 24 1945 in Provincetown which is on Cape Cod.

7. His sister Frances an A+ student is always kidding him about his marks but he doesn't seem to let her worry him.

8. Do you remember George where you found the pamphlets books and other articles?

9. Miss Brown take a letter to Professor John Mills 221 West Seventh Street Conniston North Carolina.

10. This school in the opinion of many parents provides expert instruction in the classrooms on the playing fields and in the gymnasiums.

11. Yes we have hotel reservations in Winter Park Florida from Friday February 1 to Saturday March 1.

12. A worker who is able to increase his output receives a special bonus but no one is charged for decreasing his output.

13. Cut off from us by the storm the animals in the barn whinnied and brayed and grunted all night.

14. When I sailed for Europe my friend Allan who is older than I gave me some valuable advice.

15. Jerry who won the contest last year is in the opinion of many one of the boys who will be chosen this year.

16. Well on the morning of our eighteenth day at sea we sighted the land and everyone rushed on deck.

17. Slowly silently the darkened vessel covered by a starless night slipped out to sea.

18. Mr. Adams who was recently elected to the City Council told parents teachers and taxpayers that he approved of a new school building.

19. Your letter reached me April 1 1956 and as you will recall gave me renewed hope.

20. Through the long hot lazy afternoon I watched the workmen in the old quarry where I used to work.

● REVIEW EXERCISE C. Referring to the *Summary of Uses of the Comma* on page 454, write a sentence to illustrate each of the rules, including all seven of the interrupters.

● REVIEW EXERCISE D. Spend half an hour going through a newspaper or magazine to find examples of as many *different* uses of the comma as you can. Cut out the examples — the entire sentence in each case — and paste them on paper to bring to class. Under each write the rule the sentence illustrates.

● REVIEW EXERCISE E. *End Marks and Commas.* Copy the following sentences, inserting end marks and commas as needed.

1. "Good heavens" exclaimed Miss Ruley the new teacher
2. What I wondered do all these facts figures and experiences mean
3. For weeks I think we ate nothing but beans and pork and Harry Evans the cook became very unpopular
4. Jimmy rose to his feet was recognized by the chairman and asked what had happened to the treasury
5. "Why I never heard of such a thing John" exclaimed Mrs Bellis shaking her head in dismay
6. The boys who are on the baseball team will I understand be excused early on Friday May 4 and Wednesday May 9
7. On the contrary Mr Sanford the coach told us that our chances were good
8. The dinner that the girls served consisted of lentil soup baked ham and escalloped potatoes fresh peas a green salad and apple pie
9. Andy who is very particular about food asked for a second helping of ham and peas and pie
10. It was at the carnival in Youngstown Ohio that I saw that thin young man who had six fingers on each hand
11. If you want to improve your marks you will have to do your English and science and social studies homework more carefully

CHAPTER 22

Punctuation

THE SEMICOLON

A semicolon [**;**], as you can see by looking at it, is part period and part comma. It is a very useful mark of punctuation. It says to the reader, "Stop here a little longer than you stop for a comma, but not so long as you stop for a period."

22a. Use a semicolon between main clauses not joined by *and, but, or, nor, for, yet*.

RIGHT   The taxpayers voted in favor of a new school building**;** a site for the structure will be chosen next week.

In cold weather she spent her afternoons on the skating pond**;** on warmer days she went to the indoor rink.

In this use the semicolon acts like a period, for each main clause is really a complete sentence. Where the thoughts of the clauses are very closely connected, as in the examples above, a semicolon is better than a period.

● EXERCISE 1. Read the following and decide where semicolons may be used. Copy on your paper the word preceding each semicolon, and write the semicolon after it. In some sentences you may prefer to use a period. Be prepared to tell why.

1. Each boy in our shop class was making a piece of furniture everyone had common problems to solve everyone was interested in the others' work.

2. Plans were drawn up each boy worked out a drawing of his project.

3. Cutting the boards and planing them down required more brawn than brains the opposite was true of fitting the pieces together.

4. Joining boards together to make wider panels requires experience many of the boys had a hard time getting the boards to fit smoothly.

5. My project was a table on a pedestal turning out the pedestal on the lathe was a lot of fun the wood under the sharp chisel was easy to work.

6. My hardest job was finishing the wood so that it would look smooth and shining it seemed that I used reams of sandpaper my hands and arms were sore from the exercise.

7. When all was ready, I asked Mr. Lacey if I could stain the wood he told me to go ahead he showed me how to do it.

8. The staining was fun too I got more stain on myself than on the wood.

9. After staining the wood, I had to rub filler into it to bring out the grain this is done with hard woods like the walnut I was using.

10. Finally the job was done I assembled my table I carried it home very proudly.

22b. **Use a semicolon between main clauses joined by the words** *besides, accordingly, moreover, nevertheless, furthermore, otherwise, therefore, however, consequently, also, thus, instead, hence.*

▶ NOTE: When immediately preceded by a semicolon, these words may or may not be followed by a comma with the exception of *however,* which is always followed by a comma. In general, omit the comma unless you wish to indicate a pause after the connective.

RIGHT   I thought the book much too long; however, I decided to read it all.

22c. Use a semicolon between main clauses if there are commas within the clauses.

RIGHT   This car, a revolutionary model, was invented by one of our engineers; but the high cost of manufacture prohibits large-scale production, and public demand would be too small to justify it.

Helen Burgess, the girl who is running for president of the senior class, has an excellent chance to win; and if she does win, she will be the first girl ever to achieve that position.

22d. Use a semicolon before *for example, namely, that is, for instance, in fact, on the contrary,* when they join main clauses.

▶ NOTE: When preceded by a semicolon, these expressions are followed by a comma.

RIGHT   He came to the meeting quite unprepared; that is, he had forgotten his notes.

● EXERCISE 2.   List on your paper, in the order in which they appear in the sentences below, all words which you think should be followed by a semicolon or a period. After each word place the mark you decide on. Be able to explain your decision. Number your list by sentences, keeping the words from each sentence together.

EXAMPLES   1. Someone left a coat in the locker room it was blue with white buttons.
2. Barbara had no room for us in her car however, we got a ride with Ethel there was plenty of room in her car.

1. room;
2. car;
   Ethel.

22
b-d

1. The first task was to decide what the class should make we found this a harder job than we had anticipated.

2. Our sewing class had only ten girls in it nevertheless, the teacher couldn't give any of us all the individual help we needed.

3. We had to choose our own materials furthermore she insisted that we pick out our patterns ourselves.

4. When we had finally bought what we wanted, she let us lay the pattern on the cloth she said planning where a pattern should be put was the most important part of the job.

5. Cutting into our precious material was the first thing that really scared us Miss Ames watched us like a hawk as our scissors somewhat crookedly found their mark.

6. Making skirts, we discovered, was very complicated we soon learned the importance of accurate measurements.

7. After the cutting, we continued with the job of basting that is, we put the skirts together tentatively — very tentatively.

8. Apparently my measuring hadn't been too good for instance, I was very much surprised to find the pieces didn't quite match in places.

9. I became very much absorbed in cutting I was determined to achieve a good skirt out of this mess.

10. Finally the pieces all came out even I was at last making progress.

11. The machine sewing was easier than any step to date moreover, the work went very quickly from then on.

12. After the finishing touches, I proudly presented my masterpiece to Miss Ames I had actually made a skirt I could wear!

● REVIEW EXERCISE. *Commas, Semicolons, and End Marks.* Copy the following sentences, inserting necessary punctuation.

1. How fascinating astrology is

2. Astrology which is the ancient art or science of predicting the fate of people from the positions of the stars is I understand widely practiced today

3. Most of us have heard of the word *astrology* but how many realize I wonder just what it can mean

4. People believed in astrology centuries before Christ the doctrine I think had spread from Babylonia to Greece before 400 B.C.

5. Famous and infamous people alike have believed in astrology however fearing the laughter of those who scoffed they did not always make their beliefs public

6. Adolf Hitler the German dictator never acted until his astrologer had told him the signs were right nevertheless his belief in the art didn't do him much good did it

7. When we asked him about astrology Mr. Thomas our science teacher grinned he said it was too advanced for us were we insulted

8. My sister Eileen reads the daily column "Your Horoscope" in the paper hoping her horoscope will be given her birthday is in March and she says the predictions are already given for people born up to February 15 1945

9. "Eileen what's come over you" asked my mother one day "You surely don't believe these absurd ridiculous horoscopes" [1]

10. Well I think we should try to control our own futures by working first on the present for instance our job now is to get our lessons done properly

11. My birthday is July 13 1944 I was according to the astrologers born under the zodiac sign of Cancer the Crab

12. At 32 Reeves Street San Francisco California is an office sign reading *Know Your Future* do you think many people go there

13. The office which is a small room upstairs doesn't look very prosperous they'd probably like to know their own future

14. I know mine already in fact it's settled now I'm going to be an orthodontist a specialist in straightening teeth

[1] For the position of punctuation marks with quotation marks, see Rule 24e, page 476.

15. Our Dr. Smith is one and he says the training is hard moreover you have to go to school for years even after college
16. I hope to be a veterinarian Mother says I'm awfully good at taking care of cats and dogs and horses
17. Your hours will be easy compared with those of most doctors no dog I think has ever gotten a vet out of bed in the middle of the night
18. Yes imagine us fifteen years from now having our own offices imagine hanging out our own shingles
19. I'd like to imagine our math homework was done but since it isn't let's get to work
20. Oh all right you win however I'd much rather talk wouldn't you

CHAPTER 23

Punctuation

COLONS, DASHES, PARENTHESES, ITALICS

The Colon

The usual purpose of a colon is to call the reader's attention to what comes next. A colon means, "Notice the following."

23a. Use a colon after the salutation of a business letter.

RIGHT   Dear Mr. Bernstein:
          Dear Sir:
          Gentlemen:

Do not use a colon after the salutation of a *friendly* letter. The salutation of a friendly letter is followed by a comma.

23b. Use a colon before a list of appositives or a list of items, especially when the list comes after expressions like *as follows* and *the following*.

RIGHT   At our school we have all the spring sports: baseball, track, lacrosse, tennis, and golf. [appositives]
          Congress is considering several ways of raising money: a property tax, a sales tax, and an increased income tax. [appositives]
          In his pockets we found the following: a piece of

465

23 a-b

string, a broken jackknife, six marbles, and several small sticks of wood.

The five largest cities of the United States are rated in size as follows: New York, Chicago, Philadelphia, Los Angeles, Detroit.

▶ NOTE: Do not use a colon in a sentence like the following, in which there is no pause before the series.

RIGHT   I went swimming with Henry, Sam, and Walter.

23c. Use a colon before a long and formal statement.

RIGHT   The President summed up his remarks with the following words: "Never, in all our history, have Americans faced a job so well worth while. May it be said of us in the days to come that our children and our children's children rise up and call us blessed."

23d. Use a colon between the numbers when you are writing the time.

EXAMPLES   4:30 p.m.
3:00 a.m.

▶ NOTE: A colon is also used to divide the numbers of Biblical chapters and verses:

Proverbs 15:3, Romans 2:11.

● EXERCISE 1.   Decide where colons may be used in the following sentences and be able to explain why.

1. We read the following poets last month Robert Frost, Carl Sandburg, Amy Lowell, and E. A. Robinson.
2. Many kinds of people jammed the trains at holiday time boys and girls going home from college, soldiers on a 72-hour pass, traveling salesmen hurrying to their families.
3. Essays have been handed in by the following students Mary Bohn, Eleanor Lord, Harold Weinberg, and Bill Mitchell.

4. The plane was due at 4 15, but it arrived at 4 30.
5. The box was filled with candy, nuts, fruit, and five-cent toys.
6. I should like to order the following articles a bicycle basket, a carrier for the rear fender, and a Super-ray lamp.
7. The principal began as follows "There are several important matters that must be discussed at this time . . ."
8. He offered the following excuses for his tardiness the poor condition of the roads, engine trouble, and his mother's illness.
9. At 11 00 P.M. the Weather Bureau issued this announcement "Storm warnings are posted along the entire Atlantic seaboard, and all small vessels have been advised to seek port."
10. The following meats appeared on the menu roast beef, roast lamb, broiled steak, southern fried chicken, and lamb chops.

The Dash

23e. Use the dash to indicate an important break in thought.

RIGHT   I suddenly decided — the decision still surprises me when I look back upon it — to become an aviator.
We ran toward the edge of the road — the road was especially narrow at this point — and looked with horror over the edge.

23f. Use the dash to mean *namely, in other words, that is*, and similar expressions which come before explanations.

RIGHT   He showed himself to be one of the bravest of men — he dared to stand up to the skipper and say exactly what he thought. [*that is*]
These historical novels were more exciting reading than the other novels I read this year — they had

**23
c-f**

more action and more interesting characters. [*in other words,* or *that is*]

The traffic policeman has many duties other than directing traffic ── he must watch people's faces, keeping an eye out for suspicious characters; he must watch for stolen cars; he must give information to strangers. [*namely*]

▶ NOTE: The dash and the colon are frequently interchangeable in this kind of construction.

Parentheses

23g. Use parentheses to enclose matter which is added to a sentence but is not of great importance.

The comma, the dash, and parentheses may all be used in this way. It is good practice to use this kind of construction sparingly.

RIGHT   I approached Mr. Sandle (I knew him by his long red nose) and asked for a word with him.

Several of the new planes (they are not yet available to the public) have such excellent safety devices that almost anyone can fly them safely.

● EXERCISE 2.   Decide where in the following sentences colons, dashes, and parentheses should be used. You will find some places where any one will be acceptable.

1. There are many more people backstage than the average audience ever thinks about electricians, prop boys, scenery movers, prompters, wardrobe mistresses, and stand-ins.
2. Trotting merrily down the center of Main Street no one knew exactly where they all came from was an

amazing collection of assorted dogs two purebred collies, all sorts of terriers, one Boston bull, one battered dachshund, and three obvious mutts.

3. Peter said and no one ever knew where he picked up these facts that the Senior Dance had been postponed on account of the flu epidemic.

4. At 4 31 we dashed headlong up the platform, hoping against hope the 4 30 train hadn't left an optimistic thought soon shattered.

5. Clearing his throat, the speaker began to quote "When in the course of human events . . ."

6. Ford was certainly the school's outstanding athlete captain of the football team, center on the basketball team, star hurler on the championship baseball team.

7. Mr. Shipman has many things on his mind the school enrollment, the schedules of several hundred students, and the sports program.

8. Mabel said she'd be glad if she had nothing more important to do to come over tomorrow.

9. Many imported products English bicycles, Italian motor scooters, Japanese toys are now available.

10. The list of sundaes looked tempting Forbidden Fruit, Hot Fudge with crushed walnuts, Pineapple and Marshmallow, and the old favorite Banana Split.

11. The Dean told us as though we didn't already know it that we'd be having many new subjects in college philosophy, psychology, anthropology, etc.

12. This year I'm taking the following subjects English, plane geometry, American history, French, and Latin.

13. Last year I took English, ancient history, general science, algebra, and Latin.

14. Barry wanted to invite Marcia she's the new girl from Hartford to go to the party with him, but he'd already asked another girl.

15. Trains leave here every night at 6 00, 8 42, and 11 30 p.m.

16. We grabbed our hats somebody had thoughtfully mixed them all up on the piano and flew out the door.

23g

Italics

23h. Italics are printed letters which lean to the right.

EXAMPLE   *This sentence is printed in italics.*

When you are writing or typing, indicate italics by underlining the words you want italicized. If your composition were to be printed, the typesetter would set the underlined words in italics.

The two Dickens books I have read are <u>David Copperfield</u> and <u>A Tale of Two Cities</u>.

Your sentence would then be printed like this:

The two Dickens books I have read are *David Copperfield* and *A Tale of Two Cities.*

(1) Use italics (underlining) for titles of books, works of art (pictures, musical compositions, statues, etc.), names of newspapers, magazines, and ships.

EXAMPLES   *The Adventures of Tom Sawyer*
the Boston *Herald* or the *Boston Herald*
the *American Boy*
the *Queen Mary*

► NOTE: When written in a composition, the words *a, an,* and *the* before a magazine or newspaper title are not italicized.

EXAMPLES   I was looking at cartoons in the *New Yorker.*
He is a reporter for the *Herald Tribune.*

ITALICS AND QUOTATION MARKS

In general, the use of quotation marks for titles is going out of practice; the tendency is toward italics. Magazine articles, chapter headings, and titles of poems, when referred to in the course of a composi-

tion, may be placed in quotation marks. (Titles of
book-length poems, of course, are treated like book
titles.) All other titles (books, works of art, magazines,
newspapers, ships) are italicized (underlined).

EXAMPLE   I studied Chapter IV, "Tom Comes Home," in
George Eliot's novel *The Mill on the Floss;* and
I read an article in *Cosmopolitan* entitled "They
Are a Funny Race."
Have you read "Renascence," a poem by
Millay?

**(2) Use italics (underlining) for foreign words, words
referred to as words, and letters referred to as letters.**

Picking your teeth at the table is not *comme il faut.*
There are four *and*'s in this sentence.
Dot the *i*'s and cross the *t*'s.

● EXERCISE 3.   List on your paper all words and
word groups in the following paragraph which should
be italicized. Underline each. List also those titles
which should be enclosed in quotation marks. Place
quotation marks around them.

1. Fourth period I went into the library to get an article
on modern gold mining.   2. It was in the Saturday Evening Post and was entitled Canada's New Gold Boom.
3. While I was looking for the Post, I saw the new Reader's
Digest.   4. I picked it up, read Picturesque Speech and
Patter, an article on the superliner Queen Mary, and another on the famous statue, the Venus de Milo.   5. Lying
on the table next to me were the New York Times and the
home town Herald.   6. I skimmed an editorial on scrap-
ping old ships such as the Aquitania and the Paris.   7. Jack
came in and asked me to help him with his book report on
Craig's Danger Is My Business, which I read last month.
8. "How many s's in business?" he asked.
9. "Three," I replied and, picking up Principles of Physics and my notebook, dashed off to class.

23h

● REVIEW EXERCISE A.   *Commas, semicolons, colons, dashes, parentheses, italics.* Copy the sentences below, inserting punctuation.

I

1. Beret a character in O. E. Rölvaag's novel Giants in the Earth was unable to endure the long lonely barren winters on the prairie.

2. The small sod huts which the settlers built were cold and ugly and hard to keep clean but the women managed to raise healthy children to keep their homes tidy and to make the huts livable.

3. Although their land cost the pioneers nothing the cost of lumber glass and other building materials was hard for them to meet they had almost no ready cash furthermore such things had to be brought in by wagon from distant towns.

4. A trip to town which took several days was a big event the pioneer could spare little time from his farming except in winter and then the snow made any journey hazardous.

5. Each settler had to be many things farmer blacksmith handyman doctor teacher and priest.

6. Entirely dependent on his crops the settler feared above all else drought locusts and hail against these he had no defense and they could destroy in days the labors of a year.

7. Their pleasures were simple but they were deep and lasting for example the pleasure of watching their farms grow the joy of creating something from nothing the satisfaction of harvest time.

8. Some settlers in fact preferred the rugged adventurous life as soon as civilization caught up with them they moved westward and opened more new land.

9. Daniel Boone according to S. E. White's book Daniel Boone Wilderness Scout was a man who disliked civilization that is he loved freedom which he said only the wilderness afforded.

Review 473

10. Boone the most famous American backwoodsman was born November 2 1734 near Reading Pennsylvania and he died the exact date is not known in September 1820 already a legendary figure.

II

1. On July 20 1956 I remember the day perfectly Don Harry and I set out from Sudbury Ontario on a camping trip.
2. At Jamieson's a campers' supply store we had obtained our supplies canned goods fishing tackle extra blankets it was hard to think of blankets that hot day mosquito netting and a first-aid kit.
3. Don who was in charge of supplies almost forgot the matches and I much to the alarm of the others almost left our ax behind.
4. Our guide an experienced woodsman was recommended by my Uncle George who had been out with him several times twice last year and once this year Uncle George you see is crazy about fishing.
5. Since we didn't want to be kidded on our return we had never referred to our trip as a fishing trip we had merely said we were going camping.
6. In all our plans however fish played a big part we didn't take rods and flies and bait along for the fun of carrying them.
7. The long deep pine-bordered lake was beautiful the water was unbelievably clear and on bright days it was unbelievably blue.
8. Because the water was cold we did no voluntary swimming however Harry and I took an involuntary swim which scared us badly.
9. Early one morning Harry the proud fisherman went to sleep in the boat and while he was dozing a big fish started off with his line.
10. Harry grabbed for the rod but as he wasn't fully awake he reached a little too far lost his balance and fell overboard.

474   Punctuation

● REVIEW EXERCISE B.   *Commas, semicolons, colons, dashes, parentheses, italics, end marks.* Where there are quotation marks *in this exercise,* place other punctuation *inside* the quotation marks.

1. As we listened to the bad news the prospect of easy victory faded suddenly we were being told that the star hitter the catcher and the team captain were all too ill to play
2. The following equipment will be issued paper drawing boards pens ink textbooks and a T square
3. My friend Caroline who is always well dressed helped me pick out a new dress she did not realize however that I am not a millionaire
4. Those students who made the honor roll may be excused at 2 30 on Monday Wednesday and Friday all others must remain until 3 15
5. The school according to Mr Barnes has many needs a new field tennis and handball courts a new gym floor
6. If the weather changes Mr Sommers who has a new sailboat will take us sailing if it rains we will go to the Paramount my favorite theater
7. "Well you have certainly made a mess of the house" exclaimed Mother returning after her vacation
8. Mr Simpkins waiting uneasily for his turn to shoot grew more and more nervous finally when the gun was handed to him he pointed it at the target closed his eyes and pulled the trigger
9. "A bull's eye" exclaimed the proprietor then he handed Mr Simpkins the first prize a beautiful blanket
10. Although the train was not to leave until 4 30 everyone who was going on the excursion was on the platform at 4 15 therefore we were able to see who was going with us
11. The Saturday Review recommended Charles Evart's latest book The Man from Mars

CHAPTER 24

Punctuation

QUOTATION MARKS

24a. Use quotation marks to enclose a direct quotation — a person's exact words. Do not use quotation marks to enclose an indirect quotation — not a person's exact words.

DIRECT QUOTATION Harry said, **"I am going to ask Betty for a date."** [the speaker's exact words]

INDIRECT QUOTATION Harry said that he was going to ask Betty for a date. [not the speaker's exact words]

▶ NOTE: Place quotation marks at both the beginning and the end of the quotation. Omission of quotation marks at the end of a quotation is a common error.

24b. A direct quotation begins with a capital letter.

RIGHT She said, **"Ask your father."**
Father asked, **"What did your mother say?"**
"She said I should ask you," I replied.

▶ NOTE: If the quotation is only a fragment of a sentence, do not begin it with a capital letter.

RIGHT He denied the Senator's accusation that he was a **"two-faced scoundrel."**

475

24c. When a quoted sentence is divided into two parts by such interrupting expressions as *he said, she replied, Jack added,* etc., the second part begins with a small letter.

RIGHT   "I think," said Mary, "that you are mistaken."
"One afternoon last week," she explained, "our teacher kept us after school."
"We tried to do what was expected of us," he said; "however, the work was too hard."

If the second part of a broken quotation is a new sentence, it begins with a capital.

RIGHT   "The feature has just started," he said. "You will see almost all of it."

24d. A direct quotation is set off from the rest of the sentence by commas.

RIGHT   "You shouldn't have left school," said the principal, "without getting my permission."

24e. Other marks of punctuation when used with quotation marks are placed according to the following rules:

(1) Commas and periods are always placed inside the closing quotation marks.

RIGHT   "I know the right answer," he said, "but I don't know how to get it."

(2) Colons and semicolons are always placed outside the closing quotation marks.

RIGHT   Miss Crane said to us, "You are all in danger of failing"; what she said after that I was too dazed to hear.
The following students have, in the words of the superintendent, "surpassed all expectations": Homer Earll, Don McCurry, Jack Kenmore.

(3) Question marks and exclamation points are placed inside the closing quotation marks if the quotation is a question or an exclamation; otherwise they are placed outside.

RIGHT   "What are your reasons?" challenged the speaker.
Did he say, "Turn west" or "Turn left"?
Never say, "It can't be done"!

24f. When you write dialogue (two or more persons carrying on a conversation) begin a new paragraph every time the speaker changes.

"Hello, mates," said Captain Handy softly, "what can I do for you now?"

"You can turn over the ship to me," replied the first mate, his voice filled with tension. "I'll promise you fair treatment and a safe voyage home."

Handy looked with deliberation at the crowd of mutineers. "So it's mutiny, is it, you blackguards? You can't get away with it!" he roared.

"We have got away with it, sir," replied the mate, the automatic "sir" emerging in spite of himself.

"And we'll thank you for stepping down and turning over the ship at once," added Johnson, impatience in every word.

24g. Use quotation marks to enclose titles of chapters, articles, poems, and other parts of books or magazines.

For the correct way of indicating titles of books and magazines see page 470.

RIGHT   Chapter II, "Capital Letters and Punctuation," is very valuable.

RIGHT   The captain recommended an article in *Harper's,* "The Control of Science."

**24
c-g**

24h. Use *single* quotation marks to enclose a quotation within a quotation.

RIGHT   George said, "As I remember, his exact words were, 'Meet me at the bank.' "

Helen said, "I liked Henley's poem 'Invictus' very much."

● EXERCISE 1. The following exercise is designed to test your ability to use quotation marks and the other marks of punctuation used with quotation marks. Copy it on your paper, inserting quotation marks and other necessary punctuation. Watch your paragraphing.

Hello, Harry said Mr. Morgan, slapping me too hard on the back. Hello, Mr. Morgan I said. Let's see now he said your big brother is in college this year, isn't he? Well, I don't have a brother I replied. You're probably thinking of my sister Jane. Oh, yes Mr. Morgan exclaimed. Jane is the one. She went to Southern State. How does she like college? She likes college fine I told him only she's at the university. Why, of course he answered, trying to recover himself a little. I forgot for a moment. That was your father's college, wasn't it? No, sir I had to reply. Dad went to Cornell. Is that so? Mr. Morgan answered, realizing he was getting in deeper and deeper. Anyway, it's good to have a talk with you. I always like to keep in touch with our students and alumni. Goodbye, George. Goodbye, Mr. Morgan, I said, not bothering to tell him that my name is John.

● EXERCISE 2. Using quotation marks correctly, write one original sentence containing each of the following:

1. a direct quotation beginning with *he said*
2. a direct quotation ending with *he said*
3. an indirect quotation
4. a direct quotation not beginning with a capital letter

5. a direct quotation interrupted with *he replied*
6. a question mark inside quotation marks
7. a question mark outside quotation marks
8. an exclamation point inside quotation marks
9. the title of an article or a short poem
10. the title of a short poem within a direct quotation

● EXERCISE 3. Try your hand at writing an interesting dialogue. Select two characters for your conversation, put them in a special situation, and make them talk. Two high school boys in the locker room, two girls sitting next to each other in the library or study hall, a student making thin excuses for being an hour late to school, you and your father after you have presented him with your report card. These are suggestions. How can you work the characters' actions into your dialogue? Remember how to paragraph dialogue.

24h

CHAPTER 25

Punctuation

THE APOSTROPHE

The Possessive Case

NOUNS

The possessive case of a noun or a pronoun is used to indicate ownership or relationship.

OWNERSHIP   the **woman's** hat

                 her hat   (the hat is *hers*)

                 my dog and **Jane's** cat

RELATIONSHIP   **John's** aunt

                 this **morning's** paper

                 his sneezing

In the English language the possessive case of *nouns* is formed by adding an apostrophe and an *s* or, in some words, merely an apostrophe, to the noun.

RIGHT   this man's coat
        Fred's bicycle
        both girls' hats

In forming the possessive of most nouns you will encounter no difficulty at all. Your problem, as you may already have discovered, will be *remembering* to put in the apostrophe. In other words, carelessness is responsible for most errors in omitting apostrophes.

25a. To form the possessive case of a singular noun, add an apostrophe and an s.[1]

RIGHT   the boy's hat
Bill's excuses
Gus's baseball bat
Ulysses' adventures

25b. To form the possessive case of a plural noun not ending in s, add an apostrophe and an s.

RIGHT   men's club
children's playground

25c. To form the possessive case of a plural noun ending in s, add the apostrophe only.

RIGHT   ladies' handbags
girls' sports

▶ NOTE: Do not use an apostrophe to form the *plural* of a noun.

WRONG   Three day's elapsed.
RIGHT   Three *days* elapsed.

WRONG   The plane's were left in hangar's.
RIGHT   The *planes* were left in *hangars*.

Study the following examples of the application of these rules. Explain each.

SINGULAR	SINGULAR POSSESSIVE	PLURAL	PLURAL POSSESSIVE
car	car's bumper	cars	cars' bumpers
Mr. Barnes	Mr. Barnes's car	the Barneses	the Barneses' car
woman	woman's child	women	women's children

[1] Many writers prefer to use only the apostrophe with words ending in *s*, but you will find the use of apostrophes easier if you always use the *'s* (' and *s*) with any singular word, whether the word ends in *s* or not. A proper name of more than one syllable requires the apostrophe only.

**25
a-c**

SINGULAR	SINGULAR POSSESSIVE	PLURAL	PLURAL POSSESSIVE
American	an American's pride	Americans	the Americans' pride
dog	dog's tail	dogs	dogs' tails
baby	baby's rattle	babies	babies' rattles
policeman	policeman's uniform	policemen	policemen's uniforms
book	book's cover	books	books' covers
army	army's equipment	armies	armies' equipment
doctor	doctor's prescription	doctors	doctors' prescriptions

PRONOUNS

25d. **The possessive pronouns *his, hers, its, ours, yours, theirs,* and *whose* do not require an apostrophe.**

The lists below show the nominative and possessive forms of those pronouns. Note that there are *no* apostrophes.

NOMINATIVE CASE	POSSESSIVE CASE
you	yours
he	his
she	hers
it	its
we	ours
they	theirs
who	whose

25e. **The pronouns *one, everyone, everybody,* etc., form their possessive case in the same way as nouns.**

RIGHT   everybody's eyes

● EXERCISE 1.   On your paper make a four-column chart like that on page 481, using these words: *enemy, laborer, coach, monkey, child, Mr. Jones, friend, teacher, fireman, clerk.* If you do not know how to spell the plural form of any of these words, look it up in the dictionary. The plural of *Jones* is *Joneses.*

● EXERCISE 2. List on your paper in the order in which they appear in the following paragraphs the words requiring apostrophes. After each word with an apostrophe write the thing possessed. Before each word write the number of the sentence in which it appears. Remember that the only nouns requiring just an apostrophe are plural words ending in *s.*

EXAMPLE   1. At Marians party the girls costumes were very funny.

     1. Marian's party
        girls' costumes

(The paragraphs are apostrophe exercises; they are not intended as models of good English.)

1. At Walters suggestion our boys club decided to build a club house in the Bergs back yard.   2. Everyones basement was searched, and Jimmys and ours yielded some useful crates.   3. (Jimmys uncle in Florida had been sending crates of Floridas best fruit to the Wrights all winter.) 4. The crates and some lumber from Fishers old fence were all we needed, according to our architects plans. 5. While we hunted, the other boys got shovels and spades from Mr. Greens tool shed and dug a hole for the foundation.   6. Then came the problem of nails and saws. 7. McGregors Department Store had plenty of nails, but the cost was a problem.

8. Someone remembered that Mrs. Longs lawn needed mowing, and everybodys lawn mower was rushed into action on the Longs yard.   9. Of course, Mrs. Long approved, and the mowers profits were soon turned over to our treasurers safekeeping.   10. Johns tool kit was raided for hammer and saw, and under Walters able direction, the house was begun.   11. By evening the neighborhoods

**25
d-e**

interest was centered in the new project, and Franks father,
together with Georges and mine, was out there helping.

12. In two days our clubs new house was finished.

● EXERCISE 3.   List in order on your paper the
words requiring apostrophes. After each word with
an apostrophe write the thing possessed. Before each
word write the number of the sentence in which it appears. Remember that the only nouns requiring just
an apostrophe are plural words ending in *s*.

1. Meanwhile Bills sister had brought several friends
of hers to see our clubs new quarters.   2. Janes first
idea was to have a house for their girls club too, but the
boys spirit failed when they were asked to build another.
3. Helens suggestion that the girls could use the attic
of her house seemed popular.   4. We all traipsed over to
the Browns home and filed up the attic stairs.   5. The
girls request that we boys put up a partition was granted;
and after getting Mrs. Browns consent, we set to work
like experts.   6. With boards and old blankets the partition was built.   7. The new room was larger than our
new house, and the girls originality in furnishing it far ex-
ceeded ours.   8. Our clubs furniture consisted of old boxes
and crates, but theirs was old articles gathered from the
girls homes.   9. They found an old rocker in the Wrights
attic, two porch chairs in the Longs basement, and a folding
cot.   10. The cots springs sagged pretty badly, and no
ones home yielded a mattress.   11. The suns rays beating
on the roof above the attic raised the temperature pretty
high, and the girls decided their room would be used only
on rainy days.   12. They said they would use ours on
nice days!

25f. In compound words, names of business firms, and words showing joint possession, only the last word is possessive in form.

COMPOUND WORDS   brother-in-*law*'s home
                   sergeant at *arms*'s gun

NAMES OF BUSINESS FIRMS   Marble and Wood's Furniture Store
Harcourt, Brace and Company's office

JOINT POSSESSION   Ken and Joe's jalopy
Alison and Jean's room

25g. When two or more persons possess something individually, each of their names is possessive in form.

RIGHT   Ken's and Joe's tennis rackets

25h. The words *minute, hour, day, week, month, year,* etc., when used as possessive adjectives, require an apostrophe. Words indicating amount in *cents* or *dollars*, when used as possessive adjectives, require apostrophes.

RIGHT   ten minutes' delay
an hour's wait
a month's vacation
two cents' worth
a dollar's worth

● EXERCISE 4.   List in order on your paper all words requiring apostrophes. Before each word write the number of the sentence in which it appears.

1. As it was an hours walk to Burgum and Barrs store we accepted my sister-in-laws offer of a ride.   2. Mothers and Dads cars were both in use.   3. After three days delay, Ruth and I were finally getting around to exchanging Ruths birthday present.   4. At her sisters suggestion I had bought her one of Burgum and Barrs teen-ager handbags.   5. But good things, it seems, come in bunches, and Ruth got three of them.   6. Before her birthday Ruths junk was always cluttering up others handbags.   7. Mine was known as "Ruth and Marys bag"; no one knew really whose bag it was.   8. When my plans agreed with hers, our joint ownership of a bag worked out all

**25
f-h**

right; however, if Ruths plans took her downtown and mine took me over to Andys, we didn't do so well. 9. Now that she had three bags and large gold *R*'s had been stamped on two of them, she had decided to exchange the one I gave her.

● EXERCISE 5.   List in order on your paper all words requiring apostrophes. Before each word write the number of the sentence in which it appears.

1. As we completed our ten minutes ride, I explained that she could exchange the bag for three dollars worth of something. 2. She said she wanted a scarf like Jeans or a pair of gloves like her sisters. 3. Jeans and Barbaras scarves were alike, but that didn't bother Ruth, whose mind was made up. 4. "I never see Jean and her anyway," she argued. 5. We went straight to the girls sportswear counter, caught the clerks eye, and looked for a scarf. 6. To Ruths delight, we found what she wanted, a scarf like Jeans and Barbaras; then, to the clerks surprise, Ruth handed over the handbag as payment. 7. After about an hours delay, while the manager and everyone else struggled with red tape, we got the exchange straightened out. 8. Now that it was hers, she put the scarf on her head, and we went over to Klipps Drug Store for a coke. 9. The first people we saw there were Jean and Barbara, both wearing their scarves too! 10. Ruths face was red, but I grinned.

Contractions

25i. Use an apostrophe to indicate where letters have been left out in a contraction. A contraction is a word made up of two words combined into one by omitting one or more letters.

What words have been contracted and what letters have been omitted from the following?

We can't go.
It's going to rain.
They're staying at home.

● EXERCISE 6. Study the following contractions. Be able to write them when your teacher dictates to you the words in the numbered column.

1. should not	shouldn't	10. has not	hasn't
2. they have	they've	11. she will	she'll
3. of the clock	o'clock	12. he is	he's
4. is not	isn't	13. I am	I'm
5. they would	they'd	14. they will	they'll
6. have not	haven't	15. let us	let's
7. we are	we're	16. who is	who's
8. were not	weren't	17. he would	he'd
9. that is	that's	18. they had	they'd

19. Bill is	Bill's
20. does not	doesn't
21. will not (other changes in the spelling here)	won't
22. shall not	shan't
23. did not	didn't
24. we would	we'd
25. they are	they're

● EXERCISE 7. Copy the following sentences, inserting apostrophes wherever necessary.

1. Hed met televisions greatest personalities.
2. Well get Mothers permission.
3. The boys bicycles werent all the same size.
4. The theaters policy wasnt clear.
5. Andersons Department Store announced that theyll be closed tomorrow.
6. Im sure hell accept Marys invitation.
7. Its three oclock according to Jacks watch.
8. Youll get a special price on the book because its cover isnt in good condition.

25i

9. I havent met Annes brother.
10. Didnt you think wed be on time for Helens party?

ITS AND IT'S

The word *its* is the possessive form of the personal pronoun *it*. As you know, personal pronouns do not require an apostrophe in their possessive forms.

The word *it's* is a contraction of *it is*. The apostrophe takes the place of an omitted letter.

● EXERCISE 8. This exercise is designed to give you practice in using *its* and *it's*. You should be able to do the exercise perfectly. Copy the sentences, inserting apostrophes where needed.

1. Its likely that the storm has already spent its fury.
2. If its lucky, the ship will make port without its rudder.
3. The box was in its proper place, but its contents were missing.
4. According to its author its a true story.
5. At its best its an exciting sport; at its worst its very dull.
6. Although its frame is too big, its a beautiful picture.
7. Its a letter for you even though its addressed to me.
8. The firm increased its salaries when its profits went up.
9. The team is doing its best, but its too late to win.
10. With its large print and many pictures, its an easy book to read.

25j. Use the apostrophe and *s* to form the plural of letters, numbers, and signs, and of words referred to as words.

RIGHT There are two *r*'s and two *s*'s in *embarrass*.
He shot two 3's and two 2's in the first round.
I had five +'s and seven 0's in this exercise.
There are too many *and*'s in your sentence.

● EXERCISE 9. Copy the following paragraphs, inserting apostrophes where needed.

1. Nancys a whirlwind.   2. Shes never idle.   3. Its not unusual when weve finished a hard days work to hear Nancys deep voice calling up someone to go swimming at Morgans Pond or bowling at Johnson and Johnsons bowling alleys.   4. The chances are that shell be late for supper, argue her way out of doing the dishes, and be off again to Bettys or Joans or maybe out on the Wilsons lawn playing croquet.   5. Shes always borrowing her brothers things.   6. The other day she was wearing Harolds varsity sweater and Jims slacks, and riding Andys bike.   7. I guess youd say Nancys a tomboy.

8. Last spring Frank and Henry bought a little sailboat which they kept at Jessups Landing.   9. One day Nancy arrived, hopped aboard, untied the boat, and pushed off. 10. She knew whose boat it was, and in spite of Mr. Jessups warning that it was Frank and Henrys, she hoisted its sail and set out up Drakes Creek.   11. After three hours cruising, she came gaily back to find Frank and Henry waiting anxiously for her on the dock.   12. Theyd arrived a few minutes after shed left, and Jessup had told them whod taken their boat.   13. Its a wonder they didnt throw her into the river.   14. Nancys innocent air and laughing eyes only increased the owners rage as they pointed out that the boat was theirs, not hers; but she got them to drive her back to town in their car, and they even bought her a soda at Petes on the way.   15. Thats typical of Nancys power over males.   16. Now the boys keep the sail locked up in the boathouse — they alone have the key.   17. Theyd never trust anyone else, after having fallen victims to Nancys charm.

● REVIEW EXERCISE A.   *All Punctuation.*   Copy the following sentences on your paper, inserting all necessary punctuation.

1. Saturdays game which was played at Baker Field was the last of the season

25j

2. At six oclock in the morning Don plays his cornet and Lois practices her piano lessons

3. At 3 15 oclock school was dismissed and everyone went home

4. Where I asked have Billy Helen and Jane gone

5. Mr Hall the truant officer knew we had been to Kornfields Drug Store were we surprised

6. If the gloves are yours Mike youll have to identify them

7. Whose book is this Jean I asked its not mine

8. Barry on the contrary is a tall handsome young man

9. My friend Alex and Johns brother Jim are going to the movies with us however theres plenty of room in Freds station wagon for you and Hal and Jud

10. Gee I exclaimed leaping to the curb that was a close call

11. Dr Hardy who is our family doctor came here from Boise Idaho many years ago

12. The letter that I saw was addressed to Gerald Kahn 25 Cedar Lane Omaha Nebraska it was dated July 6 1956

13. Pupils who wish to take this test must bring the following articles drawing paper pencils and a compass

14. Well youd better hurry warned Miss Huss were late already

15. Its never too late George said his father when I was a boy I made many mistakes

● REVIEW EXERCISE B.   *All Punctuation.*   Copy the following paragraphs, inserting all necessary punctuation.

1. School luckily for me was dismissed at 11 45 oclock this I thought was an undeserved break as English math and science are my afternoon classes the night before my sister Jane and I had asked Mary Sue and Evelyn to come over to do science and math with us they arrived right after the dishes were done it was Janes turn to wash and when they left at ten we hadnt even mentioned homework the books notebooks and pens which they had brought along lay untouched on the hall table with spring vaca-

tion less than one day away how could we think about school

2. Well it was a warm bright April day and as I walked home I could feel spring fever coming on I thought of things to do after lunch go over to Helens and play records go downtown shopping take a lazy sun bath I might even finish A Tale of Two Cities which I was supposed to have finished today yes it was going to be a wonderful afternoon

3. Mother however had another idea spring cleaning now dear she said in her customary businesslike tone Im going to need you this afternoon Aunt Alice is coming for the week end and the house has to be thoroughly cleaned furthermore Mrs Lake our new neighbor and I are going shopping while were gone I want you and Jane to straighten up the house wash the living room windows and above all clean out your rooms Im putting Aunt Alice in yours Jane

4. Oh Mother I protested its such a nice day why do I have to stay indoors well be home all next week couldnt the cleaning wait besides I want to get that hat at Blumbergs yes I got nowhere I could see my own expression in Janes face

5. By five oclock when Mother returned the work was done and the best thought of the day occurred to me at least tomorrow we wont have to clean house

6. Hello girls Mothers cheerful voice came from the hall my how nice the windows look wed better do the rest of them tomorrow and by the way you can wash the living room curtains for me in the morning too Mrs Lakes curtains are all done and ours look frightful

● REVIEW EXERCISE C. *Capital Letters and Punctuation.* Copy the following sentences, inserting capital letters and punctuation.

1. My brother George who spent the summer at camp wildwood near burlington vermont likes new england summers
2. While Sally went shopping Mary set the table Helen dusted and I did the french homework for all of us
3. The mississippi river drains the middle west and its

tributaries the ohio river and the missouri river reach as far into the northwest as montana and as far east as new york

4. The bergen electric company on market street had filled its showroom with new merchandise toasters irons washing machines lamps and a variety of radios

5. Yes I remember judge lamberts home said the old resident it was a big ugly brick house at the end of cherry street it stood where the first national bank now stands

6. On the southern shore of long island the surf is usually heavy on the northern side which is not on the atlantic ocean but on long island sound theres very little surf

7. You will Im sure be impressed by the beauty of yellowstone national park but nothing that youll see will surpass the grand canyon of the colorado

8. The sunnyside laundry on east state street advertised in the millville daily news for saturday march 3 that it would provide overnight service without extra cost

9. Come to my office at 3 45 said mr Atkins the mayor to patrolman Johnson so that I may hear your story of the robbery at the Hansen milling company

10. Its true said coach Horton that the team will do its best to win its last game against washington academy

11. Stewart Lister graduated from west high school in june and after studying at the university of chicago during the summer entered college in the fall as a sophomore

12. The players club of our high school rented the franklin theater for its production of Thornton Wilders play our town

CHAPTER 26

Spelling

Learning to Spell

By the time you reach high school you know whether or not you are a good speller. Really good spellers are rare people. If you are one of them, thank your lucky stars. If you are not and know you are not, you are like most of us who have to work at our spelling. You can improve your spelling if you want to, but you must make an effort. No one else can be of much help to you. *Learning to spell is your own personal responsibility.*

There is no one way to learn to spell. There are many ways, and you should learn what they are. By using a combination of several methods, you can in time become a good speller. Some of these ways, which have helped many students, are listed below. Read them over; put them into practice.

1. In your notebook, keep a list of the words you misspell.
2. Get the dictionary habit.
3. Proofread your papers before handing them in.
4. Learn to spell words by syllables.
5. Learn to pronounce words correctly.
6. Use your ears, eyes, and pencil when learning to spell a word.
7. Learn lists of commonly misspelled words.
8. Learn to spell by making associations.
9. Learn a few helpful spelling rules and apply them.

1. *In your notebook, keep a list of the words you misspell.*

Set aside a few pages in your notebook for listing words you have misspelled. This list, if kept up faithfully and reviewed frequently, will be the best means of removing your spelling errors. This method tests your will power. To copy down in your notebook all the misspelled words on your school papers *in all subjects* takes time and may seem a nuisance to you. But if you aren't willing to do that much to improve your spelling, you really don't have much desire to be a better speller.

One way to record your words is to prepare a spelling sheet with four columns. In the first column, correctly spell the word you missed. (Never enter a misspelled word on your spelling page.) In the second column, write the word again, this time divided into syllables. In the third column, write the word once more, circling the spot that gives you trouble. In the fourth column, give the reason for your mistake, or set down any comment that will help you to learn the word.

1. surprise	sur-prise	su(rp)rise	Pronounce correctly.
2. recommend	rec-om-mend	re(c)ommend	Study Rule 26b.
3. together	to-geth-er	to(get)her	This word has three small words in it: *to get her.*

2. *Get the dictionary habit.*

The dictionary is the authority on correct spelling. Whenever you wish to write a word that you think you can't spell, you may try to solve your problem in several ways. You may simply take a chance and guess at the spelling. This has an element of sportiveness in it, keeps you in suspense until the teacher has corrected your paper. Besides, it is by far the easiest way — the easiest way to misspell a word!

You may ask someone how to spell the word you

want. This method, like all methods which depend on others, has one big drawback. You have probably already discovered what the drawback is.

A third solution to your problem is to look up the word in a dictionary. You may quite reasonably wonder how you can look up the spelling of a word when you don't know how to spell it. This is sometimes an impossible task, but most of the time you can guess well enough to find the word; and once you have found it, you are really sure of the correct spelling, something you can never be sure of when you use the "guess" or "ask somebody" system. Furthermore, the very experience of looking up the word helps you to fix the word in your mind so that you'll remember it longer.

3. *Proofread your papers before handing them in.*

"Proofreading" is the process of rereading carefully for errors whatever you have written. Proofreading is the best cure for carelessness in punctuation, using capital letters, spelling, etc. It takes only a few minutes, yet it makes a great difference in the correctness of your work.

4. *Learn to spell words by syllables.*

A syllable is a word part which can be pronounced by itself. For instance, the word *af'ter* has two syllables; the word *bas'ket·ball* has three syllables; the word *an·ti·sep'tic* has four syllables. How many syllables has each of the following words? What are they?

1. apartment
2. friend
3. jumper
4. America
5. understand
6. villain
7. information
8. break
9. superintendent
10. sacrifice

When you divide a long word into its syllables, you are really making a number of shorter words out of it (these shorter words may have no meaning by themselves) and since short words are easy to spell, you make spelling easier. The word *congratulate*, for example, is a long word that may prove hard to spell unless you can divide it into syllables. Then it becomes much easier: *con·grat'u·late*. Dividing a word accurately into its syllables can be done only if you can pronounce the word correctly.

5. *Learn to pronounce words correctly.*

Faulty pronunciation may lead to faulty spelling. The boy who says *ath·a·let'ics* for *athletics* will probably *spell* the word incorrectly. He will add an extra syllable. *Incorrect pronunciation* of *arctic* (as *artic*) will result in *incorrect spelling*, leaving out the first *c*. You need to learn the correct pronunciation of a word in order to spell it correctly.

Study the pronunciation of the words in the following list. Notice how incorrect pronunciation could lead to incorrect spelling.

film	[*not* fil'*u*m]
lib·ra·ry	[*not* lib*a*ry]
light·ning	[*not* light*e*ning]
mis'chie·vous	[*not* mischiev'*i*ous]
prob·a·bly	[*not* pro*bly* or pro*bally*]
sur·prise	[*not* *su*pprise]
priv·i·lege	[*not* priv*lege*]
per·for·mance	[*not* *pre*formance]
per·spi·ra·tion	[*not* *pre*spiration]
bound·a·ry	[*not* bound*ry*]
can·di·date	[*not* can*i*date]
rep·re·sen·ta·tives	[*not* represen*tives*]

6. *Use your ears, eyes, and pencil when learning to spell a word.*

When you undertake to master the correct spelling of a word, there are three steps you should take.

First, *pronounce the word*, noting its syllables. As you know, thinking of a word syllable by syllable makes the spelling easier.

Second, *study the word*, noting especially any letters which might make the spelling difficult. Notice, for instance, the two *c*'s and one *s* in **occasion;** the fact that there is no *e* after the *u* in **argument;** that there is an *e* in **description,** etc. After you have *seen and studied* the word, close your eyes and try to *visualize* it.

Third, *write the word*. Spelling is of use only in writing. The movement of your hand in making the letters will help to fix the spelling in your mind.

7. *Learn lists of commonly misspelled words.*

The majority of the spelling errors made by students are made on a relatively few, frequently written words. Many of these words will appear easy to you. They should. But they *are*, nevertheless, so often misspelled that anyone wishing to improve his spelling should master them, and misspelling any of them should be counted as a serious error.

ONE HUNDRED SPELLING DEMONS

ache	busy	does
again	buy	done
always	can't	don't
among	choose [present	early
answer	tense; *chose* is	easy
any	past tense]	enough
been	color	every
beginning	coming	February
believe	cough	forty
blue	could	friend
break (to shatter)	country	grammar
built	dear	guess
business	doctor	half

having

hear (ear)

heard

here (*there* — a place)

hoarse (frog in your throat)

hour

instead

just

knew

know

laid

loose (adjective and verb)

lose (verb — to *lose* money)

making

many

meant

minute

much

often

once

piece (a part of something)

raise

read [spelling is same for all tenses]

ready

said

says

seems

separate

shoes

since

some

straight

sugar

sure

tear

their (ownership — *heir*)

there (*here* — a place)

they

though

through

tired

tonight

too (too much; also)

trouble

truly

Tuesday

two (2)

used

very

wear

Wednesday

week (52 in a year)

where

whether (. . . or not)

which

whole (sum of all parts)

women

won't

would

write

writing

wrote

A list of other commonly misspelled words will be found on pages 516–518.

8. *Learn to spell by making associations.*

Make any kind of association that will help you to remember a difficult word. For example, the word *recognize* has the word *cog* in it; *definite* has *finite*. You can link rhyming words, putting an easy word with a hard one: *aid, paid; hose, chose; lawful, awful.* You may think of absurd but useful sentences such as the following:

1. *Witches* have nothing to do with sand*wiches*.
2. A br*agger* ex*agger*ates.

3. A *hateful* person is seldom *grateful*.
4. *Existence* in a *cemetery* is *eerie* — all *e*'s.

What associations can you make in order to remember the spelling of *across, written, cafeteria, conscience?*

9. *Learn a few helpful spelling rules and apply them.*

Once you have memorized some of the more useful spelling rules, you can "figure out" correct spelling. Most spelling, to be sure, is learned by memorizing, yet many people find rules helpful. The rules given below are the kind that will be of most help.

26a. Write *ie* when the sound is $\overline{ee}$, except after *c*.

EXAMPLES   bel**ie**ve, th**ie**f, f**ie**rce; c**ei**ling, rec**ei**ve, dec**ei**ve
EXCEPTIONS s**ei**ze, **ei**ther, w**ei**rd, l**ei**sure, n**ei**ther, financ**ie**r

Write *ei* when the sound is not $\overline{ee}$, especially when the sound is $\overline{a}$.

EXAMPLES   fr**ei**ght, n**ei**ghbor, w**ei**gh, h**ei**ght
EXCEPTIONS fr**ie**nd, misch**ie**f, handkerch**ie**f

● EXERCISE 1. Write the following words, supplying the missing letters (*e* and *i*) in the correct order. Explain how the rule applies to each.

1. for...gn	9. p...ce	17. bel...ve
2. br...f	10. rec...ve	18. w...rd
3. rel...ve	11. retr...ve	19. rec...pt
4. conc...ve	12. sl...gh	20. s...ge
5. v...l	13. ach...ve	21. s...ze
6. n...ce	14. handkerch...f	22. bel...f
7. c...ling	15. perc...ve	23. f...nd
8. gr...f	16. th...f	24. l...sure

26b. When the prefixes[1] *il–, in–, im–, un–, dis–, mis–, re–,* and *over–* are added to a word,

[1] A prefix is a letter or group of letters added to the *beginning* of a word to change its meaning.

26 a-b

500   *Spelling*

the spelling of the word itself remains the same.

il + legal = **il**legal
in + elegant = **in**elegant
im + movable = **im**movable
un + necessary = **un**necessary
un + excused = **un**excused
dis + appear = **dis**appear
dis + satisfied = **dis**satisfied

mis + understood = **mis**understood
mis + spell = **mis**spell
re + commend = **re**commend
over + run = **over**run
over + eat = **over**eat

26c. **When the suffixes** [2] **-*ness* and -*ly* are added to a word, the spelling of the word itself remains the same.**

EXAMPLES   mean + ness = mean**ness**; final + ly = final**ly**
EXCEPTIONS   true + ly = tru**ly**
Words ending in *y* change the *y* to *i* before a suffix: ready — read**ily**; heavy — heav**iness**; happy — happ**iness**.

● EXERCISE 2.   Spell correctly the words indicated.

1. *rate* with the prefix *over*
2. *usual* with the suffix *ly*
3. *agree* with the prefix *dis*
4. *green* with the suffix *ness*
5. *mature* with the prefix *im*
6. *approve* with the prefix *dis*
7. *used* with the prefix *mis*
8. *general* with the suffix *ly*
9. *natural* with the prefix *un*
10. *practical* with the suffix *ly*
11. *able* with the prefix *un*
12. *mean* with the suffix *ness*
13. *logical* with the prefix *il*

[2] A suffix is a letter or group of letters added to the *end* of a word to change its meaning.

14. *accurate* with the prefix *in*
15. *able* with the prefix *dis*
16. *moral* with the prefix *im*
17. *construct* with the prefix *re*
18. *efficient* with the prefix *in*
19. *similar* with the prefix *dis*
20. *stern* with the suffix *ness*
21. *step* with the prefix *mis*
22. *use* with the prefix *mis*
23. *opened* with the prefix *un*
24. *brutal* with the suffix *ly*

26d. Drop the final e before a suffix beginning with a vowel.

EXAMPLES   care + ing = car**ing**   use + able = us**able**

EXCEPTIONS Keep the final *e* before *a* or *o* if necessary to retain the soft sound of *c* or *g* preceding the *e*: noti**ce**able, coura**ge**ous.

dye + ing = dye**ing** (to prevent confusion with *dying*)

26e. Keep the final e before a suffix beginning with a consonant.

EXAMPLES   care + ful = care**ful**   care + less = care**less**

EXCEPTIONS true + ly = tru**ly**   argue + ment = argu**ment**

● EXERCISE 3.   Write correctly the words formed as follows:

1. cure + ing
2. hope + ing
3. fame + ous
4. approve + al
5. nine + ty
6. change + able
7. prepare + ing
8. name + less
9. write + ing
10. singe + ing
11. desire + able
12. love + ing
13. hope + less
14. move + ing
15. true + ly

26
c-e

THE PLURAL OF NOUNS

26f. Observe the rules for spelling the plural of nouns.

(1) The regular way to form the plural of a noun is to add an s.

EXAMPLES   chair, chairs   book, books

(2) The plural of some nouns is formed by adding es.

The *e* is necessary to make the plural form pronounceable in the case of words ending in *s*, *sh*, *ch*, and *x*.

EXAMPLES   dress, dresses   bush, bushes
            birch, birches   box, boxes

(3) The plural of nouns ending in y *following* a consonant is formed by changing the y to i and adding es.

EXAMPLES   fly, flies   lady, ladies
            enemy, enemies   salary, salaries

(4) The plural of nouns ending in y *following* a vowel is formed in the usual way.

EXAMPLES   monkey, monkeys   donkey, donkeys

(5) The plural of most nouns ending in f or fe is formed by adding s. The plural of some nouns ending in f or fe is formed by changing the f or fe to v and adding es.

EXAMPLES   Add *s*: roof, roofs   dwarf, dwarfs
                     chief, chiefs

            Change *f* or *fe* to *v* and add *es*:
                     knife, knives   calf, calves
                     loaf, loaves   wharf, wharves
                     leaf, leaves

(6) The plural of nouns ending in o *following a vowel* is formed by adding s. The plural of most nouns ending in o *following a consonant* is formed by adding es, except nouns related to music.

EXAMPLES   *o* following a vowel:

        rodeo, rodeos   radio, radios

      o following a consonant:

        hero, heroes   potato, potatoes
        mosquito, mosquitoes

      nouns related to music:

        piano, pianos   soprano, sopranos
        solo, solos

(7) The plural of a few nouns is formed by irregular methods.

EXAMPLES

child, children	tooth, teeth	woman, women
mouse, mice	ox, oxen	goose, geese

(8) The plural of compound nouns (more than one word) is formed by making the *principal word* plural.

The "principal" word is the word modified; for instance, in *mother-in-law*, *mother* is the word modified by the phrase *in-law;* in *court martial*, *court* is the word modified by the adjective *martial*.

EXAMPLES   mother-in-law, mothers-in-law
           man-of-war, men-of-war
           court martial, courts martial
           lieutenant colonel, lieutenant colonels
           passer-by, passers-by

(9) The plural of compound nouns ending in *–ful* is formed by adding s to the end of the word.

26f

EXAMPLES   cupful, cupfuls   handful, handfuls

(10) The plural of foreign words is sometimes formed as in the foreign language.

EXAMPLES   alumnus (man), alumni (men)
alumna (woman), alumnae (women)
datum, data
analysis, analyses
bacillus, bacilli
crisis, crises

(11) The plural of other foreign words may be formed either as in the foreign language or by adding s or es.

EXAMPLES   index, indices or indexes
appendix, appendices or appendixes

(12) The plural of numbers and letters is formed by adding an apostrophe and s.

EXAMPLES   There are ten 5's in this column.
There are two s's in *necessary*.

(13) Some nouns are the same in the singular and plural.

EXAMPLES   sheep, deer, trout, species, Chinese

● EXERCISE 4.   Write the plural form of each of the following nouns. After each write the number of the rule that applies.

1. bench
2. boy
3. gas
4. potato
5. hoof
6. torch
7. cry
8. man
9. house
10. key
11. cargo
12. fox
13. brother-in-law
14. goose
15. radio
16. shelf
17. editor in chief
18. bacillus
19. wolf
20. spoonful

● EXERCISE 5.   Write the plural form of each of the following nouns. After each write the number of the rule that applies.

1. candy	11. fly
2. sheep	12. alto
3. piano	13. father-in-law
4. valley	14. calf
5. alumnus	15. century
6. library	16. major general
7. handkerchief	17. mouthful
8. crisis	18. hero
9. lady	19. knife
10. tomato	20. brush

HYPHENATING

As you know, the hyphen is used to divide words (between syllables) at the end of a line. It has other uses, some of which are covered by the rules below. You will find these rules helpful in many instances, but not in all. If you are in doubt about whether a word is hyphenated, consult your dictionary.

26g.   Hyphenate compound numbers from twenty-one to ninety-nine. Hyphenate fractions when used as adjectives before the word they modify.

RIGHT   twenty-nine delegates
RIGHT   two-thirds majority (but *two thirds* of the delegates)

26h.   Hyphenate a compound adjective.

RIGHT   a two-ton truck
RIGHT   a room-to-room search

▶ NOTE: When one of the words is an adverb ending in –*ly*, omit the hyphen.

RIGHT   a recently invented improvement

**26
g-h**

26i. Use a hyphen with all prefixes before a proper noun and with the prefixes *self-*, *ex-*, and *all-* before any noun.

RIGHT   anti-Russian   ex-student
         pro-British   self-respect
         Pan-American   all-star

● EXERCISE 6. By referring to the rules you have learned, explain orally the spelling of each of the following:

1. receive
2. un-American
3. coming (*e* dropped)
4. niece
5. contraltos
6. misstate
7. drunkenness
8. peaceable
9. belief
10. ladies
11. unnoticed
12. alumnae
13. naturally
14. seize
15. writing (*e* dropped)
16. overrule
17. thirty-one
18. weigh
19. loaves
20. ex-president

Words Frequently Confused

Mastery of the words in the lists on the following pages — their meaning and their spelling — will greatly improve your spelling. Study only a few at a time, and really master them.

all right   This is the only acceptable spelling. The spelling *alright* has not yet come into good usage.

already   *previously*
I had *already* finished my homework before you called.

all ready   *all are ready*
We were *all ready* at the same time.

all together *everyone in the same place*
We were *all together* at Christmas.

altogether *entirely*
He doesn't *altogether* approve of me.

capital Correct spelling for all uses except when the word means *a government building*
Washington is our national *capital*.
Capital punishment.
He invested his *capital* in oil stock.

capitol *building*
The *capitol* stands at the end of a broad avenue

clothes *what you wear*
She has a wardrobe full of expensive *clothes*.

cloths *pieces of cloth*
Try the new cleaning *cloths*.

coarse *rough, crude*
He wore a suit of *coarse* cloth and used *coarse* language.

course *path of action;* also used with *of* to mean *as was to be expected*
He followed a straight *course*.
The golf *course* and the race *course* are outside of town.
Soup was the first *course*.
I am taking a *course* in cooking.
Of *course*, I will write to you.

des′ert *a dry region*
We flew across the *desert*.

desert′ *to leave*
He *deserted* his family.

dessert′ *what you eat last*
The *dessert* was ice cream.

26i

● EXERCISE 7.   Number on your paper from 1 to 15. Write after the proper number the correct one of the words given in parentheses in the sentences below.

1. The mail had (already, all ready) been collected.
2. You were (altogether, all together) in the gym when the alarm sounded.
3. What city is the (capitol, capital) of Virginia?
4. This wood seems to have a very (coarse, course) grain.
5. I expected a delicious (dessert, desert) after such a good dinner.
6. She spends her money on (cloths, clothes).
7. We had our picture taken on the steps of the (capital, capitol).
8. I wasn't (all together, altogether) sure of myself.
9. Everything seems to be (alright, all right).
10. The painters used these (cloths, clothes) for cleaning.
11. Henry is taking the commercial (course, coarse).
12. The (desert, dessert) was an almost impossible barrier to the pioneers.
13. We are (all ready, already) to begin.
14. The doctor said I was (all right, alright).
15. The new golf (coarses, courses) will be laid out here.

● EXERCISE 8.   Write sentences in which you use correctly each of the words just studied.

hear	*using your ears* I *hear* him coming.
here	*this place* He promised to wait *here*.
its	possessive of *it* The village is proud of *its* school.
it's	*it is* *It's* a long way.

lead	present tense — *to go first* You *lead* us and we will follow.
led	past tense of *lead* He *led* the army to victory.
lead	[pronounced lĕd] *a heavy metal;* also *graphite* in a pencil The industrial uses of *lead* are many.
loose	*free, not close together* The animals broke *loose.* He stumbled in the *loose* sand.
lose	[pronounced lo͞oz] *to suffer loss* When did you *lose* your books?
moral	*good;* also *a lesson of conduct* His good conduct showed him to be a *moral* person. The class understood the *moral* of the story.
morale	*mental condition, spirit* The *morale* of the army is high.
passed	verb, past tense of *pass* They *passed* me on the way to school. She *passed* the note around the class.
past	noun or adjective or preposition He found the *past* more interesting than the present. From *past* experience I knew we had to go *past* the mountain to find the best hunting.
peace	*opposite of strife* Everyone prefers *peace* to war.
piece	*a part of something* They ate every *piece* of cake.

● EXERCISE 9. Number on your paper from 1 to 15. Write after the proper number the correct one of the words given in parentheses in the sentences below.

1. They are all (here, hear) now.
2. He (led, lead) his horse into the clearing.
3. Did you (loose, lose) your bag?
4. The first boat (past, passed) the point at noon.
5. Our class (morale, moral) has been higher since the last class meeting.
6. A (peace, piece) of the kite was hanging from the telegraph pole.
7. At the first turn, Harry (lead, led) the field.
8. I (hear, here) you are going on a trip.
9. (It's, Its) a good day for a picnic.
10. A bolt is (lose, loose) on my bicycle.
11. We hope (peace, piece) will last a long time.
12. As we approached the city, we noticed that (its, it's) skyscrapers could be seen for miles.
13. I'll give her a (piece, peace) of my mind.
14. If (its, it's) required, I'll take Latin next year.
15. He (passed, past) the final examination.

● EXERCISE 10. Write sentences in which you use correctly each of the words just studied.

personal	*individual*
	He gave his *personal* opinion.
personnel	*a group of people employed in the same place*
	The *personnel* of the company ranged in age from 16 to 64.
plain	*not fancy;* also *a flat area of land;* also *clear*
	She lives in a very *plain* home.
	We crossed the *plains* in two days.
	Our problem is quite *plain*.
plane	*a flat surface;* also *a tool;* also *an airplane*
	Plane geometry is a study of imaginary flat surfaces.
	The carpenter used a *plane*.
	A *plane* circled the airport.

principal   *head of a school;* also, as adjective, *main* or *most important*
He was sent to the *principal's* office.
The *principal* cause of accidents is carelessness.

principle   *a rule of conduct;* also *a main fact or law*
The judge accused the criminal of having no *principles.*
He understands the *principles* of mathematics.

shone   past tense of *shine*
The sun *shone* all day.

shown   *revealed*
We were *shown* several unusual exhibits at the museum.

stationary   *in a fixed position*
The classroom desks are *stationary.*

stationery   *writing paper*
I received three boxes of *stationery* at Christmas.

than   *a conjunction, used for comparisons*
I like okra better *than* peas.

then   an adverb or conjunction indicating *at that time* or *next*
He was a great quarterback *then.*
First, put the ribs in deep fat; *then* add salt.

their   *possessive* of *they*
The pupils bring *their* own lunches.

there   *a place;* also an expletive (see page 39)
We were *there* at two o'clock.
There were four of us.

they're   *they are*
They're going with us.

● EXERCISE 11.   Number on your paper from 1 to 15. Write after the proper number the correct one of the words given in parentheses in the sentences below.

1. My (principle, principal) difficulty is learning irregular verbs.
2. The child's face (shown, shone) with delight.
3. The Indian remained (stationery, stationary) in his canoe.
4. No one works harder (then, than) Jane.
5. In geometry we're studying (planes, plains) and angles.
6. My (personal, personnel) opinion should not influence you.
7. The movies were (shown, shone) in the school auditorium.
8. If (their, they're, there) going with us, they had better hurry.
9. "It is a matter of (principle, principal)!" the judge declared.
10. The queen, according to her portraits, had a (plain, plane) face.
11. As usual, I have no (stationery, stationary) left.
12. (Their, They're, There) schoolbooks were strewn all over the floor.
13. The (personal, personnel) manager was very sympathetic with the employees.
14. The (principle, principal) of our school went to college in Ohio.
15. "(Their, They're, There) making an awful racket," complained Mother.

● EXERCISE 12. Write sentences in which you use correctly each of the words just studied.

threw	*hurled*	
	Somebody *threw* a stone at the dog.	
through	*in at one side and out at the opposite side*	
	The stone went *through* a window.	

to	preposition; and part of the infinitive form of a verb Give the book *to* me, please. We will have *to* leave early.
too	adverb *also, too much* I am a sophomore, and George is a sophomore *too.* There were *too* many problems in one homework assignment.
two	*one + one* We had only *two* dollars.
weather	*conditions outdoors* The *weather* was stormy all week end.
whether	as in *whether or not* I don't know *whether* or not he meant what he said.
who's	*who is, who has* *Who's* coming? *Who's* been here?
whose	*possessive* of *who* *Whose* coat is this?
your	*possessive* of *you* Is this *your* coat?
you're	*you are* *You're* out!

● EXERCISE 13. Number on your paper from 1 to 15. Write after the proper number the correct one of the words given in parentheses in the sentences below.

1. Who (threw, through) that eraser?
2. (Your, You're) going to have to study hard tonight.
3. (Whether, Weather) you can go or not depends on your behavior this week.

4. (Too, Two, To) of us trailed out to the car together.
5. (Who's, Whose) going to go with us?
6. (You're, Your) father said we could drive over with him.
7. The boat shot (threw, through) the water at 60 knots.
8. "May I come (too, to, two)?" Marie asked.
9. (Whose, Who's) rubbers were left here in the hall?
10. We will be there (weather, whether) it rains or not.
11. The (weather, whether) has been fine this spring.
12. It's (your, you're) responsibility to pass the course.
13. I don't know (whose, who's) clothes these are.
14. (To, Two, Too) many of us tried out for football; we weren't all accepted.
15. I don't believe she knows (whose, who's) invited.

● EXERCISE 14.   Write sentences in which you use correctly each of the words just studied.

● REVIEW EXERCISE.   Number on your paper from 1 to 50. Select the correct one of the words in parentheses in each sentence and write it after the proper number.

1. Down the (Capitol, Capital) steps came the President and his cabinet.
2. Red flags marked the race (course, coarse).
3. How long have you been (here, hear)?
4. When you are (all ready, already), let me know.
5. The fire may have started in a pile of oily dust (cloths, clothes).
6. (Its, It's) never too late to mend.
7. The navy found that good food was an excellent (morale, moral) builder.
8. When we were (altogether, all together) we had our picture taken.
9. I can't remember (whether, weather) John was here or not.
10. A country's largest city is not always its (capital, capitol).
11. The seats in this room are (stationery, stationary).

12. You are (all ready, already) late.
13. There were only twenty-one years of (peace, piece) between World Wars I and II.
14. He teaches two classes in (plain, plane) geometry.
15. Our guide (led, lead) us to the top of the monument.
16. (Their, They're, There) the best friends I have.
17. You will (lose, loose) your money if you are not careful.
18. You came (to, too, two) late for the show.
19. The sun had (shown, shone) all day.
20. Do you weigh more (than, then) Phil?
21. Watch where (your, you're) going!
22. The (coarse, course) in physics nearly finished me.
23. Forgetting her weight, she devoured two rich (deserts, desserts).
24. He was wearing a (lose, loose) cape.
25. The (principal, principle) speaker was the Governor.
26. We couldn't tell (whether, weather) the ball was a foul or not.
27. I am sure he will be (all right, alright).
28. When he (through, threw) the ball, everyone ducked.
29. He is liable to (lose, loose) his temper.
30. She has a wardrobe of the finest (clothes, cloths).
31. Buffalo Bill scoured the (plain, plane) for wild animals.
32. He is a man (whose, who's) friendships are few but lasting.
33. By ten o'clock we were (all ready, already).
34. If you start fast, (you're, your) sure to win.
35. The (desert, dessert) is no longer a serious obstacle to travel.
36. We studied the (principals, principles) of good writing.
37. The house sank as (its, it's) foundations gave way.
38. (Whose, Who's) in charge of the dance?
39. The coats were made of (coarse, course) material.
40. If you (desert, dessert) us now, we won't forgive you.
41. He seemed (altogether, all together) sure of himself.
42. I gave him a (piece, peace) of cake.
43. Dr. Michael is (principal, principle) of our school.
44. Do you know (whose, who's) this is?
45. The prisoner had low (morale, moral) standards.

46. We asked for information regarding the factory's (personnel, personal).
47. I thought I'd (lose, loose) my mind!
48. He (past, passed) me just before the finish line.
49. The yearbook staff has (its, it's) own office.
50. Each officer uses business (stationary, stationery).

THREE HUNDRED SPELLING WORDS [3]

absence
abundance
accidentally
accommodate
accurate
acknowledgment
acquaintance
across
advice
advise

aerial
aisle
all right
almost
amateur
among
analyze
annual
anonymous
apologize

appearance
appetite
appreciate
appropriate
approval
arctic
argument

arrange
assistant
association

athletics
attach
attacked
attention
awful
awfully
bachelor
banana
bargain
basketball

beautiful
beginning
believe
bicycle
biscuit
bookkeeper
brake
break
breathe
bruise

bulletin
bureau
buried

business
cafeteria
calendar
campaign
candidate
captain
caricature
catastrophe
cemetery
certain
character
college
column
coming
commission
committee
comparatively
completely
complexion
conquer
conscience
conscious
convenience
copies
cordially
corps
correspondence
courageous

[3] This list includes some but not all the spelling words taken up as individual problems elsewhere in this chapter.

courteous
courtesy
criticism
criticize
customer
cylinder
defense
definitely
descent

description
despair
desperate
develop
dictionary
dining
disappear
disappointment
discipline
disease

dissatisfied
doesn't
dutiful
earnest
economical
ecstasy
efficient
eighth
embarrass
endeavor

equipment
equipped
especially
etiquette
exaggerate
excellent
exercise
exhausted

existence
explanation

extension
extraordinary
familiar
fascinating
fatigue
February
fierce
fiery
finally
foreign

forfeit
forty
fourth
fragile
gasoline
genius
government
governor
grammar
grateful

guarantee
gymnasium
handkerchief
happened
haven't
height
heroes
hoping
hospital
humorous

imitation
immediately
indispensable

influence
initial
irresistible
knowledge
laboratory
laid
license

lightning
likelihood
loneliness
losing
luxurious
lying
maneuver
marriage
martyr
matinee

meant
medicine
medieval
mentioned
microphone
minimum
mischievous
missile
misspelled
monotonous
mortgage
movable
municipal
necessarily
necessary
nickel
ninety
ninth
nuisance
occasionally

occurred
o'clock
omitted
opinion
opportunity
optimistic
orchestra
original
paid
parachute

parallel
particularly
pastime
perhaps
permanent
personally
perspiration
picnic
picnicking
planning

pleasant
pneumonia
possess
possibility
practice
precede
prejudice
prisoner
privilege
probably

procedure
professor
pronunciation
propeller
purpose
pursue
questionnaire

quiet
quite
realize

really
receive
recognize
recommend
referred
rehearse
reign
relief
repetition
representative

restaurant
rhythm
sandwich
satisfactorily
schedule
scissors
seize
semester
separate
sergeant

siege
shining
similar
sincerely
sophomore
souvenir
specimen
speech
strategy
stretch

subtle
success
sufficient

suggestion
superintendent
superior
surgeon
surprised
syllable
sympathy

symphony
synonym
tariff
television
temperament
thoroughly
tomorrow
tournament
traffic
tragedy

transferred
truly
twelfth
tying
tyranny
umbrella
undoubtedly
unforgettable
unnecessary
until

using
vacuum
vengeance
vicinity
villain
waist
waste
Wednesday
weird
writing

PART SIX

VOCABULARY

CHAPTER 27

Enlarging Your Vocabulary

Diagnostic Test

Before you start to work on your vocabulary, take the following test to see how good your vocabulary is now. When this test was given to 200 high school sophomores, the median mark was 16. How do you compare with them?

Number from 1 to 25 on your paper. After the proper number, write the letter of the word which is a synonym for the word at the left.

1. **affluent**   *a.* verbose   *b.* wealthy   *c.* friendly
2. **assuage**   *a.* make easier   *b.* rub   *c.* make brighter
3. **brevity**   *a.* position   *b.* goodness   *c.* shortness
4. **circumvent**   *a.* evade   *b.* surround   *c.* open
5. **denizen**   *a.* lair   *b.* inhabitant   *c.* bear
6. **explicit**   *a.* proud   *b.* apologetic   *c.* definite
7. **flay**   *a.* arrange in line   *b.* cast a rod   *c.* strip off skin
8. **gregarious**   *a.* sickly   *b.* sociable   *c.* cheerful
9. **hierarchy**   *a.* system of ranks   *b.* sound of music   *c.* ancient manners
10. **indolent**   *a.* unrefined   *b.* sorrowful   *c.* lazy
11. **jeopardize**   *a.* risk   *b.* assist   *c.* stripe
12. **lucrative**   *a.* profitable   *b.* bright   *c.* creative
13. **miscreant**   *a.* sneak   *b.* hobo   *c.* villain
14. **nebulous**   *a.* indistinct   *b.* difficult   *c.* villainous
15. **onerous**   *a.* rich   *b.* burdensome   *c.* poor

520

16. **plebeian**   *a.* aristocratic   *b.* common   *c.* military
17. **preclude**   *a.* prevent   *b.* preview   *c.* prevail
18. **quaff**   *a.* guffaw   *b.* drink   *c.* tremble
19. **repugnance**   *a.* dislike   *b.* insolence   *c.* desire
20. **sinecure**   *a.* easy job   *b.* hard job   *c.* technical job
21. **subjugate**   *a.* sublet   *b.* submit   *c.* subdue
22. **turgid**   *a.* cloudy   *b.* unusual   *c.* swollen
23. **vacillate**   *a.* waver   *b.* impart   *c.* empty
24. **wreak**   *a.* destroy   *b.* inflict   *c.* stretch
25. **zenith**   *a.* heavenly body   *b.* highest point   *c.* beautiful tower

How Do You Learn New Words?

Words are learned from the dictionary, as you have seen in Chapter 13, "Finding Information," but you know the meaning of many words that you have never looked up. You learned the meanings of most of the words you know by hearing others use the words or by reading passages containing them. At first, you may have had to guess; later you were sure, and the word became part of your vocabulary.

When you read, the clue to the meaning of a word may be the other words used with it, called the *verbal context;* when you listen, the clue may be the situation in which the word is spoken, called the *physical context;* whether you are reading or listening, the clue may be the resemblance of the word to another word that you know. After you have guessed, you should check in a good dictionary.

27a. Consider the verbal and physical context in determining the meaning of a word.

How good are you at guessing the meaning of words in context?

● EXERCISE 1. Number from 1 to 20 on your paper. Copy each word in heavy type in the passage

27a

below, and write the meaning next to it. When you have completed the exercise, check with dictionary meanings, rewrite those you had wrong, and analyze the context which you missed.

Oblivious of the danger, the rescuers made the **hazardous** climb up the **precipitous** cliff to the injured boy. Desiring no **remuneration**, they sought only to **extricate** the victim from his **precarious** perch on the narrow ledge to which he had fallen. The last ten feet of the climb were almost perpendicular, and the **distraught** mother watched with **trepidation** as the three brave men pushed toes and fingers into the tiny **fissures** which gave them their only hold. After what seemed like an **interminable** time, the highest climber hoisted himself to a position beside the boy. In a moment the two others joined them, and in close **proximity** they **improvised** a rope sling to hold the boy. The **crucial** moment came as, with **concerted** effort, they hoisted him over the side and slowly lowered him to safer ground. **Encumbered** by their equipment and his weight, they carried him over a long and **circuitous** route to the first-aid hut. In a few moments the doctor's **cursory** examination was completed and he assured the mother that her son would suffer no **detrimental** effects. The mother **eulogized** the rescuers, to their great embarrassment, and the entire affair **culminated** happily.

Making New Vocabulary Permanent

There are two ways in which you can help to make new words a permanent part of your vocabulary. One is to keep a vocabulary list, including the meaning, pronunciation, and derivation of each new word.[1] Start your list now in your notebook, using the words which you have learned in the diagnostic test on page 520 and in Exercise 1.

The second way to make new words a part of your

[1] It may be advisable to review at this time the dictionary method of indicating derivation. See page 289.

permanent vocabulary is to use them in speech and in writing on the day you learn them. If you do not list and use them, you will probably forget them. *Follow these two practices with all the words you learn from now on in this book and elsewhere.*

27b. List new words with their meanings in your notebook, and use them in speaking and writing.

● EXERCISE 2. Number on your paper from 1 to 20. Next to the appropriate number copy the correct synonym from the three words to the right. When you have checked your answers in the dictionary, write in your notebook the words you missed, giving their pronunciation, meaning, and derivation.

1. to **abrogate** a law — pass, repeal, amend
2. *Pilgrim's Progress* is an **allegory** — story which teaches, story which thrills, story which amuses
3. the **adamant** judge — learned, wordy, unyielding
4. cows in a **bucolic** scene — rustic, drab, colorful
5. a **clandestine** elopement — secret, hurried, silent
6. to **condone** the crime — expose, punish, excuse
7. a **despot** on the throne — figurehead, tyrant, fool
8. a **dubious** honor — earned, royal, doubtful
9. hanged in **effigy** — haste, image, public
10. a **fortuitous** occurrence — chance, planned, natural
11. an **impetuous** boy — spoiled, hasty, mischievous
12. an **irascible** old man — feeble, amiable, irritable
13. sunk in **lethargy** — despair, mud, drowsiness
14. with **naive** charm — unaffected, unnatural, studied
15. a **protracted** siege — violent, extended, brief
16. his **reticent** manner — resentful, overpolite, shy
17. **retribution** for his action — praise, excuse, punishment
18. **sanctioned** by the priest — overlooked, blessed, approved

27b

19. with the **tenacity** of a lion — firmness, ferocity, violence

20. a **verbose** speech — oral, wordy, violent

● EXERCISE 3.   Each of the words in the list below will fit meaningfully into one of the following sentences. Number on your paper from 1 to 10 and write after the proper number the word which you think fits the corresponding sentence. Then look up the words in the dictionary and rearrange your list accordingly. You may find that a word has several meanings in the dictionary. The exercise sentence (the context) will help you select the appropriate meaning.

remonstrate	paragon
detriment	repugnance
querulous	sophisticate
infringement	tumult
malingerer	veracity

1. The ——— was discharged from the school infirmary when they discovered that he was pretending to be sick.

2. He posed as a ——— who had experienced everything in life.

3. The students ——— about the amount of work expected of them.

4. The story of the cherry tree is a legend about George Washington's ———.

5. The sick man complained in a ———— tone.

6. Fred's low marks were a ——— to him when he tried to get into college.

7. A great ——— accompanied the clash between the demonstrators and the police.

8. The picnickers looked with ——— at the large caterpillars.

9. Galahad was the ——— among King Arthur's knights.

10. The judge decided that the two books were so different that there had been no ——— of the copyright.

● EXERCISE 4. Copy the following adjectives onto your paper. Using the dictionary, write next to each word the meaning as implied in the paragraph below. Each of the adjectives fits into one of the numbered blanks in the paragraph. After each adjective, write the number of the blank in which it fits.

ascetic	perfidious
humanitarian	primitive
passive	relentless
malign	utopian
momentous	laudatory

The __1__ first half of the twentieth century has produced its share of men and women whose names will go down in history. Among the noblest figures are the __2__ Gandhi, advocating a policy of __3__ resistance, and the __4__ Albert Schweitzer, devoting his talents and energies to a __5__ tribe in Africa. Among the most ignoble men are the ranting Hitler, spewing hatred and violence; the __6__ Mussolini, breaking his word to every side; and the __7__ Stalin, seeking and destroying every enemy. It is impossible to speak in too __8__ a manner of the first two and their benign influence, while the __9__ influence of the three tyrants cannot be adequately condemned. A __10__ world can be achieved only when the spirit of Gandhi and Schweitzer prevails over the spirit of cruelty and selfishness.

Latin Prefixes and Roots

Many words now in the English language were originally borrowed from another language. Latin has contributed most, and a student of Latin can tell the meanings of many words in English which still resemble their Latin ancestors. Even those who have not studied Latin, however, may enrich their vocabularies by learning parts of words from Latin which are now used in English words. Because the same

Latin element may be found in many English words, learning that element helps in studying English.

Short elements which come before the main part of a word are called prefixes; *contra* and *pro* are common prefixes. The main part of the word is called the root; *–dict–* and *–duct–* are roots. The part which is added at the end of the main part of a word is the suffix; *–ion* and *–ive* are suffixes. *Contradiction* and *productive* are words formed from these elements.

27c. **Learn the origin and meaning of the prefix and root of each word you look up in the dictionary.**

LATIN PREFIXES

The Latin prefixes in the following lists have been selected because they occur frequently in English words. Learn them as preparation for doing the exercises which follow.

LATIN PREFIX	MEANING
ab–, a–	from
ad–	to
bi–	two
circum–	around
com–, con–	with, together

● EXERCISE 5. Give the meaning of the prefix printed in heavy type. Then, by referring to the dictionary, show how each of the prefixes is related to the meaning of the word.

EXAMPLE   advent = **ad** (to) + **vent** (come) = arrive

1. **ab**erration
2. **ad**here
3. **bi**annual
4. **circum**vent
5. **con**coct

Learn the meaning of the following prefixes.

LATIN PREFIX	MEANING
contra–	against
de–	from
di–, dis–	away, from
e–, ex–	out of
in–, im–	in, into, not
inter–	between, among
intra–	within
non–	not

● EXERCISE 6.   Follow the directions in Exercise 5.

1. **contra**band
2. **dis**integrate
3. **ex**cavate
4. **in**carnate
5. **inter**pose
6. **intra**mural

MORE LATIN PREFIXES

LATIN PREFIX	MEANING
per–	through
post–	after
pre–	before
pro–	before
re–	back, again
retro–	back
semi–	half
sub–	under
super–	above
trans–	across

● EXERCISE 7.   Using the dictionary, write the meaning of each word in the following list. Be prepared to give the meaning of each prefix and to explain how it is related to the meaning of the word.

1. **per**ennial
2. **post**humous
3. **pre**empt
4. **pro**fane
5. **re**voke
6. **retro**active
7. **semi**annual
8. **sub**jugate
9. **super**human
10. **trans**lucent

27c

LATIN ROOTS

● EXERCISE 8.   Each Latin root in the list below is used in *one* of the two words following the root. Number from 1 to 10 on your paper. Referring to your dictionary, write the word in which the root occurs and the meaning of the word. Be prepared to explain in class the relation of the root to the meaning.

EXAMPLE 1.   **–port–**   *carry;* portrait, import
              1.   *import–*   to carry in

1. **–ced–**   *go;* cedar, recede
2. **–cid–**   *kill;* insecticide, cider
3. **–cur–**   *run;* cursory, current
4. **–duc–**   *lead;* induce, duckling
5. **–gen–**   *kind;* genuflect, generic
6. **–miss–**   *send;* transmission, misshapen
7. **–sent–**   *feel;* absent, sentiment
8. **–jac–**   *throw;* ejaculate, jacket
9. **–ven–**   *come;* venal, convene
10. **–vis–**   *see;* viscount, visual

Learn the meanings of the following Latin roots in preparation for the exercise that follows.

LATIN ROOTS	MEANING
–dic–, dict–	say, speak word
–fac–, fact–	do, make
–junct–	join
–pon–, –pos–	place, put
–scrib–, –script–	write
–spec–, –spic–	look, see
–spir–	breath
–vert–, vers–	turn
–voc–	call
–volv–	roll, turn

● EXERCISE 9.   Copy the words in heavy type onto your paper. Referring to the dictionary, underline the root of each word, write the meaning of each root, and give the meaning of the word as it is used in the paragraph.

The governor read the letter which the secretary handed him, and began to dictate an answer in faultless **diction**. His **facile** delivery was not marked by any hesitation for thought as he explained his **position**. "At this critical **juncture** in the affairs of our state," he said, "we place confidence in the integrity of our legislators. We do not all **subscribe** to the same party policies, but we rely on one another's **perspicuity** to see the issues clearly. The **conspiracy** to **subvert** the public welfare is bound to fail, and in the face of the public outrage which has been **provoked**, we will do the duty that **devolves** upon us."

● EXERCISE 10.   Number from 1 to 10 on your paper, skipping two lines after each number. For each word in heavy type below write the prefix (if there is one) after the proper number and give its meaning. On the next line write the root and its meaning, and on the third line write the whole word and give its meaning as it is used in the phrase. Ignore the suffixes. Refer to the dictionary if necessary.

EXAMPLE   robins, the **precursors** of spring

pre– — before

–curs– — run

precursors — forerunners

1. a business **recession**
2. **controverted** by the facts
3. **extrasensory** impressions
4. without **provocation**
5. **transcribe** the notes
6. the **induction** of the officers
7. **contended** bravely
8. **convolutions** of the brain
9. an ancient **progenitor**
10. to **intervene** on his behalf

Greek Prefixes and Roots

The following Greek prefixes and roots are found in many words in English as well as other languages. Learn them for the exercise that follows.

GREEK PREFIX	MEANING
anti–	against
hyper–	over, above
em–, en–	in
hemi–	half

● EXERCISE 11.   In a numbered list on your paper, write each prefix and, on the line below, each word. After each prefix write its meaning. By referring to the dictionary, give a definition of each word.

1. antibiotic
2. hypercritical
3. emphasis
4. endemic
5. hemisphere

● EXERCISE 12.   By referring to the dictionary, define the following words by showing the relationship of the Greek prefix to the meaning.

1. **hypo–**   (under) + **tension** =
2. **para–**   (beside) + **phrase** =
3. **peri–**   (around) + **meter** =
4. **pro–**   (before) + **logue** =
5. **syn–**   (together) + **thesis** =

GREEK ROOTS

● EXERCISE 13.   Learn the following Greek roots and their meanings. By referring to a dictionary, show in written definitions how the meanings of the words in the third column are found in the meanings of their roots.

GREEK ROOT	GENERAL MEANING	WORD
1. anthrop–	man	anthropology
2. chron–	time	chronometer

3. gen–   birth   genealogy
4. geo–   earth   geology
5. hetero–   different   heterogeneous

Study the meaning of these Greek roots.

GREEK ROOT	MEANING
–homo–	same
–hydr–	water
–log–	speak, science
–morph–	form
–mon–, mono–	one

● EXERCISE 14.   Using the Greek roots above, define the following words by dividing each word into parts. Refer to a dictionary.

EXAMPLE   **mono** (one) + **gamy** (marriage) = one marriage

1. homogeneous   4. monologue
2. hydrophobia   5. metamorphosis
3. biology

MORE GREEK ROOTS

GREEK ROOT	MEANING
–neo–	new
–pan–	all
–phon–	sound
–psych–	mind
–scop–	seeing
–tech–	skill
–tele–	far

● EXERCISE 15.   Copy the following words on your paper. Underline the Greek roots. By referring to a dictionary, give the meaning of the words.

1. neolithic   4. polytechnic
2. panorama   5. telescope
3. psychology   6. phonograph

● EXERCISE 16.   Number from 1 to 5 on your paper. By referring to the following list of prefixes, complete the word in each sentence below by filling in the blank with the correct prefix.

EXAMPLE   **The distance around an area is the ——meter.**
       1. perimeter   around

pro–, hetero–, hypo–, hyper–, syn–

1. The patient's symptoms which developed later proved the doctor's ——gnosis was correct.
       before
2. His ——dox opinions were met with disapproval.
       different
3. The doctor injected a ——dermic needle into his arm.
       under
4. Making two things happen together is called ——chron-izing things.   together
5. ——bolic statements can sometimes be used effectively
   over
   in writing.

● EXERCISE 17.   Number from 1 to 15 on your paper. Using the lists of Greek roots on pages 530–531, copy the elements in heavy type and write their meanings in the words below. Then, by referring to the dictionary, write the meanings of the entire word.

EXAMPLE   **live in a demo**cracy; demo– — people; demo-
       cracy — rule of the people.

1. **anthro**poid ape.
2. **psycho**somatic ailment
3. a **hydr**aulic jack
4. an a**morph**ous substance
5. wearing a **mon**ocle
6. a beautiful **pan**orama
7. the science of eu**gen**ics
8. **phon**etic symbols
9. a famous **geo**physicist
10. the **ortho**pedist operated
11. mental **tele**pathy
12. the **chron**ology of history
13. of wide **scope**
14. the words are **homo**nyms
15. a **neo**phyte in a convent

● REVIEW EXERCISE. Divide each of the following words into prefixes and roots and explain how these parts make up the meaning of the word.

EXAMPLE   predict = **pre** (before) + **dict** (say) = to say beforehand

1. circumspect	11. transport
2. retrospect	12. interpose
3. repose	13. symbiosis
4. aspect	14. permeate
5. subordinate	15. induce
6. adjacent	16. recede
7. controversial	17. posthumous
8. conspicuous	18. parasite
9. bipartisan	19. homonym
10. diverge	20. periscope

Words with Interesting Histories

● EXERCISE 18.   Each of the following words in heavy type is derived from the name of a mythological or actual person. Number from 1 to 10 on your paper. Referring to your dictionary give the meaning and origin of the words in heavy type below.

EXAMPLE   The outraged citizens resolved to **boycott** the store of the quarrelsome merchant.

boycott — refuse to buy — from Captain Boycott, the first man so treated.

1. The **chauvinistic** statesman made a warlike speech.
2. The winner said his **mentor** deserved more credit than he did.
3. The woman hammer-throwing champion was built like an **Amazon**.
4. His **jovial** manner deserted him as he grew weary.
5. Rip Van Winkle's wife was a **termagant**.
6. The quiz contestant met his **nemesis**.
7. Only **herculean** strength could have accomplished the feat.

8. It is sometimes difficult for a slow person to get along with one of **mercurial** disposition.
9. Faced by a **titanic** task, the man had the inclination to give up.
10. **Panic** was prevented by the quick thinking of the policeman.

Borrowed Words in English

● EXERCISE 19.   Refer to the dictionary to find the meaning of each foreign word or phrase in column A. Copy column A on your paper. After each item write the name of the language it comes from; then write the letter of the matching item in column B.

A	B
1. nom de plume	a. a dabbler in the arts
2. junta	b. a stroke of good luck
3. dilettante	c. noninterfering
4. bonanza	d. pen name
5. laissez-faire	e. a secret council

● EXERCISE 20.   Consult your dictionary; write the meaning of the following words on your paper and use them in a sentence. Be prepared to give the correct pronunciation in class.

EXAMPLE   **à la carte** — with a stated price for each dish. Because he wanted a special combination of food, he ordered his meal à la carte.

1. à la mode
2. entre nous
3. fait accompli
4. reveille
5. tour de force

● EXERCISE 21.   Consult your dictionary; write the meaning of the following words and use them in a sentence.

1. bona fide
2. ex officio
3. gratis
4. tempus fugit
5. terra firma

● EXERCISE 22. Number on your paper from 1 to 10. Look up each word in column A in your dictionary. Write after each number the letter of the item in column B that expresses the meaning of the word.

A	B
1. alma mater	a. sudden and decisive move
2. con amore	b. principal woman singer in opera
3. blitzkrieg	c. slip in manners
4. denouement	d. farewell
5. hoi polloi	e. one's school or college
6. smörgåsbord	f. outcome of a play or story
7. coup d'état	g. the masses
8. prima donna	h. a variety of side dishes
9. auf wiedersehen	i. with tenderness
10. faux pas	j. violent offensive in war

● EXERCISE 23. Number on your paper from 1 to 10. Looking up the following words in the dictionary, select the appropriate word for each blank in the sentences below, and write it after the proper number.

anagram	metabolism
epilogue	orthodontist
epitome	philanthropist
hypodermic	neolithic
lithograph	protozoan

1. A concluding section added to a literary work is called an ——.
2. The later Stone Age is referred to as the —— age.
3. A dentist who specializes in straightening and adjusting teeth is called an ——.
4. Many adults dislike the sight of a —— needle.
5. A microscopic, one-celled animal is called a ——.
6. A word formed from another by transposing the letters is called an ——.
7. A person who loves and does good for mankind is called a ——.

8. A picture made from a stone or a plate is called a ——.

9. The process of building up food into living matter is called ——.

10. A condensed account or summary is called an ——.

● EXERCISE 24.   Copy column A on your paper. Referring to your dictionary, write next to each word the letter of the best meaning from column B.

A	B
1. anarchy	a. the slaying of a king
2. anathema	b. a speech of praise
3. epitaph	c. a device for measuring
4. eulogy	d. a box for storing things
5. euthanasia	e. stopping and starting again
6. indictment	f. an implied comparison
7. intermittent	g. absence of a system of government
8. metaphor	h. a mass of stone
9. regicide	i. legal accusation by the grand jury
10. repository	j. painless killing
	k. a person or a thing accursed
	l. a short statement on a tombstone

Word List for Grade 10

As a result of your study of this chapter, you will recognize many of the words in the following list. You will find that a great many contain familiar prefixes and roots. Make it a regular practice to learn new words from the list. Add them to the list in your notebook, giving the pronunciation, meaning, and derivation as you find them in the dictionary. Ten words a week will be as many as you can handle efficiently. After learning the words, use them as often as you can in your writing and speaking.

aberration
abrogate
abstract
accrue
acrimony
adamant
adequate
adherence
adjunct
admonish

advent
affluent
allegory
altruistic
ambiguous
amorphous
anagram
analogy
anarchy
anathema

anatomist
anthropoid
anthropology
antibiotic
antidote
arbiter
ascetic
aspect
assuage
astute

averse
boycott
brevity
brochure
bucolic
buoyant

bureaucracy
capitulate
caustic
chauvinistic

chronometer
circuitous
circumnavigate
circumspect
circumvent
clandestine
concerted
concoct
condone
consequential

conspectus
contend
contravene
controvert
convene
convolution
copious
crucial
culminate
cursory

cynic
denizen
despot
deteriorate
detrimental
dexterity
dilettante
disintegrate
disparage
dissenting

distraught
diverge

dubious
dynamic
effigy
embellish
encroach
encumber
entity
ephemeral

epicurean
epilogue
epitaph
epitome
equanimity
eugenics
eulogize
euphony
expedient
explicit

extraneous
extricate
facile
fallacy
fastidious
fervent
fissure
flay
fortuitous
frustrated

furtive
genealogy
generic
geophysicist
gregarious
hazardous
herculean

heterodox
heterogeneous
homogeneous

humanitarian
hydraulic
hydrophobia
hyperbolic
hypercritical
hypertension
hypochondriac
hypothesis
imperious
impetuous

improvise
inculcate
indictment
indolent
induction
infringement
inhibition
interminable
intermittent
interpose

intervene
intramural
introvert
irascible
jeopardize
juncture
laudatory
lethargy
lithograph
lucid

lucrative
malign

malingerer
maudlin
mentor
mercenary
mercurial
metabolism
metamorphosis
metaphor

miscreant
mitigate
monocle
monogram
naive
nebulous

nemesis
neolithic
nomenclature
nondescript

nonentity
oblivious
onerous
orthodontist
orthopedist
ostentation
panic
panorama
paradox
paragon

paraphrase
parasite
passive
pecuniary
pedagogue
pediatrician
pensive
perennial

perfidious
perimeter

permeate
pernicious
perspicuity
perturb
philanthropist
phonetics
plebeian
polytechnic
posthumous
postscript

precarious
precipitous
preclude
precursors
predatory
predilection
preempt
presumptuous
primitive
profane

prognosis
propriety
proscriptive
protozoa
protracted
provocation
proximity
psychosomatic
querulous
recession

reconcile
regicide
reiterate

relentless
relevant
remuneration
replenish
repository
repugnance
residual

respiration
reticent
retribution
retroactive
retrograde
sanctioned
satiate
scope
secular

sedentary

sedulous
sophisticate
stringent
subjugate
subvert
succinct
symbiosis
synchronize
synonym
telepathy

tenacity
tenure
termagant
titanic

transcribe
translucent
transmission
trepidation
tumult
turgid

unanimity
utopian
vacillate
valid
veracity
verbose
vicissitude
wreak
zenith
zodiac

Review Exercises

The purpose of this section is to provide additional exercises in grammar, usage, sentence structure, and mechanics. Use of these exercises after the chapters in Part One, Part Two, and Part Five have been studied will help to prevent your forgetting what you learned in those chapters. From time to time your teacher will assign an exercise from this section as a drill or test to help you remember what you have studied.

Chapter 1: The Word

● EXERCISE 1. Number on your paper from 1 to 25. Write the italicized words in the following paragraphs after the proper number. After each word, write what part of speech it is.

During the (1) *winter*, basketball is the (2) *most* (3) *popular* sport in the United States. The game was invented (4) *by* James Naismith (5) *about* (6) *seventy-five* years ago. (7) *He* wanted a game (8) *that* could be played (9) *indoors* between the (10) *end* of the (11) *football* season (12) *and* the start of (13) *spring* sports. For a long time the game was played (14) *exclusively* in America, (15) *but* now (16) *it* has become (17) *international*, and teams are sent to the Olympics by many countries.

Small communities throughout the Middle West (18) *always* (19) *show* a tremendous (20) *enthusiasm* for (21) *their* high school basketball teams. A town (22) *with* a (23) *winning* team is a happy town and finds the (24) *weekly* or biweekly game a sure cure for the dullness of (25) *winter* life.

Chapter 2: The Sentence

● EXERCISE 2. The basic pattern of each of the following sentences consists of subject, verb, and complement. Number on your paper from 1 to 10. After the proper number, write the three parts of the base of each sentence. After the complement, tell what kind of complement it is: object (direct or indirect), predicate nominative, or predicate adjective.

1. At the end of the day most of the students are rather tired.
2. Some of the parents offered their services.
3. This year's production was decidedly superior to past performances.
4. In March the Drama Club always produces either a play or a musical.
5. Both teachers and students usually give us an excellent demonstration of their talents.
6. Working together in a dramatic production provides good training in co-operation.
7. Which act of the play are you directing?
8. Mr. Woodward, our teacher, was once a professional actor.
9. Take one of the boys with you.
10. The same person controls the lighting and directs the raising and lowering of the curtain.

Chapter 3: The Sentence *(continued)*

● EXERCISE 3. Make a column on your paper and copy the prepositional phrases in each of the following sentences. Identify each as an adjective or adverb phrase.

1. The boys strapped their camping equipment to the luggage racks on their bicycles and rode away at 5 A.M.
2. On level ground they pedaled with ease, but they found the roads through the hills very tiring.

3. A steep rise in the road sometimes forced them off their bicycles, which they pushed to the top of the hill.
4. As they coasted down the hills at high speed, they careened around curves in the road and narrowly missed ditches and trees.
5. A stray dog from a nearby farm or a chicken in their path might necessitate the sudden application of brakes, followed by a quick skid in the gravel or a dive over the handle bars.

● EXERCISE 4.   List the verbal phrases in the following sentences and label each as participial, gerund, or infinitive.

1. Falling behind in homework is fatal to a student who is trying for good grades.
2. Characteristically doing his best at all times, Allan managed to raise his average, bringing it well above B.
3. Explaining the secret of his success, Allan told us it was using available time profitably.
4. Miss Temple, working in the laboratory, offered to help anyone needing assistance.

● EXERCISE 5.   List on your paper the subordinate clauses in the following sentences. After each clause, tell whether it is an adjective clause, an adverb clause, or a noun clause.

1. When the jury returns, they will tell us whether the defendant is guilty.
2. Although he had the missing money, I do not believe that he stole it.
3. Any man who tells the truth need not fear reprisal unless he admits his guilt.
4. The crime that this man committed baffled the police, who worked for a year to discover who the culprit was.

● EXERCISE 6.   Number on your paper from 1 to 10. After the proper number, tell what kind of sentence each of the following is: simple, compound, complex, compound-complex.

1. While your manners are faultless, your attitude leaves something to be desired.
2. Mrs. Bauer played the piano, and Mr. Henry played the drums.
3. If it takes as long to explore the moon as it did to explore America, none of us will be around when the job is finished.
4. Finally, after the war, statesmen sat down together and settled their differences.
5. With the admission of so many new nations, the balance of power in the United Nations shifted in favor of the world's small countries.
6. When you can see both sides of an issue equally well, you find it difficult to take a stand, but everyone insists you must stand on one side or the other.
7. Although new media of communication bring nations closer together, new ideologies tend to keep them apart.
8. Pride is a powerful factor in an individual's behavior; it is also the cause of much disharmony among nations.
9. Prosperity derives from economic strength, but security depends on military strength.
10. Competition, which is the life of trade, is also the cause of much of the tension that exists between nations.

Chapter 4:   Writing Complete Sentences

● EXERCISE 7.   Read the following paragraphs carefully. They contain sentence fragments and run-on sentences. Copy the passage, removing all fragments and run-ons by changing the punctuation and capital letters.

Our national bird is the great bald eagle. As most Americans know. Similar to the bald eagle is the golden eagle. Which has a wingspread up to seven and a half feet. The national bird is protected by law but the golden eagle is not, the result is that hunters are rapidly diminishing the number of these great birds. If the golden eagles are not also given the protection of the law, they may become extinct. In a few years.

The National Audubon Society says that the annual slaughter of golden eagles is a national disgrace. Some hunters bagging hundreds of eagles a year. Texas and Oklahoma are the principal hunting territories, the birds are often shot from airplanes by gunners. Who are paid by both sheep ranchers and manufacturers. Who want the feathers. Sheep ranchers claim the eagles menace sheep, tourists buy the feathers. Protecting the golden eagle will also provide further protection for the bald eagle. Because hunters often mistakenly kill bald eagles. Which, at a certain stage in growth, resemble golden eagles.

The golden eagle migrates to Texas and Oklahoma from northern regions. Such as Canada, and Alaska, and our other Northwestern states. Golden eagles will be protected. If Congress amends the Bald Eagle Act. To include golden eagles.

Chapter 5: Making Words Agree

● EXERCISE 8. Number on your paper from 1 to 25. If a sentence contains an error, or errors, in agreement, write the correct form after the sentence number on your paper. If a sentence is correct, write a *C* after the proper number.

1. Each of these record players play stereo as well as hi-fi recordings.
2. Neither of these books have a happy ending.
3. Everyone in the two cars was injured.
4. Either Charles or Ken are sure to be there.
5. If one of the girls offer to help, send them to me.
6. The principal, as well as the two coaches, is going with us.
7. Where's the letters that came for me?
8. One of our hardest problems are keeping the halls quiet.
9. Neither the boss nor his men seem interested in the job.
10. The height of all ceilings are eight feet.
11. Both my father and mother like to ski.
12. Whenever anyone looks sleepy in class, Mr. Lord calls on them.

13. Although some of my answers was correct, I failed the test.
14. Do you want some of these kind?
15. Neither my brothers nor my father ever go fishing.
16. Who reads this kind of book for pleasure?
17. Where's Betty and Alice?
18. Have either of the sponsors given their permission?
19. Everyone did what they could to help us.
20. The length of these races put a severe strain on the runner.
21. The reason for our delay were the bad roads.
22. Is twenty minutes enough time?
23. Mr. Sage told everyone to help themselves.
24. Frank or Luke own their own horse.
25. Here comes your brother and sister.

Chapter 6:   Using the Correct Case of Pronouns

● EXERCISE 9. Number on your paper from 1 to 25. If a sentence contains an incorrect pronoun, write the correct form after the proper number on your paper. For each correct sentence, write *C* after the corresponding number.

1. I don't know whom it was.
2. You should do better than her.
3. Don and him play in the backfield.
4. Can you tell the difference between his brother and him?
5. No one knew whom the article referred to.
6. Mr. Keene gave Bill and I a ride home.
7. Ask Sam and they when they are leaving.
8. Jane and me will take turns.
9. Gary is better prepared than I.
10. I will take whomever wants to come.
11. I don't know who I should believe.
12. Betty and her can make up their work.
13. If it was them, you will soon know it.
14. The boat was built by Jack and he.
15. There are some students whom no teacher can interest.

16. Kurt and I decided not to bother you and them.
17. Art and we discovered whom the thief was.
18. Is there any mail for Dorothy or I?
19. I am sure that us boys will be criticized.
20. He is a man whom everyone likes.
21. I met Fred and she at the bus station.
22. Jim and he are not so successful as them.
23. Is Phil expecting you or I?
24. Please tell Keith and I what she said.
25. If you expect we boys to help you, you must help us.

Chapter 7:   Using Verbs Correctly

● EXERCISE 10.   Number your paper from 1 to 25. If all verbs in a sentence are correct, place a *C* after the corresponding number on your paper. If a sentence contains an incorrect verb, write the correct form of the verb.

1. What happened when the teacher come into the room?
2. Why he done it is a mystery.
3. Books are not to be left laying about the corridors.
4. Have you driven this route before?
5. The rocket raised slowly from the launching pad.
6. If he had asked me, I would have went with him.
7. Some people seem unable to set still.
8. She thought I should have written to her.
9. Carl swum bravely to the rescue.
10. The dress shrunk when it was washed.
11. Overloaded, the plane could not have rose from the runway.
12. How long has he lain here?
13. Jim run a good race until the last hundred yards.
14. The show begun on time.
15. Has anyone broke John's record?
16. Rising from his chair, the judge demanded order.
17. We were sitting directly behind you.
18. Laying in a hospital day after day is dull as well as weakening.

19. The committee's decision don't seem fair.
20. I was surprised when she come to the door.
21. To conceal their presence, the scouts had to lay still.
22. Jerry drunk three milk shakes.
23. I seen him at the game.
24. When the tire burst, it made a loud noise.
25. During the day the temperature raised thirty degrees.

Chapter 8: Using Modifiers Correctly

● EXERCISE 11. Most of the following sentences contain errors in the use of modifiers (words, phrases, clauses). Rewrite such sentences, correcting the faulty modifiers. If a sentence is correct, write *C* after its number on your paper.

1. While doing my homework, the telephone interrupted me five times.
2. Two bodies were discovered by firemen lying on the floor of the living room.
3. Replying to reporters, the coach said this year's team is better than any other team he has coached.
4. Helen plans to work after she gets married for a little while.
5. While Harry's essay was the most funniest, it was not written so good as John's.
6. Listen very careful to the two recordings and tell me which one you like best.
7. By working as slow as possible, the job was made to last all day.
8. Students are excused from last-period study halls that have a B+ average.
9. An award was presented to Gus Dugan for a job well done by the principal.
10. During the two-week examination period, all extra-curricular activities are canceled.
11. We were told when the bell rang to return to our home rooms.
12. Marion can't sing as good as Judy because, of the two, Judy has the truest voice.

13. Because Jimmy obviously felt bad about his grades, his father did not scold him severely.
14. Teachers will accompany their classes to designated areas during fire drills outside the building.
15. Bob gave a good talk on training your dog in English class this morning.
16. Approaching the capitol from the south, a long flight of stone steps confronts the visitor.
17. Although the captain is faster than any player on the team, he didn't play so good in last night's game.
18. Of the three brothers, Stan is the smartest, but Gene is the most popular.
19. Henry tried to describe the girl to the boys that he had asked for a date.
20. One of the men was picked up by a policeman who had been acting suspiciously.

Chapter 9:   Sentence Variety

● EXERCISE 12.   Demonstrate your ability to put several ideas into one effective sentence by combining each group of short sentences into one long sentence. Use subordinate clauses with appropriate subordinating conjunctions, introductory phrases, appositives, and compound subjects and verbs. Write very few compound sentences.

1. Mary went skating. I went with her. We went to Skateland. It is a large outdoor rink. It wasn't big enough for both of us. We collided and nearly knocked ourselves out.
2. Dacron is a synthetic fiber. It is the ideal material for boat sails. It is strong and water repellent.
3. Spray soaks a sail. A cotton sail becomes heavy with absorbed water. It may stretch out of shape. A Dacron sail sheds water. It keeps its shape.
4. Parents guide students. Teachers guide students. There is too much guidance. As a result, the sparks of curiosity and imagination in students are extinguished.

5. Guidance is telling a child what to do. The child's decisions are made for him. He is not prepared for later life. Then he must make his own decisions.
6. A mutt is cheaper than a pedigreed dog. He is friendlier. He is not so high-strung. He is a better pet.
7. The headlinesman is one of several officials in a football game. He is stationed near the side line. He keeps track of the number of downs and the advance of the ball. He watches for infractions of the offside rule.
8. Parents have political views. The political views are given to their children. The children grow up. They think like their parents and vote like their parents.
9. Newspapers like sensational news stories. Crimes committed by young people are sensational. They make the front page. The good things young people do are not sensational. Newspapers ignore them.
10. We had planned a five-hundred-mile drive. A snow storm was predicted. We canceled our plans. We spent the next day shoveling three feet of snow from our driveway.

Chapter 10: Special Problems in Good Usage

● EXERCISE 13. Most of the following sentences contain errors in usage. Rewrite correctly each sentence containing a usage error. If a sentence is correct, write *C* after its number on your paper.

1. These statistics infer that less students are studying science than formally.
2. Irregardless of my advice, Mrs. Larch tried to learn her child how to read.
3. Grandfather just wants to be let alone so that he can lie in the hammock or sit in his rocking chair all day.
4. Being as she is an alumnus of this school, she hadn't ought to have no trouble getting into college.
5. My great-grandparents immigrated to this country in 1870, bringing with them all their children except my Uncle Don.

6. When you went to school, did you bring that there note to the principal like I asked you to?
7. Don't a rocket raise as good in bad weather as in fair weather?
8. In spite of my advice, my brother he nearly drownded himself swimming out too far; he couldn't hardly swim good enough to get back to shore.
9. What is the affect of the poet's frequent allusions to mythology, history, and etc.?
10. I could of laid there another hour without suffering no ill effects.
11. A compromise is when both sides make concessions in order to reach agreement.
12. He seems to be under the allusion that everywheres he goes, the girls will fall for him.
13. Who beside Jean and me excepted your invitation?
14. You might of won if you had made less errors.
15. From the speaker's remarks, I inferred that he was an alumnus of Harvard.
16. Frances must of gone somewheres with her brother because he wouldn't leave her go out alone at night.
17. How has the recent emigration of people from England effected the country?
18. I sat beside Joe until the teacher he changed our seats.
19. Until the fog raised, we didn't know where we were at.
20. How does having fewer students in the class affect the teaching?
21. Jeff is competing in several events beside the 100-yard dash and the high jump.
22. Since we reorganized the shipping department many less orders get mixed up than formally.
23. Although there wasn't scarcely enough ammunition to go around, the captain decided to try to hold the position.
24. For the use of the furniture, the books, and the painting, the producer wants to thank the Breakfront Furniture Company, the Towne Stationery Store, and the Little Gallery, respectfully.
25. The new governor has effected several tax reforms which can't help but benefit the poor people in this state.

Cumulative Review

● EXERCISE 14. The following groups of sentences contain errors in usage, sentence structure, and mechanics (capitals and punctuation). Revise and rewrite each group in good English.

1. One of New Yorks finest hospitals are the animal medical center an ultramodern hospital and research institution. Which cost more than $4,000,000. It is located at sixty-second street and east river drive, the hospital has a staff of veterinarians and accommodations for nearly 300 patients with operating rooms and diagnostic and research laboratories.
2. Milk is our most complete food. Containing all the vitamins required by man. Americans drink less quarts of milk annually than do people in some other countries per capita, in fact the united states ranks eighth in milk consumption. Finland drinks the most milk and switzerland eats the most cheese. Which is a milk product.

   Milk also supplies us with casein. Which is used in the manufacture of paint glossy paper automobile tires and glue. Another milk product is lactic acid, it is used in medicines in dyeing textiles and soft drinks. In Toronto Ontario an ice-skating rink was flooded with 250 gallons of surplus milk, finding that it did not chip so easy as frozen water, frozen milk pleased the skaters.

552

554

Capitalization Style Sheet

Mexico City — a city in Mexico
Ocala National Forest — our national forests
Twenty-ninth Street — across the street
Houghton Lake — a shallow lake
the South — a mile south
North America — northern Wisconsin
the Explorers' Club — a club for explorers
Ford Motor Company — an automobile company
Central High School — a new high school
Pomona College — four years in college
the American Revolution — a successful revolution
the Wrigley Building — a Chicago building
the Fourth of July — the fifth of July
the Senior Ball — a ball given by seniors
the Freshman Class — freshman classes
English, French, Latin — social studies, physics, art
History II — a course in world history
Winter's frosty breath — spring, summer, winter, fall
Principal Langley — Mr. Langley, the principal
the President (U.S). — the president of our club
the Senator — a senator's duties
God made His will known — tribal gods of the Indians
Don't tell Mother (*or* mother) — Don't tell my mother
Uncle Bill — my uncle
Ivory soap
the Democratic party
a Negro, a Presbyterian, a Swede
The Last of the Mohicans
the Reader's Digest

Correction Symbols

ms	error in manuscript form or neatness	**nc**	not clear
cap	error in use of capital letters	**ll**	run-on sentence, begin sentence here
p	error in punctuation	**gr**	error in grammar
sp	error in spelling	**w**	error in word choice
frag	sentence fragment	**¶**	Begin a new paragraph here.
ss	error in sentence structure	**t**	error in tense
k	awkward sentence	**∧**	You have omitted something.

Index

KEY TO SUPPLEMENTARY DRILL

If additional drill is required, see Blumenthal and Warriner's ENGLISH WORKSHOP, **New Series**, Grade 10. The rule numbers in this text are keyed below to appropriate lessons in the Workshop.

Text Rule No.	Workshop Lesson No.	Text Rule No.	Workshop Lesson No.
1a	1	5d	68
1b	1	5f	66
1c	1	5g	68
1d	2	5h	68
1e	3	5k	69
1f	4	5n	70
1g	4	5p	71
1h	5		
1i	5	6a	76-7
1j	6	6b	76-7
		6c	76-7
2a	15	6d	76-7
2b	15	6f	78
2c	15		
2d	16	7a	84-90
2e	15		
2f	15	8a	93
2j	17	8g	98
2k	17		
2l	17	10c	95
2m	18		
		11a	102
3f	34-5	11b	102-06
3g	34-5		
3h	36	12a	107-16
3i	36		
3j	36	15a	117-18
3k	36	15c-d	119
3l	28		
3m	28	19c	9-10
3n	28	19d	12
3o	30	19e	11
3p	30-1		
3q	28-9	21a	40
3r	32	21b	41-5
3s	33	21c	46
		21d	47
4a	51		
4b	51	24a-b	62
4c	52	24c	63
4d	51-2	24d-e	62
4e	55-7		
		25a	22
5a	67	25b-c	22
5c	67	25d	24
		25h	23
		25i	25
		25j	25